# NEW
# STRUCTURAL
# ECONOMICS

D1557142

# NEW STRUCTURAL ECONOMICS
## A FRAMEWORK FOR RETHINKING DEVELOPMENT AND POLICY

JUSTIN YIFU LIN

**THE WORLD BANK**
Washington, D.C.

© 2012 International Bank for Reconstruction and Development / International Development Association or
The World Bank
1818 H Street NW
Washington DC 20433
Telephone: 202-473-1000
Internet: www.worldbank.org

1 2 3 4 15 14 13 12

This volume is a product of the staff of The World Bank with external contributions. The findings, interpretations, and conclusions expressed in this volume do not necessarily reflect the views of The World Bank, its Board of Executive Directors, or the governments they represent.

The World Bank does not guarantee the accuracy of the data included in this work. The boundaries, colors, denominations, and other information shown on any map in this work do not imply any judgment on the part of The World Bank concerning the legal status of any territory or the endorsement or acceptance of such boundaries.

ISBN (paper): 978-0-8213-8955-3
ISBN (electronic): 978-0-8213-8957-7
DOI: 10.1596/978-0-8213-8955-3

Library of Congress Cataloging-in-Publication Data

Lin, Justin Yifu, 1952-
New structural economics : a framework for rethinking development / by Justin Yifu Lin.
    p. cm.
  Includes bibliographical references and index.
  ISBN 978-0-8213-8955-3 -- ISBN 978-0-8213-8957-7 (electronic)
  1. Economic development. 2. Neoclassical school of economics. I. Title.
HD75.L56 2012
338.9--dc23

2011050744

Cover design and photo illustration: Critical Stages

# CONTENTS

## Box

## Figures

## Tables

# Acknowledgments

This volume presents the key findings of my research program on New Structural Economics (NSE), which I conducted during my tenure as Chief Economist and Senior Vice President of the World Bank from 2008 to 2011. This contribution to development economics and policy would not have been possible without the overall guidance and support of Robert Zoellick, President of the World Bank Group. I am grateful to Bob for his encouragement and valuable advice over my tenure.

I am also very thankful to K. Y. Amoako, Alice Amsden, Ha-Joon Chang, Anne Krueger, Wonhyuk Lim, Howard Pack, Dani Rodrik, Joseph Stiglitz, Suresh Tendulkar, and Dirk Willem te Velde for providing insightful and detailed comments on the NSE framework. Their contributions fueled a thought-provoking and enriching debate about the framework and are presented in this book.

In addition, I would like to thank my many friends and colleagues who provided thoughtful inputs and suggestions on various aspects of the work presented here and throughout the research process. In particular, I am grateful to Shaida Badiee, Gary Becker, Otaviano Canuto, Ha-Joon Chang, Robert Cull, Augusto de la Torre, Christian Delvoie, Asli Demirgüç-Kunt, Shantayanan Devarajan, Hinh Dinh, Doerte Doemeland,

Shahrokh Fardoust, Ariel Fiszbein, Robert Fogel, Alan Gelb, Indermit Gill, Ann Harrison, James Heckman, Vivian Hon, Jiandong Ju, Auguste Tano Kouame, Aart Kraay, John Litwack, Norman Loayza, Frank Lysy, Shiva Makki, William Maloney, Célestin Monga, Mustapha Nabli, Vikram Nehru, Ngozi Okonjo-Iweala, Howard Pack, Luiz Pereira da Silva, Nadia Piffaretti, Claudia Paz Sepulveda, Brian Pinto, Zia Qureshi, Martin Ravallion, David Rosenblatt, Sergio Schmukler, Luis Servén, Sunil Sinha, Hans Timmer, Volker Treichel, Harald Uhlig, Lixin Colin Xu, Yong Wang, and the many others whom I have had the pleasure and opportunity to collaborate with during the production of the manuscript. I would like to express special thanks to Doerte Doemeland, who worked closely with me in the finalization and editing of the manuscript.

The research on NSE evolved from my previous work on economic development and transition at the China Center for Economic Research at Peking University. Several papers produced during that period are also included in this volume. I would like to take this opportunity to thank my former colleagues, Qiang Gong, Demin Huo, and Ho-Mou Wu, and former students, Binkai Chen, Shudong Hu, Feiyue Li, Yongjun Li, Zhiyun Li, Mingxing Liu, Peilin Liu, Xifang Sun, Zhaoyang Xu, and Pengfei Zhang for their support and collaboration in the research.

Last, the World Bank's Office of the Publisher provided excellent editorial, design, and printing services under the direction of Carlos Rossel. In this context, I would like to thank Santiago Pombo-Bejarano, Patricia Katayama, Aziz Gökdemir, Andrés Meneses, and Martha Gottron.

# ABBREVIATIONS

| | |
|---|---|
| CAD | comparative-advantage-defying |
| CAF | comparative-advantage-following |
| DC | developed countries |
| GDP | gross domestic product |
| GIFF | Growth Identification and Facilitation Framework |
| GMM | Generalized Method of Moments |
| HRS | Household Responsibility System |
| IEF | Index of Economic Freedom |
| IMF | International Monetary Fund |
| LDC | less developed countries |
| NIE | newly industrialized economies |
| NSE | New Structural Economics |
| R&D | research and development |
| TCI | Technology Choice Index |
| TFP | total factor productivity |
| TVE | township and village enterprises (China) |
| UNU-WIDER | United Nations University – World Institute for Development Economics Research |

# INTRODUCTION

The quest for sustainable growth has been the most intriguing topic in the world for economists and policy makers since Adam Smith's *An Inquiry into the Nature and Causes of the Wealth of Nations* was published in 1776. Measured by today's living standards, all countries in the world were poor at the beginning of the 18th century. Their economies were predominately based on agriculture. Growth of gross domestic product (GDP) per capita had lingered at around 0.05 percent a year for millennia. Only after the onset of the Industrial Revolution did per capita income growth in the now advanced countries accelerate, jumping to around 1 percent a year in the 19th century and doubling to about 2 percent in the 20th century. This was an unimaginable change. While it took about 1,400 years for world income to double before the 18th century, the same process took only about 70 years in the 19th century and only 35 years in the 20th century for the now advanced countries (Maddison 1995). Nevertheless, the acceleration of growth was largely limited to the United Kingdom, where the Industrial Revolution began, a few western European economies, and Britain's "offshoots": Australia, Canada, New Zealand, and the United States (Maddison 1982). The result was a great divergence in income levels as the ratio of the top few to the majority bottom-income countries increased from 8.7 in 1870 to 38 by 1960 (Pritchett 1997).

After World War II, most countries in the developing world gained economic and political independence and started their postwar or post-independence reconstruction. By the end of the 20th century, a small set of developing countries was able to achieve prolonged high growth, catching up with or significantly narrowing their gap with the advanced industrial economies. Japan, in 1950 a developing country with a per capita income one-fifth of the United States, reached 63 percent of U.S. income by 1970 and became the world's second-largest economy. Japan's rise was the result of an impressive annual growth performance of 9.6 percent during the 1950s and 1960s, driven by the transformation from an agrarian to an industrial economy and continuous upgrading in key manufacturing sectors. Using an outward-oriented, market-friendly development strategy, the Asian Tigers—Hong Kong SAR, China; the Republic of Korea; Singapore; and Taiwan, China—grew in excess of 7 percent annually between the early 1960s and the early 1990s, demonstrating that it is possible to maintain impressive growth rates and to close the gap with advanced economies. More recently, growth in several large economies, such as China, Brazil, and India, has taken off, turning them into new global growth poles (World Bank 2011). These high growth rates have led to a significant reduction in poverty. Between 1981 and 2005, the percentage of people living below US$1.25 a day was halved, falling from 52 percent to 26 percent. This drop in poverty was nowhere as apparent as in my home country, China. In 1981 a staggering 84 percent of Chinese lived in poverty. By 2005 this proportion had fallen to 16 percent—well below the average for the developing world.

Although the occurrence of high, sustained growth further diversified in the 21th century to some Sub-Saharan African and Latin American countries, such growth still remains the exception rather than the rule. Most developing countries suffered from prolonged uninterrupted spells of anemic growth (Reddy and Minoui 2009). Between 1960 and 2009, only about one third of low-income countries reached at least middle-income status. Despite the rising weight of middle-income countries in supporting global growth, many of them have been stuck in the "middle-income trap." Of the countries that were independent and had middle-income status in 1960, almost three-fourths remained middle-income or had regressed to low-income by 2009. The ones that made it to high-income status are countries in Western Europe, Japan, the Asian Tigers, and two island econ-omies in Latin America (Barbados and Trinidad and Tobago). If we can learn from the failed development attempts by most developing countries and especially the few successes, explore the nature and determinants of economic growth, and provide policy makers with the tools to unleash their country's growth potential, poverty could become within a generation or two a memory of the past.

Sustained economic growth cannot happen without structural changes (Kuznets 1966). All countries that remain poor have failed to achieve structural transformation, that is, they have been unable to diversify away from agriculture and the production of traditional goods into manufactur-ing and other modern activities. In Sub-Saharan Africa, which constitutes the core of the development challenge today, agriculture continues to play a dominant role, accounting for 63 percent of the labor force. Its share of manufacturing in 2005 was lower than in 1965 (Lin 2011). Recent empiri-cal work confirms that the bulk of the difference in growth between Asia and developing countries in Latin America and Africa can be explained by the contribution of structural change to overall labor productivity (McMillan and Rodrik 2011).

Development economics first became an independent subdiscipline of modern economics after World War II. Various schools of first-generation development economists in fact emphasized the importance of structural change and saw structural differences as a result of market failures. Not surprisingly, they proposed to use government interventions to facilitate structural change through import substitution and gave priority to mod-ern advanced industries. It was a period when new protective devices such as quantitative restrictions on imports and exchange controls to manage the balance of payments were first used on a large scale by most coun-tries. Using Keynesianism as the main intellectual foundation for their analyses, early development economists advocated a "dirigiste dogma" (Lal 1983), positing as the central tenant of their theories that develop-ing countries were irremediably different from industrial countries. Most developing countries and multilateral development institutions followed these policy recommendations. From Latin America to Europe, Asia, and Africa, results were disappointing, and the gap with the industrialized countries widened.

The failure of the government interventions inspired by the first-wave development thinking generated a new wave, which highlighted government failures and adopted an astructural approach toward economic development that emphasized the essential function of markets in allocating resources and providing incentives for economic development, ignored the structural differences among countries at different levels of development in their policy recommendations, and expected the structural change to happen spontaneously in a country's development process.

Keynesian macroeconomics was also challenged by the emergence of stagflation in the 1970s, the Latin American debt crisis, and the collapse of the socialist planning system in the 1980s. The rational expectations theory became the dominant intellectual framework for development and helped refute the structuralist theoretical foundation for the state's role in using fiscal, monetary, and trade policy for economic development. The new development thinking emphasized getting the price right, creating a stable market environment, strengthening the institutions necessary for markets to function well (property rights, good governance, business environment, and the like), and building human capital (education and health) to supply the increasingly skilled labor required by advances in technology.

Multilateral institutions and development agencies were the main advocates for this wave of thinking and influenced economic policies in developing countries through their programs. They based much of their policy advice and conditionality on stabilization and structural adjustment programs that reflected the new dominant paradigm and promoted economic liberalization, privatization, and the implementation of rigorous stabilization programs. The results of these policies for growth and employment generation were at best controversial.

Something strange and unexpected happened in the recent history of economic development: it was observed that developing countries that succeeded during the second half of the 20th century did not follow the dominant development thinking or the policy prescriptions of the first and second wave. That puzzling fact convinced researchers to revisit some of the big assumptions underlying theories of economic development.

As pointed out, countries that have led the world growth since the Industrial Revolution and developing countries that have successfully converged with developed countries all experienced profound structural changes in the composition of employment and the relative contribution of primary, secondary and tertiary sectors to aggregate growth. Drawing lessons from the intellectual advances, controversies, and disappointments of development economics, a third wave of development thinking, advanced by a small group of economists such as Dani Rodrik, Ricardo Hausmann, Andres Velasco, Philippe Aghion, Michael Spence, Ann Harrison, Célestin Monga, myself, and a few others is well under way. It aims at bringing structural change back to the core of development studies, and it emphasizes the important roles for the market and the state in the process of promoting economic development. These economists all agree that the market should be the basic mechanism for resource allocation, but that government must play an active role in coordinating investments for industrial upgrading and diversification and in compensating for externalities generated by first movers in the dynamic growth process.

The "New Structural Economics" presented in this book is an attempt to set out this third wave of development thinking. Taking into account the lessons learned from the growth successes and failures of the last decades, it advances a neoclassical approach to study the determinants and dynamics of economic structure. It postulates that the economic structure of an economy is endogenous to its factor endowment structure and that sustained economic development is driven by changes in factor endowments and continuous technological innovation.

The factor endowments in a country are given at any specific time and changeable over time. A country's comparative advantages and thus its optimal industrial structure are determined by its factor endowments. Upgrading the industrial structure in a given country requires the upgrading of the factor endowment structure from one that is relatively abundant in labor and natural resources to one that is relatively abundant in capital, the introduction of new technologies, and the corresponding improvement in infrastructure to facilitate economic operations. The new structural economics argues that the best way to upgrade a country's endowment structure is to develop its industries at any specific time according to the comparative advantages determined by its given endowment structure at that time. The economy will be most competitive, the economic surplus will be the largest, and the capital accumulation and the upgrading of factor endowment structure will be the fastest possible. For the private enterprises in a country to enter industries according to the country's comparative advantages, relative factor prices must fully reflect the relative abundance of those factors, and those prices can be determined only through competition in a well-functioning market. Therefore, the market should be the basic institution of the economy.

For the introduction of new technologies, developing countries can turn their backwardness into an advantage by borrowing or adapting technologies that have already matured in richer economies. In contrast, advanced economies must produce at the global technology frontier and have to invest continuously in new R&D to achieve technological innovation. Hence developing countries have the potential to achieve a rate of technological innovation several times higher than that of advanced countries.

Upgrading the industrial structure as well as the corresponding improvement in infrastructure, however, entails coordination of investments and compensation for externalities generated by first movers that cannot be internalized by private enterprises. Without this coordination and compensation, the process of economic development will slow. The government should therefore play an active role in facilitating structural change through mitigating the coordination and externality problem.

Chapter I reviews the evolution of development thinking and presents the main arguments and extensions of New Structural Economics. This chapter also includes insightful comments on the framework from my colleagues Anne Krueger, Dani Rodrik, and Joseph Stiglitz and my rejoinder to their comments.

Chapter II shows how the New Structural Economics complements previous thinking on development and growth. It compares the predictions derived from the New Structural Economics with the stylized facts of successful countries identified by the Growth Report issued in 2008 by the Commission on Growth and Development and discusses the policy lessons that can be drawn from the New Structural Economics. The principle of comparative advantage and the role of the state in facilitating structural transformation, which are key aspects of the framework, are further discussed in a subsequent debate between Ha-Joon Chang and myself.

The Growth Identification and Facilitation Framework (GIFF), which lays out a step-by-step approach for policy makers to facilitate structural change based on the framework of the New Structural Economics, is presented in chapter III. It guides policy makers on how to identify new industries consistent with a country's latent comparative advantage. It also presents information, coordination, and externality issues intrinsic to industrial upgrading and discusses government policies that can help overcome these constraints. Explaining why industrial policy has often failed in the past, the chapter also warns against government policies that are aimed at protecting selected firms and industries that defy a country's comparative advantage. Dirk Willem te Velde, Suresh Tendulkar, Alice Amsen, K. Y. Amoako, Howard Pack, and Wonhyuk Lim provide thought-provoking comments on the approach. The chapter concludes with a rejoinder.

Chapter IV illustrates how to apply the GIFF in developing countries. Using the example of Nigeria, the chapter identifies appropriate comparator countries and selects a wide range of industries in which Nigeria may have latent comparative advantage as the comparator countries may be losing theirs. The chapter argues that these industries, which include food processing, light manufacturing, suitcases, shoes, car parts, and petrochemicals, may lend themselves to targeted interventions of the government. The paper also discusses binding constraints to growth in each of these industries' value chains as well as mechanisms through which governance-related issues in the implementation of industrial policy could be addressed.

Chapter V focuses on the question of financial structure and development. Financial structure varies significantly across countries and, within a country, at different levels of development. The chapter argues that the optimal financial structure in an economy is endogenous to real demand for financial services based on industrial structure, which in turn hinges on a country's comparative advantages. Historically, the financial literature has argued that financial depth rather than financial structure matters for economic development. This chapter provides an overview of theoretical and empirical advances that support the notion that financial structure is important for economic development and endogenous to its industrial structure. It also discusses the circumstances under which the actual financial structure deviates from its optimal structure.

The New Structural Economics argues that countries that pursue a comparative-advantage-following development strategy perform better than other countries. In chapter VI, the book presents empirical evidence to support this notion. It shows that countries that follow their comparative advantage have higher growth, lower economic volatility, and less inequality. It argues that the failure of most developing countries to converge with advanced economies can be explained largely by their governments' inappropriate development strategies. In the past, governments placed priority on the development of certain capital-intensive industries rather than focusing their efforts on upgrading a country's endowment structure and creating an enabling environment for the development of sectors aligned with a country's comparative advantage.

Chapter VII points out that as wages rise rapidly in dynamically growing emerging market economies, such as China, India, Brazil, Indonesia and others, in the multipolar growth world of the 21st century, the labor-intensive industries in those emerging market economies will be losing comparative advantages and provide golden opportunities for other low-income countries to enter. China alone currently has 85 million manufacturing jobs in labor-intensive industries. If low-income countries in Africa and other parts of the world are able to seize these jobs, they will be able to grow dynamically, reduce poverty, and improve living standards quickly. Lower-income countries should therefore turn their late-comer status to their advantage by identifying mature industries in carefully selected lead countries and facilitating the entry of their own private enterprises or foreign direct investments from the comparator countries into those industries. This chapter also summarizes key policy messages and provides concluding thoughts.

As stated in the annual UNU-WIDER Lecture that I delivered in Maputo on May 4, 2011, I believe that every developing country, including those in Sub-Saharan Africa, can grow at 8 percent or more continuously for several decades, significantly reducing poverty and becoming middle- or even high-income countries in the span of one or two generations, if its government has the right policy framework to facilitate the private sector's development along the line of its comparative advantages and tap into the late-comer advantages (Lin 2011). I hope that the publication of this book will make a contribution toward the realization of that goal in the developing world.

# References

Kuznets, S. 1966. *Modern Economic Growth.* New Haven, CT: Yale University Press.

Lal, Deepak. 1983. "The Poverty of 'Development Economics.'" Institute of Economic Affairs, London.

Lin, Justin Yifu. 2011. "From Flying Geese to Leading Dragons: New Opportunities and Strategies for Structural Transformation in Developing Countries." WIDER Annual Lecture 15, Helsinki: UNU-WIDER. (A shorter version of this paper is forthcoming in *Global Policy.*)

Maddison, Angus. 1982. *Phases of Capitalist Development.* Oxford, UK: Oxford University Press.

———. 1995. *Monitoring the World Economy, 1820–1992.* Paris: OECD.

McMillan, Margaret, and Dani Rodrik. 2011. "Globalization, Structural Change and Productivity Growth," Kennedy School of Government, Harvard University, Cambridge, MA., http://www.hks.harvard.edu/fs/drodrik/ Research%20papers/Globalization,%20Structural%20Change,%20and%20 Productivity%20Growth.pdf.

Pritchett, Lant. 1997. "Divergence, Big Time." *Journal of Economic Perspectives* 11 (3): 3–17.

Reddy, Sanjay, and Camelia Minoiu. 2009. "Real Income Stagnation of Countries 1960–2001." *Journal of Development Studies* 45 (1): 1–23.

Spence, M. 2011. *The Next Convergence: The Future of Economic Growth in a Multispeed World.* New York: Farrar, Straus and Giroux.

World Bank. 2011. *Global Development Horizons—Multipolarity: The New Global Economy.* Washington, DC: World Bank.

# New Structural Economics: A Framework for Rethinking Development

# NEW STRUCTURAL ECONOMICS: A FRAMEWORK FOR RETHINKING DEVELOPMENT*†

Several decades from now, when economic historians look back on the story of the past hundred years, it is very likely that they will be intrigued by the mystery of diverging performances by various countries, especially during the second half of the twentieth century. On the one hand, they will be amazed by the rapid growth path followed by a small number of countries such as Brazil, Chile, China, Indonesia, India, Korea, Malaysia, Mauritius, Singapore, Thailand, and Vietnam, where the industrialization process quickly transformed their subsistence, agrarian economies

* Adapted from "New Structural Economics: A Framework for Rethinking Development," by Justin Yifu Lin, originally published in *The World Bank Research Observer* (2011) 26 (2): 193–221, published by Oxford University Press on behalf of the International Bank for Reconstruction and Development / The World Bank. © 2011 The International Bank for Reconstruction and Development/ The World Bank.

and lifted several hundred million people out of poverty in the space of one generation. On the other hand, they will be puzzled by the apparent inability of many other countries, where more than one-sixth of humanity remained trapped in poverty, to generate sustainable growth. They will also notice that with the exception of a few successful economies, there was little economic convergence between rich and poor countries in spite of the many efforts made by developing countries and despite the assistance of many multilateral development agencies.

Long-term sustainable and inclusive growth is the driving force for poverty reduction in developing countries, and for convergence with developed economies. The current global crisis, the most serious one since the Great Depression, calls for a rethinking of economic theories. It is therefore a good time for economists to reexamine development theories as well. This paper discusses the evolution of development thinking since the end of World War II and suggests a framework to enable developing countries to achieve sustainable growth, eliminate poverty, and narrow the income gap with the developed countries. The proposed framework, called a neoclassical approach to structure and change in the process of economic development, or new structural economics, is based on the following ideas:

First, an economy's structure of factor endowments evolves from one level of development to another. Therefore, the industrial structure of a given economy will be different at different levels of development. Each industrial structure requires corresponding infrastructure (both tangible and intangible) to facilitate its operations and transactions.

Second, each level of economic development is a point along the continuum from a low-income agrarian economy to a high-income post-industrialized economy, not a dichotomy of two economic development levels ("poor" versus "rich" or "developing" versus "industrialized"). Industrial upgrading and infrastructure improvement targets in developing countries should not necessarily draw from those that exist in high-income countries.

Third, at each given level of development, the market is the basic mechanism for effective resource allocation. However, economic development as a dynamic process entails structural changes, involving industrial upgrading and corresponding improvements in "hard" (tangible) and "soft" (intangible) infrastructure at each level. Such upgrading and improvements require an inherent coordination, with large externalities to firms' transaction costs and returns to capital investment. Thus, in addition to an effective market mechanism, the government should play an active role in facilitating structural changes.

The remainder of the paper is organized as follows: the next section examines the evolution of development thinking and offers a critical review of some of its main schools of thought. I then outline the basic principles and conceptual framework of the new structural economics, the function of the market, and the roles of a facilitating state. In the next section I highlight similarities and differences between old and new structural economics, and discuss some preliminary insights on major policy issues based on this new approach.

## A Short Review of Development Thinking and Experiences

The process of sustainable per capita income increase and economic growth, characterized by continuous technological innovation and industrial upgrading, is a modern phenomenon. From Adam Smith to the early twentieth century, most economists believed that laissez-faire was the best vehicle for achieving sustainable growth in an economy. It was assumed that in thriving economies all decisions about resource allocation are made by economic agents interacting in markets free of government intervention. The price system determines not only what is produced and how but also for whom. Households and firms pursuing their own interests would be led, "as if by an invisible hand," to do things that are in the interests of others and of society as a whole. Although the laissez-faire approach was challenged by Marxist economists and others, it became the dominant intellectual framework for the study of growth in all countries and remained so for a long time. It certainly provided many good insights on the process of economic development but it missed the importance of the process of continuous, fundamental technological changes and industrial upgrading, which distinguishes modern economic growth from premodern economic growth (Kuznets 1966).

The study of economic development proceeds in two related but separate tracks: growth theories and development theories. While some of the key ingredients of modern growth theory such as competitive behavior, equilibrium dynamics, the importance of physical capital and human capital, the possibility of diminishing returns, and the impact of techno-logical progress can be found in the work of classical economists (Ramsey 1928; Schumpeter 1934), systematic modeling only started in the 1940s when some pioneers used primary factors to build generic models based on aggregate production functions. Harrod (1939) and Domar (1946) trig-gered extensive research along these lines. Following their initial work, the Solow-Swan model sparked the first major wave of systematic growth analysis. The objective was to understand the mechanics of growth, iden-tify its determinants, and develop techniques of growth accounting, which would help explain changes in the momentum and role of economic policy. That first generation of growth researchers highlighted the centrality of capital. One important prediction from these models was the idea of con-ditional convergence, derived from the assumption of diminishing returns to capital—poor economies with lower capital per worker (relative to their long-run or steady-state capital per worker) will grow faster. While that assumption allowed the model to maintain its key prediction of conditional convergence, it also seemed odd: technology, the main determinant of long-run growth, was kept outside of the model (Lin and Monga 2010).

A new wave of growth modeling had to come up with a convincing theory of technological change. Endogenous growth theory, as it came to be known, maintained the assumption of nonrivalry because technology is indeed a very different type of factor from capital and labor—it can be used indefinitely by others, at zero marginal cost (Romer 1987, 1990; Aghion and Howitt 1992). But it was important to take the next logical step and to understand better the public good characterization of technology and think of it as a partially excludable nonrival good. The new wave there-fore reclassified technology not just as a public good but as a good that is subject to a certain level of private control. However, making it a partially excludable nonrival good and therefore giving it some degree of exclud-ability or appropriability was not sufficient to ensure that incentives for its production and use were socially optimal. The move away from perfect competition was therefore necessary. It has yielded high methodological payoffs. While neoclassical models of growth took technology and factor accumulation as exogenous, endogenous growth models explain why tech-nology grows over time through new ideas and provide the microeconomic underpinnings for models of the technological frontier.

Another important question has been to understand how technological diffusion takes place across countries and generates or sustains growth—and why it does not take root in others. Various interesting possibilities have recently been explored in an attempt to answer that critical question (Jones 1998; Acemoglu, Johnson, and Robinson 2001; Glaeser and Shleifer 2002). Both on the theoretical and empirical fronts, progress has been made in our understanding of growth in recent decades. However, growth research still faces significant methodological difficulties and challenges in identifying actionable policy levers to sustain and accelerate growth in specific countries. Intellectual progress has been even slower in the particular domain of development theories. It took a paper by Rosenstein-Rodan (1943) to bring development issues to the forefront of the discipline. The paper suggested that the virtuous circle of development depended essentially on the interaction between economies of scale at the level of individual firms and the size of the market. Specifically, it assumed that modern methods of production can be made more productive than traditional ones only if the market is large enough for their productivity edge to compensate for the necessity of paying higher wages. But the size of the market itself depends on the extent to which these modern techniques are adopted. Therefore, if the modernization process can be started on a very large scale, then the process of economic development will be self-reinforcing and self-sustaining. If not, countries will be indefinitely trapped in poverty.

Rosenstein-Rodan's framework sparked a wave of similar ideas (Chang 1949; Lewis 1954; Myrdal 1957; Hirschman 1958) which came to be known as the structuralist approach to economic development. These early development theories held that the market encompassed insurmountable defects and that the state was a powerful supplementary means to accelerate the pace of economic development (Rosenstein-Rodan 1943; Nurkse 1953; Hirschman 1958). The slump of international trade in the Great Depression led to export pessimism in the post-War period. In Latin America, for instance, political leaders and social elites were influenced strongly by the deterioration in the terms of trade, the economic difficulty encountered during the Great Depression in the 1930s, and the thesis developed by Prebisch (1950) and Singer (1950). They believed that the decline in the terms of trade against the export of primary commodities was secular and led to the transfer of income from resource-intensive developing countries to capital-intensive developed countries. They argued that the way for a developing country to avoid being exploited by developed countries was to develop domestic manufacturing industries through a process known as import substitution. Moreover, the emergence of previous colonies or semi-colonies as newly independent states in Asia and the Middle East, and later in Africa, was accompanied by strong nationalist sentiments.

The results were disappointing in many cases. In many developing countries, well-intended government interventions failed. This was the case across Latin American, African, and South Asian countries in the 1960s and 1970s when import substitution and protection were essential features of the development strategy. One of the main reasons for the failure of many former socialist and developing countries to achieve dynamic growth in their transitional processes was the fact that they attempted to defy the comparative advantage determined by their endowment structures and gave priority to development of capital-intensive heavy industries when capital in their economies was scarce. In order to implement such strategies, developing-country governments had to protect numerous nonviable enterprises in their priority sectors (Lin 2009a; Lin and Li 2009).

By shielding unsustainable industries from import competition, developing countries also imposed various types of other costs on their economies. Protection typically led to: (i) an increase in the price of imports and import-substituting goods relative to the world price and distortions in incentives, pushing the economy to consume the wrong mix of goods from the point of view of economic efficiency; (ii) the fragmentation of markets, as the economy produced too many small-scale goods, which resulted again in loss of efficiency; (iii) decreased competition from foreign firms and support for the monopoly power of domestic firms whose owners were politically well connected; and (iv) opportunities for rents and corruption, which raised input and transaction costs (Krueger 1974; Krugman 1993).

As government-led economic development strategies based on the structuralist teachings failed in many countries, the free market approach appeared to triumph and influence development thinking. This trend was reinforced by a new revolution in macroeconomics. The prevailing Keynesian macroeconomics was challenged by the stagflation in the 1970s, the Latin American debt crisis, and the collapse of the socialist planning system in the 1980s. The so-called rational expectations revolution emerged and refuted the structuralist theoretical foundation for the state's role in using fiscal and monetary policy for economic development.

The Latin American debt crisis began in 1982 when international financial markets realized that the collapse of the Bretton Woods system had put some countries with unlimited access to foreign capital in a situation where they could not pay back their loans. The crisis was precipitated by a number of interrelated exogenous shocks that toppled the Mexican and several other Latin American economies, which were already overburdened with a substantial percentage of the world's outstanding debt (Cardoso and Helwege 1995). It prompted multilateral lending institutions and bilateral lenders—especially the United States—to call for a comprehensive set of reforms of Latin American economies and to advocate a set of free-market policies that followed the canons of the neoclassical paradigm, later known as the Washington Consensus (Williamson 1990).

The Washington Consensus quickly came to be perceived as "a set of neoliberal policies that have been imposed on hapless countries by the Washington-based international financial institutions and have led them to crisis and misery" (Williamson 2002). It promoted economic liberalization, privatization, and the implementation of rigorous stabilization programs. The results of these policies in terms of growth and employment generation were at best controversial (Easterly, Loayza, and Montiel 1997; Easterly 2001). By the end of the 1990s and parallel to the dismissal of structuralism and the prevalence of the free market approach, the development economics research community was witnessing the end of an era dominated by cross-country regressions, which attempted to identify growth determinants. That approach had been to focus on the independent and marginal effects of a multitude of growth determinants. This led to the linearization of complex theoretical models. Yet, the general view was that growth determinants interact with each other. To be successful, some policy reforms must be implemented with other reforms. There was a general perception that the policy prescriptions stemming from such regressions did not produce tangible results.

An alternative perspective on non-linearities was the Growth Diagnostics or Decision Tree approach suggested by Hausmann, Rodrik, and Velasco (2005). They recognized the central role of structural change in economic development and argued that there are "binding constraints" on growth in each country. These authors suggested that binding constraints can vary over time and across countries. They concluded that identification of the binding constraint was therefore key in practice. This framework highlighted pragmatically the inability of governments to reform everything and stressed the need to prioritize reforms, which should be done through the information revealed by shadow prices. It should be noted that the Growth Diagnostics approach is not operational unless one assumes away reform complementarities, which is the feature of linear growth regressions.

The divergence in growth performance between developed and developing countries, despite predictions of convergence from mainstream economic theory, has led to controversy. Some have concluded that the policy prescriptions, or expectations about their effectiveness, or both, were wrong. Others have observed that growth researchers had paid limited attention to heterogeneity (the specific characteristics of each country). The suggestion that cross-country distribution may be multimodal (with the existence of "convergence clubs") did not settle the debate about which new directions were needed for growth research. Instead, many basic questions have come back on the agenda: Are development economists looking in the wrong place in their quest for the determinants of growth? Should the focus be on institutions (institutional outcomes), instead of or in addition to policies? And, assuming that they are not reflecting other factors, how can good institutional outcomes be generated?

These unanswered questions were on the agenda for a long time. Starting in the 1980s, many development economists tried to understand better the causality of relationships and the various transmission channels through which policies, institutional changes, or foreign aid affect growth. They were also the rationale for an increased focus of growth research on microbehavior issues at the household and firm levels, with two goals: (i) allowing for heterogeneity in the economy (across and within countries); and (ii) investigating how constraints to growth operate at the microlevel.

The growing disappointment and disillusionment with aid effectiveness also led to the quest for rigorous impact evaluation of development projects and programs. This has generated a new approach to development led by economists at the MIT Poverty Lab, whose goal is "to reduce poverty by ensuring that policy is based on scientific evidence" through the use of randomized control trials (RCT) or social experiments. Although RCT are good tools for understanding the effectiveness of some specific microprojects, they often do not start from a clear strategic assessment of how a particular method would fit the knowledge gaps of highest priority (Ravallion 2009). All too often, research looks for topics "under the light." The positive outcomes for policymaking are more often the occasional by-products of research than its objective from the outset.

Recent microempirical studies may have indeed shed light on some important problems, such as the impact of the investment climate on firm performance or the impact of household behavior on productivity (Rosenzweig and Wolpin 1985). But "there is a risk the bulk of present-day research in development economics appears to be too narrowly focused and/or of too little generalizability to help much in the fight against poverty and to facilitate structural change and sustained growth" (World Bank 2010).

The time has come to reexamine the state of development economics, to learn from past experiences and previous knowledge, and to offer new thinking and a new framework. Drawing lessons from past experience and from economic theories, the next section presents the key principles of a new structural economics, which is a neoclassical approach to economic structure and dynamic change in the process of economic development.[1]

## A Neoclassical Approach to Structure and Change

The starting point for the analysis of economic development is an economy's endowments. Endowments are a given in an economy at any specific time and are changeable over time. Following the tradition of classical economics, economists tend to think of a given country's endowments as consisting only of its land (or natural resources), labor, and capital (both physical and human).[2] These are in fact factor endowments, which firms in an economy can use in production. It should be noted that the analysis of new structural economics focuses on the dynamics of the capital/labor ratio. This is because land is exogenously given in any realistic discussion of a country's development and natural resources, such as mining resources, exist underground in fixed quantity and their discovery is often random. Conceptually, it is useful to add infrastructure as one more component in an economy's endowments. Infrastructure includes hard (or tangible) infrastructure and soft (or intangible) infrastructure. Examples of hard infrastructure are highways, port facilities, airports, telecommunication systems, electricity grids, and other public utilities. Soft infrastructure consists of institutions, regulations, social capital, value systems, and other social, economic arrangements. Infrastructure affects the individual firm's transaction costs and the marginal rate of return on investment.

Countries at different levels of development tend to have different economic structures due to differences in their endowments. Factor endowments for countries at the early levels of development are typically characterized by a relative scarcity of capital and relative abundance of labor or resources. Their production activities tend to be labor intensive or resource intensive (mostly in subsistence agriculture, animal husbandry, fishery, and the mining sector) and usually rely on conventional, mature technologies and produce "mature," well-established products. Except for mining and plantations, their production has limited economies of scale. Their firm sizes are usually relatively small, with market transactions often informal, limited to local markets with familiar people. The hard and soft infrastructure required for facilitating that type of production and market transactions is limited and relatively simple and rudimentary.

At the other extreme of the development spectrum, high-income countries display a completely different endowment structure. The relatively abundant factor in their endowments is typically capital, not natural resources or labor. They tend to have comparative advantage in capital intensive industries with economies of scale in production. The various types of hard infrastructure (power, telecommunication, roads, port facilities, etc.) and soft infrastructure (regulatory and legal frameworks, cultural value systems, etc.) that are needed must comply with the necessities of national and global markets where business transactions are long distance and large in quantity and value.

Economic development requires continuous introduction of new and better technology to an existing industry. Most people in low-income countries depend on agriculture for their livelihood. Improvements in agricultural technology are key to increasing farmers' income and reducing poverty. However, economic development also requires continuous diversifying and upgrading from existing industries to new, more capital-intensive ones. Without such a structural change, the scope for sustained increase in per capita income will be limited. Therefore, the discussion in this paper will focus mostly on issues related to industrial upgrading and diversification.

Developing countries have the advantage of backwardness in the upgrading process and a whole spectrum of industries with different levels of capital intensity available for them to choose. However, they must first upgrade their factor endowment structure, which requires their stock of capital to grow more rapidly than the labor force (see Ju, Lin, and Wang 2009). When they move up the industrial ladder in the process of economic development, they also increase their scale of production—because of the indivisibility of capital equipment. Their firms become larger and need a bigger market, which in turn necessitates correspondent changes in power, transportation, financial arrangements, and other soft infrastructure.

The process of industrial upgrading and diversification also increases the level of risk faced by firms. As firms move closer to the global technology frontier, it becomes increasingly difficult for them to borrow mature technology from advanced countries. They increasingly need to invent new technologies and products and thus face more risk. The idiosyncratic risk of a firm has three components based on risk sources: technological innovation, product innovation, and managerial capacity. At the early level of development, firms tend to use mature technologies to produce mature products for mature markets. At that level, the main source of risk is the managerial ability of firms' owner-operators. At a higher level of development, firms often invent new technologies to produce new products for new markets. In addition to managerial capacity, such firms face risks arising from the maturity of technology and markets. Therefore, while technological innovation, product innovation, and managerial capacity all contribute to the overall level of risk associated with firms, their relative importance varies greatly from one industry to another and from one level of economic development to another.

With changes in the size of firms, scope of the market, and nature of risk, along with the upgrading of the industrial structure, the requirements for infrastructure services, both hard and soft, also change. If the infrastructure is not improved simultaneously, the upgrading process in various industries may face the problem of x-inefficiency, a phenomenon discussed by Leibenstein (1957). Because the industrial structure in an economy at a specific time is endogenous to its given relative abundance of labor, capital, and natural resources at that time, the economy's factor endowment will change with capital accumulation or population growth, pushing its industrial structure to deviate from the optimal determined by its previous level.[3]

When firms choose to enter industries and adopt technologies that are consistent with the comparative advantage determined by changes in the country's factor endowments,[4] the economy is most competitive.[5] As competitive industries and firms grow, they claim larger domestic as well as international market shares and create the greatest possible economic surplus in the form of profits and salaries. Reinvested surpluses earn the highest return possible as well, because the industrial structure is optimal for that endowment structure. Over time, this approach allows the economy to accumulate physical and human capital, upgrading the factor endowment structure as well as the industrial structure and making domestic firms more competitive over time in more capital- and skill-intensive products.

Firms care about profits. For them spontaneously to enter industries and choose technologies consistent with the economy's comparative advantage, the price system must reflect the relative scarcity of factors in the country's endowment. This only happens in an economy with competitive markets (Lin 2009a; Lin and Chang 2009). Therefore, a competitive market should be the economy's fundamental mechanism for resource allocation at each level of its development. That kind of comparative-advantage-following approach in economic development may appear to be slow and frustrating in countries with major poverty challenges. In reality, it is the fastest way to accumulate capital and upgrade the endowment structure, and the upgrading of industrial structure can be accelerated by better access to technology and industries already developed by and existing in more advanced countries. At each level in their development, firms in developing countries can acquire the technologies (and enter the industries) that are appropriate for their endowment structure, rather than having to reinvent the wheel (Gerschenkron 1962; Krugman 1979). This possibility to use off-the-shelf technology and to enter into existing industries is what has allowed some of the East Asian newly industrialized economies to sustain annual GDP growth rates of 8 and even 10 percent.

As a country climbs up the industrial and technological ladder, many other changes take place: the technology used by its firms becomes more sophisticated, and capital requirements increase, as well as the scale of production and the size of markets. Market transactions increasingly take place at arm's length. A flexible and smooth industrial and technological upgrading process therefore requires simultaneous improvements in educational, financial, and legal institutions, and in hard infrastructure so that firms in the newly upgraded industries can reduce transaction costs and reach the production possibility frontier (Harrison and Rodríguez-Clare 2010). Clearly, individual firms cannot internalize all these changes cost effectively, and spontaneous coordination among many firms to meet these new challenges is often impossible. Change in infrastructure requires collective action or at least coordination between the provider of infrastructure services and industrial firms. For this reason, it falls to the government either to introduce such changes or to coordinate them proactively.

Successful industrial upgrading in responding to change in an economy's endowment structure requires that the pioneer firms overcome issues of limited information regarding which new industries are the economy's latent comparative advantages determined by the changing endowment structure. Valuable information externalities arise from the knowledge gained by pioneer firms in both success and failure. Therefore, in addition to playing a proactive role in the improvements of soft and hard infrastructures, the government in a developing country, like that in a developed country, needs to compensate for the information externalities generated by pioneer firms (Rodrik 2004; Lin 2009a; Lin and Monga 2011; Harrison and Rodríguez-Clare 2010).[6]

## What Is "New" About the New Structural Economics?

Like all learning ventures, economic development thinking is bound to be a continuous process of amalgamation and discovery, continuity, and reinvention. The existing stock of knowledge has been the result of many decades of work by thinkers from various backgrounds and disciplines and has come to light through several waves of theoretical and empirical research. It is therefore only natural that the proposed new structural economics has some similarities to and differences from previous strands in the development economics literature. Its main value-added should be assessed on the new policy insights it provides and the pertinence of the research agenda ahead.

### Difference with Earlier Literature on Structural Change

Earlier thinking on structural change in the context of economic development is mostly associated with Rostow (1990 [1960]) and Gerschenkron (1962). In trying to understand how economic development occurs and what strategies can be adopted to foster that process, the former suggested that countries can be placed in one of five categories in terms of their level of growth: (i) traditional societies, characterized by subsistence economy, with output not traded or even recorded, the existence of barter, high levels of agriculture, and labor-intensive agriculture; (ii) societies with preconditions to growth, where there is an increase in capital use in agriculture, the development of mining industries, and some growth in savings and investment; (iii) societies in take-off mode, with higher levels of investment and industrialization, accumulation of savings, and a decline in the share of the agricultural labor force; (iv) societies that drive to maturity and where wealth generation enables further investment in value adding industry and development—growth becomes self-sustaining, industry is diversified, and more sophisticated technology is used; and (v) mass-consumption societies that achieve high output levels and where the services industry dominates the economy.

Gerschenkron questioned Rostow's proposition that all developing countries pass through a similar series of levels and its implication that it is possible to generalize the growth trajectory of different countries. For the new structural economics, economic development from a low level to a high level is a continuous spectrum, not a mechanical series of five distinguished levels. Although the change in an economy's industrial structure reflects the changes in that economy's endowment structure, the development of industries in different countries with a similar endowment structure can be achieved in different and nonlinear ways. This is especially true with the increased globalization of markets, the rapid development of new products, and constant technological change, as countries can exploit opportunities that were not available in the past and specialize in industries that are likely to vary from one economy to another.

The new structural economics also provides a framework for understanding the endogeneity and exogeneity issues surrounding the key stylized facts of modern growth analysis that have been outlined by the Growth Commission (2008) and Jones and Romer (2009): an economy that follows its comparative advantage in the development of its industries will be most competitive in domestic and world markets. As a result, the economy will generate potentially the largest income and surplus for savings. Capital investment will also have the largest possible return. Consequently, households will have the highest savings propensity, resulting in an even faster upgrade of the country's endowment structure (Lin and Monga 2010).

## Similarities to and Differences from Old Structural Economics

In terms of similarities, the "new" and the "old" structural economics are both founded on structural differences between developed and developing countries and acknowledge the active role of the state in facilitating the movement of the economy from a lower level of development to a higher one. However, there are profound differences between these two approaches regarding their targets and the modalities of state intervention. The old structural economics advocates development policies that go against an economy's comparative advantage and advise governments in developing countries to develop advanced capital-intensive industries through direct administrative measures and price distortions. By contrast, the new structural economics stresses the central role of the market in resource allocation and advises the state to play a facilitating role to assist firms in the process of industrial upgrading by addressing externality and coordination issues.

The differences between the two frameworks derive from their dissimilar views on the sources of structural rigidities: old structural economics assumes that the market failures that make the development of advanced capital-intensive industries difficult in developing countries are exogenously determined by structural rigidities due to the existence of monopolies, labor's perverse response to price signals, and/or the immobility of factors. By contrast, the new structural economics posits that the failure to develop advanced capital-intensive industries in developing countries is endogenously determined by their endowments. The relative scarcity in their capital endowment and/or the low level of soft and hard infrastructure in developing countries make the reallocations from the existing industries to the advanced capital-intensive industries unprofitable for the firms in a competitive market.

Old structural economics assumes a dual and restrictive view of the world, with a binary classification of only two possible categories of countries: "low-income, periphery countries" versus "high-income, core countries." As a result, it views the differences in the industrial structure between developed and developing countries as expressing a dichotomy. Contrary to that vision, the new structural economics considers these differences as the reflection of a whole spectrum that includes many different levels of development. The new structural economics also rejects dependency theories. In an increasingly globalized world, it sees opportunities for developing countries to counter negative historical trends by diversifying their economy and building industries that are consistent with their comparative advantage so as to accelerate growth and achieve convergence by exploiting the advantage of backwardness in an open, globalized world.

Another major difference between the new and the old structural economics is the rationale for using key instruments of economic management. Old structural economics sees systematic government intervention in economic activities as the essential ingredient in the modernization objective. Among the key instruments used to move from "developing" countries to "industrialized" countries are generalized protectionism (such as government-imposed tariffs on imports to protect infant industries), rigid exchange-rate policies, financial repression, and the creation of state-owned enterprises in most sectors.

By contrast, the new structural economics recognizes that import substitution is a natural phenomenon for a developing country climbing the industrial ladder in its development process, provided that it is consistent with the shift in comparative advantage that results from changes in its endowment structure. But it rejects conventional import-substitution strategies that rely on the use of fiscal policy or other distortions in low-income, labor- or resource-abundant economies to develop high cost, advanced capital-intensive industries that are not consistent with the country's comparative advantage. It also stresses the idea that the industrial upgrading process in a developing country should be consistent with the change in the country's comparative advantage that reflects the accumulation of human and physical capital and the change in its factor endowment structure—this ensures the viability of firms in new industries. The new structural economics concludes that the role of the state in industrial diversification and upgrading should be limited to the provision of information about the new industries, the coordination of related investments across different firms in the same industries, the compensation of information externalities for pioneer firms, and the nurturing of new industries through incubation and encouragement of foreign direct investment (Lin 2009a; Lin and Chang 2009; Lin and Monga 2011). The state also needs to assume effectively its leadership role in the improvement of hard and soft infrastructure in order to reduce transaction costs on individual firms and so facilitate the economy's industrial development process.

## New Structural Economics: Some Policy Insights

The ultimate goal of development thinking is to provide policy advice that facilitates the quest for sustainable and inclusive economic and social progress in poor countries. Although specific policy measures to be derived from the new structural economics approach will require further research and depend very much on country context and circumstances, in this section I will make some conjectures about a few preliminary insights on various topics.

*Fiscal Policy.* Until Britain's very high unemployment of the 1920s and the Great Depression, economists generally held that the appropriate stance for fiscal policy was for governments to maintain balanced budgets. The severity of the early twentieth-century crises gave rise to the Keynesian idea of counter-cyclicality, which suggested that governments should use tax and expenditure policies to offset business cycles in the economy. By contrast, neoclassical economics offers doubts about the implicit assumption behind the Keynesian model of a multiplier greater than one[7] and its implication that governments are able to do something that the private sector has been unable to do: mobilize idle resources in the economy (unemployed labor and capital) at almost zero social cost, that is, with no corresponding decline in other parts of GDP (consumption, investment, and net exports). Instead, they warn against the possibility of the so-called

Ricardian equivalence trap and point to the fact that households tend to adjust their behavior for consumption or saving on the basis of expectations about the future. They suggest that expansionary fiscal policy (stimulus packages) is perceived as immediate spending or tax cuts that will need to be repaid in the future. They conclude that the multiplier could be less than one in situations where the GDP is given and an increase in government spending does not lead to an equal rise in other parts of GDP. The neoclassical paradigm even suggests the possibility of some rare instances where multipliers are negative, pointing to situations where fiscal contractions become expansionary (Francesco and Pagano 1991).

From the viewpoint of new structural economics, the effects of fiscal policy may be different in developed and developing countries due to the differences in opportunities of using counter-cyclical expenditure for making productivity-enhanced investments. Physical infrastructure in general is a binding constraint for growth in developing countries, and governments need to play a critical role in providing essential infrastructure to facilitate economic development. In such contexts, recessions are typically good times for making infrastructure investments, for three main reasons. First, such investments boost short-term demand and promote long-term growth.[8] Second, their investment cost is lower than in normal times. And third, the Ricardian equivalence trap can be avoided because the increase in future growth rates and fiscal revenues can compensate for the cost of these investments (Lin 2009b).

If a developing country government follows the new structural economics approach of facilitating the development of industries according to the country's comparative advantage, its economy will be competitive and the fiscal position and the external account are likely to be sound, thanks to the likelihood of strong growth, good trade performance, and the lack of nonviable firms that the government has to subsidize. Under this scenario, the country will face fewer homegrown economic crises. If the economy is hit by external shocks such as the recent global crisis, the government will be in a good position to implement a counter-cyclical fiscal stimulus and invest in infrastructure and social projects. Such public investments can enhance the economy's growth potential, reduce transaction costs on the private sector, increase the rate of return on private investment, and generate enough tax revenues in the future to liquidate the initial costs.

In addition to its different stance on fiscal stimulus, the new structural economics approach also offers a different strategy for managing natural resource wealth. In resource-abundant countries, it would recommend that an appropriate share of revenues from commodities be used to invest in human capital, infrastructure, social capital, and compensation for first movers in new nonresource sectors so as to facilitate the structural transformation. To accomplish this with the greatest effect, these resources should finance investment opportunities that remove binding constraints on industrial diversification and upgrading, especially in the infrastructure and education sectors. Microeconomic analyses show that even when factory floor costs are comparable, inefficiencies in infrastructure can make it impossible for poor countries to compete on international markets. Freight and insurance costs in African countries are 250 percent of the global average,[9] with road freight delays two to three times as long as in Asia. Lacking financial resources and the appropriate policy frameworks, many of these countries are often unable to sustain much needed investment and maintenance expenditures. In such contexts, the effective fiscal strategy would not be to keep natural resource revenues in sovereign funds and invest in foreign equity markets or projects but, rather, to use a substantial portion of the revenues for financing domestic or regional projects that facilitate economic development and structural change—i.e., projects that stimulate the development of new manufacturing industries, diversify the economy, provide jobs, and offer the potential of continuous upgrading.[10]

*Monetary Policy.* Old structural economics suggested that monetary policy should be under government control (not independent central banks) and directed at influencing interest rates and even sector credit allocation. But it also acknowledged that many other factors that influence the investment demand-schedule in developing countries are too powerful for monetary policy alone to achieve sufficient levels of investment, channel resources in strategic sectors, and combat unemployment.

Building on lessons from the rational expectations revolution, neoclassical economists doubted the idea that monetary policy could be used to support industrial development. They recommended that its main goal be price stability, and advocated the use of short-term interest rates by independent central banks to maintain the general level of prices (or to control money supply growth), and not to stimulate economic activity and trigger inflation.

The new structural economics envisions the possibility of using interest rate policy in developing countries as a counter-cyclical tool and as an instrument to encourage infrastructure and industrial upgrading investments during recessions—measures that may contribute to productivity growth in the future. Monetary policy is often ineffective for stimulating investment and consumption in recessions and excess capacity situations in developed countries, especially when nominal interest rates hit the zero bound in a context of limited profitable investment opportunities, pessimistic expectations, high unemployment rates, low confidence about the future, and the likelihood of liquidity traps. It should be noted, however, that developing countries are less likely to encounter such liquidity traps. Even when faced with excess capacity in existing domestic industries, their scope for industrial upgrading and diversification is large. Their firms have incentives to undertake productivity-enhancing, industrial-upgrading investments during recessions if interest rates are sufficiently low. Furthermore, they tend to have many infrastructure bottlenecks. Lowering interest rates in such contexts would also encourage investments in infrastructure.

The objective of monetary policy should be much broader than traditionally conceived under neoclassical economics—in economic slumps, it should aim at encouraging investment that removes bottlenecks on growth. In practical terms, this implies not just that interest rates should be lowered in the slump, as would be the case in most circumstances under a standard Taylor rule. It also implies that monetary authorities should resort to temporary interest rate subsidies, flexible credit allocation rules, or similar time-bound devices, targeting infrastructure projects identified by development banks as binding constraints, preferably in specific geographic locations where the payoff is the largest and where political economy constraints can be more easily managed.

*Financial Development.* There is ample consensus that financial development is essential to sustaining economic growth. There is, however, much less agreement on the specific role it plays in that process. Starting with the observation that one of the major constraints facing developing countries was limited capital accumulation, old structural economics regarded the problems of the financial sector in underdeveloped economies as resulting from widespread market failures that could not be overcome by market forces alone.[11] They recommended that governments adopt a hands-on approach in that process, mobilize savings, and allocate credit to support the development of advanced capital-intensive industries. This very often led to financial repression (McKinnon 1973; Shaw 1973). In some countries, especially in Sub-Saharan Africa, the belief in soft-budget constraints led governments to accumulate deficits in state-owned financial institutions and created a pervasive business culture of self-repression not only for banks, but also for private enterprises (Monga 1997). Drawing consequences from such analyses, neoclassical economists advocated financial liberalization. They contended that bureaucrats generally do not have the incentives or expertise to intervene effectively in credit allocation and pricing, and that a well-defined system of property rights, good contractual institutions, and competition would create the conditions for the emergence of a sound financial system. They recommended that government exit from bank ownership and lift restrictions on the allocation of credit and the determination of interest rates (Caprio and Honohan 2001).

While agreeing with the need to address the deleterious effects of financial repression, the new structural economics would emphasize the fact that those distortions are often designed to protect nonviable firms in priority sectors in developing countries. It would then stress the importance of an appropriate sequencing of liberalization policies in domestic finance and foreign trade so as to achieve stability and dynamic growth simultaneously during transition. The new structural economics also posits that the optimal financial structure at a given level of development may be determined by the prevailing industrial structure, the average size of firms, and the usual type of risk they face, all factors that are in turn endogenous to the economy's factor endowments at that level. Observing that national policies frequently favor large banks and the equity market regardless of the structure of the economy, it would suggest that low-income countries choose small, local banks as the backbone of their financial systems, instead of trying to replicate the financial structure of advanced industrialized countries. This would allow small-scale firms in agriculture, industry, and the service sector to gain adequate financial services. As industrial upgrading takes place and the economy relies increasingly on more capital-intensive industries, the financial structure will change to give greater weight to large banks and sophisticated equity markets (Lin, Sun, and Jiang 2009).

*Foreign Capital.* In a world that they thought was characterized by the core-periphery relationship, old structural economists tended to view foreign capital mainly as a tool in the hands of industrialized countries and their multinational firms to maintain harmful control over developing countries. They rejected the idea that free capital movements among countries could deliver an efficient allocation of resources and considered foreign direct investment flows to poor countries as an instrument for foreign ownership and domination. They advocated tight restrictions on virtually all forms of international financial flows.

Neoclassical economic theory argues that international capital mobility serves several purposes: it allows countries with limited savings to attract financing for productive domestic investment projects; it enables investors to diversify their portfolios; it spreads investment risk more broadly; and it promotes intertemporal trade—the trading of goods today for goods in the future (Eichengreen and others 1999). Therefore, the theory generally favors open or liberalized capital markets, with the expectation of more efficient allocation of savings, increased possibilities for diversification of investment risk, faster growth, and the dampening of business cycles. It should be noted, however, that some neoclassical economists also argue that liberalized financial markets in developing countries can be distorted by incomplete information, large and volatile movements in and out of the system, and many other problems leading to suboptimal consequences that are damaging for general welfare.

The new structural economics approach considers foreign direct investment to be a more favorable source of foreign capital for developing countries than other capital flows because it is usually targeted toward industries consistent with a country's comparative advantage. It is less prone to sudden reversals during panics than bank loans, debt financing, and portfolio investment, and does not generate the same acute problems of financial crises as do sharp reversals of debt and portfolio flows. In addition, direct investment generally brings technology, management, access to markets, and social networking, which are often lacking in developing countries and are yet crucial for industrial upgrading. Thus, liberalizing inward direct investment should generally be an attractive component of a broader development strategy. By contrast, portfolio investment that may move in and out quickly, in a large quantity, tends to target speculative activities (mostly in equity markets or the housing sector) and create bubbles and fluctuations. It should not be favored.[12] The new structural economics approach may also shed new light on the puzzle raised by Lucas (1990) about the flow of capital from capital scarce developing countries to capital abundant developed countries. Without improvement of infrastructure and upgrading to new comparative advantage industries, the accumulation of capital in a developing country may encounter diminishing returns, causing lower returns to capital in developing countries, and justifying the subsequent outflow of capital to developed countries.

*Trade Policy.* There have been various old structural economics approaches to external trade. But one constant feature is the belief that integration into the global economy is bound to maintain the existing world power structure, with Western countries and their multinational corporations dominating poorer countries and exploiting their economies. In order to break the dependency trap, old structural economics thinkers have suggested that priority be given to import-substitution strategies, with developing economies closed and protected until their modern industries can compete with advanced industrialized countries in world markets.

A radically different view was adopted by economists in the 1980s. Observing that macroeconomic crises in developing countries almost always have an external dimension, they considered that their immediate cause was the lack of foreign exchange to service debts and purchase imports. They recommended trade liberalization and export promotion as a solution to generate foreign exchange through export earnings. This was also consistent with the view that, in the long term, outward oriented development strategies are more effective than inward looking policies. This view was bolstered further by the argument that such a strategy would increase demand for unskilled labor and hence unskilled wages, as had happened in successful East Asian countries (Kanbur 2009).

The analysis from the new structural economics would be consistent with the view from neoclassical economics that exports and imports are endogenous to the comparative advantage determined by a country's endowment structure (they are essential features of the industrial upgrading process and reflect changes in comparative advantage). Globalization offers a way for developing countries to exploit the advantages of backwardness and achieve a faster rate of innovation and structural transformation than is possible for countries already on the global technology frontier. Openness is an essential channel for convergence. The new structural economics approach recognizes, however, that many developing countries start climbing the industrial ladder with the legacy of distortions from old structural economics strategies of import-substitution. It would therefore suggest a gradualist approach to trade liberalization. During transition, the state may consider providing some temporary protection to industries that are not consistent with a country's comparative advantage, while liberalizing at the same time entry to other more competitive sectors that were controlled and repressed in the past. The dynamic growth in the newly liberalized sectors creates the conditions for reforming the old priority sectors. This pragmatic, dual-track approach may achieve the goal of growth without losers in the transition process (Naughton 1995; Lau, Qian, and Roland 2000; Subramanian and Roy 2003; Lin 2009a).

*Human Development.* Old structural economics generally said little about the role of human development in economic growth. By contrast, neoclassical economics has shown that the continuing growth in per capita incomes of many countries during the nineteenth and twentieth centuries was mainly due to the expansion of scientific and technical knowledge that raised the productivity of labor and other inputs in production. Economic theory has demonstrated that growth is the result of synergies between new knowledge and human capital, which is why large increases in education and training have accompanied major advances in technological knowledge in all countries that have achieved significant economic growth. Education, training, and health, which are the most important investments in human capital, are considered to be the most important driving force for economic development (Becker 1975; Jones and Romer 2009).

The new structural economics considers human capital to be one component of a country's endowment. For economic agents, risks and uncertainty arise during the process of industrial upgrading and technological innovation that accompanies economic development. As various firms move up the industrial ladder to new, higher capital-intensity industries and get closer to the global industrial frontier, they face higher levels of risks.

Human capital increases workers' ability to cope with risk and uncertainty (Schultz 1961) but its formation requires a long time. A person who loses the opportunity to receive education at a young age may not be able to compensate for that loss at a later age. In a dynamic growing economy, it is important to plan ahead and make human capital investments before the economy requires the set of skills associated with new industries and technologies. However, improvements in human capital should be commensurable with the accumulation of physical capital and the upgrading of industry in the economy. Otherwise, human capital will either become a binding constraint for economic development if it is under-supplied because of insufficient investment, or the country will have many frustrated highly educated youths if the industrial upgrading of the economy is not progressing fast enough to provide skilled jobs.

A well-designed policy on human capital development should be an integral part of any country's overall development strategy. The new structural economics goes beyond the neoclassical generic prescription for education and suggests that development strategies include measures to invest in human capital that facilitates the upgrading of industries and prepares the economy to make full use of its resources. The key components of such strategies should follow Lucas's (2002) suggestion to allow human capital to have both a quality and a quantity dimension. It should also include alternative policies for promoting skill formation that are targeted to different levels of the life cycle,[13] with the government and the private sector working closely together to anticipate or respond to the skills needs in the labor market. Singapore, one of the 13 high-growth economies[14] that have been able to grow at more than 7 percent for periods of more than 25 years since World War II, provides a successful example of human capital development as a national strategy (Osman-Gani 2004), which goes beyond the schooling decision and recognizes that on-the-job training is an important component of aggregate human capital. Its human resource strategies have been continuously revised and adjusted in conjunction with other national strategic economic policies.

## Concluding Thoughts

The new structural economics approach highlights the importance of endowments and differences in industrial structures at various levels of development and the implications of distortions stemming from past, misguided, interventions by policymakers whose belief in old structural economics led them to over-estimate governments' ability to correct market failures. It also points out the fact that policies advocated under the Washington Consensus often failed to take into consideration the structural differences between developed and developing countries and ignored the second-best nature of reforming various types of distortions in developing countries.

The proposed new structural economics attempts to develop a general framework for understanding the causality behind the observed stylized facts of sustained growth. Specifically, the new structural economics proposes to: (i) develop an analytical framework that takes into account factor and infrastructure endowments, the levels of development, and the corresponding industrial, social, and economic structures of developing countries; (ii) analyze the roles of the state and the market at each development level and the mechanics of the transition from one level to another; and (iii) focus on the causes of economic distortions and the government's strategies for exit from the distortions. It is not an attempt to substitute another ideologically based policy framework for those that have dominated development thinking in past decades, yet showing little connection to the empirical realities of individual countries. Rather, it is an approach that brings attention to the endowment structure and level of development of each country and suggests a path toward country-based research that is rigorous, innovative, and relevant to development policy. This framework stresses the need to understand better the implications of structural differences at various levels of a country's development—especially in terms of the appropriate institutions and policies, and the constraints and incentives for the private sector in the process of structural change.

The current state of development economics and the severe impact of the global crisis on the economies of developing countries have generated strong demand for a new framework for development thinking. The research agenda of the new structural economics should enrich research and enhance the understanding of the nature of economic development. This would help assist low- and middle-income countries in achieving dynamic, sustainable, and inclusive growth, and in eliminating poverty.

## Notes

† The paper was presented as the Kuznets Lecture at the Economic Growth Center, Yale University on March 1, 2011. The main arguments of this paper were first presented at DEC's fourth Lead Economists Meeting and at Lin's first anniversary at the Bank on June 2, 2009. A shorter version of the paper was presented at the conference on "Challenges and Strategies for Promoting Economic Growth," organized by the Banco de México in Mexico City on October 19–20, 2009, and at public lectures at Cairo University on November 5, 2009, Korean Development Institute on November 17, 2009, OECD on December 8, 2009, UNU-WIDER on January 19, 2010, Stockholm Institute of Transitional Economics on January 21, 2010, National University of Management in Cambodia on September 8, 2010, Bank of Italy on April 26, 2011, and University of Dar es Salaam on April 29, 2011.

Célestin Monga provided invaluable help in preparing this paper. The paper also benefits from discussions and comments from Gary Becker, Otaviano Canuto, Ha-Joon Chang, Luiz Pereira Da Silva, Augusto de la Torre, Christian Delvoie, Asli Demirgüç-Kunt, Shantayanan Devarajan, Hinh T. Dinh, Shahrokh Fardoust, Ariel Fiszbein, Robert Fogel, Alan Gelb, Indermit S. Gill, Ann Harrison, James Heckman, Aart Kraay, Auguste Tano Kouame, Norman V. Loayza, Frank J. Lysy, Shiva S. Makki, William F. Maloney, Mustapha Kamel Nabli, Vikram Nehru, Howard Pack, Nadia Piffaretti, Mohammad Zia M. Qureshi, Martin Ravallion, Sergio Schmukler, Claudia Paz Sepúlveda, Luis Serven, and Harald Uhlig. I am also grateful for the editor and three referees for helpful comments and suggestions.

1. I will refer to the early contributions by structuralist economists such as Prebisch (1950) and Furtado (1964, 1970) and recent contributions by structuralist economists such as Taylor (1983, 1991, 2004) and Justman and Gurion (1991) as old structural economics.

2. The total endowments at a specific time—the economy's total budgets at that time and the endowment structure, together with the households' preferences and firms' available production technologies—determine the relative factor and product prices in the economy. Total budgets and relative prices are two of the most fundamental parameters in economic analysis. Moreover, the endowments are given at any specific time and are changeable over time. These properties make endowments and the endowment structure the best starting point for analysis of economic development. Except in Heckscher-Ohlin trade theory, the economic profession has not given sufficient attention to the implications of factor endowments and endowment structure.

3. The proposition that the industrial structure is endogenous to an economy's endowment structure at each level of its development has been the subject

of extensive theoretical studies. For instance, Lin and Zhang (2009) develop an endogenous growth model that combines structural change with repeated product improvements to discuss the endogeneity of industrial structure, the appropriate technology, and economic growth in a less developed country (LDC) in a dynamic general-equilibrium framework. They use a two-sector model in which technological change in the traditional sector takes the form of horizontal innovation based on expanding variety as suggested in Romer (1990) while technological progress in the modern sector is accompanied by incessantly creating advanced capital-intensive industry to replace backward labor-intensive industry. This requires an intentional investment of resources by profit-seeking firms or entrepreneurs (Grossman and Helpman 1994). The model shows that: (i) the optimal industrial structure in LDCs should not be the same as that in developed countries (DCs); (ii) the appropriate technology adopted in the modern sector in LDCs ought to be inside the technology frontier of the DCs; and (iii) a firm in an LDC that enters a capital-intensive, advanced industry (by DC standards) would be nonviable owing to the relative scarcity of capital in the LDC's factor endowment. Ju, Lin, and Wang (2009) develop a dynamic general equilibrium model to show that industries will endogenously upgrade toward the more capital-intensive ones as the capital endowment becomes more abundant. The model features a continuous inverse-V-shaped pattern of industrial evolution driven by capital accumulation: As the capital endowment reaches a certain threshold, a new industry appears, prospers, then declines, and finally, disappears. While the industry is declining, a more capital-intensive industry appears and booms. Capital is mobile in an open economy. It is unlikely that the mobility of capital will equalize the capital–labor ratio in high-income, capital-abundant countries and low-income, labor-abundant countries. This is because there are two main purposes for the capital to flow from a higher-income country to a lower-income country. The first one is to exploit the lower-income country's comparative advantage of abundant labor (or natural resources) so as to use the lower-income country as its export base. For this purpose, the industry must be consistent with the recipient, lower-income country's comparative advantage determined by its factor endowment, although the technology used by the foreign-invested firms may be somewhat more capital intensive than the indigenous firms. The second purpose of capital flow from a higher-income country is to get access to a lower-income country's domestic markets. For this type of capital flow, the foreign-invested industries will be more capital intensive than the indigenous firms but only the types of production activities that are consistent with the host country's comparative advantage, for example assembly of parts into final products, will be located in the lower-income country. Therefore, the theoretical insights derived from the assumption that the relative abundance of capital in a country is given at any specific time will hold even with capital mobility.

4.  For nontradable goods and services, the nature of least-cost production tech-
    nology will also be endogenously determined by the endowment structure.
    That is, as capital becomes relatively abundant, the technology used to pro-
    duce nontradable goods and services will also become relatively capital inten-
    sive, just as happens in the tradable goods sector. For simplicity, the discussion
    in the paper will focus on the tradable sector.

5.  Porter (1990) made the term "competitive advantage" popular. According to
    him, a nation will have competitive advantage in the global economy if the
    industries in the nation fulfill the following four conditions: (1) their indus-
    tries intensively use the nation's abundant and relatively inexpensive factors of
    production; (2) their products have large domestic markets; (3) each industry
    forms a cluster; and (4) the domestic market for each industry is competitive.
    The first condition in effect means that the industries should be the economy's
    comparative advantage determined by the nation's endowments. The third and
    the fourth conditions will hold only if the industries are consistent with the
    nation's competitive advantage. Therefore, the four conditions can be reduced
    to two independent conditions: comparative advantage and domestic market
    size. Of these two independent conditions, comparative advantage is the most
    important because if an industry corresponds to the country's comparative
    advantage, the industry's product will have a global market. That is why many
    of the richest countries of the world are very small (Lin and Ren 2007).

6.  Industries in advanced developed countries today are typically located on the
    global frontier and face uncertainty as to what the next frontier industries
    will be. This explains why government policy measures to support pioneer
    firms in such countries are usually in the form of general support to research
    in universities (which has externalities to private firms' R&D), patents,
    preferential taxes for capital investments, mandates, defense contracts, and
    government procurement. Support in the form of preferential taxes, defense
    contracts, and government procurement are industry or product-specific.
    Government support to basic research also needs to be prioritized for certain
    types of potential industries or products because of budget constraints. How-
    ever, government support to pioneer firms in developing countries, especially
    low-income countries, often fails. One of the most important reasons is the
    attempt by low-income countries governments to support firms in industries
    that are inconsistent with the economy's comparative advantages (Lin 2009a;
    Lin and Chang 2009).

7.  Barro (2009) calls active fiscal policy of the Keynesian type "the extreme
    demand-side view" or the "new voodoo economics."

8.  Recent research suggests that economic returns on investment projects in devel-
    oping countries average 30–40 percent for telecommunications, more than 40
    percent for electricity generation, and more than 200 percent for roads. In

Thailand, production loss due to power outages represented more than 50 percent of the total indirect costs of doing business in 2006. Firms often rely on their own generators to supplement the unreliable public electricity supply. In Pakistan, more than 60 percent of homes destroyed by fire surveyed in 2002 owned a generator. The cost of maintaining a power generator is often high and burdensome, especially for small and medium-size firms, which are important sources of employment. Yet, while these costs must be privately borne, their benefits are felt across the economy.

9. This is percentage of cost (UNCTAD Statistical Database).

10. The exploitation of natural resources can generate a large amount of revenues but it is generally very capital intensive and provides limited job opportunities. In a recent visit to Papua New Guinea, I observed that the Ok Tedi copper and gold mine in Tabubil generates almost 80 percent of the country's export revenues and 40 percent of government revenues but provides only 2,000 jobs. A proposed liquefied natural gas project will double Papua New Guinea's national income after its completion in 2012, but the project will only provide 8,000 jobs. The majority of Papua New Guinea's 6.5 million population still live on subsistence agriculture. The contrast between the standard of living of a few elite workers in modern mining and that of subsistence farmers is becoming a source of social tensions. A similar observation can be made about Botswana: the failure to diversify the economy from diamond mining and to generate employment opportunities may explain the widening disparity and deterioration of various human and social indicators, despite the diamond industry's great success in sustaining Botswana's growth miracle over the past 40 years.

11. Gerschenkron (1962) made a similar point, arguing that the private sector alone cannot effectively address the problems of access to finance in weak institutional environments.

12. A sudden large inflow of portfolio capital is most likely to be invested in speculative sectors rather than in productive sectors. The reason is twofold: a large increase in investment in existing industries may encounter diminishing returns to capital, and the potential for quick and large industrial upgrading is limited by human capital, as well as soft and hard infrastructure constraints.

13. Carneiro and Heckman (2003) have demonstrated the importance of both cognitive and noncognitive skills that are formed early in life in accounting for gaps in schooling among social groups and other dimensions of socioeconomic success. They have provided empirical evidence of a high return to early interventions and a low return to remedial or compensatory interventions later in life.

14. The list includes: Botswana; Brazil; China; Hong Kong SAR, China; Indonesia; Japan; Korea; Malaysia; Malta; Oman; Singapore; Taiwan, China; and Thailand.

# References

Acemoglu, D., S. Johnson, and J.A. Robinson. 2001. "The Colonial Origins of Comparative Development: An Empirical Investigation." *American Economic Review* 91: 1369–401.

Aghion, P., and P. Howitt. 1992. "A Model of Growth through Creative Destruction." *Econometrica* 60(2): 323–51.

Barro, R.J. 2009. "Government Spending Is No Free Lunch." *The Wall Street Journal*, January 22.

Becker, Gary S. 1975. *Human Capital: A Theoretical and Empirical Analysis, with Special Reference to Education.* 2nd ed. New York: Columbia University Press for NBER.

Caprio, G., and P. Honohan. 2001. *Finance for Growth: Policy Choices in a Volatile World.* New York: World Bank and Oxford University Press.

Cardoso, E., and A. Helwege. 1995. *Latin America's Economy.* Cambridge, MA: MIT Press.

Carneiro, P., and J.J. Heckman. 2003. "Human Capital Policy." IZA Discussion Papers 821, Institute for the Study of Labor (IZA).

Chang, P.K. 1949. *Agriculture and Industrialization.* Cambridge, MA: Harvard University Press.

Domar, E. 1946. "Capital Expansion, Rate of Growth, and Employment." *Econometrica* 14 (April): 137 – 47.

Easterly, W. 2001. *The Elusive Quest for Growth: Economists' Adventures and Misadventures in the Tropics.* Cambridge, MA: MIT Press.

Easterly, W., N. Loayza, and P.J. Montiel. 1997. "Has Latin America's Post-Reform Growth Been Disappointing?" World Bank Policy Research Paper 1708, World Bank, Washington, D.C., August.

Eichengreen, B., M. Mussa, G. Dell'Ariccia, E. Detragiache, G.M. Milesi-Ferretti, and A. Tweedie. 1999. "Liberalizing Capital Movements: Some Analytical Issues." Economic Issues no. 17. IMF, Washington, D.C.

Francesco, G., and M. Pagano. 1991. "Can Severe Fiscal Contractions Be Expansionary?—Tales of Two Small European Countries." In O.J. Blanchard and S. Fischer, *NBER Macroeconomics Annual 1990.* Cambridge, MA: MIT Press.

Furtado, C. 1964. *Development and Underdevelopment.* Los Angeles: University of California Press.

———. 1970. *Economic Development of Latin America.* London: Cambridge University Press.

Gerschenkron, A. 1962. *Economic Backwardness in Historical Perspective: A Book of Essays.* Cambridge, MA: Belknap Press of Harvard University Press.

Glaeser, E., and A. Shleifer. 2002. "Legal Origins." *Quarterly Journal of Economics* 117 (November): 1193–229.

Grossman, G.M., and E. Helpman. 1994. "Endogenous Innovation in the Theory of Growth." *Journal of Economic Perspectives* 8(1): 23–44.

Growth Commission. 2008. "The Growth Report: Strategies for Sustained Growth and Inclusive Development." Washington, D.C.

Harrison, A., and A. Rodríguez-Clare. 2010. "Trade, Foreign Investment, and Industrial Policy for Developing Countries." In D. Rodrik (ed.), *Handbook of Economic Growth*, Vol. 5. Amsterdam, The Netherlands: North-Holland, p. 4039–213.

Harrod, R.F. 1939. "An Essay in Dynamic Theory." *The Economic Journal* 49(193): 14–33.

Hausmann, R., D. Rodrik, and A. Velasco. 2005. "Growth Diagnostics." In J. Stiglitz and N. Serra (eds.), *The Washington Consensus Reconsidered: Towards a New Global Governance*. Oxford: Oxford University Press.

Hirschman, A.O. 1958. *The Strategy of Economic Development*. New Haven, CT: Yale University Press.

Jones, C.I. 1998. *Introduction to Economic Growth*. New York: W.W. Norton.

Jones, C.I., and P.M. Romer. 2009. "The New Kaldor Facts: Ideas, Institutions, Population, and Human Capital." NBER Working Paper Series 15094.

Ju, J., J.Y. Lin, and Y. Wang. 2009. "Endowment Structures, Industrial Dynamics, and Economic Growth." Policy Research Working Papers Series 5055, World Bank, Washington, D.C.

Justman, M., and B. Gurion. 1991. "Structuralist Perspective on the Role of Technology in Economic Growth and Development." *World Development* 19(9): 1167–83.

Kanbur, R. 2009. "The Crisis, Economic Development Thinking, and Protecting the Poor." Presentation to the World Bank's Executive Board, July.

Krueger, A. 1974. "The Political Economy of Rent-Seeking Society." *American Economic Review* 64(3): 291–303.

Krugman, P. 1979. "A Model of Innovation, Technology Transfer, and the World Distribution of Income." *Journal of Political Economy* 87(2): 253–66.

———. 1993. "Protection in Developing Countries." In R. Dornbusch (ed.), *Policymaking in the Open Economy: Concepts and Case Studies in Economic Performance*. New York: Oxford University Press, 127–48.

Kuznets, S. 1966. *Modern Economic Growth: Rate, Structure and Spread*. New Haven, CT: Yale University Press.

Lau, L.J., Y. Qian, and G. Roland. 2000. "Reform without Losers: An Interpretation of China's Dual-track Approach to Transition." *Journal of Political Economy* 108(1): 120–43.

Leibenstein, H. 1957. *Economic Backwardness and Economic Growth: Studies in the Theory of Economic Development*. New York: Wiley.

Lewis, W.A. 1954. "Economic Development with Unlimited Supplies of Labor." The Manchester School, May.

Lin, J.Y. 2009a. *Economic Development and Transition: Thought, Strategy, and Viability.* Cambridge: Cambridge University Press.

———. 2009b. "Beyond Keynesianism." *Harvard International Review* 31(2): 14–17.

Lin, J.Y., and H. Chang. 2009. "DPR Debate: Should Industrial Policy in Developing Countries Conform to Comparative Advantage or Defy It?" *Development Policy Review* 27(5): 483–502. (Reprinted as the debate in chapter II of this volume.)

Lin, J.Y., and F. Li. 2009. "Development Strategy, Viability, and Economic Distortions in Developing Countries." Policy Research Working Paper 4906, World Bank, Washington, D.C., April.

Lin, J.Y., and C. Monga. 2010. "The Growth Report and New Structural Economics." Policy Research Working Papers Series 5336, World Bank, Washington, D.C. (Reprinted in chapter II of this volume.)

———. 2011. "DPR Debate: Growth Identification and Facilitation: The Role of the State in the Dynamics of Structural Change." *Development Policy Review* 29(3): 259–310. (Reprinted in chapter III of this volume.)

Lin, J.Y., and R. Ren. 2007. "East Asian Miracle Debate Revisited" (in Chinese). *Jingji Yanjiu* (Economic Research Journal) 42(8): 4–12.

Lin, J.Y., and P. Zhang. 2009. "Industrial Structure, Appropriate Technology and Economic Growth in Less Developed Countries." Policy Research Working Paper 4906, World Bank, Washington, D.C., April.

Lin, J.Y., X. Sun, and Y. Jiang. 2009. "Towards a Theory of Optimal Financial Structure." Policy Research Working Papers Series 5038, World Bank, Washington, D.C.

Lucas Jr., R.E. 1990. "Why Doesn't Capital Flow from Rich to Poor Countries?" *American Economic Review* 80(2): 92–96.

———. 2002. *Lectures on Economic Growth.* Cambridge, MA: Harvard University Press.

McKinnon, R.I. 1973. *Money and Capital in Economic Development.* Washington, D.C: Brookings Institution.

Monga, C. 1997. *L'argent des autres—Banques et petites entreprises en Afrique: le cas du Cameroun.* Paris: LDGJ-Montchretien.

Myrdal, G. 1957. *Economic Theory and Under-developed Regions.* London: Duckworth.

Naughton, B. 1995. *Growing Out of Plan: Chinese Economic Reform 1978–1993.* Cambridge: Cambridge University Press.

Nurkse, R. 1953. *Problems of Capital Formation in Underdeveloped Countries.* New York: Oxford University Press.

Osman-Gani, A.M. 2004. "Human Capital Development in Singapore: An Analysis of National Policy Perspectives." *Advances in Developing Human Resources* 6(3): 276–87.

Porter, M.E. 1990. *The Competitive Advantage of Nations.* New York: Free Press.

Prebisch, R. 1950. *The Economic Development of Latin America and its Principal Problems*. New York: United Nations. Reprinted in *Economic Bulletin for Latin America* 7(1): 1–22.

Ramsey, F.P. 1928. "A Mathematical Theory of Saving." *Economic Journal* 38 (152): 543–59.

Ravallion, M. 2009. "Evaluation in the Practice of Development." *The World Bank Research Observer* 24(1): 29–53.

Rodrik, D. 2004. "Industrial Policy for the Twenty-First Century." Cambridge, MA. [http://ksghome. harvard.edu/~drodrik/unidosep.pdf].

Romer, P.M. 1987. "Growth Based on Increasing Returns Due to Specialization." *American Economic Review* 77(2): 56–62.

———. 1990. "Endogenous Technological Change." *Journal of Political Economy* 98(5, Part 2): *The Problem of Development: A Conference of the Institute for the Study of Free Enterprise Systems*, October, pp. S71–S102.

Rosenstein-Rodan, P. 1943. "Problems of Industrialization of Eastern and Southeastern Europe." *Economic Journal* 111(210–11, June–September): 202 –11.

Rosenzweig, M.R., and K.I. Wolpin. 1985. "Scientific Experience, Household Structure and Intergenerational Transfers: Farm Family Land and Labor Arrangements in Developing Countries." *Quarterly Journal of Economics* 100, Supplement.

Rostow, W.W. 1990 [1960]. T*he Stages of Economic Growth: A Non-Communist Manifesto*, 3rd edn. New York: Cambridge University Press.

Schultz, T.W. 1961. "Investments in Human Capital." *American Economic Review* 51 (1): 1–17.

Schumpeter, J., 1934. *The Theory of Economic Development*. Cambridge, MA: Harvard University Press.

Shaw, E. 1973. *Financial Deepening in Economic Development*. New York: Oxford University Press.

Singer, H. 1950. "The Distribution of Gains between Investing and Borrowing Countries." *American Economic Review* 40(May): 473–85.

Subramanian, A., and D. Roy. 2003. "Who Can Explain the Mauritian Miracle? Mede, Romer, Sachs, or Rodrik?" In. D. Rodrik (ed.), In *Search of Prosperity: Analytic Narratives on Economic Growth*. Princeton: Princeton University Press, 205–43.

Taylor, L. 1983. *Structuralist Macroeconomics: Applicable Models for the Third World*. New York: Basic Books..

———. 1991. *Income Distribution, Inflation and Growth: Lectures on Structuralist Macroeconomic Theory*. Cambridge, MA: MIT Press.

———. 2004. *Reconstructing Macroeconomics: Structuralist Proposals and Critiques of the Mainstream*. Cambridge, MA: Harvard University Press.

UNCTAD Statistical Database. http://www.unctad.org/templates/page .asp?intItemID=2364&lang=1.

Williamson, J. 1990. "What Washington Means by Policy Reform."
    In J. Williamson (ed.), *Latin American Adjustment: How Much Has
    Happened?* Washington, D.C.: Institute for International Economics.
———. 2002. "Did the Washington Consensus Fail?" [http://www.peterson
    institute.org/publications/papers/paper.cfm?ResearchID=488].
World Bank. 2005. *Economic Growth in the 1990s: Learning from a Decade of
    Reform.* Washington, D.C.
———. 2010. "Research for Development: A World Bank Perspective on Future
    Directions for Research." Policy Research Working Paper 5437,
    Washington, D.C.

# COMMENTS

## Anne Krueger[*][†]

Ever since development economics became a field, there has been a search for "the" key to development. Physical capital accumulation, human capital, industrial development, institutional quality, social capital, and a variety of other factors have been the focus at one time or another. As each became the focal point, there was a parallel explicit or implied role of government.

If I understand Justin Lin correctly, he is saying that the "new structural economics" (NSE) accepts that earlier thought ignored comparative advantage, which should be market determined, but that growth requires improvements in 'hard' (tangible) and 'soft' (intangible) infrastructure at each stage. Such upgrading and improvements require coordination and inhere with large externalities to firms' transaction costs and returns to capital investment. Thus, in addition to an effective market mechanism, the government should play an active role in facilitating structural change (p. 28).

He seems also to believe that growth depends almost entirely on industry growth and believes that constant "upgrading" or moving up the value added chain is the central challenge. He says that "the laissez-faire approach... missed the importance of the process of continuous,

---

* Adapted from "Comments on "New Structural Economics' by Justin Lin," by Anne Krueger, originally published in *The World Bank Research Observer* (2011) 26 (2): 222–26, published by Oxford University Press on behalf of the International Bank for Reconstruction and Development/The World Bank. © 2011 The International Bank for Reconstruction and Development / The World Bank.

fundamental technological changes and industrial upgrading, which distinguishes modern economic growth from premodern economic growth" (p. 15).

It is questionable whether such changes and upgrading must take place early in the development process. In many countries, unskilled labor has moved to unskilled-labor-intensive industries, with expansion of those industries' outputs for a period during which more and more workers acquired acquaintance with modern factory techniques, and exports of the unskilled-labor-intensive goods increased. Only later in the development process did upgrading become a major part of industrial growth once there had been significant absorption of rural labor, and much of it happened in existing firms in response to rising real wages, lower capital costs, and learning through exposure to the international market.

However, in most countries rural labor could be absorbed only as agricultural productivity increased; Lin's NSE seems to equate growth with industrial expansion, ignoring the importance of increased productivity of the large fraction of the labor force (and of land) in rural areas. Failure to invest in agricultural research and development and in rural health and education has been a major weakness of many countries' development strategies. While strides have been made in reducing discrimination against agriculture, the NSE as exposited by Lin would appear to support the industrial and urban bias that has itself constituted a very large distortion in some countries.

It will come as no surprise that I agree that the market should be used to determine comparative advantage, and that governments have responsibilities for insuring an appropriate incentive framework and provision of infrastructure (both hard and, as he terms it, "soft").

But there is nothing new in that. What purports to be the "new" part is the assertion that coordination and upgrading of infrastructure should in some way be related to particular industries. It is at this point where a question arises: most economists would accept the view that cost–benefit analysis should be used in the choice of infrastructure projects. If "externalities" and "coordination" are important, are they important for specific industries or for the entire industrial economy? If the former, how are those industries to be identified, and how would the externalities be estimated in cost–benefit analysis? Or would they? If infrastructure is seen to be industry-specific, it is not clear what it is. As with the possible existence of infant industries, it is one thing to believe that there are such industries (perhaps) and quite another to identify ahead of time which they are. And even if such industries exist and are identified, questions arise as to the incentives that would be appropriate for the government to foster these industries. (Would they be firm-specific treatment? Tariffs? Subsidies to firms or industries? Each has huge problems.) And if it is more "conventional," what is new? If infrastructure is specific to industry (or a group of industries), the same questions must be addressed.

Some hints are given as to what Lin has in mind: "successful industrial upgrading in responding to change in an economy's endowment structure requires that the pioneer firms overcome issues of limited information regarding which new industries are the economy's latent comparative advantages determined by the changing endowment structure. Valuable information externalities arise from the knowledge gained by pioneer firms in both success and failure. Therefore, in addition to playing a proactive role in the improvements of soft and hard infrastructures, the government in a developing county, like that in a developed country, needs to compensate for the information externalities generated by pioneer firms" (p. 25).

Here, the infant industry concerns arise again. How can these externalities be forecast? As Baldwin (1969) pointed out, there are major difficulties with this argument, quite aside from the identification of such externalities. And firms producing unskilled-labor-intensive goods and exporting them have usually learned of the opportunities provided by the international market and chosen to upgrade as their experience has increased. Learning does not seem to have been a major issue for firms in South Korea, Taiwan, and elsewhere.

Another hint as to what Lin has in mind comes from his advocacy of coordination of infrastructure investments. According to him, "Change in infrastructure requires collective action or at least coordination between the provider of infrastructure services and industrial firms. For this reason, it falls to the government either to introduce such changes or to coordinate them proactively."(p. 25) How this would be carried out is unclear; Lin insists that infrastructure must be upgraded with growth as long as it is consistent with the evolving future direction of comparative advantage, but does not elaborate on how that future direction should be identified.

Involving individual firms and industries in decisions as to infrastructure investments would appear to offer far too much scope for individual firms' and industries' influence over these investments.

Although it is certainly true that not everything can be done at once, focus on selected areas for large investments at the neglect of the rest of the economy is a highly questionable strategy. Why it would be preferable to allocate scarce capital so that some activities have excellent infrastructure while others must manage with seriously deficient infrastructure is not clear: without further evidence, it would appear to be a distortion. Further, questions can also be raised as to why "soft infrastructure," such as the "business environment" (which consists of such things as the commercial code, the structure of taxes and subsidies, regulations, and so on), cannot be economy wide. And the criteria by which there would be designation of a given area, or the types of industries that would be eligible, as the recipient of special treatment are not discussed. What the hard infrastructure is that does not consist of items such as roads and ports, and is industry specific, is not discussed.

But all of this hinges on the proposition that decisionmakers in the public sector can ascertain the appropriate rate of "upgrading" and the extent of the supposed externalities. This raises a host of issues. There is, first, the consideration that even if one could know which activities would have comparative advantage, that advantage often develops as small firms enter, some of which are successful and grow larger. Any strategy of "upgrading" would inevitably favor larger, established firms, and hence encounter the same sorts of problems as did the older import-substitution strategy which, as Lin recognizes, failed. "Picking winners" as industries is difficult; it cannot be firm specific or the usual problems of corruption and cronyism arise. And yet supporting an industry or industries as an undifferentiated entity is difficult: are textiles an industry? Or is synthetic fiber an industry? Or is nylon an industry? And, of course, the breakdown could go further. And as capital and skills per person accumulate, how is it to be decided where the industrial park or export processing zone should be? And which firms should be eligible to enter it?

Another strand of Lin's argument pertains to the role of distortions. He appears to be saying that countries that earlier adopted import-substitution strategies have distorted industrial structures that should affect policy.

In particular, he says: "many developing countries start climbing the industrial ladder with the legacy of distortions from old structural strategies of import-substitution. [The new structural economics] would therefore suggest a gradualist approach to trade liberalization. During transition, the state may consider some temporary protection to industries that are not consistent with a country's comparative advantage, while liberalizing at the same time entry to other more competitive sectors that were controlled and repressed in the past" (p. 36).

Here, as elsewhere, little guidance is given as to how much protection industries would be provided with; how long that protection would last; how industries to be protected would be chosen; and so on. But even more important, one can imagine the political pressures for greater protection for longer periods. Protection of some industries is disprotection of others, as is well known, so reform efforts would clearly be dampened. Even worse, a major challenge for liberalizing reform is for it to be credible that the altered policies are not reversible. Lin's prescription would greatly increase the challenge of creating credibility, and a slower transition would be a longer period during which growth was slow and political pressures opposing liberalization at all were mounting.

In all, there is much in Lin's analysis with which most would agree, but focus on governmentally led identification of industries with "latent comparative advantage" and industry-specific provision of infrastructure is not convincing. Lin calls for much research. A first task should be to show that there are industry (or industry-cluster) externalities, how they could be identified and measured ex ante, and what sorts of government support would improve potential welfare and growth prospects without generating the same sorts of rent-seeking opportunities as import substitution policies did.

Until that research is undertaken, the NSE will, it is to be feared, be taken as a license for governments to support specific industries (and worse yet, perhaps even firms), in ways that may be no more conducive to growth than were the old, failed, import-substitution policies.

## Note

† Anne Krueger is Professor of International Economics in the School of Advanced International Studies (SAIS) at Johns Hopkins University and a Senior Fellow at the Stanford Center for International Development.

## Reference

Baldwin, Robert E. 1969. "The Case against Infant Industry Protection." *Journal of Political Economy* 77(3): 295–305.

## Dani Rodrik[*][†]

Justin Lin wants to make structuralist economics respectable again, and I applaud him for that. He wants to marry structuralism with neoclassical economic reasoning, and I applaud this idea too. So he has two cheers from me. I withhold my third cheer so I can quibble with some of what he writes.

The central insight of structuralism is that developing countries are qualitatively different from developed ones. They are not just radially shrunk versions of rich countries. In order to understand the challenges of under-development, you have to understand how the structure of employment and production—in particular the large gaps between the social marginal products of labor in traditional versus modern activities—is determined and how the obstacles that block structural transformation can be overcome.

The central insight of neoclassical economics is that people respond to incentives. We need to understand the incentives of, say, teachers to show up for work and impart valuable skills to their students or of entrepreneurs to invest in new economic activities if we are going to have useful things to say to governments about what they ought to do. (And of course, let's not forget that government officials must have the incentive to do the economically "correct" things, too.)

If we put these two sets of ideas together, we can have a useful development economics, one that does not dismiss the tools of contemporary economic analysis and yet is sensitive to the specific circumstances of developing economies. This is the kind of development economics that is appropriately nuanced in its take on government intervention. It doesn't presume

* Adapted from "Comments on "New Structural Economics' by Justin Lin," by Dani Rodrik, originally published in *The World Bank Research Observer* (2011) 26 (2): 227–29, published by Oxford University Press on behalf of the International Bank for Reconstruction and Development/ The World Bank. © 2011 The International Bank for Reconstruction and Development / The World Bank.

omniscience or altruism on the part of governments. It has a healthy respect for the power and effectiveness of markets. But it does not blithely assume that development is an automatic process that takes care of itself as long as government stays out of the picture.

So as Lin rightly emphasizes, the state has a useful role to play in promoting industrial diversification and upgrading. He lists among desirable functions the provision of information about new industries, the coordination of investments across firms and industries, the internalization of informational externalities, and the incubation of new industries through the encouragement of foreign direct investment. Policies of this kind may be unnecessary or superfluous in advanced economies, but they are essential if poor countries are to progress.

To distinguish his brand of structuralist development economics from old-style structuralism, Lin writes that a key difference is that the old school advocated policies that go against an economy's comparative advantage. The new approach, by contrast, "stresses the central role of the market ... and advises the state to play a facilitating role to assist firms in the process of industrial upgrading by addressing externality and coordination issues." Lin argues that government policies should "follow" comparative advantage, rather than "defy" it.

Here is where I quibble with Lin's argument. It seems to me that Lin wants to argue both for and against comparative advantage at the same time, and I cannot quite see how this can be done. If one believes that externality and coordination problems need to be addressed, as Lin apparently does, one must believe that such problems are preventing firms from investing appropriately. One must believe that markets are sending entrepreneurs the wrong signals—invest here, not there—and that allocating resources according to comparative advantage, as revealed by market prices, would be socially suboptimal. Comparative advantage has practical meaning for firms only insofar as it gets reflected in prices.

So when Lin asks governments to step in to address market failures and recommends the type of policies I have listed above—the coordination of investments, the incubation of new industries, etc.—he too is asking them to defy comparative advantage as revealed in market prices. In this respect, there is less difference between what the old school said and what the new school is saying.

Lin doesn't want governments to employ "conventional" import substitution strategies to build capital-intensive industries which "are not consistent with the country's comparative advantage." But isn't building industries that defy comparative advantage what Japan and South Korea did, in their time? Isn't it what China has been doing, and quite successfully, for some time now? According to my calculations, the export bundle of China is that of a country between three and six times richer. If China, with its huge surplus of agricultural labor, were to specialize in the type of products that its factor endowments recommend, would it now be exporting the advanced products that it is?

Some people draw a distinction between static and dynamic comparative advantage in this context, but I don't think that is the relevant distinction. Market failures drive a wedge between market prices and social marginal valuations, and distort the relative costs that signal comparative advantage. Whether these distortions are introduced into intertemporal relative prices or today's relative prices is largely secondary. The policies that Lin recommends are meant to offset such market distortions, and their intended effect is to induce firms to make choices that defy comparative advantage.

I suspect that my difference with Lin is mainly methodological—and perhaps even just terminological—and may have little practical import. What Lin probably has in mind is that today's industrial policies need to have a softer touch than that which structuralists of old tended to recommend. They must be more respectful of markets and incentives; they must show greater awareness of the potential of government failures; and they must focus specifically on market failures rather than vague shortcomings of the private sector. I would agree with all this.

But a deeper question relates to the policy implications one draws from all this. In principle, market failures need to be addressed with appropriately targeted policies. So if the problem is one of information spillovers, the first-best is to subsidize the information generating process. If the problem is lack of coordination, the first-best is for the government to bring the parties together and coordinate their investments. In practice, though, the relevant market failures cannot be always closely identified and the directly targeted remedies may not be available. The practical reality is that the type of policies structuralism calls for—whether of the traditional or the contemporary type—have to be applied in a second-best setting. And in such a setting, nothing is all that straightforward anymore.

Presumably this is the reason why Lin recommends, for example, a gradual approach to trade liberalization. Such an approach is, at best, a second-best remedy to some loosely specified market failures that either cannot be precisely identified ex ante or cannot be fully treated with first-best Pigovian interventions. But how different is this from the old structuralist approach? Didn't most structuralists also view protection as a temporary expedient, to be done away with once the requisite industrial capabilities were built?

To repeat, my differences with Justin Lin are second order, and they are swamped by our areas of agreement. My quibbles are a bit like the internal doctrinal debates waged among communists—does the revolution require the intensification of the class struggle, or can that stage be skipped?—when much of the rest of the world is on a different wavelength altogether.

As a fellow traveler, I am greatly encouraged by what Justin Lin is trying to do. It is high time that the common sense exhibited in his approach reclaimed its mantle in development economics.

## Note

† Dani Rodrik is professor of international political economy at Harvard University's John F. Kennedy School of Government.

## Joseph E. Stiglitz[*][†]

Twelve years ago, when I was chief economist of the World Bank, I suggested that the major challenge to development economics was learning the lessons of the previous several decades: a small group of countries, mostly in Asia, but a few in other regions, had had phenomenal success, beyond anything that had been anticipated by economists; while many other countries had experienced slow growth, or even worse, stagnation

---

* Adapted from "Rethinking Development Economics," by Joseph Stiglitz, originally published in *The World Bank Research Observer* (2011) 26 (2): 230–36, published by Oxford University Press on behalf of the International Bank for Reconstruction and Development / The World Bank. © 2011 The International Bank for Reconstruction and Development / The World Bank.

and decline—inconsistent with the standard models in economics which predicted convergence. The successful countries had followed policies that were markedly different from those of the Washington Consensus, though they shared some elements in common; those policies had not brought high growth, stability, or poverty reduction. Shortly after I left the World Bank, the crisis in Argentina—which had been held up as the poster child of the country that had followed Washington Consensus policies—reinforced the doubts about that strategy.

The global financial crisis, too, has cast doubt over the neoclassical paradigm in advanced industrial countries, and rightly so. Much of development economics had been viewed as asking how developing countries could successfully transition toward the kinds of market-oriented policy frameworks that came to be called "American style capitalism." The debate was not about the goal, but the path to that goal, with some advocating "shock therapy," while others focused on pacing and sequencing—a more gradualist tack. The global financial crisis has now raised questions about that model even for developed countries.

In this short essay, I want to argue that the long-term experiences in growth and stability of both developed and less developed countries, as well as the deeper theoretical understanding of the strengths and limitations of market economies, provide support for a "new structural" approach to development—an approach similar in some ways to that advocated by Justin Lin in his paper, but markedly different in others. This approach sees the limitations of markets as being greater than he suggests—even well functioning market economies are, on their own, neither efficient nor stable. The only period in the history of modern capitalism when there has not been repeated financial crises was the short period after the Great Depression when the major countries around the world adopted, and enforced, strong financial regulations. Interestingly this was also a period of rapid growth and a period in which the fruits of that growth were widely shared.

But government not only has a restraining role; it has a constructive and catalytic role—in promoting entrepreneurship, providing the social and physical infrastructure, ensuring access to education and finance, and supporting technology and innovation.

The perspective that I am putting forward differs not only in its view of the efficiency and stability of unfettered markets, but also in what it sees as the primary driver of economic growth. Since Solow's pioneering work more than a half-century ago (Solow 1957), it has been recognized that the major source of increases in per capita income are advances in technology.[1]

The argument that improvements in knowledge are a primary source of growth is even more compelling for developing countries. As the *World Development Report* for 1998–99 emphasized, what separates developing and developed countries is not just a gap in resources, but a disparity in knowledge. There are well understood limits to the pace with which countries can accumulate capital, but the limitations on the speed with which the gap in knowledge can be closed are less clear.

But the view that creating a learning society, focusing on absorbing and adapting, and eventually producing knowledge, provides markedly different perspectives on development strategies than those provided by the neoclassical model. That model centered attention on increasing capital and the efficient allocation of resources. Since the appropriate sectoral structure of the economy naturally depends on the resource endowment, there will be a natural evolution of the economy's structure over time. Markets allocate resources efficiently, enabling the structure to change as the (endogenous) endowments change. A government's main role, in this view, is not to put impediments in the market.

The standard market failures approach criticized these conclusions by focusing on a variety of market imperfections: For instance, imperfections in capital markets meant that finance was often not available for new enterprises that were required as part of this sectoral adjustment. Individuals on their own couldn't finance their education. There are pervasive externalities—not only environmental externalities but also those associated with systemic risk, so evidenced in the current crisis. Research over the past 20 years has explored the consequences of market failures like imperfect capital markets, traced these imperfections back to problems of imperfect and asymmetric information, and proposed a set of remedies, which in some countries, in some periods, have worked remarkably well. Good financial regulations in countries like India protected them against the ravages of the global financial crisis.

But the perspective of the "learning society"—or, as Greenwald and I call it, the "infant economy"—adds a new dimension to the analysis

(Greenwald and Stiglitz 2006). Knowledge is different from an ordinary commodity. The accumulation of knowledge is inherently associated with externalities—knowledge spillovers. Knowledge itself is a public good. If the accumulation, absorption, adaptation, production, and transfer of knowledge are at the center of successful development, then there is no presumption that markets, on their own, will lead to successful outcomes. Indeed there is a presumption that they will not.

The "new structuralist approach" advocated by Justin Lin is perfectly aligned with this perspective. Lin provides guidance as to how governments should direct the economy; he emphasizes that they should strive to shape the economy in a way that is consistent with its comparative advantage. The problem is that some of the most important elements of comparative advantage are endogenous. Switzerland's comparative advantage in watch-making has little to do with its geography.

Standard Heckscher-Ohlin theory (emphasizing that trade in goods was a substitute for movement in factors) was formulated in a period before globalization allowed the kinds of flows of capital that occur today. With fully mobile capital, outside of agriculture, natural resource endowments need not provide the basis for explaining patterns of production and specialization.[2] In short, there is no reason for countries to need to limit themselves to patterns dictated by endowments, as conventionally defined. More important is the "endowment" of knowledge and entrepreneurship. A major focus of policy should be on how to enhance and shape those endowments.

Even if a government would like to avoid addressing these issues, it cannot; for what the government does (or does not do) has consequences, positive and negative, for the development of the "learning society." This is obviously so for investments in infrastructure, technology, and education; but also for financial, trade, intellectual property rights and competition policies.

At the center of creating a learning society is the identifying of sectors that are more amenable to learning, with benefits not captured by firms themselves, so that there will be underinvestment in learning. Elsewhere Greenwald and I have argued that an implication of this is the encouragement of the industrial sector, which typically has large spillovers. This approach provides an interpretation of the success of Asia's export-led growth. Had Korea allowed market forces on their own to prevail, it would not have embarked on its amazing development successes. Static efficiency entailed that Korea produced rice; indeed the country might today have been among the most efficient rice farmers—but it would still be a poor country. As Arrow pointed out (1962), one learns by doing (and one learns how to learn by learning [Stiglitz 1987]).

This discussion highlights the fundamental difference with neoclassical approaches emphasizing short-run efficiency. The fundamental trade-offs between static and dynamic efficiency should be familiar from the debate over patent laws.

A major concern with these industrial policies[3] concerns implementation—do developing countries have the requisite capacities? We need to put this question in context. There is probably no country that has grown successfully without an important role, not just in restraining and creating markets, but also in promoting such industrial policies, from the countries of East Asia today to the advanced industrial countries, not just during their developmental stages, but even today. The task is to adopt policies and practices—to create institutions like an effective civil service—that enhance the quality of the public sector. The successful countries did so. Policies that either intentionally or unintentionally weaken the state are not likely to do so.

Economic policies have to reflect the capacity of the state to implement them. One of the arguments in favor of exchange rate policies that encourage export industries is that they are broad based: the government does not have to pick particular "strategic" sectors to support. As always, there are trade-offs: efficiency might be enhanced if the sectors with the largest externalities could be targeted.

There are other broad-based policies, such as a development-oriented intellectual-property regime, and investment and financial policies that encourage transfer of technology and the promotion of local entrepreneurship, that can help promote a learning and innovation society (Hausmann and Rodrik 2003; Stiglitz 2004; Emran and Stiglitz 2009; Hoff 2010). Some forms of financial and capital market liberalization may be counterproductive.

Interventions will never be perfect, nor need they be to effect an improvement in economic performance.[4] The choice is not between an imperfect government and a perfect market. It is between imperfect governments and imperfect markets, each of which has to serve as a check on the other; they need to be seen as complementary, and we need to seek a balance between the two—a balance which is not just a matter of assigning certain tasks to one, and others to the other, but rather designing systems where they interact effectively.

While I have been discussing the economics of development, that subject cannot be separated from broader aspects of societal transformation (Stiglitz 1998), as Hirschman emphasized in his writings (1958, 1982). Race and caste are social constructs that effectively inhibit the human development of large parts of the population in many parts of the world. The study of how these constructs get formed, and how they change, is thus a central part of developmental studies (Hoff and Stiglitz 2010). In this article, I have emphasized the creation of a learning society. The economics of doing so entails policies that change sectoral composition. But at the root of success is the education system and how it inculcates attitudes toward change and skills of learning. Other policies (for example legal systems, gender-based microcredit schemes, affirmative action programs) can also play an important role. Before concluding, I want to make two further remarks. The first concerns the relationship between growth and poverty reduction. While growth may be necessary for sustained poverty reduction, it is not sufficient. Not all development policies are pro-poor; some are anti-poor. Policies like financial and capital market liberalization have, at least in some countries, contributed to greater instability, and a consequence of that instability is more poverty.[5] Contractionary monetary and fiscal policies in response to crises exacerbate the downturns, leading to higher unemployment and a higher incidence of poverty. Policies to promote a learning economy too can either be pro- or anti-poor, but the most successful policies will necessarily be broad-based, engendering a transformation of the learning capacities of all citizens, and will therefore be pro-poor.

The second comment relates to the broader objectives of development, which should be sustainable improvements in the well-being of the citizens of the country, and the metrics we use to assess success.[6] Our metrics don't typically capture the increase in the wealth of a country that is a result of the learning strategies advocated here. It is only gradually, over time, that the benefits are realized and recognized.

The aftermath of the global financial crisis should be an exciting time for economists, including development economists, since it dramatically revealed flaws in the reigning paradigm. This paradigm has had enormous influence in development economics, though that influence was already waning, because its prescriptions had failed. Fortunately there are alternative frameworks already available—a plethora of ideas that should provide the basis for new understandings of why a few countries have succeeded so well and some have failed so miserably. Out of this understanding, perhaps we will be able to mold new policy frameworks that will provide the basis of a new era of growth—growth that will both be sustainable and enhance the well-being of most citizens in the poorest countries of the world.

## Notes

† Joseph Stiglitz is a professor of finance and business at Columbia University and chair of the university's Committee on Global Thought. This article was originally a paper prepared for a World Bank symposium, based on Justin Yifu Lin's paper, "New Structural Economics" (chapter I in this book). The perspective taken here is based on joint work with Bruce Greenwald (2006; forthcoming). Stiglitz is indebted to Eamon Kirchen-Allen for research assistance.

1. Even before Solow, Schumpeter had argued that the strength of a market economy resided in its ability to promote innovation and invention; and, shortly after Solow's work, there developed a large literature on endogenous growth, associated with names like Arrow, Shell, Nordhaus, Atkinson, Dasgupta, Uzawa, Kennedy, Fellner, and Stiglitz, followed on in the 1980s and 1990s by the work of Romer. (See for example Atkinson and Stiglitz, 1969; Dasgupta and Stiglitz, 1980a and 1980b; Fellner, 1961; Kennedy, 1964; Nordhaus, 1969a and 1969b, Romer, 1994; Shell, 1966 and 1967; Uzawa, 1965.) The earlier work on endogenous (sometimes referred to as induced) innovation addressed not only the rate of innovation but its direction. For a discussion of more recent contributions in this line of research, see Stiglitz (2006).

2. Indeed, the work of Krugman has emphasized that today most trade is not related in fact to differences in factor endowments.

3. I use the term broadly to embrace any policy attempting to affect the direction of the economy.

4. Indeed, if all projects were successful, it suggests that the government is undertaking too little risk.

5. As I have also noted, such policies may have an adverse effect in enhancing domestic learning capacities.

6.  The International Commission on the Measurement of Economic Performance and Social Progress emphasized the failures of GDP to reflect either sustainability or well-being (Fitoussi, Sen, and Stiglitz 2010). GDP per capita does not say anything about how well most citizens are doing; it can be going up even though most citizens' incomes are declining (as has been happening in the United States). GDP focuses on production in the country, not on incomes earned by those in the country, and takes no account of environmental degradation or resource depletion, or, more broadly, of sustainability. The United States and Argentina both provide examples of countries whose growth appeared to be good—but both were based on unsustainable debts, used to finance consumption booms, not investment.

## References

Arrow, Kenneth J. 1962. "The Economic Implications of Learning by Doing." *Review of Economic Studies* 29:155 –73.

Atkinson, A.B., and J.E. Stiglitz. 1969. "A New View of Technological Change." *The Economic Journal* 79(315): 573–8.

Dasgupta, P., and J.E. Stiglitz. 1980a. "Industrial Structure and the Nature of Innovative Activity." *The Economic Journal* 90(358): 266–93.

———. 1980b. "Uncertainty, Market Structure and the Speed of R&D." *Bell Journal of Economics* 11(1): 1–28.

Emran, S., and J.E. Stiglitz. 2009. "Financial Liberalization, Financial Restraint, and Entrepreneurial Development." Working paper, Institute for International Economic Policy Working Paper Series Elliott School of International Affairs The George Washington University, January (www2.gsb.columbia.edu/faculty/jstiglitz/download/papers/2009_Financial_Liberalization.pdf).

Fellner, W. 1961. "Two Propositions in the Theory of Induced Innovations." *The Economic Journal* 71(282): 305–8.

Fitoussi, J., A. Sen, and J.E. Stiglitz. 2010. *Mismeasuring Our Lives: Why GDP Doesn't Add Up*. New York: The New Press. (The Report of the Commission in the Measurement of Economic Performance and Social Progress, also known as the Sarkhozy Commission.)

Greenwald, B., and J.E. Stiglitz. 2006. "Helping Infant Economies Grow: Foundations of Trade Policies for Developing Countries." *American Economic Review: AEA Papers and Proceedings* 96(2): 141–6.

———. Forthcoming. *Creating a Learning Society: A New Paradigm For Development and Social Progress*. New York: Columbia University Press.

Hausmann, R., and D. Rodrik. 2003. "Economic Development as Self-Discovery." *Journal of Development Economics* 72(2): 603–33.

Hirschman, A.O. 1958. *The Strategy of Economic Development*. New Haven, CT: Yale University Press.

————. 1982. "The Rise and Decline of Development Economics."
In M. Gersovitz, and W.A. Lewis, eds., *The Theory and Experience of Economic Development*. London: Allen and Unwin: 372–90.

Hoff, K. 2010. "Dysfunctional Finance: Positive Shocks and Negative Outcomes." Policy Research Working Paper 5183, The World Bank Development Research Group Macroeconomics and Growth Team, January.

Hoff, K., and J.E. Stiglitz. 2010. "Equilibrium Fictions: A Cognitive Approach to Societal Rigidity." *American Economic Review* 100(2): 141–6.

Kennedy, C. 1964. "Induced Bias in Innovation and the Theory of Distribution." *Economic Journal* 74(295): 541–7.

Nordhaus, W.D. 1969a. "An Economic Theory of Technological Change." *American Economic Association Papers and Proceedings* 59: 18–28.

————. 1969b. *Invention, Growth and Welfare: A Theoretical Treatment of Technological Change*, Cambridge, MA: MIT Press.

Romer, P. 1994. "The Origins of Endogenous Growth." *The Journal of Economic Perspectives* 8(1): 3–22.

Shell, K. 1966. "Toward a Theory of Inventive Activity and Capital Accumulation." *American Economic Association Papers and Proceedings* 56: 62–8.

————. ed. 1967, *Essays on the Theory of Optimal Economic Growth*. Cambridge, MA: MIT Press.

Solow, Robert M. 1957. "Technical Change and the Aggregate Production Function." *Review of Economics and Statistics* 39(3): 312–20.

Stiglitz, J.E. 1987. "Learning to Learn, Localized Learning and Technological Progress." In P. Dasgupta and P. Stoneman, eds., *Economic Policy and Technological Performance*. Cambridge, New York: Cambridge University Press: 125–53.

————. 1998. "Towards a New Paradigm for Development: Strategies, Policies and Processes." The 9th Raul Prebisch Lecture delivered at the Palais des Nations, Geneva, October 19, UNCTAD. Also Chapter 2 in Ha-Joon Chang, ed., *The Rebel Within*. London: Wimbledon Publishing Company, 2001: 57–93.

————. 2004. "Towards a Pro-Development and Balanced Intellectual Property Regime." Keynote address presented at the Ministerial Conference on Intellectual Property for Least Developed Countries, World Intellectual Property Organization, Seoul, October 25. http://www2.gsb.columbia.edu/faculty/jstiglitz/download/2004_TOWARDS_A_PRO_DEVELOPMENT.htm.

———. 2006. "Samuelson and the Factor Bias of Technological Change." In M. Szenberg, L. Ramrattan, and A.A. Gottesman, eds., *Samuelsonian Economics and the Twenty-First Century.* New York: Oxford University Press: 235–51.

Uzawa, H. 1965. "Optimum Technical Change in an Aggregate Model of Economic Growth." *International Economic Review* 6(1): 18–31.

# DEVELOPMENT THINKING 3.0: THE ROAD AHEAD

Development economics appeared after World War II with the intention of helping developing countries industrialize their economies, reduce poverty, and narrow their income gaps with advanced countries. However, the developing countries that followed its recommendations to formulate their development policies failed to achieve the intended goals. In a paper on *New Structural Economics: A Framework for Rethinking Development* published in the most recent issue of the *World Bank Research Observer* [and reprinted as chapter I in this book], I took up the challenge of synthesizing half a century of various approaches proposed by development economics, and suggested a way forward. I am very fortunate and honored that my paper was critically discussed in the same issue of the journal by Anne Krueger, Dani Rodrik, and Joseph Stiglitz, who are among the best minds and most respected experts in the profession—two of them happen to be my predecessors as Chief Economist at the World Bank.

I basically argue that early researchers who launched development economics as a sub-discipline of modern economics focused on market failures and advocated old structuralist, state-led development policies. These policies did not properly account for comparative advantage and failed to create competitive industries. In reaction, a second wave of development thinking inspired by neo-liberalism focused on government failures and recommended Washington Consensus–type policies that also failed to deliver sustainable, inclusive growth and poverty reduction in developing countries.

Looking at the economic history of all successful economies since the Industrial Revolution, I have suggested a general framework for engaging in a third phase of development thinking that focuses on structural change, driven by changes in endowment structure and comparative advantages. That framework, encapsulated in the idea of New Structural Economics (NSE), would help the state play a proactive facilitating role in structural transformation. It would also require policy makers to be more disciplined in designing and implementing strategies around the function of the market.

As could be expected, Anne Krueger, Joseph Stiglitz, Dani Rodrik, and I all agree on the importance and need to reignite the debate on development recipes—especially in light of the current global financial and economic crisis. But we also have subtle and important differences of ideas on the true lessons from economic history and economic theory.

My biggest divergence of views is with Anne Krueger, who questions whether the fundamental technological changes and industrial upgrading— which I consider to be at the heart of, and crucial to, the mechanics of growth—must take place early in the economic development. She contends that "only later in the development process did upgrading become a major part of industrial growth once there had been significant absorption of rural labor, and much of it happened in existing firms in response to rising real wages, lower capital costs, and learning through exposure to the international market" (p. 49). My view of economic development is slightly different: The migration of unskilled rural labor to unskilled labor-intensive industries is a form of structural change that may not occur spontaneously. I believe that proactive action must be taken by policy makers to manage the demand for labor: Indeed it is necessary for the government to facilitate the growth of existing and emerging unskilled labor-intensive industries along the line argued in the NSE. Without such action, many rural out-migrants will be unemployed as has been the case in Africa, Latin America and many other developing countries. On the supply side of the labor market, the government also needs to provide basic education and training to enhance the rural out-migrants' ability to adapt to the new working environment and requirements in the industrial sector. Moreover, successful catching-up countries may start their upgrading process long before their rural surplus labor is exhausted. One example is China. With 39.1 percent of China's labor force still working in the primary sector in 2009, that issue is hotly debated in academic circles: some economists wonder whether China has reached the so-called Lewis turning point and depleted its labor surplus. However, the quick and continuous upgrading of China's industries is still going on, exemplified by the quality and varieties of China's exports to the U.S. market. A similar situation was observed in 1980 when 34 percent of Korea's labor force was still in agriculture. However, Korea had already entered not only industries such as consumer electronics, but also shipbuilding, automaking, and memory chips by that time.

I fully agree with Anne that agricultural productivity needs to be improved in parallel with industrialization (p. 48). But again, in order to improve agricultural productivity and increase farm income, the government must play a proactive role in making new agricultural technology available, providing extension services, improving irrigation, and expanding market channels. The government also needs to create conditions to facilitate the diversification of agriculture into new, higher-value-added cash crops.

While Anne agrees that "the market should be used to determine comparative advantage, and that governments have responsibilities for insuring an appropriate incentive framework and provision of infrastructure, both hard and soft," she objects, most notably, to government intervention aiming at fostering the development of specific industries and doubts "why it would be preferable to allocate scarce capital so that some activities have excellent infrastructure while others must manage with seriously deficient infrastructure" (p. 51).

In fact, identification of new industries and prioritization of government's limited resources to facilitate the development of those industries are both essential for successful growth strategies in developing countries. Why? Because the infrastructure improvements required are often industry specific. One simply has to look at the list of recent success stories in African countries to understand the necessity for identification: textiles in Mauritius, apparel in Lesotho, cotton in Burkina Faso, cut flowers in Ethiopia, mango in Mali and gorilla tourism in Rwanda all required that governments provide *different* types of infrastructure. The refrigeration facilities needed at the airport and regular flights to ship Ethiopia's cut flowers to the auctions in Europe are obviously quite different from the improvements required at the port facilities for textile exports in Mauritius. Similarly, the type of infrastructure needed for the garment industry in Lesotho is distinct from the one needed for mango production and export in Mali or for attracting gorilla tourism in Rwanda. Because fiscal resources and implementation capacity are limited, the government in each of those countries had to prioritize and decide which particular infrastructure they should improve or where to optimally locate the public services to make those success stories happen. Deng Xiaoping explained that pragmatic wisdom at the beginning of China's transition to a market economy when he advocated allowing a few regions and people to get rich first so as to achieve common prosperity for all people in the nation. The dynamic growth in those regions and industries would increase fiscal revenues, giving the government more resources to improve infrastructure for other regions in the nation later.

Identification of new sectors or lines of business and prioritization of infrastructure investment are also necessary because to be competitive in the globalized world, a new industry not only must align with the country's comparative advantage so that its factor costs of production can be at the lowest possible level but it also must have the lowest possible transaction-related costs. Why? Suppose a country's infrastructure and business environment are good and industrial upgrading and diversification happen spontaneously. Without government coordination, firms may enter into too many different industries that are all consistent with the country's comparative advantage. As a result, most industries may not form clusters that are sufficiently large and will not be competitive in the domestic and international markets. A few clusters may emerge eventually after many failures. Such a "trial and error" process is likely to be long and costly, reducing the individual firms' expected returns and incentives to upgrade or diversify to new industries, and slowing down the country's economic development. It is therefore imperative for a facilitating state in a developing country to identify and select new industries that are consistent with comparative advantage, use its limited resources to improve infrastructure for a limited number of carefully selected industries, provide adequate incentives for first movers, and coordinate private firms' related investments in those industries so that clusters can be formed successfully and quickly. Whether the government plays the identification and facilitation role may explain why some developing countries can grow at 8 percent or more for several decades while most others fail to have a similar performance.

I agree with Anne that cost-benefit analysis is indeed an excellent tool that should be used for evaluating the potential merits of every single infrastructure *project* (p. 49). Such an analysis sheds light on the validity of competing alternatives and can help make better public investment decisions. It forces policy makers to provide quantitative data to back up qualitative arguments and is therefore an invaluable technique for increasing social welfare. But it is microeconomic by nature. Without the identification of potentially successful industries and their likely location and needed infrastructure, policy makers are confronted with too many possible feasible projects that all need careful cost-benefit analysis. Moreover, for every public investment project, there are many benefits and costs that are intangible and therefore difficult to value. It is also well known that the results of that analysis can be very sensitive to the choice of the discount rate, and that the information used to determine future benefits and costs is limited by current knowledge.

In her discussion of infant industries, Anne observes that firms that produce and export unskilled-labor-intensive goods have usually learned from the opportunities arising from the dynamics of international market. She notes that "learning does not seem to have been a major issue for firms in South Korea, Taiwan, and elsewhere" (p. 50). Learning may not be an issue if it is a by-product of the firms' business activities, but if it is not such a spontaneous element of their activities, firms may not have the incentives to invest in it. A low-income country should have comparative advantage in the production of many unskilled, labor-intensive manufacturing products that it still imports. Such product market information should be available freely to any entrepreneur in the country. But production information about where to buy the equipment and intermediate inputs to manufacture these imported products, and knowledge about how to operate a firm to produce them, are relatively costly to obtain for most entrepreneurs in low-income countries. Furthermore, the coordination of related investment in infrastructure, access to finance for investment and operation, or the availability of foreign exchange for importing equipment for developing the new industry may still be serious issues for private firms even if learning about product market and production information is not a problem.

Anne's skepticism of all industry-specific interventions—a skepticism widely shared in the mainstream economic profession and Washington-based development institutions—results from the pervasive failures of government's attempts to pick winners in the past. Those failures were mostly due to the misguided attempts by many governments to develop industries that were inconsistent with their countries' comparative advantages. Firms in those industries were not viable in open, competitive markets, and their investment and survival depended on heavy government protection, large subsidies, and direct resource allocations through measures such as monopoly rent, high tariffs, quota restrictions, and subsidized credits. The large rents embedded in those measures created many distortions and easily became the targets of political capture. All this created difficult governance problems. The likelihood of these problems arising is much reduced when the government facilitates the development of new industries that are consistent with the country's changing comparative advantage determined by the change in its endowment structure, as suggested in the NSE.

Anne also worries that the identification of any new industry for upgrading "would inevitably favor larger, established firms and hence encounter the same sorts of problems as did the older import-substitution strategy" (p. 51). Her worry is valid for the old structuralist import-substitution strategy because the industries favored went against the comparative advantages of the countries that adopted it. Such industries were too capital intensive and only a few rich and politically well-connected firms could enter them. However, if the identified new industries are consistent with the country's comparative advantages, capital intensive or not, many firms will be able to enter and contest the dominance of large firms, as exemplified by the auto industry in Japan in the 1960s, the textile industry in Mauritius and electronics in Taiwan, China, in the 1970s, and the garment industry in Bangladesh and salmon-farming in Chile in the 1980s.

The type of government incentives for the first movers advocated in the NSE is limited to compensating for the externalities generated by the first movers rather than supporting nonviable firms, as in the case of old structuralist import-substitution strategy. Therefore, tax holidays for first movers for a few years, and preferential access to credit and foreign exchange (in countries where lack of access is a binding constraint) would be enough.

Finally, Anne questions the uncertainty surrounding the scope, depth, and length of government protection and points out the risk of political capture and rent-seeking in situations where a government adopts a dual-track approach during its transition from a heavily distorted economy to a well-functioning market economy. She argues that "a major challenge for liberalizing reform is for it to be credible that the altered policies are not reversible. Lin's prescription would greatly increase the challenge of creating credibility, and a slower transition would be a longer period during which growth was slow and political pressures opposing liberalization at all were mounting" (p. 52). The credibility argument was used to support the shock therapy in the transitions of East Europe and the former Soviet Union in the early 1990s. However, even though those firms were privatized, governments in transition economies were very often forced to provide other disguised and less efficient forms of subsidies and protection to ward off large unemployment and subsequent social and political instability. As a result, most transition economies encountered the awkward situation of "shock without therapy." Instead of a "J-curve" recovery as promised by the proponents of shock therapy, those economies encountered an "L-curve" growth path (a prolonged sluggish growth after a sharp decline in the GDP) during their transition. By contrast, good performers such as China, Vietnam, Laos, Slovenia, and Uzbekistan have reformed their distorted economies by adopting a more pragmatic, dual-track approach, which consists of progressively phasing out government support to "nonviable" firms in priority sectors and at the same time liberalizing the entry of formerly repressed private enterprises, joint ventures, and foreign direct investment in sectors aligned with their comparative advantages. The lesson is clear: for any developing country confronted with severe distortions and poor growth performance, the best way to gain confidence and credibility in its liberalization reforms is to achieve stability and dynamic growth in the transition process.

The comments by Joe Stiglitz and Dani Rodrik on my paper reveal more differences of emphasis and style than divergence on substance. I agree with Dani's assessment that our difference "is mainly methodological—and perhaps even just terminological—and may have little practical import" (p. 55). However, there are a few differences that are worth highlighting.

Beyond the traditional need for regulation, Joe sees a catalytic role for governments "in promoting entrepreneurship, providing the social and physical infrastructure, ensuring access to education and finance, and supporting technology and innovation" (p. 57). He strongly challenges the belief in the efficiency and stability of unfettered markets, and stresses the need for advances in technology as a key condition for increases in per capita income. Consequently, he favors public action for the creation of a "learning society" (p. 58).

I agree with Joe on the importance of learning. However, the content and mechanism of learning may be different for countries at different levels of development. Developing countries that are still at the early phase of their development generally do not have the necessary human and physical capital to leapfrog into capital-intensive, high-tech industries. The more effective route for their learning and development is to exploit the advantages of backwardness and upgrade and diversify into new industries according to the changing comparative advantages determined by the changes in their endowment structure. The subsequent dynamics of growth, accumulation of human and physical capital, and industrial and technological upgrading eventually open up possibilities to enter and master capital- and knowledge-intensive industries at the global frontier. The need to generate new knowledge through indigenous innovations in an economy increases with its economic development and the narrowing of the knowledge gap (the distance to the global technology/industrial frontier). Therefore, the learning and the enhancement of human capital should be commensurate with the level of economic development. Otherwise the attempt to create a "learning society" by increasing education alone may not correspond to the emergence of new, dynamic sectors consistent with the comparative advantage reflected in its endowment structure. Should this happen, the educated young people will not find suitable employment opportunities, causing a waste of scarce human and educational resources and, most likely, social tensions, as has happened in North African and many other developing countries.

Joe points out that "some of the most important elements of comparative advantage are endogenous" and contends that "Switzerland's comparative advantage in watch-making has little to do with its geography" (p. 59). The fact is that watch-making was a new industry in the 16th century.

Switzerland goldsmiths started making watches in 1541 and formed the first watch-makers' guild in 1601.[1] According to Maddison's (2010) estimations, Switzerland's per capita income in 1600 was 750 measured in 1990's international dollars, which was 77 percent of Britain's in the same year. Therefore, Switzerland was one of the "high-income" countries in the world at that time. To continue its income growth, it had to upgrade its industries to some new higher-value-added industries.

While Switzerland's comparative advantage in watching-making has little to do with its geography, as Joe pointed out, geography may be a crucial reason for its leadership in this industry since the 16th century. Watches are small, light, and high value added, with potential for continuous technology improvements. Such an industry is particularly suitable for a landlocked country like Switzerland. This may explain why Switzerland has kept its watch-making industry by maintaining technology leadership through continuous innovations since the 16th century but gave up other industries, such as garments, textiles, and footwear, which flourished in Switzerland in its early history.

Joe may be a bit too optimistic when he suggests that full capital mobility in a globalized world allows countries to free themselves from patterns dictated by endowments, as conventionally defined. He postulates that "with fully mobile capital, outside of agriculture, natural resource endowments need not provide the basis for explaining patterns of production and specialization" (p. 59). However, short-term capital flows are too volatile to be a reliable source for long-term productive investments in developing countries. We observed that during the East Asian financial crisis of the late 1990s. By contrast, foreign direct investments are more reliable because they are motivated by the search for profits. They mostly go to tradable sectors or production activities which are consistent with a host country's comparative advantage so as to use that location as an export base, or to enter the host country's domestic market—except when they are driven by occasional cases of privatization of large non-tradable sectors such as utilities and telecommunication. Because of his optimism about the mobility of capital, Joe highlights the importance of knowledge and entrepreneurship endowment. The importance of knowledge and entrepreneurship cannot be overemphasized. They are indeed driving forces for industrial upgrading and diversification in a dynamically growing economy. Nevertheless, as discussed above, the type of new knowledge that is useful for a country's development depends on the needs of new industries that align with the country's comparative advantage. An entrepreneur's investment in an open, competitive market is unlikely to be successful if he or she invests in industries that do not align with the country's comparative advantage.

Joe proposes the undervaluation of the exchange rate as a broad-based policy for encouraging the upgrading of tradable industries (p. 60). This is a delicate issue: it may help exports but it always makes imports of equipment more expensive, which is an obstacle for industrial upgrading and diversification (because firms need new capital equipment from abroad to upgrade or diversify into new industries). Therefore such a policy may help existing industries' exports but may not be conducive to long-term growth. Successful developing countries seem to have adopted a policy of undervaluation of real exchange rate if the Balassa-Samuelson theorem is used as a reference. However, the explanation may be the following: these countries typically converge from a dual economy with large surplus labor to a modern economy with a unified national labor market. At some point that theorem does not apply: before the depletion of surplus labor, the wage rate in the tradable and non-tradable sectors will not increase, which is a required mechanism for real appreciation in the theorem. What then looks like undervaluation may actually be an equilibrium exchange rate.

Dani's quibble with my approach seems to be related to his assumption that coordination and externality issues only exist in situations where markets send entrepreneurs the wrong signals. He therefore suggests that I may be arguing "both for and against comparative advantage" (p. 55). This deserves a clarification: Comparative advantage is determined by factor endowment. If an industry is consistent with a country's comparative advantage, the factor cost of production will be lower than otherwise. But for that industry to be competitive in its domestic and international markets, transaction-related costs should also be reduced to their lowest possible level. Yet, individual firms cannot internalize the reduction of many of the transaction-related costs arising from issues such as provision of infrastructure, logistics, finance, educated labor and so forth. Without government coordination and facilitation to reduce such costs and compensate for the externalities generated by the first mover, these industries are likely to simply remain as the *latent* comparative advantage of the economy. An illustration of this problem is the fact that low-income countries typically have comparative advantages in most unskilled, labor-intensive industries but few of them are able to be competitive in those industries—precisely because governments fail to effectively play their facilitating role. Therefore, the answer to Dani's objection lies in the distinction between a country's *latent* comparative advantage, which determines the factor costs of production, and its *actual* comparative advantage (or, in Michael Porter's term, competitive advantage), which requires in addition the reduction of transaction-related costs. My recommendation that governments step into the economic process and address market failures should therefore not be misunderstood as an attempt to defy an economy's "natural" or "inexorable" comparative advantage as revealed in market prices but as a way of opening the black box of business competitiveness, converting an economy's potential into reality, and igniting the march of domestic firms toward market success.

The differences between Dani's and my understanding of the government's role arise to a large extent from our diverging interpretations of experiences in successful countries such as Japan, Korea and China. He regards the successful catching up in Japan and South Korea as evidence for the need to defy a country's comparative advantage (p. 55). When Japan embarked upon its industrialization path in the early years of the Meiji period (1868–1912), it was an agrarian society in which farming, forestry and fishing employed more than 70 percent of the working population and represented over 60 percent of national output. Throughout the Meiji, Taisho (1912–26) and pre-war Showa (1926–36) periods, the top exports were raw silk yarn, tea, and marine products. The main market for these commodities was the United States. Historians remind us that along with the opening up of Japanese ports, demand for these primary commodities quickly ballooned and domestic producers greatly profited from it. Silk in particular brought wealth to rural areas and generated much coveted foreign exchange. Also, mining, which had continued from the previous Edo Period, was largely requisitioned by the government and later sold off to the private sector to become one of Japan's principal industries. The success of these sectors allowed Japan's per capita income to increase 40 percent from $737 in 1870 to $1,012 in 1890 and again to $2,026 at the onset of Great Depression in 1929 (Maddison 2010).[2] From the point of view of NSE, that success contributed to capital accumulation and changed Japan's endowment structure and comparative advantage. In the words of Japanese historian Kenichi Ohno, "the industrialization of the Meiji Period was a *light* industrial revolution, which made its way from importing to domestic production and then onto exporting. Within this transition, cotton production played a central role. The iron and steel, shipbuilding and chemical industries, as well as the manufacture of electrical machinery and appliances were in their infancy and the country was still in the process of learning by imitating the West... By late Meiji, private-sector production in the areas of shipbuilding, railway carriages and machine instruments had slowly emerged."[3] Japan's industrialization proceeded in a flying-geese pattern, moving step by step from simple, labor-intensive manufacturing goods to more capital- and technology-intensive manufacturing goods (Akamatsu 1962).

Korea also adopted a realistic approach to industrial upgrading and adjusted its strategy to enter industries that were consistent with its latent (and evolving) comparative advantage. In the 1960s Korea developed and exported labor-intensive products such as garments, plywood, and wigs. With capital accumulation and a change in its endowment structure due to success, Korea upgraded to more capital-intensive sectors such as the automotive sector. But at the initial stage, domestic manufacturers concentrated mostly on assembly of imported parts, which was labor-intensive and in line with their comparative advantage at the time. Similarly, in electronics, the focus was initially on household appliances, such as TVs, washing machines and refrigerators before the country moved to the production of memory chips, the least technologically complex segment of the information industry. Korea's technological ascent has been rapid, at a pace commensurate to changes in underlying comparative advantage. Such changes reflected rapid accumulation of physical and human capital resulting from the dynamic growth, which could only occur because the country's main industrial sectors remained consistent with its existing comparative advantage.

Similarly, Dani's observation that China has been defying its comparative advantage successfully, with its export bundle resembling that of a country between three and six times richer, neglects the fact that these are mostly processed products. China only provides value-added in labor-intensive assembly and accessories. Empirical research (Wang and Wei 2010) shows that China's exports are consistent with China's comparative advantage.

Dani also questions the differences between my recommendation for gradual trade liberalization and the old structuralist policies. The latter approach advocated protection and subsidies to build new industries that were not aligned with comparative advantage, whereas the dual-track, gradual approach for trade liberalization that I recommend advises governments in transition economies to provide temporary protection or subsidies to old industries that were not viable in an open, competitive market but were established under the misguided old structuralist strategy. The pragmatic dual-track approach helps a transition economy avoid unnecessary and costly economic and social disruption, and eventually leads to a system of market-based prices and resource allocation as explained in my response to Anne's comments.

Summing up, it appears that Anne's questions about the practicality of my framework arise mostly from interrogations on how to identify new industries that are consistent with a country's latent comparative advantage, and how to administer the coordination and incentives for the first movers. Joe's and Dani's advocacy of broad-based interventions such as undervalued real exchange rates to support the trade sector but reluctance to embrace the idea of sector-specific policies are also related to the puzzle about how to identify industries aligned with latent comparative advantage. Those questions are addressed in a companion paper entitled "Growth Identification and Facilitation," co-authored with Célestin Monga and published in *Development Policy Review* (chapter III of this book). Based on economic analysis and historical experiences, the growth identification and facilitation framework that we propose suggests that policy makers identify dynamic tradable industries in fast-growing countries with similar endowment structures, and with a *per capita* income about double their own. If domestic private firms in these sectors are already present, policy makers should identify them and remove constraints on those firms' technological upgrading or on entry by other firms. In industries where no domestic firms are present, policy makers could aim to attract foreign direct investment from the countries being emulated or organize programs for incubating new firms. The government should also pay attention to the development by private enterprises of new and competitive products, and support the scaling up of successful private-sector innovations in new industries. In countries with a poor business environment, special economic zones or industrial parks can facilitate firm entry, foreign direct investment, and the formation of industrial clusters. Finally, the government might help pioneering firms in the new industries by offering tax incentives for a limited period, co-financing investments, or providing access to land or foreign exchange.

I am grateful to Anne, Joe, Dani, and many others who have provided comments and constructive criticism of my paper. Despite our differences, there seems to be an emerging consensus on the need to reconcile lessons from the first two major waves of development thinking (structuralism and neo-liberalism) into a new synthesis that recognizes and defines the proper roles of state and markets. The road ahead towards that third wave (which might be termed "Development Thinking 3.0") will obviously involve healthy and useful intellectual disagreements. Because, as Confucius once said, "Real knowledge is to know the extent of one's ignorance."

## Notes

1. http://www.fhs.ch/en/history.php.
2. Dollars are 1990 dollars adjusted for Geary-Khamis purchasing power parity.
3. Translated excerpts from the book *Tojokoku no Globalization: Jiritsuteki Hatten wa Kanoka* (Globalization of Developing Countries: Is Autonomous Development Possible?) by Toyo Keizai Shimposha (2000), quoted by Japan's National Graduate Institute for Policy Studies (GRIPS). See http://www.grips .ac.jp/forum-e/pdf_e01/eastasia/ch5.pdf.

## References

Akamatsu, K. 1962. "A Historical Pattern of Economic Growth in Developing Countries," *The Developing Economies* (Tokyo), supplement issue no. 1: 3–25.

Maddison, A. 2010. "Historical Statistics of the World Economy: 1–2008 AD" (www.ggdc.net/maddison/Historical_Statistics/vertical-file_02-2010.xls).

Wang, Z., and S. Wei. 2010. "What Accounts for the Rising Sophistication of China's Exports," in "China's Growing Role in World Trade," eds. R, Feenstra and S. Wei. Chicago: University of Chicago Press.

# THE GROWTH REPORT AND NEW STRUCTURAL ECONOMICS

# THE GROWTH REPORT
# AND NEW STRUCTURAL
# ECONOMICS

## WITH CÉLESTIN MONGA[†]

## 1. Introduction

Economists have always been conflicted between the need to understand the dynamics of business cycles, and the study of long-term growth—both of which are important for human welfare. The world economy has just experienced a severe financial and economic crisis,[1] which has justified the intellectual focus on stabilization policies, especially given the role that coordinated and decisive monetary and fiscal policies have played in preventing the global recession from becoming a worldwide depression. But the persistence of poverty in many parts of the world and the potential long-term impact of the crisis on global poverty reduction also highlight the importance of policies that are conducive to sustainable and inclusive growth.[2] Economic growth is indeed the main source of divergences in living standards across countries and regions of the world. As Barro and Sala-i-Martin (1995) observe, "if we can learn about government policy options that have even small effects on long-term growth rates, we can contribute much more to improvements in standards of living than has been provided by the entire history of macroeconomic analysis of countercyclical policy and fine tuning."

In fact, economic growth may be the single most important issue confronting economists today. The differences in output per worker and national income across countries are still puzzling. According to calculations by Maddison (2001), world population rose 22-fold over the past millennium. Per capita income increased 13-fold, world GDP nearly 300-fold. This contrasts sharply with the preceding millennium, when world population grew by only a sixth, and there was no advance in per capita income. Measured in today's living standards, all countries in the world were poor in the beginning of the 18th century. Sustained growth in income per capita only picked up after 1820: per capita income rose more than eightfold.

A well-known fact confirmed by the recent crisis is the observation that countries that have sustained high rates of growth have also performed well despite the global meltdown. Their dynamic performance has made them more resilient. With strong external balance sheets and ample room for fiscal maneuver before the crisis, they were able to implement countercyclical policies to combat external shocks. "A crisis is a terrible thing to waste," said Paul Romer, one of the preeminent theorists of growth. Despite its heavy human, financial and economic cost, the recent recession provides a unique opportunity to reflect on the knowledge from several decades of growth research, draw policy lessons from the experience of successful countries, and explore new approaches going forward.

Looking at the data, one may be surprised to note that the recession has obscured the broader economic narrative of our time, which is the remarkable economic performance of many poor countries, especially in the past ten years. Leaving aside the United States, which ranks third, the four most populous countries of the world (Brazil, China, India, Indonesia), have made great strides, averaging annual growth rates well over 6 percent a year. That is a vast improvement in the standards of living for more than 40 percent of the world's population. The same trends are in place in many other South American countries (Chile, Colombia, Peru) and in some African countries (Botswana, Mauritius, Tunisia, Ghana).

To be sure, poverty reduction is still a very challenging development issue. In an increasingly globalized world where fighting poverty is not only a moral responsibility but also a strategy for confronting some of the major problems (diseases, malnutrition, insecurity and violence) that ignore boundaries and contribute to global insecurity, thinking about new ways of generating and sustaining growth is a crucial task for economists. It is therefore essential to continue searching for new ideas on the mechanics of wealth creation. Over the last 50 years, much progress has been made, most recently with the work of the Growth Commission Report.[3] But beyond a consensus on broad principles and the rejection of one-size-fits-all approaches, economists still face significant challenges in identifying actionable policy levers that are directly relevant to specific countries.

This paper reassesses the evolution of knowledge on growth and suggests a new structural approach to the analysis. Section 2 offers a brief, critical review of lessons learned from growth research and examines the remaining challenges—especially from the policy standpoint. Section 3 highlights the important recent contribution of the Growth Commission Report and the identification of stylized facts associated with sustained and inclusive growth. Section 4 provides a consistent framework for understanding its key findings through the lenses of new structural economics. Section 5 offers some concluding thoughts.

## 2. The Quest for Growth: An Unfinished Journey

Economic historians who have examined the evolution of growth performance throughout history tend to divide it into three distinct periods: The first one, which spanned most of human history up to the middle of the 18th century, was marked by static living standards, despite population growth—the so-called Malthusian conditions. The second one, which lasted from about 1750 to the 1820s, was characterized by some improvement in living standards, and changes in demographic trends (higher fertility rates and lower mortality rates). The third epoch, observed initially in England at the end of the first quarter of the 19th century, has been that of modern economic growth (Cameron, 1993). Deciphering the mystery of modern economic growth and explaining convergence and divergence have been major topics of research, especially since the 1950s. While much progress has been achieved on theoretical and empirical grounds, much remains to be understood on the policy front.

## Growth Analysis in Historical Perspective

The analysis of growth—and the specific factors that have sustained it and accompanied the structural changes associated with it—became a major topic of interest for thinkers in general and economists in particular in the early 18th century. David Hume, whom Rostow claims to be "the first modern economist" (1990: 18) placed economic analysis at the center of his analysis of the human condition. He also offered economic concepts that are considered to "form a reasonably coherent and consistent theory of the dynamics of growth." Classical economists who followed in his footsteps—such as Adam Smith, Alfred Marshall, David Ricardo and Allyn Young—were also obsessed with economic growth. Perhaps because of their fascination with the idea of human progress celebrated during the Enlightenment, they explored the determinants of economic development, and the role that policymakers could play in fostering prosperity. Their pioneering work highlighted important notions such as factor accumulation, factor substitution, technical change, or specialization, which are at the core of modern growth theory.

But growth analysis slowed down after the Great Depression, as the intellectual focus shifted from long-run to short-run issues. In fact, with the notable exception of the pioneering work of Robert Solow, for much of the 20th century and certainly through the 1960s and 1970s, macroeconomists tended to study business cycles issues that characterized the post-War period. As they tried to better understand stabilization policies—monetary and fiscal measures to avoid disruptive and costly inflation—few resources were devoted to the analysis of the long-run determinants of growth.

Things changed in the 1980s when many prominent researchers focused their attention on differences in economic performance among countries. Surveys of economic growth and levels of performance in different parts of the world economy show that growth has indeed been uneven across countries and regions: between 1900 and 2001, per capita GDP in Western Europe increased by a factor of 6.65 (6.7 in Western offshoots), compared to 5.2 in Latin America, 4.2 in Eastern Europe, and only 2.5 in Africa.[4] The number of people living in high-growth environments or in countries with

OECD per capita income levels has increased in the past 30 years by a factor of four, from 1 billion to about 4 billion (Growth Commission, 2008).

Following the initial work by Harrod and Domar, the Solow-Swan model sparked the first major wave of systematic growth analysis. The objective was to understand the mechanics of growth, identify its determinants, and to develop techniques of growth accounting, which would help explain changes in the momentum and the role of economic policy. That first generation of growth researchers highlighted the centrality of capital. Their models featured neoclassical forms of production functions with specifications that relied on constant returns to scale, diminishing returns and some elasticity of substitution between inputs. In order to present a general equilibrium model of the economy, these researchers adopted a constant saving rate rule. This was a crude assumption but a major step forward in tool building, as it offered a clear demonstration that general equilibrium theory could be applied convincingly to real world issues. One important prediction from these models was the idea of conditional convergence, derived from the assumption of diminishing returns to capital— poor economies with lower capital per worker (relative to their long-run or steady state capital per worker) will grow faster.[5]

The major strength of that line of growth research was the explicit introduction of technology—in addition to capital and labor—in the theoretical and empirical analysis. But the limited toolkit available at the time created a major shortcoming to that approach: technology was presented as an exogenously given public good. The major prediction of the model based on the assumption of diminishing returns to capital was the idea that per capita growth will cease in the absence of continuous improvements in technology. While that assumption allowed the model to maintain its key prediction of conditional convergence, it also seemed odd: technology, the main determinant of long-run growth, was kept outside of the model.[6]

A new wave of growth modeling had to come up with a convincing theory of technological change—one that frees up the neoclassical model from the exogeneity of the main determinant of long-term growth. A first step was to design a theory of continuous growth fuelled by non-diminishing returns to investment on a broad class of physical and human capital. The process could go on indefinitely if returns do not diminish as economies grow (Romer 1986). A second, more effective approach was to move away from the straightjacket of perfect competition, and incorporate imperfect competition and R&D theories in growth modeling—the rationale here being that such bold methodological moves helped explain why the economy would not run out of new ideas, and growth rates could be kept positive in the long run (Romer 1987, 1990; Aghion and Howitt, 1992).

Endogenous growth theory, as it came to be known, maintained the assumption of nonrivalry because technology is indeed a very different type of factor from capital and labor—because it can be used indefinitely by others, at zero marginal cost. But it was important to take the next logical step and to better understand the public good characterization of technology, and think of it as a partially excludable nonrival good. The new wave therefore reclassified technology not just as a public good but as a good that is subject to a certain level of private control. By making it a partially excludable nonrival good and therefore giving it some degree of excludability or appropriability, it was possible to ensure that incentives matter for its production and use. The move away from perfect competition was therefore necessary. It has yielded high methodological payoffs. While neoclassical models of growth took technology and factor accumulation as exogenous, endogenous growth models explain why technology grows over time through new ideas, and provide the microeconomic underpinnings for models of the technological frontier.

Another important question has been to understand how technological diffusion takes place across countries and generates or sustains growth—and why it does not take root in others. Various interesting possibilities have recently been explored in an attempt to answer that critical question: one option has been to add an avenue for technology transfer as a new component to the endogenous growth model, that is, "endogenizing" the mechanism by which different countries achieve the ability to use various intermediate capital goods (Jones, 1998). Another popular route is to try to identify the fundamental determinants of growth through political economy models. Contrary to previous waves of growth modeling, this line of research focuses not on the proximate determinants of growth but on the impact on growth of such factors as institutions or the quality of governance (Acemoglu and Robinson, 2001; Glaeser and Shleifer, 2002). Several other approaches to growth research have yielded various insights to the mystery of modern economic growth (Barro and Sala-i-Martin 2003; Jones 1998).

## Challenges of Explaining Convergence—and Divergence

On both the theoretical and empirical fronts, progress has been made in our understanding of growth in recent decades. On the theoretical front, the analysis of endogenous technical innovation and increasing returns to scale has provided economists with a rich general framework for capturing the broad picture and the mechanics of economic growth. From Solow's work, we know the importance of the role of capital accumulation (both physical and human) and technical change in the growth process. From contributions by Becker, Heckman, Lucas[7] and many others, we also learned about the importance of human capital through diffusion of new knowledge or on-the-job learning, often stimulated by trade, and the so-called college wage premium. From work by North (1981), with supporting theoretical and empirical analyses exemplified by the works of Acemoglu and Robinson (2001), Greif (1993), and Glaeser and Shleifer (2002), we have learned that growth is in large part driven by innovation and institutions that have evolved in countries where innovative activity is promoted and conditions are in place for change to take place. From Romer and the endogenous growth theorists, we have understood the need to change the focus of growth theory from accumulation to knowledge creation and innovation. In sum, we know quite a lot about some of the basic ingredients of growth.

On the empirical side, the availability of standardized data sets—especially the Penn World tables—has stimulated interest in cross-country work that highlights systematic differences between high-growth and low-growth countries with regard to: (i) Initial conditions such as productivity, human capital, demographic structure, infrastructure, financial development, or inequality; (ii) Policy variables of various sorts such as trade openness, macroeconomic stability, levels and composition of public spending, taxation, or regulation; and (iii) Institutional variables such as general governance indicators, administrative capacity, rule of law, protection of property rights, or corruption.

However, growth research still faces significant methodological difficulties, and challenges in identifying actionable policy levers to sustain and accelerate growth in specific countries.[8]

Deaton (2009) expresses the general sentiment of despair among economists when he notes that "empiricists and theorists seem further apart now than at any period in the last quarter century. Yet reintegration is hardly an option because without it there is no chance of long-term scientific progress." Despite many decades of theoretical advances and the development of new techniques to help policymakers in developing countries identify systematically constraints to growth, the intellectual and policy agenda ahead is indeed still daunting.

Contrary to the prediction of most neoclassical models, convergence among world economies has been a limited phenomenon (Pritchett 1997). In 2008, GDP per capita in the United States (the world's richest country) was three times higher than per capita income in neighboring Mexico, 16 times higher than the per capita income in India, and 145 times the per capita income of the Democratic Republic of Congo. That gap is still widening. In most of the past century, incomes in developing countries have fallen far behind those in developed countries, both proportionately and absolutely.[9]

Yet, empirical observation reveals that divergence between industrialized and developing countries is not inexorable: in the past two centuries, some countries have been able to catch up with the most advanced economies (most notably Germany, France, and the USA in the late 19th century, and the Nordic countries, Japan, and the 13 economies analyzed in the Growth Commission Report in the 20th century). After the Industrial Revolution began in England in the mid-eighteenth century, experiments conducted in laboratories became the major source of technological invention and innovation (Lin, 1995). This was especially true for those macro-inventions that consisted of radical new ideas and involved large, discrete, novel changes, as defined by Mokyr (1990). For developed countries, such inventions were essential to technological advances. With investment in research and development, innovation became endogenous (Romer, 1986; Lucas, 1988). Industrial structures were upgraded continuously and productivity increased. As a result, developed countries began to take off and the divergence between the North and the South appeared (Baumol, 1994).

Historical evidence suggests that the growth process followed a similar pattern in developing economies such as the four East Asian dragons (Korea, Singapore, Taiwan, Hong Kong), which converged to the income levels of advanced western countries in the second half of the 20th century. The same process subsequently allowed countries as diverse as China,

Vietnam, Botswana, or Mauritius to achieve rapid and sustained growth in the 1980s and 1990s (Lin, 2003, 2009; Rodrik, 2005). Except for that select group, most developing countries have failed to achieve their economic growth ambitions since World War II. In fact, many have encountered frequent crises despite efforts from their governments and assistance from international development agencies. Yet, their experiences highlight the need to understand how developing countries can create the conditions for facilitating the flow of technologies and unleash growth, even in the context of sub-optimal microeconomic policies, weak institutions, and the absence of full-fledged private property rights.

The failures of growth research to predict divergence on a large scale indicates that the proposed theories did not capture the fundamental factor(s) that determines whether or not a developing country will converge. Some researchers have recently argued that the evolution of economic performance of nations is determined by conditional convergence—the idea that countries converge when all other macroeconomic variables that proxy for differences in steady-state characteristics are held constant—or to put it differently, the distribution of world income reveals the existence of convergence clubs among countries.[10] But the puzzle of diverging performances may be more easily sorted out through comparative analysis based on in-depth country studies and historical experience: the key ingredients for convergence of successful economies seem to lie in their ability to change their endowment structure, increase the pace of adoption of new ideas, speed up the process of industrial upgrading, and improve institutions simultaneously. Understanding and replicating the economic strategies and policies that allowed latecomers to catch up with the most advanced economies is still a major challenge for economists and policymakers around the world.

## New Directions in Applied Growth Research

The disappointments of growth research—most notably from the perspective of policymakers seeking specific action plans to generate prosperity—have led to a reassessment of the validity and usefulness of existing knowledge, and to the development of radically new approaches. An important study by the World Bank (2005) that focused on lessons of the 1990s highlighted the complexity of economic growth and recognized that it is not amenable to simple formulas. The report also noted that the reforms carried out in many developing countries in the 1990s focused too narrowly on the efficient use of resources, not on the expansion of capacity and growth. While they enabled better use of existing capacity, thereby establishing the basis for sustained long-run growth, they did not provide sufficient incentives for expanding that capacity.[11] The report concluded that there is no unique, universal set of rules to guide policymakers. It recommended less reliance on simple formulas and the elusive search for "best practices," and greater reliance on deeper economic analysis to identify each country's one or two most binding constraints on growth.

That line of research is exemplified by the Growth Diagnostics framework, which aims at identifying the one or two most binding constraints on any developing economy, and then focusing on lifting those. The main rationale is to ensure that economic reforms are contingent on the economic environment. "Presented with a laundry list of needed reforms, policymakers have either tried to fix all of the problems at once or started with reforms that were not crucial to their country's growth potential. And, more often than not, reforms have gotten in each other's way, with reform in one area creating unanticipated distortions in another area. By focusing on the one area that represents the biggest hurdle to growth, countries will be more likely to achieve success from their reform efforts" (Hausmann, Rodrik and Velasco, 2008). The proposed approach offers a decision tree methodology to help identify the relevant binding constraints for each country. While it does not specifically identify the political costs and benefits of various reform strategies, its focus on alternative hypotheses can help clarify the options available to policymakers for responding to political constraints. "We are concerned mainly with *short-run* constraints. In this sense, our focus is on igniting growth and identifying constraints that inevitably emerge as an economy expands, not on anticipating *tomorrow's* constraints on growth" (Hausmann, Rodrik and Velasco, 2008).

A key lesson from that approach is the notion that different countries (or even the same country at different points in time) require different policy choices to facilitate growth, and that the 'big principles' that growth requires—sound money, property rights, openness, free markets—can take many forms and that achieving them requires country-specific context and information. In particular, these principles need not take any one precise institutional or policy form. Each country is assumed to have some binding constraints to its growth potential, and failure to identify and remove them would impede economic performance, even if every other production factor is satisfactory. The Growth Diagnostics approach is certainly an important advance in growth analysis. However, its model does not fully flesh out the notion of "binding constraint."[12] The variable definitions are deliberately left quite imprecise, which makes it challenging to operationalize them.

Another influential new approach is the one adopted by researchers at the MIT Poverty Lab, who suggest that the quest for growth be re-centered on assessing the impact of a development project or program (against explicit counterfactual outcomes). Starting with the idea that credible impact evaluations are needed to ensure that the most effective programs are scaled up at the national or international levels, they design randomized control trials (RCTs) or social experiments that can be used to leverage the benefits of knowing which programs work and which do not (Duflo and Kremer, 2003). Their approach is based on the notion that the standard aggregate growth paradigm relies, to a large extent and mistakenly, on the assumption of a rational representative agent. Stressing heterogeneity in country circumstances and among micro agents, this new wave of research attempts to explicitly account for the heterogeneity of individual households and firms in development analysis and policy.[13] It has produced some useful tools for understanding the effectiveness of some specific micro projects. But even assuming that they can actually transfer lessons from localized development experiences to different geographic or cultural areas,[14] RCTs still fall short in providing useful overall guidance to policymakers confronted with the design of development strategies.

While these new approaches to growth research have shed light on important questions, they have not provided sufficient guidance on how policymakers could foster the process of industrial upgrading and structural change. It would be desirable to complement them with structural analyses of the determinants of growth—specifically the identification of factors that would allow poor economies to move from one stage of development to another.

## 3. The Unique Contribution of the Growth Report

Despite intellectual progress, some of the key questions on the growth research agenda today remain the same as those that confronted previous generations of researchers: If growth is driven in large part by innovation, why are some countries successful at innovating and adapting to change, while others are not? What are the forces that drive convergence and what are the factors that stifle material progress? What are the conditions for the kind of structural change that allow low-income countries to become middle-income and then high-income economies? What are the most important determinants of growth (initial conditions, institutions, and policies)? What is the appropriate role for governments and markets in the growth dynamics?

Faced with the difficulty of providing clear answers to such pressing questions and the impossibility of deriving actionable policy recommendations from growth analyses, some growth researchers have found it useful to avoid searching for robust determinants of growth, and to look instead for the stylized facts that can guide economic policy in developing countries. This approach goes back several decades, most notably to Kaldor's (1961) six characteristics of 20th century growth, derived from United States and United Kingdom macroeconomic data: (i) sustained rate of increase in labor productivity; (ii) sustained rate of increase in capital per worker; (iii) stable real interest rate or return on capital; (iv) stable ratio of capital to output; (v) stable shares of capital and labor as fractions of national income; and (vi) a wide variation in the rate of growth of fast growing economies, of the order of 2-5 percent.

More recently, Jones and Romer (2009) have identified a different set of stylized facts: (i) increases in the extent of the market—via globalization and urbanization; (ii) acceleration of the pace of growth over time, from virtually zero to relatively rapid rates; (iii) variation in the rate of growth of GDP per capita, which increases with the distance from the technology frontier; (iv) large income and total factor productivity differences; (v) increases in human capital per worker; and (vi) long-run stability of relative wages.

*The Growth Report: Strategies for Sustained Growth and Inclusive Development*, a landmark study issued in 2008 by the Commission on

Growth and Development, followed a similar approach but took it to a new level. It built on the findings of several other empirical studies initiated by the World Bank during the past two decades to reassess the past theories of economic growth and poverty reduction, and rethink its policy advice to developing countries.[15] Launched in April 2006, the Commission brought together 22 leading practitioners from government, business and policymaking arenas, mostly from the developing world. It was chaired by Nobel Laureate Michael Spence and Danny Leipziger, a World Bank Vice-President. Over a period of two years the Commission sought to "gather the best understanding there is about the policies and strategies that underlie rapid and sustained economic growth and poverty reduction."

The Commission was established to take stock of the state of theoretical and empirical knowledge on economic growth with a view to drawing implications for policy, and avoiding the trap of purely theoretical exercises. It provides the following motivation for its work: (i) the sense that poverty cannot be reduced in isolation of economic growth, and that this link has been missing in many development strategies; (ii) increasing evidence that the economic and social forces underlying rapid and sustained growth are much less well understood than generally thought—economic advice to developing countries has been given with more confidence that justified by the state of knowledge; (iii) realization that the accumulation of highly relevant (both successful and unsuccessful) growth experiences over the past 20 years provides a unique source of learning; and (iv) growing awareness that, except for China and India, and other rapidly growing economies in East Asia, developing countries need to accelerate their rates of growth significantly for their incomes to catch up with income levels in industrialized countries, and for the world to achieve a better balance in the distribution of wealth and opportunity.

The uniqueness of the Commission lies not only in its very diverse composition but also in the way it has reexamined growth analysis. Its approach has been to "try to assimilate and digest the cumulative experience of growth and development as well as careful and thoughtful policy analysis in a wide spectrum of fields. We then seek to share this understanding with political leaders and policymakers in developing countries, including the next generation of leaders; with an international community of advisors; and with investors, policymakers and leaders in advanced countries and international institutions who share the same goals"[16] (Growth Commission, 2008, p. x).

The Report starts with the observation that "fast, sustained growth does not happen spontaneously. It requires long-term commitment by a country's political leaders, a commitment pursued with patience, perseverance, and pragmatism" (Growth Commission, 2008, p. 2). It then identifies some of the distinctive characteristics of 13 high-growth economies[17] that have been able to grow at more than 7 percent for periods of more than 25 years since World War II. At that pace of expansion, an economy almost doubles in size every decade.[18] The Report then asks how other developing countries can emulate them. Observing that each country has specific characteristics and historical experiences that must be reflected in its growth strategy, it does not attempt to provide a generic formula for policymakers to apply. However, it offers a framework that can help policymakers design a growth strategy. While it does not lay out a full set of answers, it suggests the right questions to be addressed.

The conclusion is an optimistic one: rapid, sustained growth is not a miracle confined to certain parts of the world. It can be achieved by all developing countries. More important than the list of "growth ingredients," which includes a wide range of policy prescriptions whose validity depends on specific contexts and conditions, the Report lists "five striking points of resemblance" among all highly successful countries:

- *Openness to the global economy.* During their periods of fast growth, all the successful economies made the most of the global economy. They did so in at least two ways: first, they imported ideas, technology and know-how from the rest of the world—a world that has become more open and more tightly integrated since the end of World War II. Second, they exploited global demand, which provided an almost infinite market for their goods. In sum, successful economies "all imported what the rest of world knew, and exported what it wanted." The unsuccessful countries did the opposite. The lesson here is clear: in order to achieve sustained and dynamic growth, a developing country must: (i) rely on its comparative advantage (that is, export what the rest of the world needs and upgrade its industries step by step at a pace consistent with the change in its endowment structure so as to make its economy competitive); and (ii) tap the potential of advantage of backwardness (imported ideas, technology and know-how from the rest of the world in the process of its industrial upgrading).

- *Macroeconomic stability.* The second stylized fact of high-growth countries is their maintenance of stable macroeconomic environments. During their most successful periods, all 13 countries avoided the kind of unpredictability in fiscal and monetary policies that damage private sector investment. While growth was sometimes accompanied by moderate inflation in some of them (Korea in the 1970s, China in the mid-1990s), budget deficits or even high ratios of debt-to-GDP, the situation never got out of control.
- *High saving and investment rates.* Another characteristic of high-growth countries is their willingness to forgo current consumption in pursuit of higher levels of incomes in the future. High saving rates were matched by high investment rates. The fact that countries such as Singapore or Malaysia adopted mandatory saving schemes have led some researchers to stress the importance of deliberate saving policies as the main cause for these high saving and investment rates (Montiel and Serven, 2008). In fact, the main explanation may be the ability of these countries to produce large economic surplus and to generate rates of return on investment that were high enough to provide strong incentives to save. In the 1970s, Southeast Asia and Latin America had similar savings rates. Twenty years later, the Asian rate was about 20 percentage points higher.
- *Market allocation.* The Report notes that the 20th century saw many experiments with alternatives to a market system. They all failed to help developing countries achieve sustained growth. While successful countries may differ in the intensity and strength of their property rights systems, they all adopted a well-functioning market mechanism that provided adequate price signals, transparent decision-making and good incentives. Their governments also did not resist the market forces in the reallocation of capital and labor from sector to sector, industry to industry.
- *Leadership and governance.* Sustained growth that can help overcome poverty is typically a multi-decade process, which only takes place in a stable and functional investment environment. It requires political leadership and effective, pragmatic and sometimes activist governments.

The Growth Commission Report also identifies a series of "bad ideas" to be avoided by policymakers in their search for growth. The non-exhaustive list includes: subsidizing energy; relying on the civil service to deal with joblessness; reducing fiscal deficits by cutting expenditures on infrastructure investment; providing open-ended protection to domestic firms; imposing price controls to stem inflation; banning exports for long periods of time; resisting urbanization and measuring educational progress through infrastructure; ignoring environmental issues as an "unaffordable luxury"; adopting regulation of the banking system; or allowing the exchange rate to appreciate excessively.

Summing up, it can be said that the Report represents a major step forward as it provides a practical approach to help policymakers today understand the economic dynamics of catching up, and to identify the precise (and probably country-specific) mechanics of creating the appropriate infrastructures, incentive systems, and institutions to facilitate and sustain the evolving growth process. It also offers a new challenge to growth researchers, who must come up with a conceptual framework for making sense of its main findings.

## 4. A New Structural Analysis of the Growth Report

The stylized facts identified by the Growth Commission Report can be either endogenous or exogenous variables to the growth process. In order to disentangle causes and effects, and prioritize public policies, it is useful to go beyond the mere association that these stylized facts suggest, and reflect on the dynamics of possible causal relationships. As Zellner (1979) pointed out, this requires some generally acceptable economic theory. The new structural economics approach provides such a framework.

### Principles of New Structural Economics

The new structural economics framework (Lin, 2010) is based on the analysis of the growth process in modern times and across continents. It starts with the observation that the main feature of modern economic development is continuous technological innovation and structural change. The optimal industrial structure in an economy, that is, the industrial structure that will make the economy most competitive domestically and internationally at any specific time, is endogenous to its comparative advantage, which in turn is determined by the given endowment structure of the economy at that time.[19] Economies that try to grow simply by adding more and more physical capital or labor to the existing industries eventually run into diminishing returns; and economies that try to deviate from their comparative advantage are likely to perform poorly.

Because the optimal industrial structure at any given time is endogenous to the existing factor endowments, a country trying to move up the ladder of technological development must first change its endowment structure. With capital accumulation, the economy's factor endowment structure evolves, pushing its industrial structure to deviate from the optimal determined by its previous level. Firms then need to upgrade their industries and technologies accordingly in order to maintain market competitiveness.

If the economy follows its comparative advantage in the development of its industries, its industries will be most competitive in domestic and world markets. As a result, they will gain the largest possible market share and generate potentially the largest surplus. Capital investment will also have the largest possible return. Consequently, households will have the highest savings propensity, resulting in an even faster upgrade of the country's endowment structure.

A developing country that follows its comparative advantage to develop its industries can also benefit from the advantage of backwardness in the upgrading process and grow faster than advanced countries. Enterprises in developing countries can benefit from the industrial and technological gap with developed countries by acquiring industrial and technological innovations that are consistent with their new comparative advantage through learning and borrowing from developed countries.

The main question then is how to ensure that the economy grows in a manner that is consistent with its comparative advantage. The goal of most firms everywhere is profit maximization, which is, *ceteris paribus,* a function of relative prices of factor inputs. The criterion they use to select their industries and technology is typically the relative prices of capital, labor and natural resources. Therefore, the precondition for firms to follow the comparative advantage of the economy in their choice of technologies and industries is to have a relative price system which can reflect the relative scarcity of these production factors in the endowment structure. Such a relative price system exists only in a competitive market system. In developing countries where this is not usually not the case, it is necessary that government action be taken to improve various market institutions so as to create and protect effective competition in the product and factor markets.

In the process of industrial upgrading, firms need to have information about production technologies and product markets. If information is not freely available, each firm will need to invest resources to search for it, collect it, and analyze it. For individual firms in developing countries, industrial upgrading is therefore a high-reward, high-risk process. First movers who attempt to enter new industries can either fail—because they target the wrong industries—or succeed—because the industry is consistent with the country's new comparative advantage. In the case of success, their experience offers valuable and free information to other prospective entrants. They will not have monopoly rent because of competition from new entry. Moreover, these first movers often need to devote resources to train workers on the new business processes and techniques, who may be then hired by competitors. First movers generate demand for new activities and human capital which may not have existed otherwise. Even in situations where they fail, their bad experience also provides useful knowledge to other firms. Yet, they must bear the costs of failure. In other words, the social value of the first movers' investments is usually much larger than their private value and there is an asymmetry between the first movers' gain from success and the cost of failure. Successful industrial upgrading in an economy also requires new types of financial, legal, and other "soft" (or intangible) and "hard" (or tangible) infrastructure to facilitate production and market transactions and allow the economy to reach its production possibility frontier. The improvement of the hard and soft infrastructure requires coordination beyond individual firms' decisions.

Economic development is therefore a dynamic process marked with externalities and requiring coordination. While the market is a necessary basic mechanism for effective resource allocation at each given stage of development, governments must play a proactive, facilitating role for an economy to move from one stage to another. They must intervene to allow markets to function properly. They can do so by (i) providing information about new industries that are consistent with the new comparative advantage determined by change in the economy's endowment structure; (ii) coordinating investments in related industries and the required improvements in infrastructure; (iii) subsidizing activities with externalities in the process of industrial upgrading and structural change; and (iv) catalyzing the development of new industries by incubation or by attracting foreign direct investment to overcome the deficits in social capital and other intangible constraints.

In sum, the new structural economics framework is three-pronged: it includes an understanding of a country's comparative advantage defined as the evolving potential of its endowment structure; reliance on the market as the optimal resource allocation mechanism at any given stage of development; and the recognition of a facilitating role of the state in the process of industrial upgrading. It helps explain the economic performance of the most successful developing countries.

### Key Findings of the Growth Commission: A New Structural Analysis

The new structural economics provides a framework for understanding the endogeneity and exogeneity issues surrounding the five stylized facts of the Growth Commission Report: (i) exploiting the world economy through openness; (ii) maintaining macroeconomic stability; (iii) keeping high rates of saving and investment; (v) using markets to allocate resources; and (v) having committed, credible, and capable governments. The first three stylized facts are logical outcomes of a country following its comparative advantage determined by its factor endowments in each stage of development. The fourth stylized fact, the market mechanism, is the precondition for a country to follow its comparative advantage. The last stylized fact, a committed, credible, and capable government, is a prediction as well as a consequence of following comparative advantage.

First, if a country follows its comparative advantage in its development strategy,[20] it will have an open economy, and produce whatever is consistent with its existing endowment structure and export to the international market,[21] while importing whatever goods and services are not in its comparative advantage. Its trade dependency ratio will be endogenous to its comparative advantage and will be larger than would be the case otherwise. Its economy will become competitive and its endowment

102 | New Structural Economics

structure and industrial structure will be upgraded at the fastest pace possible. In the industrial upgrading process, the country will be able to tap into the advantage of backwardness by borrowing technologies and industries from advanced countries. The country will achieve a much faster rate of growth than the advanced countries, as its innovation cost will be smaller than that of countries already on the global technology frontier. Its economy will therefore achieve convergence with high-income countries. From that perspective, exploiting the world economy through openness (*stylized fact 1*) is a result of the growth strategy that facilitates industrial upgrading according to the comparative advantage determined by the country's endowment structure.

Macroeconomic stability (*stylized fact 2*) is also a consequence of a country following comparative advantage in its development strategy. If a country does so, its economy will be competitive. Its industries will be viable in an open, competitive market (Lin 2009). The upgrading of industries will mainly rely on its own capital accumulation process. The government will have a strong fiscal position, for several reasons: first, it will reap the benefits of dynamic growth; second, there will be no need for subsidizing non-viable firms; and third, the economy will generate more job opportunities and less unemployment. The country will also be much less exposed to homegrown crises due to uncompetitive industries, currency mismatch, or fiscal crises. Because of its external competitiveness and limited reliance on capital inflows for growth, the country is also likely to have strong external accounts. Therefore, the government will be in a strong position to adopt countercyclical measures if there are shocks to the economy from global crises.

Recording high rates of saving and investment (*stylized fact 3*) is another logical result of the new structural economics approach of developing industries that are consistent with comparative advantage. Such a strategy allows a developing economy to be most competitive and produce the largest possible economic surplus (profits). This yields the highest savings for the economy. Competitive industries also imply high return on investment, which in turn provides additional incentives to save and invest. Moreover, good public investments can enhance the economy's growth potential, reduce transaction costs on the private sector, increase the rate of return on private investment, and generate enough tax revenues in the future to liquidate the initial costs.

Adopting a market system to allocate resources (*stylized fact 4*) is a necessary condition for an economy to follow comparative advantage in its development. Most firms are set up to pursue profits. They will follow the economy's comparative advantage in their decisions regarding the adoption of technology and entry into industries if relative prices reflect the relative scarcity of each factor in the endowment structure. This only happens in an economy with competitive markets (Lin 2009; Lin and Chang 2009). Therefore, a competitive market is the economy's optimal mechanism for resource allocation at each stage of its development.

Building committed, credible, and capable governments (*stylized fact 5*), that is, creating a facilitating state, is also a condition for an economy to adopt a comparative-advantage-following strategy in its development process. For a developing economy to upgrade from one industrial structure to another, the government needs to play a facilitating role in improving soft and hard infrastructures and in overcoming the information, coordination and externality issues. Therefore, a committed, credible and capable government is a precondition for sustainable growth. But capable states can also be seen as a consequence of that strategy: if the government's goal is to facilitate a development process that is consistent with the country's comparative advantage, its intervention will be implemented more easily and more successfully, which will strengthen its credibility. So a committed, credible and capable state can also be viewed as the outcome of the country's following its comparative advantage in its development.

Beyond those stylized facts, the Growth Commission Report also identified "bad ideas" to be avoided by policymakers in developing countries. While the Report prudently offers the caveat that there are situations and circumstances that may justify limited or temporary resort to some of the policies listed under that category, it notes that "the overwhelming weight of evidence suggests that such policies involve large costs and their stated objectives—which are often admirable—are usually much better served through other means" (p. 68). These "bad ideas" include costly or unsustainable policy decisions such as subsidizing energy, relying on the civil service to deal with joblessness, providing open-ended protection,

reducing fiscal deficits by cutting expenditures on infrastructure investment, or allowing the exchange rate to appreciate excessively.

Policy recommendations derived from the new structural economics
approach would help developing country governments avoid such "bad
ideas." Energy subsidies for instance are adopted in most countries to support nonviable firms (political economy rationale), or to help the poor
(equity rationale). Large, costly and unsustainable government subsidies
in developing countries arise from the fact that development strategies
deviate substantially from their optimal industrial structure. If a country
follows its comparative advantage in its development strategy, few of its
state-owned or private enterprises will be nonviable, and there will be
no need to provide subsidies to firms. Its economy will achieve dynamic
growth, which would allow poverty to be reduced rapidly. There will be
little need to subsidize the poor through price distortions. By growing fast,
the economy will create many job opportunities. Viable private firms offer
the best insurance against joblessness, so there will be no need to use public
employment as a tool to deal with joblessness. Moreover, the government
will not have to use open-ended protection to support or subsidize nonviable firms.

Thanks to the country's good economic performance, the government's
fiscal position is likely to be strong and there will be no justification for the
kind of erratic budget policies (expenditure cuts, public investment delays,
payment arrears, salary freezes, etc.) that are often caused by large fiscal deficits. Likewise, a government that implements a development strategy consistent with the country's comparative advantage will not have to
resort to an overvalued exchange rate as a means for subsidizing nonviable
firms that are created in the framework of comparative-advantage-defying,
import-substitution policies.

## 5. Conclusion

The quest for economic growth has preoccupied economists and policy-
makers since at least the 18th century. Much progress has been achieved
over the past 50 years, most notably on theoretical and empirical grounds.
On the theoretical front, the analysis of endogenous technical innovation and increasing returns to scale has provided economists with a rich

general framework for capturing the broad picture and the mechanics of economic growth. On the empirical side, the availability of standardized data sets such as the Penn World Tables has stimulated interest in cross-country work that highlights systematic differences between high-growth and low-growth countries with regard to initial conditions, and policy and institutional variables.

Yet, despite progress, policymakers around the world—especially in developing countries, still face difficulty in identifying specific actionable policy levers that can help ignite and sustain the type of dynamic growth rates that are necessary to reduce poverty. In recent years, growth researchers have responded to their concerns by trying to address various new challenges: the lack of convergence among countries; the identification of robust determinants of economic performance; the design of the supporting institutions for innovation and technological change, which are widely acknowledged to be the foundations for structural change and prosperity; and the identification of binding constraints to growth, the evaluation of successful development programs through randomized control trials, with the goal of scaling them up whenever possible.

By adopting a radically different approach to growth analysis, the Growth Report has made an important contribution to knowledge. It has identified five stylized facts (openness, macroeconomic stability, high rates of saving and investment, market mechanism, committed, credible and capable government) that can guide policymaking in developing countries. But in doing so, the Report has not disentangled causes and consequences.

The new structural economics framework proposed in Lin (2010) helps explain the endogeneity and exogeneity issues surrounding these five stylized facts. A central proposition that runs through this paper is that, developing countries that implement economic policies in contradiction with their comparative advantage tend to perform poorly and suffer macroeconomic instability. They do not exploit the benefits of globalization to the fullest. Typical features of such strategies are large budget deficits due to government support of nonviable firms, inflationary policies caused by excessive consumption, financial repression, and over-valued exchange rates in the context of low productivity. By contrast, countries that adopt comparative-advantage-following strategies are typically in the position to achieve dynamic growth. They rely on the market as the key mechanism for allocating resources at any given stage of development, and they have credible and capable governments. As a consequence of following their comparative advantage, they have an open economy, achieve macroeconomic stability, and record high rates of saving and investment.

## Notes

† Célestin Monga, a native of Cameroon, is a Senior Advisor to the World Bank Senior Vice President and Chief Economist. In his 13-year career in the World Bank, he has held positions in both operations and in the research department. He has also served on the Board of Directors of MIT's Sloan School of Management (Sloan Fellows) and taught at Boston University and the University of Bordeaux (France).

1. The losses precipitated by the financial crisis have been enormous. Total capitalization of world stock markets halved in 2008—about $32 trillion of wealth. The losses in household wealth during 2008 were about $11 trillion in the United States ($8.5 trillion in financial assets and $2.5 trillion in housing assets) and were estimated at $1.5 trillion in the United Kingdom ($0.6 trillion in financial assets and $0.9 trillion in housing assets). Losses of such magnitude have significant wealth effects on consumption and savings. Industrial production fell sharply in many developed and emerging countries and for the first time since 1929, world trade contracted in 2009. Data sources: Global Stability Reports; IMF Survey Magazine, June 24, 2009.

2. There were 1.4 billion people living under the international poverty line of $1.25 a day before the global crisis. Applying the country-specific growth projections to survey-based data and aggregating, World Bank experts calculate that the crisis will add 50 million people to the 2009 count of the number of people living below $1.25 a day and 57 million to the count of the number of people living under $2 a day. Given current growth projections for 2010, there will be a further impact on poverty in that year, with the cumulative impacts rising to an extra 64 million people living under $1.25 a day and 76 million more under $2 a day by 2010.

3. The report was released in 2008 and titled *The Growth Report: Strategies for Sustained Growth and Inclusive Development*. The Commission was constituted of 20 experienced policymakers and two Nobel prize-winning economists, Michael Spence and Robert Solow. Its work has been supported by the Governments of Australia, Sweden, the Netherlands, and the United Kingdom, the William and Flora Hewlett Foundation, and the World Bank Group.

4. Maddison (2007). See also *The World Economy: Historical Statistics*, available at http://www.ggdc.net/maddison/. Western offshoots, a term used in Maddison (2001), include Australia, Canada, New Zealand, and the United States.

5. Conditional convergence is a key property in Solow-Swan models. It is conditional because in these models, the steady-state levels of capital and output per worker depend on characteristics that vary across economies: saving rate, population growth rate, and the position of the production function. Many recent empirical studies have suggested that many other sources of cross-country variations such as government policies or the initial stock of human capital should be included in the analysis.

6. The Cass (1965) and Koopmans (1965) versions of the neoclassical model, which built on Ramsey's analysis of consumer optimization, attempted to provide an endogenous determination of saving rates. While this extension helped preserve conditional convergence, it did not solve the problem of long-run growth being determined by exogenous technological progress.

7. See, in particular, Becker (1992); Heckman (2006); Lucas (2004).

8. This is the case not only in development economics but also in various sub-disciplines of macroeconomics. Following the 2008-09 global crisis, a heated debate erupted among economists over the pertinence of the dominant models and their policy prescriptions. See for instance Blanchflower (2009), Krugman (2009), or Stiglitz (2009). For an assessment of controversies in development economics over methodological and policy issues, see Deaton (2009) and Ravallion (2009).

9. From 1870 to 1990, the ratio of per capita incomes between the richest and the poorest countries increased by roughly a factor of five. See Pritchett (1997).

10. That is the view expressed by Barro and Sala-i-Martin (1992); and Baumol (1986). Prescott (1999) is even more optimistic and expresses the view that continued divergence is not an option, and that the world distribution of income will eventually converge.

11. As Zagha et al. (2006) note, "whereas reforms can help achieve efficiency gains, they will not put the economy on a sustained growth path unless they also strengthen production incentives and address market or government failures that undercut efforts to accumulate capital and boost productivity." Pritchett (2006) suggests that economists abandon the quest for a single growth theory, and focus instead on developing a collection of growth and transition theories tailored to countries' particular circumstances.

12. The methodology proposed for the identification of the binding constraints to growth relies on shadow prices. Even in countries where data on shadow prices are widely available, it is not clear that this would accurately identify

areas in which progress is most needed in each country. For example, one could imagine a simple model of growth for a low income country where technology and human capital are complementary. In such a country, the returns to education and technology adoption would both be low due to low levels of human capital and technology. An exclusive focus on shadow prices and an ignorance of cross-country comparison of levels would then suggest no need to improve education levels and encourage technology adoption.

13. See Banerjee and Duflo (2005). Bourguignon (2006) offers a compelling theoretical framework for making the same case.

14. Critics of RCTs point to the fact that they often do not start from a clear strategic assessment of how a particular method would fit the knowledge gaps of highest priority. See Ravallion (2009).

15. These previous studies include, among others, the *East Asian Miracle* (1993), the *Growth in the 1990's* (2005), and the *World Development Report* on Agriculture for Development (World Bank 2007).

16. The way the Commission organized its work was also quite unusual: first, it defined themes and issues deemed important for growth and development. Then, it invited world renowned academics, practitioners and experts to author papers exploring the state of knowledge in these themes and issues; those were reviewed and discussed at workshops. A working group which interacted with academics and commissioners, reviewed and commented on papers throughout the process. The working group also supported the Chairman in drafting the final report by reviewing interim drafts and providing comments.

17. The list includes: Botswana, Brazil, China, Hong Kong (China), Indonesia, Japan, Korea, Malaysia, Malta, Oman, Singapore, Taiwan (China), and Thailand.

18. Because growth rates of this magnitude for such long periods were unheard of before the latter part of the 20th century, the authors acknowledge that their work could have been called a report on "economic miracles," except that they believe the term is a misnomer: unlike miracles, sustained high growth can be explained and repeated.

19. A country's *competitive advantage* refers to a situation where domestic industries fulfill the following four conditions: (i) They intensively use the nation's abundant and relatively inexpensive factors of production; (ii) Their products have large domestic markets; (iii) Each industry forms a cluster; and (iv) domestic market for each industry is competitive (Porter 1990). A country's *comparative advantage* is the situation in which it produces a good or service at a lower opportunity cost than that of its competitors. Such a condition is based on the country's possession of comparative advantage in that product or service determined by its endowment structure at any given time (Lin 2010).

The first condition for competitive advantage listed by Porter supposes that the industries should be the economy's comparative advantage determined by the nations' endowments. The third and the fourth conditions will hold only if the industries are consistent with the nation's competitive advantage. Therefore, the four conditions can be reduced to two independent conditions: the comparative advantage and domestic market size. Between these two independent conditions, the comparative advantage is the most important because if an industry corresponds to the country's comparative advantage, the industry's product will have a global market. That is why many of the richest countries of the world are very small (Lin and Ren 2007).

20. We define the development strategy here in the same way as Rodrik (2005), referring to policies and institutional arrangements adopted by the government in a developing country for achieving economic convergence with the living standards prevailing in advanced countries.

21. Exportable manufacturing goods are of particular importance, as they allow late-comers in the industrialization process to position themselves in industries where they have lower wages and other competitive advantages than more advanced economies.

## References

Acemoglu, D. and J.A. Robinson, 2001. "The Colonial Origins of Comparative Development: An Empirical Investigation." *American Economic Review*, September.

Aghion, P. and P. Howitt, 1992. "A Model of Growth through Creative Destruction." *Econometrica*, vol. 60, no. 2, March, pp. 323–351.

Banerjee, A. and E. Duflo, 2005. "Growth Theory through the Lens of Development Economics." In Philippe Aghion & Steven Durlauf (eds.), *Handbook of Economic Growth*, vol. 1, chapter 7.

Barro, R. J., and X. Sala-i-Martin, 1995. *Economic Growth*, Cambridge, MIT Press.

Barro, R. J. and X. Sala-i-Martin, 1992. "Convergence." *Journal of Political Economy*, vol. 100, no. 2.

Baumol, W., 1994. "Multivariate Growth Patterns: Contagion and Common Forces as Possible Sources of Convergence." In W. Baumol, R. Nelson and E. Wolf (eds.), *Convergence of Productivity, Cross-National Studies and Historical Evidence*, New York: Oxford University Press.

Baumol, W., 1986. "Productivity Growth, Convergence, and Welfare: What the Long-Run Data Show." *American Economic Review*, vol. 76, December, pp. 1072–85.

Becker, G.S., 1992. "Education, Labor Force Quality, and the Economy: The Adam Smith Address." *Business Economics*, vol. 27, no. 1, January, pp. 7–12.

Blanchflower, D., 2009. "The Future of Monetary Policy." Speech at Cardiff University, March 24.

Bourguignon, F., 2006. "Economic Growth: Heterogeneity and Firm-Level Disaggregation." PREM Lecture, Washington, D.C., World Bank, April.

Cameron, R., 1993. *A Concise Economic History of the World*, 2d ed., Oxford, Oxford University Press.

Cass, D., 1965. "Optimum Growth in an Aggregative Model of Capital Accumulation." *Review of Economic Studies*, no. 32, July, pp. 233–240.

Deaton, A., 2009. *Instruments of Development: Randomization in the Tropics, and the Search for the Elusive Keys to Economic Development*, Princeton, N.J., Princeton University Center for Health and Wellbeing, January.

Duflo, E. and M. Kremer, 2003. "Use of Randomization in the Evaluation of Development Effectiveness." Paper prepared for the World Bank Operations Evaluation Department, July.

Glaeser, E. and A. Shleifer, 2002. "Legal Origins." *Quarterly Journal of Economics*, vol. 117, November, pp. 1193–1229.

Growth Commission, 2008. *The Growth Report: Strategies for Sustained Growth and Inclusive Development*, Washington D.C.

Hausmann, R., D. Rodrik, and A. Velasco, 2008. "Growth Diagnostics." In N. Serra and J.E. Stiglitz (eds.), *The Washington Consensus Reconsidered: Towards a New Global Governance*, New York, Oxford University Press, pp. 324–354.

Heckman, J.J., 2006. "Skill Formation and the Economics of Investing in Disadvantaged Children." *Science*, vol. 312 (5782), June, pp. 1900–1902.

Jones, C.I. and P.M. Romer, 2009. *The New Kaldor Facts: Ideas, Institutions, Population, and Human Capital*, working paper no. 15094, NBER, June.

Jones, C. I., 1998. *Introduction to Economic Growth*, New York, W.W. Norton.

Kaldor, N., 1961. "Capital Accumulation and Economic Growth." In: F.A. Lutz and D.C. Hague (eds.), *The Theory of Capital*, New York, St. Martin Press, pp. 177–222.

Koopmans, T.C., 1965. "On the Concept of Optimal Economic Growth." In: *The Econometric Approach to Development Planning, Amsterdam*, North Holland.

Krugman, P., 2009. "How Did Economists Get it so Wrong?" *New York Times Magazine*, September 2.

Lin, J.Y., 2010. *New Structural Economics: A Framework for Rethinking Development*, Policy Research Working Papers, no. 5197, Washington D.C., World Bank.

Lin, J.Y. 2009. *Economic Development and Transition: Thought, Strategy, and Viability*, Cambridge, Cambridge University Press.

Lin, J.Y. 2003. "Development Strategy, Viability and Economic Convergence." *Economic Development and Cultural Change*, Vol. 53 (2), pp. 277–308. (A version of this article appears in chapter VI of this volume.)

Lin, J. Y., 1995. "The Needham Puzzle: Why the Industrial Revolution Did Not Originate in China." *Economic Development and Cultural Change*, Vol. 41 (2), 269–92.

Lin, J.Y., and H. Chang, 2009. "DPR Debate: Should Industrial Policy in Developing Countries Conform to Comparative Advantage or Defy It?" *Development Policy Review*, Vol. 27, No. 5, pp. 483–502. (Reprinted in chapter II of this volume.)

Lin, J.Y. and Ren, R., 2007. "East Asian Miracle Debate Revisited" (in Chinese). *Jingji Yanjiu* (Economic Research Journal), Vol. 42 (8), 4–12.

Lucas, R.E., 2004. *Lectures on Economic Growth*, Cambridge, MA., Harvard University Press.

Lucas, R. E., Jr, 1988. "On the Mechanism of Economic Development." *Journal of Monetary Economics*, Vol. 22, 3–42.

Maddison, A., 2007. *Contours of the World Economy 1–2030 AD: Essays in Macro-Economic History.* Oxford University Press.

Maddison, A., 2001. *The World Economy: A Millennial Perspective*, Paris, OECD.

Mokyr, J., 1990. *The Lever of Riches: Technological Creativity and Economic Progress*, New York and Oxford: Oxford University Press.

Montiel, P. and L. Serven, 2008. "Real Exchange Rates, Saving, and Growth: Is There a Link?" Background Paper, Commission on Growth and Development, Washington D.C.

North, D., 1981. *Structure and Change in Economic History.* New York: Norton.

Porter, M. E., 1990. *The Competitive Advantage of Nations*, New York: Free Press.

Prescott, E., 1999. "Interview with Edward Prescott." In B. Snowdown and H. Vane (eds.), *Conversations with Economists: Interpreting Macroeconomics*, Edward Elgar.

Pritchett, L., 2006. "The Quest Continues." *Finance and Development*, vol.43, no. 1.

Pritchett, L., 1997. "Divergence, Big Time." *Journal of Economic Perspectives*, vol. 11. No. 3, summer, pp. 3–17.

Ravallion, M., 2009. "Evaluation in the Practice of Development." *The World Bank Research Observer*, vol. 24, no. 1, February, pp. 29–53.

Rodrik, D., 2005. "Growth Strategies." In Philippe Aghion & Steven Durlauf (ed.), *Handbook of Economic Growth*, vol. 1, chapter 14, pages 967–1014, Elsevier.

Romer, P. M., 1986. "Increasing Returns and Long-Run Growth." *Journal of Political Economy*, vol. 95, no. 5, October, pp. 1002–1037.

Romer, P. M., 1987. "Growth Based on Increasing reurns Due to Specialization." *American Economic Review*, vol. 77, no. 2, May, pp. 56–62.

Romer, P. M., 1990. "Endogenous Technological Change." *Journal of Political Economy*, vol. 98, no. 5, October, part II, S71-S102.

Rostow, W.W., 1990. *Theorists of Economic Growth from David Hume to the Present—With a Perspective on the Next Century*, New York, Oxford University Press.

Stiglitz, J., 2009. *Freefall: America, Free Markets, and the Sinking of the World Economy*, New York, W. W. Norton & Co.

World Bank, 2007. *World Development Report 2008: Agriculture for Development*, Washington D.C.

World Bank, 2005. *Economic Growth in the 1990s: Learning from a Decade of Reform*, Washington D.C.

Zagha, R., I. Gill, and G. Nankani, 2006. "Rethinking Growth," *Finance and Development*, vol. 43, no. 1.

Zellner, A., 1979. "Causality and Econometrics, Policy and Policymaking," *Carnegie-Rochester Conference Series on Public Policy*, vol. 10, pp. 9–54.

# SHOULD INDUSTRIAL POLICY IN DEVELOPING COUNTRIES CONFORM TO COMPARATIVE ADVANTAGE OR DEFY IT?*

## A DEBATE BETWEEN JUSTIN LIN

## AND HA-JOON CHANG†

## Justin Lin

*Introduction: Growth and Industrial Upgrading*

At a time when cyclical turbulence threatens to distract us from the longer-run goal of promoting sustained growth and development, I welcome the chance to launch a discussion on this crucial topic with my friend Ha-Joon Chang. The Nobel laureate Robert Lucas (1988) has commented that 'Once one starts to think about them [questions of economic growth], it is hard to think about anything else'. What he had in mind was the remarkable sustained growth in productivity and living

* Adapted from "Should Industrial Policy in Developing Countries Conform to Comparative Advantage or Defy It? A Debate Between Justin Lin and Ha-Joon Chang," *Development Policy Review*, 27 (5), August 2009 (DOI: 10.111/J.1467-7679.2009.00456.X). © 2009 Justin Lin, Ha-Joon Chang.

standards that has characterised especially the countries of East Asia in recent decades, compared with the stagnation that, at least at that time, afflicted much of the rest of the developing world.

To Professor Lucas' comment, I would add that, once you start thinking about growth, it is hard not to focus on the continuous industrial and technological upgrading that is characteristic of sustained economic growth. In theory, as has long been recognised, poor countries should be able to take advantage of their backwardness, by importing modern technology and institutions developed elsewhere. But while some countries have done this well, many others have been far less successful at industrial upgrading and therefore at poverty reduction. What is it that makes it possible in one or two generations for a country to go from exporting wigs and plywood to competing in the most technologically advanced sectors?

The answer is not simply 'a dynamic private sector', though that is the ultimate driver. Historical examples make it clear that the answer must include effective government policies to catalyse private-sector growth. Governments have adopted a variety of measures to promote industrialisation and technological upgrading, with a wide variety of results. Used well, the unique powers available to governments can be wielded to initiate and support long-run sustained improvements in factors and productivity. Our central task as development economists is to learn from these historical examples, as well as from economic theory and empirics, so that we can help today's poorer countries to map out and follow a sustained growth path. In this essay, I shall argue that industrial upgrading and technological advance are best promoted by what I call a *facilitating* state—a state that facilitates the private sector's ability to exploit the country's areas of comparative advantage. As I shall explain, the key is to make use of the country's current comparative advantage—not in the factors of production that it may have someday, but in the factors of production that it has now.

### The Case for a State Role: Market Failures That Block Innovation

First, however, it is necessary to justify why the state needs to take the lead in development, because the facilitating-state approach requires government to do much more than a pure laissez-faire approach would allow. Developing economies are ridden with market failures, which cannot be ignored simply because we fear government failure. One such market failure is caused by important *information externalities*. Economic innovations—whether they succeed or fail—yield information about profitable and unprofitable market opportunities. But because much of this information is available not only to the innovators themselves but also to competitors and potential imitators, who do not bear any of the costs of the innovation, it will tend to be undersupplied by the market. Government subsidies are one possible mechanism for encouraging innovation and offsetting this first-mover disadvantage.

A second market failure is caused by *co-ordination problems*. Developing countries lag behind more developed countries, not only in technology and industrial structure, but also in human capital, infrastructure and institutions. For a country to climb up the industrial and technological ladder, a host of other changes also need to take place: technologies become more complicated, capital requirements increase, the scale of production increases, the size of markets increases, and market exchanges increasingly take place at arm's length. A flexible and smooth industrial and technological upgrading therefore requires simultaneous improvements in education, financial and legal institutions, and infrastructure. Individual firms clearly cannot internalise all these changes cost-effectively, and co-ordination among many firms to achieve these changes will often be impossible. For this reason, it falls to government either to introduce such changes itself or to co-ordinate them.[1]

In these cases, the positive externalities of firm entry and experimentation and needs for co-ordination can justify government intervention, and do so in a way that is perfectly compatible with neoclassical economic theory. It is true that the force of this argument is lessened by the high risk of government failures, but fear of poor governance does not absolve us of responsibility for trying to design effective strategies for facilitating development. Another Nobel laureate, W. Arthur Lewis (1955), correctly pointed out that '[N]o country has made economic progress without positive stimulus from intelligent governments', even as he warned of the 'mischief done to economic life by governments'. A half-century later, it remains true that there are few if any examples of governments that have succeeded with a purely laissez-faire approach that does not try to come to grips with market failures, and far more examples of rapid growth in countries whose governments have led effectively. Therefore, it is incumbent upon policy-makers and researchers to identify the most effective ways of promoting the productivity growth and change in industrial structure necessary for development.

## The Facilitating State: Helping the Private Sector Exploit Comparative Advantage

In summary, these severe market failures can provide a rationale for government intervention to kick-start growth. But what kind of intervention? The key to answering that question is recognising that the optimal industrial structure is *endogenous* to the country's endowment structure— in terms of its relative abundance of labour and skills, capital, and natural resources. Upgrading the industrial structure requires first upgrading the endowment structure, or else the resulting industrial structure will become a drag on development. Therefore the government's role is to make sure that the economy is well launched on this endogenous process of upgrading.

Let me explain this. The role of the facilitating state is to encourage the emergence of firms, industries, and sectors that, once launched, will make effective use of the country's *current* comparative advantage. In many poor countries, that will mean focusing on labour- and/or resource-intensive types of production activities and services. Even with the increased international capital flows of recent decades, low-cost capital remains relatively scarce, whereas labour and resources are relatively abundant and less costly. Focusing on labour- and resource-intensive production activities allows poor countries' firms to be competitive in domestic and international markets. The facilitating state provides the necessary co-ordination to remove the barriers to the emergence of these firms and their related industries, and gives them a helping nudge to overcome externalities, but then is able to let them grow and advance organically because of their comparative advantage.

As the competitive industries and firms grow, they will claim larger market share and create the greatest possible economic surplus, in the form of profits and salaries. When the surplus is reinvested, it earns the highest return possible as well, because the industrial structure is optimal for that endowment structure. Over time, this strategy allows the economy to accumulate physical and human capital, upgrading the endowment structure as well as the industrial structure and making domestic firms more competitive over time in more capital- and skill-intensive products.

While this *comparative-advantage-following* approach sounds gradual—and hence unsatisfying, when we consider the enormity of the poverty challenge—in fact progress is accelerated by the availability of technology and industries already developed by and existing in more advanced countries. Firms in developing countries can at each stage in their development acquire the technologies and enter into industries appropriate for their endowment structure, rather than having to do frontier innovation themselves. This ability to use off-the-shelf technology and to enter into existing industries is what has made possible the sustained annual GDP growth rates of 8 and even 10% achieved by some of the East Asian NIEs.

## The State as Midwife, not Permanent Nursemaid

Too often, developing-country policy-makers have tried to take a short cut in this endogenous process of industrial and technological upgrading. They have fixed their sights and their policies on an ideal industrial structure that they associate with modernisation, but that structure is of course usually capital- and skill-intensive and is characteristic of a higher-income country than their own. As I have argued in my Marshall Lectures (Lin, 2009), industrial strategies of the often newly-independent developing countries in the 1950s and 1960s were informed by incorrect perceptions of the binding constraints on development. These countries adopted development strategies that placed a priority on capital-intensive heavy industries, that is, industries that made intensive use of a factor that they largely lacked, and that neglected to use many of the factors that they had in great abundance, such as unskilled labour and natural resources. In effect, these policy-makers took the optimal industrial structure as something that they could impose exogenously, rather than something that results from the characteristics of the economy and changes over time.

This approach can be thought of as *comparative-advantage-defying*, and it has high costs, both financially and in terms of governance quality. To implement this strategy, governments have to provide substantial protection and subsidisation to firms that are not viable without government subsidies and protection and cannot quickly become internationally competitive. Such firms cannot generate any real surplus for society. Without a continuous flow of surplus, it will be far harder to finance improvements in the factors of production—notably, capital and skilled labour—that are in turn necessary to make a more advanced industrial structure viable over the medium term. By distorting market signals and shifting resources from competitive to noncompetitive sectors, high levels of protection and subsidies slow the country's accumulation of physical and human capital. They also encourage firms to divert their energies from productive entrepreneurship into rent-seeking, which corrupts institutions and further slows capital accumulation.

Suppose the government tries to protect and subsidise the growth of capital-intensive industries, or other industries in which it has no comparative advantage. In that case, the accumulation of capital and the upgrading of endowment structure are retarded, slowing the upgrading of its optimal technology/industrial structure. Rather than serving as midwife to healthy new industries, it is likely to find itself becoming a long-run nursemaid to sickly infant industries that never mature. The culture of rent-seeking that is likely to emerge will calcify the web of protection even more and make later reforms more difficult.

### Comparative vs. Competitive Advantage

Putting domestic firms in a position to exploit the country's comparative advantage may sound sensible but old-fashioned. How does exploiting comparative advantage compare with the promotion of 'competitive advantage', a strategy popularised by Michael Porter (1990) over the past two decades? In that literature, the four key sources of competitive advantage are:

- sectors/industries that make good use of factors that are abundant domestically;
- large domestic markets, to enable firms to achieve scale;
- industrial clusters; and
- vibrant domestic competition, to encourage efficiency and productivity growth.

But these requirements can be simplified, in my view. First, consider domestic competition: if a country's strategy defies comparative advantage, it will generally be unable to enforce competition, because non-viable firms will need to be protected. Industrial clusters will also be hard to build and sustain, because, unless the government gives subsidies and protection, firms will not enter into this industry. However, the government will not be able to give subsidies and protection to many firms in an industry at the same time so as to form an industrial cluster. And if the country follows its comparative advantage, large domestic markets become unnecessary, because the industries and firms should be able to compete on global markets. Thus these four requirements boil down largely to a single prescription: exploit your comparative advantage.

## Closing Notes

I am happy to launch this exchange with my friend and colleague Ha-Joon. We both care deeply about understanding the roots of rapid economic growth and poverty reduction, and we have both thought carefully about the East Asian growth successes of the past two generations. There will doubtless be differences in the conclusions we reach on trade and industrial policy, but it is illustrative that neither of us questions the importance of a major state role in promoting economic development. Perhaps this is because in the countries we know most intimately—China and South Korea—a crucial ingredient in growth was a capable and largely developmentally oriented state. The issue is identifying the key role played by the state in those countries and other rapid developers. My reading of these cases is that, while they took proactive steps to accelerate industrial upgrading, their success was spurred primarily by a state that made possible the effective exploitation of comparative advantage at each stage of development.

## Notes

† This is the first in an occasional series of DPR Debates, designed to illuminate specific issues of international development policy. Each debate will bring together two well-known researchers or practitioners, giving them the opportunity, over three rounds, to test and challenge each other's ideas. The debates are intended to be robust but accessible, rooted in rigorous research but useful to the wide readership of *Development Policy Review*.

Ha-Joon Chang is a reader in the Political Economy of Development, Faculty of Economics, University of Cambridge. He is the author, *inter alia*, of *Kicking Away the Ladder: Development Strategy in Historical Perspective* (Anthem

Press, 2002), and *Bad Samaritans: Rich Nations, Poor Policies, and the Threat to the Developing World* (Random House, 2007).

1. Note that this is a different argument from the co-ordination role often proposed in the past for developing-country governments. That 'big push' line of argument stressed that if each potential firm's viability depends on inputs from another firm that does not yet exist, none of the potential firms may emerge. In this case, the government can theoretically move the economy to a higher-welfare equilibrium with a big push that leads to the concurrent emergence of upstream and downstream firms (see Rosenstein-Rodan, 1961; and Murphy et al., 1989). But changing global conditions have made the traditional big-push argument less compelling. The reduction in transportation and information costs in recent decades has led to global production networks in which many countries, both developed and developing, produce only certain parts of a final product according to each country's comparative advantage.

## References

Lewis, W. Arthur (1955) *Theory of Economic Growth*. London: Allen & Unwin.

Lin, Justin Yifu (2009) *Economic Development and Transition: Thought, Strategy, and Viability*. Marshall Lectures, 2007/8. Cambridge: Cambridge University Press.

Lucas, Robert E, Jr. (1988) 'On the Mechanics of Economic Development', *Journal of Monetary Economics* 22 (1): 3–42.

Murphy, Kevin M., Shleifer, Andrei and Vishny, Robert W. (1989) 'Industrialization and the Big Push', *Journal of Political Economy* 97(5): 1003–26.

Porter, Michael E. (1990) *The Competitive Advantage of Nations*. London: Free Press.

Rosenstein-Rodan, P. (1961) 'Notes on the Theory of the "Big Push', in H. S. Ellis and H. C. Wallich (eds), *Economic Development for Latin America*. New York: St Martin's Press.

## Ha-Joon Chang

It is a pleasure to debate this issue with Justin Lin, whose intellectual interests are exceptionally wide-ranging and whose theoretical position, while firmly grounded in neoclassical economics, is never dogmatic.

In his opening essay, Justin acknowledges the importance of industrial upgrading for economic growth and development. This is a point that is often missed by today's development mainstream, which emphasises static allocative efficiency; so Justin's emphasis on industrial upgrading is really welcome.

On top of that, Justin also acknowledges the positive role that state intervention can play in promoting industrial upgrading, given important market failures that exist in the supply of new technological knowledge, such as the externalities generated by innovators experimenting with new things and the co-ordination failures across different input markets (for example, education, finance, legal institutions, and infrastructure). Justin also rightly warns against the possibility of government failure, but goes on to note that 'there are few if any examples of governments that have succeeded with a purely laissez-faire approach that does not try to come to grips with market failures, and far more examples of rapid growth in countries whose governments have led effectively'.

Up to this point, we are on the same platform. However, there are some important differences in our views. Our main difference is that, whereas Justin believes that state intervention, while important, should be basically about facilitating the exploitation of a country's comparative advantage, I believe that comparative advantage, while important, is no more than the base line, and that a country needs to defy its comparative advantage in order to upgrade its industry.

The concept of comparative advantage, first invented by David Ricardo, is one of the few concepts in economics that is more than common sense (the others include Keynes' notion of effective demand and Schumpeter's concept of innovation). The beauty of this concept is that it shows how even a country with no absolute international cost advantage in any industry may benefit from international trade by specialising in industries at which it is least bad. Indeed, it was the brilliance of Ricardo's concept that first drew me into economics. And as a guide to finding out the best way to maximise a country's current consumption opportunities, *given its current endowments*, we cannot do better than that.

As is well known, this theory, especially in the Heckscher-Ohlin-Samuelson version that Justin uses, is based on some stringent assumptions. Of course, all theories have assumptions and therefore the fact that there are some stringent assumptions in itself cannot be a point of criticism. However, we still need to ask whether the particular assumptions made by a model are appropriate for the particular questions we happen to be asking. My contention is that, while the assumptions made by the HOS theory may be acceptable when we are interested in short-term allocative efficiency (i.e., when we want to find out whether a country is exploiting its given resources with the maximum efficiency), they are not acceptable if we are interested in medium-term adjustment and long-term development.

First, let us look at the issue of medium-term adjustment. One of the key assumptions of the HOS theory is the assumption of perfect factor mobility (within each country). When this is assumed, no one loses out from changes in trade pattern caused by external shocks. So, if a steel mill shuts down because, say, the government reduces tariffs on steel, the resources employed in the industry (the workers, the buildings, the blast furnaces) will be employed (at the same or higher levels of productivity and thus higher returns) by another industry that has become relatively more profitable, say, the computer industry. No one loses from the process.

However, in reality, factors of production are usually fixed in their physical qualities. Blast furnaces from a bankrupt steel mill cannot be re-moulded into a machine making computers. Steel workers do not have the right skills for the computer industry: unless they are retrained, they will remain unemployed; at best, they will end up working in low-skill jobs, where their existing skills are totally wasted. In other words, even if the country as a whole benefits from trade liberalisation (which is not always the case even in the short run), the owners of factors of production that have low or no mobility are going to lose from it, unless there is deliberate compensation. This is why trade liberalisation has produced so many 'losers', despite the prediction of HOS theory.

This is a more serious problem in developing countries, where the compensation mechanism is weak, if not non-existent. In developed countries, the welfare state works as a mechanism partially to compensate losers from the trade-adjustment process through unemployment benefit, guarantees of health care and education, and even guarantees of a minimum income. In some countries, such as Sweden and other Scandinavian countries, there are also highly effective re-training schemes for unemployed workers. In most developing countries, however, such mechanisms are very weak and often virtually non-existent. As a result, the victims of trade adjustment in these countries are not even partially compensated for the sacrifice that they have made for the rest of society.

If the assumption of perfect factor mobility makes HOS inadequate for the analysis of medium-term adjustment, its assumption about technology makes it particularly unsuited to the analysis of long-term economic development.

The assumption in the HOS model is that there is only one best technology for producing a particular product and, more importantly, that all countries have the same ability to use that technology. So, in the HOS theory, if Ecuador should not be producing BMWs, it is not because it cannot do it, but because doing it has too high an opportunity cost, as producing BMWs will use too much of its scarce factor of production—capital.

However, this is assuming away the very thing that makes some countries developed and others not—namely, their differential abilities to develop and use technologies, or what is known as 'technological capabilities'. In the end, the rich countries are rich and the poor countries are poor because the former can use, and develop, technologies that the latter cannot use, let alone develop.

Moreover, the nature of the process of acquiring higher technological capabilities is such that a country trying to catch up with a more technologically advanced country needs to set up and protect industries in which it does not have comparative advantage. Why should that be the case? Can the country not wait until it accumulates enough physical and human capital before it enters a more advanced industry that uses physical and human capital more intensively?

Unfortunately, it cannot be done quite like that. Factor accumulation does not happen as an abstract process. There is no such thing as general 'capital' or 'labour' that a country can accumulate and that it can deploy wherever necessary. Capital is accumulated in concrete forms, such as machine tools for the car parts industry, blast furnaces, or textile machines. This means that, even if a country has the right capital-labour ratio for the automobile industry, it cannot enter the industry if its capital has been accumulated in the form of, say, textile machines. Likewise, even if a country accumulates more human capital to justify its entry into the automobile industry, it cannot start making cars if all its engineers and workers were trained for the textile industry.

Most (although not all) technological capabilities are accumulated through concrete production experiences, and at that in the forms of 'collective knowledge' embodied in organisational routines and institutional memories. Even if a country has all the right machines, engineers, and workers (which is not possible anyway, as I have just explained), they still cannot be combined into an internationally competitive firm overnight because they actually need to be put through a (potentially very lengthy) learning process before they can acquire all the necessary technological capabilities.

This is why Japan had to protect its car industry with high tariffs for nearly four decades, provide a lot of direct and indirect subsidies, and virtually ban foreign direct investment in the industry before it could become competitive in the world market. It is for the same reason that the electronics subsidiary of the Nokia group had to be cross-subsidised by its sister companies for 17 years before it made any profit. History is full of examples of this kind, from eighteenth-century Britain to late twentieth-century Korea.

Of course, Justin is absolutely right in saying that deviating too much from one's comparative advantages is to be avoided. Comparative advantage does offer a useful guideline in telling us how much the country is sacrificing by protecting its infant industries. The more you deviate from your comparative advantage, the more you pay in order to acquire capabilities in new industries.

However, this does not mean that a country should conform to its comparative advantage, as Justin puts it. As I have argued, given the nature of the process of factor accumulation and technological capability-building, it is simply not possible for a backward economy to accumulate capabilities in new industries without defying comparative advantage and actually entering the industry before it has the 'right' factor endowments.

Given this, a good neoclassical economist may be tempted to argue that a country should do a cost-benefit analysis before deciding to enter a new industry, weighing the costs of technological upgrading against the expected future returns, using comparative advantage as the measuring rod. However, this is a logical but ultimately misleading way of looking at the process. The problem is that it is very difficult to predict how long the acquisition of the necessary technological capabilities is going to take and how much 'return' it will bring in the end. So it is not as if Nokia entered the electronics industry in 1960 because it could clearly calculate that it would need to invest such and such amount in developing the electronics industry (through cross-subsidies) for exactly 17 years but then would reap huge future returns of such and such amount. Nokia probably did not think that it would take 17 years to make a profit in electronics. It probably did not know how large the eventual return was going to be. That is the nature of entrepreneurial decision-making in a world with bounded rationality and fundamental uncertainty. In other words, unless you actually enter the industry and develop it, it is impossible to know how long it will take for the country to acquire the necessary technological capabilities to become internationally competitive.

At the most general level, Justin and I share the same policy conclusions. We agree that industrial upgrading is necessary for economic development. We agree that it will not happen purely through market forces and will need government intervention. We also agree that the government should not push the economy too far away from its current structure too quickly.

However, there are some important differences between the two of us. In the theory of neoclassical comparative advantage that Justin uses, the issue of limited factor mobility is neglected, resulting in the systemic underestimation of the costs of trade liberalisation and hence the need for good redistribution mechanisms. More importantly, technological capabilities are missing from the theory, when they are really what distinguishes developed countries from developing ones. Once we realise that a lot of technological capabilities are acquired in an industry-specific manner through actual production experiences, we begin to see that it is by definition necessary to defy comparative advantage if a country is going to enter new industries and upgrade its industrial structure. And the length and the strength of such protection can be very large, as the examples of Toyota, Nokia, and countless other examples of successful infant-industry protection show, and also inherently difficult to predict.

## Justin Lin

Ha-Joon summarises well our key areas of agreement: government has a role to play in promoting technological and industrial upgrading, but there are risks in deviating too far from a country's comparative advantage. Our differences lie in how to define 'too far'—how to interpret trade models and historical evidence, and how to promote technological learning cost-effectively.

## Do Adjustment Costs and Technological Differences Really Undermine the Theory of Comparative Advantage?

Ha-Joon argues that, because of imperfect factor mobility (in effect, adjustment costs) and simplified assumptions about technology, arguments against infant-industry protection that are based on standard trade models (such as Baldwin, 1969) do not provide good guidance for policy. Clearly, there are frictions in labour-market adjustment to changes in industrial competitiveness, and physical capital is often industry-specific. Workers cannot move costlessly from one industry to another, or from one region to another, and many developing-country governments do little to compensate the losers. But adjustment costs can easily be incorporated into standard trade models, without undermining the basic theory of comparative advantage (Mussa, 1978). Moreover, when a country loses comparative advantage in the existing industry, the industry-specific capital can be relocated in the form of foreign direct investment to other countries, in what has been called a flying-geese pattern of economic development in East Asia and many other parts of the world (Akamatsu, 1962).

Ha-Joon's second point is that the Heckscher-Ohlin-Samuelson model incorrectly assumes that the same technology is available to producers in all countries. Yet the theory of comparative advantage does not hinge on having identical technology. Ricardo's original model of comparative advantage recognised that England and Portugal had different technologies for producing wine and cloth, for example. Moreover, theoretical models are intended to be simplifications; in empirical trade models, richer and poorer countries are routinely recognised to be using different technologies. Thanks to the dramatic reduction in information and transportation costs, countries at different stages of development could even concentrate on different segments of the same industry, each using different technologies and producing different products according to comparative advantages. Take the information industry as an example: high-income countries, like the US, specialise in product/technology development; middle-income countries, like Malaysia, concentrate on the fabrication of chips; and lower-middle-income countries, like China, focus on the production of spare parts and the assembly of final products.

Ha-Joon correctly observes that in reality trade liberalisation has produced many losers in the past two decades. But this is because those countries started with many industries that were inconsistent with their areas of comparative advantage, as a result of comparative-advantage-defying (CAD) strategies that their governments had adopted in the past. Removing protection in a shock-therapy manner caused the collapse of nonviable firms. However, if, in the liberalisation process, the government liberalises the entry to sectors in which the country has comparative advantage, and phases out protections to the CAD industries gradually, as argued in my Marshall Lectures (Lin, 2009), the country can obtain a Pareto improvement by achieving stability and dynamic growth simultaneously in the process. Indeed, this is how China has managed its transition from a planned to a market economy.

## What Do We Learn about Technological Upgrading from the Success Stories?

Underlying Ha-Joon's line of argument is research that he and others have done on some of the most rapid industrialisers. Here, I will comment on the case of Korea with a brief note about his Nokia example as well.

On the one hand, it is hard to argue that an active industrial and trade policy substantially hindered growth in the Republic of Korea. The country did protect certain sectors with high trade barriers, and in some cases took an aggressive approach to industrial upgrading into capital-intensive industries. And over the past 40 years, Korea has achieved remarkable GDP growth rates, and has performed impressively on industrial upgrading, into such industries as automobiles and semiconductors.

Yet we should not overstate the extent to which Korea pushed ahead of its comparative advantage. In the automotive sector, for example, early in its growth period, Korean manufacturers concentrated mostly on the assembly of imported parts—which was labour-intensive and in line with their comparative advantage at the time. Similarly, in electronics, the focus was initially on household appliances, such as TVs, washing machines, and refrigerators, and then moved on to memory chips, the least technologically complex segment of the information industry. Korea's technological ascent has been rapid, but then so has its accumulation of physical and human capital, due to the conformity of Korea's main industrial sectors to the existing comparative advantages, and hence its changes in underlying comparative advantage.

Equally important, the Korean government had a record of managing the protected sectors in ways that kept them subject to market discipline, which made large-scale deviation from the economy's comparative advantage impossible. Industries benefiting from protection and subsidisation were required to prove on export markets that their competitiveness was increasing over time. In addition, the government worked hard to make sure that Korean manufacturers could access intermediate inputs at world prices, for example through duty-drawback and exemption schemes and export-processing zones. So the government clearly recognised that comparative advantage mattered, and that successful technological upgrading depended on firms being influenced by world prices for both inputs and outputs. The evidence indicates that Korea's government served as a facilitating state, as argued in my opening contribution.

Let me add a footnote on the Nokia example, which I would interpret differently from Ha-Joon. Nokia's technological upgrading—from timber company to footwear, to manufacturing for Philips and then manufacturer of own-brand household electronics, and finally to mobile-phone powerhouse—took place roughly in line with the growth of Finland's stocks of physical and human capital. The Finnish government helped in ways that were far-sighted, but that I would interpret as consistent with the facilitating role in a comparative-advantage-following strategy. It promoted R&D and competition in the mobile-phone industry in the 1970s, creating and building on a pan-Nordic mobile network (Ali-Yrkkö and Hermans, 2004). The learning-by-doing that Nokia gained was invaluable, but the core element of this strategy was not high levels of protection of the domestic market. Nokia apparently cross-subsidised the development of its mobile-phone division through profits in other areas. However, Finland's per capita income in 1970, measured in 1990s' purchasing power parity, had already reached 9,600 international dollars, which was at a level close to Germany's 10,800 dollars in the same year (Maddison, 2006). Nokia's decision is wholly consistent with a model of technological/industrial upgrading by a profit-maximising private firm in an open, competitive, high-income country.

## Are Dynamic Comparative Advantage and Infant-Industry Protection Sound Foundations for Industrial Policy?

Finally, we should turn to the question of Ha-Joon's theoretical foundation for using trade policy as a tool for promoting industrial upgrading. His argument is based on the idea of dynamic comparative advantage and infant-industry protection. Nevertheless, if industrial upgrading proceeds step by step in conjunction with changes in comparative advantage, learning costs are lower than if the country attempts a big leap. As an analogy, think of mathematics learning. Typically, a student starts by studying algebra, then proceeds through calculus to real analysis. If instead he started with real analysis, even though he might eventually master it, the learning costs would most likely be much higher than otherwise. Similarly, if a firm begins by manufacturing bicycles, then learns to make motorcycles, and eventually moves into making automobiles, the total learning costs will probably be much lower than if it starts with the daunting task of mastering the efficient production of automobiles.

When a government chooses to provide protection or incentives to firms in sectors that may be viable only in twenty or more years, it will inevitably have to draw resources from firms in areas of current comparative advantage. This will reduce the surpluses they earn, and will therefore slow capital accumulation and the upgrading of the country's endowment structure and comparative advantage, making the infant industry stay as an infant much longer than otherwise (Baldwin, 1969; Saure, 2007).

Furthermore, excessive protection risks institutionalising a culture of rent-seeking. Given how important the quality of institutions and governance is to development, the indirect effects of protection through poor governance may be even more damaging than the direct effects.

## References

Ali-Yrkkö, Jyrki and Hermans, Raine (2004) 'Nokia: A Giant in the Finnish Innovation System', in Gerd Schienstock (ed.), *Embracing the Knowledge Economy: The Dynamic Transformation of the Finnish Innovation System.* Cheltenham: Edward Elgar Publishing.

Akamatsu, Kaname (1962) 'A Historical Pattern of Economic Growth in Developing Countries', *The Developing Economies*, Preliminary Issue No.1: 3–25.

Baldwin, Robert E. (1969) 'The Case Against Infant-Industry Tariff Protection', *Journal of Political Economy* 77 (3): 295–305.

Lin, Justin Yifu (2009) *Economic Development and Transition: Thought, Strategy and Viability.* Cambridge: Cambridge University Press.

Maddison, Angus (2006) *The World Economy.* Paris: OECD.

Mussa, Michael (1978) 'Dynamic Adjustment in the Heckscher-Ohlin-Samuelson Model', *Journal of Political Economy* 86 (5): 775–91.

Saure, Philip (2007) 'Revisiting the Infant Industry Argument', *Journal of Development Economics* 84 (1): 104–17.

## Ha-Joon Chang

Even though we come from different theoretical traditions, Justin and I agree on the broad framework for the analysis of industrial upgrading. To be sure, we have our differences. While we may both be of the view that comparative advantage is an important principle, I see it as only a 'base line', whereas Justin thinks it should be stuck to very closely, if not perfectly. We agree on the importance of adjustment costs and technological learning, but we differ in how important we think they are and we analyse them in different ways.

However, these are differences whose clarification actually helps us think through some of the finer points and advances our knowledge, rather than those that lead to unproductive bickering.

First, on adjustment costs. Justin is right in saying that these costs can be (and occasionally have been) incorporated into mainstream trade models. But my question is: if adjustments costs are important, why have they been so much neglected *in practice* by mainstream economists, who keep recommending trade liberalisation with only perfunctory, if any, attention to adjustment costs? It is not enough to say that adjustment costs can be incorporated into mainstream models. Intellectual leaders in the mainstream camp, like Justin, should encourage people actually to do it and then fully apply the results in designing trade-policy reform. The same applies to the assumption of identical technology. If it is better *not* to assume identical technology (as Justin implicitly acknowledges), why do mainstream economists keep using the HOS version of comparative advantage rather than the Ricardian version, in which differences in technology determine the comparative advantages of different nations?

As for Justin's point that even activity-specific assets do not need to lose their value entirely in the adjustment process because they can be shifted to another country, I thank him for reminding me of this important point. However, this mainly applies to physical assets and then only to a limited extent. Not all physical assets can be shipped abroad and many of them need complementary assets and skills if they are to realise their full productive potential. Moreover, workers with specific skills (or human capital, if you like) cannot move to the 'next-goose' country, except for a limited number of technicians who may be called upon to advise the factories in the new host countries. For the workers, it is cold comfort to learn that the physical assets they used to work with may preserve some of their value by moving to another country. To make things worse, the workers usually have fewer and less diversified assets (even including their own human capital) than the owners of physical assets, so they are less capable of coping with the consequences of the adjustment, even if they are subject to the same magnitude of shocks (in proportional terms) as the capitalists.

Thus seen, Justin's 'flying geese' point does not lessen the need to incorporate adjustment costs into trade policy design. If anything, it actually highlights the need to better design compensation schemes for the workers with specific skills (for example, subsidised re-training programmes).

Justin argues that trade liberalisation in the last two decades has produced many losers 'because those countries started with many industries that were inconsistent with their areas of comparative advantage' because of wrong policies in the past. This may often (although not always) have been the case, but it does not justify the way trade liberalisation has been conducted in the last two decades. If we know that a country has deviated 'too much' from its comparative advantage, the prudent course of action will be not to try to liberalise trade too much too quickly, as otherwise the adjustment costs will be very high.

Two wrongs do not make a right.

This naturally leads me to Justin's second point—the challenge of deciding how much to deviate from comparative advantage. Using the Korean and Finnish examples, he argues that these countries succeeded because they did not deviate from their comparative advantages too much. He is right in saying that Korea's move along the 'ladder' of international division of labour has often been carried out in small, if rapid, steps. Although I do not fully agree with this characterisation (for example, the moves into industries like steel and shipbuilding were big leaps, with virtually no 'intermediate' steps), I also agree that making excessive leaps can result in excessive learning costs.

Thus seen, we could suppose some kind of inverted-U-shaped relationship between an economy's deviation from comparative advantage and its growth rate. If it deviates too little, it may be efficient in the short run, but its long-term growth is slowed down, as it is not upgrading. Up to a point, therefore, increasing deviation from comparative advantage will accelerate growth. After a point, negative effects of protection (for example, excessive learning costs, rent-seeking) may overwhelm the acceleration in productivity growth that the 'infant' industries generate, resulting in negative growth overall.

I think Justin would probably agree with the above way of seeing things. However, there is one big disagreement between the two of us in applying this idea. It is the question of 'how much (deviation from comparative advantage) is too much?' (or where is the apex in the inverted-U curve?)

Using the Finnish example, Justin says that Nokia was justified in moving into the electronics industry, as Finland was already a pretty rich country, with per capita income (in international dollars) only 13% lower than that of Germany in 1970 ($9,577 vs. $10,839). However, the relevant year is not 1970 but 1960, which is when the electronics subsidiary of Nokia was set up, and in that year the income gap with Germany was much greater, at 23% ($7,705 vs. $6,230).[1] Anyway, these figures are purchasing power parity (PPP) figures, which tend to inflate a poorer country's income. PPP figures are preferable if we are interested in measuring comparative living standards, but if we are interested in comparative advantage in international trade, current dollar figures, rather than PPP figures, are better figures to use.

If we use current dollars, the picture becomes quite different.[2] In 1960, the per capita income of Finland was only 41% that of the US, the frontier country in electronics and overall ($1,172 vs. $2,881). This does not look like the case of a country sticking closely to comparative advantage. If Finland's decision regarding Nokia does not look 'wrong' enough, how about Japan? In 1961, the per capita income of Japan was a mere 19% that of the US ($563 vs. $2,934), but Japan was then protecting and promoting all sorts of 'wrong' industries—automobiles, steel, shipbuilding, and so on.

For an even more dramatic example, take the case of South Korea. Its (then) state-owned steel mill, POSCO, which had been set up in 1968, started production in 1972, when its per capita income was a mere 5.5% that of the US ($322 vs. $5,838).[3] To make it worse, in the same year, South Korea decided to deviate even further from its comparative advantage by launching its ambitious Heavy and Chemical Industrialisation programme, which promoted shipbuilding, (home-designed) automobiles, machinery, and many other 'wrong' industries. Even as late as 1983, when Samsung decided to design its own semiconductors, Korea's income was only 14% that of the US ($2,118 vs. $15,008). Does this sound like a 'comparative-advantage-conforming' strategy, as Justin calls it?

A further difficulty with Justin's argument is that in all these examples of defiance of comparative advantage, the market gave Finland, Japan, and Korea unambiguous signals that they should not promote those industries; all the companies in those industries ran losses or earned profits on paper only because they were subsidised by profitable companies in the same business group and/or by the government (directly through subsidies and indirectly through protection and entry restrictions). But if Justin thinks Nokia's experience is 'consistent with a model of technological/industrial upgrading by a profit-maximising private firm in an open, competitive, high-income country', is he saying that market signals are not to be taken seriously? Within the neoclassical framework, how else are we to judge whether or not a country is following its comparative advantage, except by looking at profits and losses made by the relevant companies?

I think that, deep down, Justin and I actually agree. We agree that countries should deviate from comparative advantage to upgrade their economy, although Justin thinks this deviation should be fairly small and I think it can be big. However, because Justin is too faithful to neoclassical economics, he has to say that a country with an income level that is only 5% of the frontier country moving into one of the most capital-intensive industries (Korea and steel) is consistent with the theory of comparative advantage. Once Justin frees himself from the shackles of neoclassical economics, our debate will be more like two carpenters having a friendly disagreement over what kind of hinges and door handles to use for a new cabinet that they are building together, on whose basic design they agree.

## Notes

1. All the PPP income figures are from Maddison (2006: Tables 1-c for Europe, 2-c for the USA, 5-c for South Korea).
2. All the current dollar income figures are from http://www.nationmaster.com/red/graph/eco_gdp_percapeconomy-gdp-per-capita, which draws on the World Bank and the CIA data.
3. Even in PPP terms, its income was only 16% that of the US ($2,561 vs. $15,944).

## Justin Lin

I've enjoyed this extended exchange, which has given us a chance to highlight our differences, while recognising our points of agreement. In response to Ha-Joon's latest submission, it is useful to focus on two points: the dynamic nature of industrial upgrading, and the role of government in promoting it.

### Industrial Upgrading as a Dynamic Process

First, let me reiterate that innovation is necessary for industrial upgrading and development, and that government has a role in supporting that innovation for the positive externalities innovation brings to an economy's development. It is hard work to climb technological ladders, to use a metaphor employed by Ha-Joon and others. The developed countries that are at the technology frontiers recognise this. They provide considerable public support to firms in their frontier industries—directly by giving a patent to a new invention and sometimes also through defence contracts; and indirectly through supporting basic research at universities, which ultimately spills over into product development and benefits firms and industries at the technological frontier. As inside-the-frontier innovations in developing countries involve similar risk and externalities, public support can be desirable and justifiable in that context too. Well-thought-out subsidisation is not only consistent with the role of a facilitating state, but is even implied. However, as pointed out in my first essay, the subsidies to compensate for an innovative firm's externality will be small compared with those that would be required to protect non-viable firms in industries that go against an economy's comparative advantage.

Second, industrial upgrading in an economy is a continuous process. Although government needs to help solve externality and co-ordination problems for the pioneer firms, their upgrading is based on the fact that the economy has successfully exploited its existing comparative advantages and its endowment structure, as well as comparative advantage shifting. When the Korean government started its world-class state-owned Pohang Iron and Steel company in 1968, to use Ha-Joon's example, that investment was built upon the success of development in garments, plywood, wigs, footwear, and other labour-intensive industries. With the success of those labour-intensive industries, Korea accumulated capital and the capital intensity of its endowment structure increased. From the perspective of the comparative-advantage-following strategy, the upgrading of a few firms into more capital-intensive industries became a necessity.

The 'flying geese' metaphor is useful in the domestic context as well as the international one: when an economy follows its comparative advantage in economic development, its endowment structure and comparative advantage change dynamically. Some firms need to play the role of a 'lead goose' so as to pioneer the upgrading into new industries. This appears to be one area of difference between Ha-Joon and me: I see the lead goose as a small but important leading wedge in a dynamic process, whereas he sees it as a more quantitatively significant part of the economy making larger discrete technological leaps. The quantitative difference can cause a qualitative difference. When the lead goose is a small wedge in the dynamic process, the nature of the economy is consistent with its comparative advantage. Unlike the upgrading in the comparative-advantage-defying strategy discussed in my first essay, the subsidies to the lead goose can derive mostly from intra-firm profits obtained in the operations of other products in competitive markets, as in the case of Samsung and Nokia.

Third, the global technological frontier is continually being pushed outward. Industries such as steel production and shipbuilding were among the most advanced industries globally in the nineteenth century, but by the mid-twentieth century they no longer held this leading-edge position. Compared with new industries, such as aviation, information, and heavy chemicals, their technologies had become mature. Investments in these mature industries required a large amount of capital, compared with traditional labour-intensive industries, but their capital intensities were much lower than in the new emergent industries. It is therefore not surprising that, with some government support for overcoming the difficulty of mobilising a large amount of capital in an economy with an underdeveloped financial sector, these industries are viable in countries that have achieved or are approaching lower-middle-income status. When Korea established Pohang Iron and Steel, its per capita income in dollar terms was just 5.5% that of the US, as pointed out by Ha-Joon. I would also like to mention that China had become the largest producer of steel in the world by 2000, at a time when its per capita income in dollar terms was only about 2.5% of the US level.[1] Korea and China were able to succeed in the steel industry at a relatively low income level because steel had become a mature and relatively low capital-intensity industry in the global industrial spectrum.

A related point is that, within industries, some segments are more accessible to developing countries than others. Manufacturing includes various stages—product R&D, design, production of complex parts, production of simpler parts, and assembly—and they all have different factor requirements and are consistent with different patterns of comparative advantage. Countries therefore scale the ladder of technological sophistication and capital intensity within industries dynamically in a flying-geese pattern as well. Samsung's entry in 1983 into the development of the 64-kilobit dynamic random access memory (DRAM) chip, which was relatively low-tech on the microchip spectrum at that time and was produced with the proprietary technology from Micron of the United States and Sharp of Japan, was built on some 15 years of successful operations in consumer electronics. It is worth noting that, in spite of the success of its entry into microchips in 1983, Samsung, on the one hand, has not entered the more complicated and advanced CPU chips and, on the other hand, has maintained its successful operations in consumer electronics.

## Facilitating Comparative Advantage, with Equal Parts Vision and Realism

To sum up my argument in this exchange, I reiterate that the comparative-advantage-following approach is dynamic in nature and the state should play a facilitating role in that process. This means that economic development in a country should exploit pragmatically the existing opportunities embedded in the country's areas of comparative advantage, while recognising the potential for industrial upgrading when those areas of comparative advantage have been exploited. Industrial upgrading is an innovation involving risks and externalities, whether in developed or developing countries, and thus requires the government to play a facilitating role. Governments in developing countries can play that role through the channels of information, co-ordination and compensation for externalities, as discussed in my first essay.

Ha-Joon's rhetorical jibe notwithstanding, neoclassical economics is simply a useful tool in all this, not a constraint. It is flexible enough to model the externalities, dynamics, and co-ordination failures that give the government a role to play, while also providing the metrics to judge whether government is supporting industries that take the economy too far from its areas of comparative advantage. Without the former, developing countries may lack the wisdom to seize opportunities to develop competitive industries and lay the foundation for sustainable industrial upgrading and development. But without the latter, as the historical record emphasises, governments can make any number of costly mistakes, most notably by funding large-scale, unrealistic and unsustainable comparative-advantage-defying projects and industries. By facilitating industrial upgrading where domestic firms will be able to survive and thrive, government can intervene in ways that yield the greatest social returns.

## Notes

1.  Here I use Ha-Joon's method of comparison based on market exchange rates, but PPP incomes are the more appropriate basis for comparison, in my view. Although market exchange rates govern international trade, PPP figures are better indicators of the level of development and capacity of an economy, and are therefore more relevant for discussions of industrial upgrading.

## Ha-Joon Chang

As the exchange shows, Justin and I agree on many things. Both of us recognise that 'climbing up the ladder' is a hard slog that involves more than 'getting the prices right'. It requires, *inter alia*, intelligent industrial policy, organisation building, and efforts to accumulate technological capabilities through R&D, training and production experiences. We agree that, in climbing up the ladder, a country can skip some rungs with the help of industrial policy, but that it can slip, fall, and even be destroyed, if it tries to jump too many rungs. The principle of comparative advantage, Justin says and I agree, can tell us what a country's 'natural' climbing ability is and thus help us to see how much risk it is taking in trying to skip a certain number of rungs.

However, we have some important differences.

Justin emphasises that neoclassical economics is flexible enough to allow us to deal with all the complex issues arising during the development process. I think it is not enough.

I agree that neoclassical economics is a lot more flexible than is usually recognised by many of its critics and that it can justify most types of state intervention, even of pretty 'unorthodox' kinds. After all, in the 1930s, the famous Marxist Oskar Lange tried to justify socialist planning with a neoclassical general equilibrium model.

However, the rational-choice, individualistic foundation of neoclassical economics limits its ability to analyse the uncertain and collective nature of the technological learning process, which is at the heart of economic development. I have emphasised the importance of bounded rationality, fundamental uncertainty (and not just calculable risk), and collective knowledge in the development process. This means that the industrial upgrading process will be messy. It will not be possible for a country to follow market signals closely and enter an industry when its factor endowments are right, as will happen with the smooth comparative-advantage-conforming strategy that Justin advocates. In the real world, firms with uncertain prospects need to be created, protected, subsidised, and nurtured, possibly for decades, if industrial upgrading is to be achieved.

In practical terms, my difference with Justin lies primarily in the extent to which we think the defiance of comparative advantage is advisable. While Justin believes that the skipping of the rungs in climbing the ladder should be very small ('comparative-advantage-conforming' in his words), I believe that it can be, and sometimes has to be, large ('comparative-advantage-defying' in his words). There is, of course, a chance that such an attempt may not succeed, but that is the nature of any venture into new activities, whether purely private or assisted by the state.

Justin is right in pointing out that Korea's forays into industries like steel, shipbuilding, and microchips were not as dramatic as they may have looked at first sight. By the time Korea entered them, steel and shipbuilding were technologically mature, although I am not sure whether that necessarily means lower capital intensity, as Justin assumes; technological maturity will increase capital intensity by leading to a greater embodiment of technologies in capital goods, while it may reduce capital intensity by lowering the relative prices of the relevant capital goods. Even in microchips, the segment that Korea entered, namely, the DRAM chip, was (and still is) technologically the easiest.

However, all these still do not mean that Korea's entry into these industries was comparative-advantage-conforming. First of all, technologically mature or not, the fact remains that industries like steel were still way too capital-intensive for Korea at the time (or, for that matter, today's China). More interestingly, Korea's success in steel was owed especially to the fact that it reaped the maximum scale economy by deliberately going for the most up-to-date and capital-intensive technology available (bought from New Nippon Steel).

Most importantly, the market clearly signalled that these were 'wrong' industries to enter, by making the producers run losses or forcing the government or the relevant business groups to manufacture 'artificial' profits by protecting and subsidising them. I do not think any version of neoclassical economic theory can justify protecting an industry for four decades (for example, Japanese and Korean cars) or cross-subsidising a loss-making subsidiary for 17 years (Nokia).

I have learned a lot from this exchange with Justin. We come from different intellectual traditions, but we have conducted a cordial and very productive debate that bears no bitterness or petty point-scoring. I wish there could be more exchanges like this in the pages of *Development Policy Review* and elsewhere.

# GROWTH IDENTIFICATION AND FACILITATION: THE ROLE OF THE STATE IN THE DYNAMICS OF STRUCTURAL CHANGE

# GROWTH IDENTIFICATION AND FACILITATION: THE ROLE OF THE STATE IN THE DYNAMICS OF STRUCTURAL CHANGE

## WITH CÉLESTIN MONGA*†

## 1. Introduction

The recent global crisis, the most serious since the Great Depression, has forced economists and policy-makers to rethink their approaches to macroeconomic management. For developing countries, in the midst of a

* Adapted from "DPR Debate: Growth Identification and Facilitation: The Role of the State in the Dynamics of Structural Change," *Development Policy Review,* 29 (3), May 2011 (DOI: 10.1111/j.1467-7679.2011.00534.x). © 2011 Lin, J., Monga, C., te Velde, D. W., Tendulkar, S. D., Amsden, A., Amoako, K. Y., Pack, H., and Lim, W. © 2011 Overseas Development Institute. Reprinted with the permission of John Wiley and Sons / Blackwell Publishing.

financial and economic turmoil not of their own making, the road ahead is likely to be rocky. Because of the sluggish recovery in high-income countries and the heavy cost of the crisis, they will have to confront a more difficult global environment for their exports and financing conditions. Yet, in order to continue tackling the enormous challenge of poverty and achieve convergence, they must return to the pre-crisis path of dynamic growth.

How to promote economic growth has been a main topic for economic discourse since the publication of Adam Smith's *The Wealth of Nations* in 1776. Market mechanisms have proved essential for valuing the basic ingredients for production and providing the right price signals and the appropriate incentive system for the efficient allocation of resources. However, modern economic growth—a fairly recent phenomenon (Maddison, 2001)—is a process of continuous technological innovation, industrial upgrading and diversification, and improvements in the various types of infrastructure and institutional arrangements that constitute the context for business development and wealth creation (Kuznets, 1966).

Historical evidence shows that all countries that have successfully transformed from agrarian to modern advanced economies—both the old industrial powers of Western Europe and North America, and the newly industrialised economies of East Asia—have had governments that played a pro-active role in assisting individual firms in overcoming the inevitable co-ordination and externality problems. In fact, the governments in high-income countries today continue to do so. However, the sad fact is that almost every government in the developing world has attempted, at some point, to play that facilitating role, but most have failed. In this article, we argue that these pervasive failures are mostly due to government inability to come up with good criteria for identifying industries appropriate for a given country's endowment structure and level of development. In fact, government propensity to target industries that are too ambitious and not aligned with a country's comparative advantage largely explains why their attempts to 'pick winners' have resulted in 'picking losers'.[1] By contrast, spontaneously or intentionally, the governments in successful developing countries have typically targeted mature industries in countries with an endowment structure similar to and a level of development not much more advanced than theirs. The main lesson is straightforward: to facilitate industrial upgrading and diversification, government policy must be anchored in industries with latent comparative advantage so that, once the new industries are established, they can quickly become competitive domestically and internationally.

This article broadens the scope of analysis of industrial policy by introducing an important distinction between two types of government interventions. First are those that facilitate structural change by aiming to provide information, compensate for externalities, and co-ordinate improvements in the 'hard' and 'soft' infrastructure[2] that are needed for the private sector to grow in a manner consistent with the dynamic change in the economy's comparative advantage. Second are those whose objective is to protect selected firms and industries that are in defiance of the comparative advantage determined by the existing endowment structure— either in new sectors that are too advanced or in old sectors that have lost comparative advantage.

The remainder of the article is structured as follows: Section 2 explains the importance of well-functioning markets and the rationale for a facilitating state in the process of dynamic economic growth. Section 3 briefly reviews some important lessons from early industrial development strategies around the world and analyses the role of the state in the process of structural change in today's advanced economies. It also examines similar attempts by developing-country governments to adopt policy interventions to facilitate industrial upgrading and economic diversification, and analyses the reasons for their success or failure. Building on the foundations of new structural economics (Lin, 2010), Section 4 provides a framework for formulating industrial policy based on a new approach entitled 'growth identification and facilitation'. Section 5 offers some concluding thoughts.

## 2. Structural Change, Efficient Markets and a Facilitating State

Economists have long been intrigued by the mystery of modern economic growth, typically observed through the seemingly divergent evolution of the change in per capita gross domestic product among countries. Since taking off sometime around 1820 (Maddison, 2001), the world growth rate has risen more or less steadily, peaking during a 'golden age' (1950–73) when it averaged almost 3% per year. But such progress has been uneven across regions, countries, and time. Sustained growth has led to improved living standards, first in Western Europe, North America and Japan, and more recently in newly industrialised (NIEs) and other emerging market economies. Cross-country income distribution that initially widened (with the proportional gap between the richest and poorest countries growing more than fivefold from 1870 to 1990) (Pritchett, 1997) has slowed in recent decades among groups of countries. With the narrowing of the top end of the distribution, there seem to be 'convergence clubs' among nations (Evans, 1996). Still, many of the poorest countries, especially in Africa, are excluded from the convergence process.

Modern growth theory has attempted to explain the diverging paths followed. Despite differences in approach and methodology, there is wide consensus that the variation of living standards across countries and time mostly reflects differences in the rate of capital accumulation and productivity growth. Empirical studies carried out from the perspective of development accounting show that, among these two broad factors, 'productivity differences among countries are the dominant explanation for income differences. Similarly, differences in productivity growth are the most important explanation for differences in income growth rates among countries' (Howitt and Weill, 2010: 43-4). Over the long term, productivity growth is associated with technological[3] and structural change, namely, to reduce the costs of producing the same outputs with better knowledge and to relocate resources from lower value-added to higher value-added industries.[4]

It can therefore be said that continuous technological innovation, industrial upgrading, economic diversification and an acceleration of income growth are the main features of modern economic growth (Kuznets, 1966; Maddison, 2006).[5] Each country at any specific time possesses given factor endowments consisting of land (natural resources), labour and capital (both physical and human), which are the total budgets that the country can allocate to primary, secondary and tertiary industries to produce goods and services. These are changeable over time, and conceptually it is useful to add both 'hard' and 'soft' infrastructure to the mix (Lin, 2010).[6] Both types are essential to the competitiveness of domestic firms because they affect transaction costs and the marginal rate of return on investment.

At any given point in time, *ceteris paribus,* the structure of a country's endowment, that is, the relative abundances of factors that the country possesses, determines the relative factor prices and thus the optimal industrial structure (Ju et al., 2009). A low-income country with abundant labour or natural resources and scarce capital will have comparative advantage and be competitive in labour- or resource-intensive industries. Similarly, a high-income country with abundant capital and scarce labour will have comparative advantage and be competitive in capital-intensive industries. The optimal industrial structure in a country, which will make it most competitive, is therefore endogenously determined by its endowment structure. For a developing country to reach the advanced countries' income level, it needs to upgrade its industrial structure relative to their capital-intensity. However, to achieve that, it must first close its endowment gap with that of the advanced countries, and the strategy to get there is to follow its comparative advantage at each stage of its development. When firms choose to enter industries and adopt technologies consistent with that country's comparative advantage, the economy is most competitive. These firms will claim the largest possible market shares and create the greatest possible economic surplus in the form of profits and salaries. Because of the competitiveness, re-invested surpluses earn the highest return, which allows the economy to accumulate even more physical and human capital over time. This dynamic can lead to a virtuous circle: it can upgrade the country's factor-endowment structure as well as the industrial structure, and also make domestic firms more competitive in more capital- and skill-intensive products over time.

A firm's objective is to maximise profit, not to exploit the economy's comparative advantage. It will follow the comparative advantage in choosing its industry and technology in the development process only if the relative factor prices reflect the relative abundances of factors in the economy (Lin, 2009; Lin and Chang, 2009). Relative factor prices of such nature will exist only in a competitive market system. An efficient market mechanism is therefore a required institution for the economy to follow its comparative advantage in the process of dynamic development.

However, in spite of the importance of the market mechanism, for the following information, co-ordination, and externality reasons, it is also desirable for the government to play a pro-active role in facilitating industrial upgrading and diversification in the development process.

First, the decision to upgrade or diversify is never an obvious choice. A pioneer firm may fail due to the lack of complementary inputs or adequate infrastructure for the new industry, or the targeted industry may simply not be consistent with the economy's comparative advantage. Industrial upgrading and diversification are therefore likely to be a costly trial-and-error exercise of discovery, even with the advantage of backwardness (Hausmann and Rodrik, 2003). In order to be successful in a competitive market, firms in a developing country need information about which industries within the global industrial frontier align with the country's latent comparative advantage.

Information has the same properties as public goods. The costs of collecting and processing information are substantial; however, the marginal cost of allowing one more firm to share the information is almost zero, once the information is generated. Therefore, the government can play a facilitating role by investing in information collection and processing and making information about the relevant new industries freely available to firms. In addition, the choice of a new industry may also shape the economy's future growth potential in a path-dependent way through the accumulation of specific human and social capital. The government is better than individual private firms at analysing information about this and making that information available to the public.

Second, technological innovation and industrial diversification and upgrading are typically accompanied by changes in capital and skills requirements for firms, as well as changes in their market scope and infrastructure needs due to the evolving nature of production embodied in the process. In other words, industrial upgrading and diversification are typically accompanied by changes in hard and soft infrastructure requirements. For example, with the change from agrarian production to manufacturing and from simple to advanced manufacturing in the development process, the scale of production and market scope become increasingly large, and with them the demand for transportation and power. Individual firms are not capable of internalising these provisions or deploying the kind of co-ordination efforts among firms in different sectors needed to meet those increasing demands.[7] Even if some large single companies were willing to finance a national road or a power network, co-ordination through the public sector would be needed to ensure consistency, efficiency and prevention of natural monopolies when the national economy grows. In addition to the hard infrastructure, in a low-income country firms in small-scale, labour-intensive agriculture and manufacturing need only an unskilled labour force and an unsophisticated financial and marketing system. But when the economy expands into modern manufacturing, high-skilled labour and large funds for lump-sum investments in equipment, working capital and/or export financing are needed, as well as new marketing arrangements. However, individual firms are usually not capable of internalising the needed changes in soft infrastructure. Here again, there is a need for the state to provide or co-ordinate some of those changes in different sectors of the economy so as to facilitate the individual firms' upgrading and diversification.[8]

Third, innovation, which underlies the industrial upgrading and diversification process, is by nature a very risky endeavour. Even when governments are willing and capable of helping by providing firms with the necessary information and co-ordination, success is not guaranteed. Firms can fail because the targeted industry is too ambitious, or the market too small, or the co-ordination inadequate. But even such cases of failure offer useful information to other firms, indicating that the targeted industries are inappropriate and should be re-examined. First-mover firms therefore pay the cost of failure and produce valuable information for other firms. And when they succeed, their experience also provides information externalities to other firms: their success proves that the new industry is aligned with the economy's new comparative advantage, thus prompting many new firms to enter the industry.[9]

The subsequent large entry of new firms eliminates the possible rents that the first mover may enjoy. From the perspective of an individual firm, the incentive to be a pioneer firm is repressed because of the asymmetry between the high cost of failure and the limited advantage of success. Unless there is compensation for the information externalities that the pioneer firm creates, few firms will have the incentive to be the first movers and thus the process of industrial upgrading and diversification as well as economic growth will be impeded (Aghion, 2009; Romer, 1990). In a developed country with global-frontier industries, a successful first mover can in general be rewarded with a patent and enjoys the rent created by a period of monopoly for its innovation. For a developing country, its new industry is most likely to be a matured industry located within the global industrial frontier. So the first mover will not be able to obtain a patent for its entry into a new industry. Some form of direct support from government to pioneer firms that are willing to take the risk to move to new industries is therefore justifiable.[10]

Compared with developed countries whose industries are located on the global frontier and their industrial upgrading and diversification rely on their own generation of new knowledge through a process of trial and error, developing countries in the catching-up process move within the global industrial frontier and have the advantage of backwardness. In other words, they can rely on borrowing the existing technology and industrial ideas from the advanced countries. This method of acquiring innovation has a lower cost and is less risky than the one used by firms in developed countries (Krugman, 1979).[11] Therefore, in a developing country committed to the market system, if firms know how to tap into the potential of the advantage of backwardness and the government pro-actively provides information, co-ordination, and externality compensation in the process of industrial upgrading and diversification, the country can grow much faster than a developed country and achieve the goal of converging with high-income countries (Lin, 2009). After all, this was the case for Britain before the eighteenth century; for Germany, France and the United States in the nineteenth century; and the Nordic countries, Japan, Korea, Taiwan-China, Singapore, Malaysia and other East Asian economies in the twentieth century (Amsden, 1989; Chang, 2003; Gerschenkron, 1962; Wade, 1990).

## 3. Picking Winners or Losers: Lessons from Experience

There is wide consensus among economic historians on the important role played by the state in facilitating structural change and helping sustain it across time and across developed countries. However, except for a few successful cases post-World War II, the governments in most developing countries have failed to play that desirable role. It is therefore essential to briefly review historical and contemporary experiences of state intervention, to draw lessons from the many failures and few successes.

### 3.1 The Role of the State in Structural Change in Advanced Economies

There is ample historical evidence that today's most advanced economies relied heavily on government intervention to ignite and facilitate their take-off and catch-up processes, which allowed them to build strong industrial bases and sustain the momentum of their growth over long periods. In his well-known survey of trade and industrial policies leading to early economic transformations in the Western world, List (1841) documented various policy instruments through which governments protected domestic industries or even intervened to support the development of specific industries—many of which became successful and provided the bedrock for national industrial development.[12]

Likewise, Chang (2003) has reviewed economic developments during the period when most of the currently advanced economies went through their industrial revolutions (between the end of the Napoleonic Wars in 1815 and the beginning of World War I in 1914). He has documented various patterns of state intervention that have allowed these countries to successfully implement their catch-up strategies. Contrary to conventional wisdom that often attributes the Western industrial successes to laissez-faire and free-market policies, the historical evidence shows that the use of industrial, trade, and technology policies was the main ingredient for their successful structural transformation. This ranged from the frequent use of import duties or even import bans for infant-industry protection to industrial promotion through monopoly grants and cheap supplies from government factories, various subsidies, public-private partnerships, and direct state investment, especially in Britain and the US (Trebilcok, 1981). All European countries trying to catch up with Britain devoted efforts to technology policy. Up to the middle of the first Industrial Revolution, the main channel for technological transfer was the movement of skilled workers who embodied new knowledge. Latecomers to the industrialisation process, such as France, attempted to acquire them on a large scale from Britain, but the British government banned the emigration of skilled workers for more than a century, starting in 1719.[13] When new technologies became embodied in machines, they too were put under government control: various laws were adopted throughout the eighteenth and nineteenth centuries to ban the export of 'tools and utensils'.

In all advanced economies, the government supported the acquisition of foreign technology, 'sometimes by legal means such as financing study tours and apprenticeships, and sometimes through illegal measures, which included support for industrial espionage, smuggling of contraband machinery, and refusal to acknowledge foreign patents' (Chang, 2003: 18).

In Germany (Prussia), for instance, Frederick the Great annexed the industrial province of Silesia and promoted the steel and linen industries. Advanced technologies such as iron-puddling, the coke furnace or the steam engine were subsequently imported from more successful countries (Kindleberger, 1978).

Government intervention took many forms in the early experiences of industrialisation. In Japan, the government created many factories ('pilot plants') in shipbuilding, mining, textiles, etc., most of which were subsequently sold off to the private sector at very low prices and further subsidised. This helped launch the process of industrialisation and diversification. Even when government-run enterprises performed poorly,[14] there were many cases of failures that generated a burgeoning private sector. This was most notably the case in Japan during the Meiji Restoration[15] when a vibrant textile industry emerged from the failure of the poorly managed state-owned enterprise. Private firms were successful because they learned the skill and management from the state-owned firms, and introduced various process innovations to replace expensive equipment with inexpensive labour, which was Japan's comparative advantage at the time (Otsuka et al., 1988).[16]

Developed-country governments continue to adopt various measures to support industrial upgrading and diversification, even though these policies may not be announced under the formal label of 'industrial policy'. Besides patent systems, which are industry-neutral, other such measures typically include support for basic research, mandates, allocation of defence contracts and large public procurements. Local governments also often provide all kinds of incentives to private firms to attract them to particular geographic areas and induce new investments. The application of all these measures needs to identify specific industries or products and amounts to 'picking winners'.

A prime example is the US, where the government has constantly offered strong incentives to private businesses and academic institutions for discovering new ideas that are valuable for sustaining growth, as well as making such ideas non-rival—besides building infrastructure in key economic sectors such as transportation and providing financing to education and training in order to build the country's skills base in various industries. This is routinely done through subsidies for research and development, and through the granting of patents and copyrights. The Advanced Technology Program, for instance, launched in 1990, has been instrumental in the research and development of promising high-risk technologies. Government subsidies can also be found in areas such as defence, energy, transportation and home construction.

The ongoing debate over the need for a US industrial policy[17] has not changed the hard facts about the important role played by the federal and state governments in industrial development in recent decades. Their interventions include the allocation of large amounts of public funding to defence-related procurements and R&D spending, which have large spill-over effects throughout the economy (Shapiro and Taylor, 1990). In fact, the share of the federal government in total R&D spending, which was only 16% in 1930, has remained between 50 and 66% during the post-World War II years (Owen, 1966; Mowery and Rosenberg, 1993). As Chang observes, 'industries such as computers, aerospace and the internet, where the U.S.A. still maintains an international edge despite the decline in its overall technological leadership, would not have existed without defence-related R&D funding by the country's federal government'. Government support is also critical in other important segments of the economy such as the health industry: public funding to the National Institutes of Health, which in turn support a large fraction of R&D by biotechnological firms, has been essential in helping the US maintain its lead in that industry.

The same is true in Europe where discussions of active industrial policy have been taking place since the end of World War II.[18] In fact, many of Europe's most remarkable industrial successes (space programme Ariane, aircraft manufacturer Airbus, etc.) were achieved in the context of intergovernmental co-operation, with decisive political support from the European Union. Since the early 1990s, the European Commission has issued several policy papers on the subject, including the 1994 report *An Industrial Competitiveness Policy for the European Union*, which set the stage for more determined government interventions. Other official strategy documents have focused on the risk of de-industrialisation, the regulatory burden, the impact of enlargement of the EU on the competitiveness of European companies and their location, etc. In the context of the review of the Lisbon Strategy in March 2005, EU Member States set the objective of 'creating a solid industrial base', and reiterated the increasing importance attached to R&D and innovation in all forms, as well as information and communication technologies.[19]

France has always favoured government-sponsored economic programmes in which the public and private sectors co-ordinate their efforts to develop new technologies and industries. The French government often provides financial support and capital to the private sector by direct subsidies, tax credits, or government-run developmental banks.[20] In Britain, the government, which defines itself as 'a market shaper', has recently released a new industrial policy aimed at: supporting enterprise and entrepreneurial activity, including the access to finance required for starting and growing firms; fostering knowledge creation and its application; helping people develop the skills and capabilities to find work and build the businesses and industries of the future; investing in the infrastructure required to support a modern low-carbon economy; ensuring open and competitive markets to drive innovation and rising productivity; and building on industrial strengths where Britain has particular expertise or might gain a comparative advantage, and where government action can have an impact (British Government, 2009).

Another interesting case is that of Finland, a late but successful state-led industrialisation. According to Jäntti and Vartiainen (2009), the economic policy that achieved this objective was a mix of heavy government intervention and private incentives. Government intervention aimed at a fast build-up of industrial capital in order to ensure a solid manufacturing base. The main features of the country's growth regime were: a high rate of capital accumulation, which often required the use of administrative rationing of credit through interest-rate controls as well as a policy of selective loan approvals for capital-equipment investment; and a high rate of investment in targeted areas of manufacturing, the paper and pulp and metalworking industries in particular. State enterprises were established in the basic metal and chemical-fertiliser industries, and in the energy sector. As late as in the 1980s, state-owned enterprises accounted for 18% of the country's total industry value-added (Kosonen, 1992).

Almost all developing countries have tried to replicate the earlier models of state-led structural change, especially after World War II. From the planned economies of Eastern Europe and Asia to left-leaning or even liberal regimes in Latin America, Asia, Africa and throughout the Arab world, many governments have adopted various policy measures to promote industrial development and industrial upgrading (Chenery, 1961). While there have been a few successes in East Asia, most of these attempts have failed to deliver the expected results (Krueger and Tuncer, 1982; Lal, 1994; Pack and Saggi, 2006). Nevertheless, the governments in developing countries will continue to attempt to play the facilitating role. It is therefore all the more important to understand better why some countries have been able to succeed while most others have failed, so that it is possible to advise the governments to do the right things and avoid the mistakes (Rodrik, 2009).

## 3.2 The Recipe for Success—or Failure

There are two main reasons for the controversies and confusion about industrial policy in developing countries. First, economists have tended to focus their attention on the failed policies implemented and not on the objectives and the broader strategic choices made in the successful cases. Second, too often very different types of government interventions are lumped together in regression analyses, with little consideration specifically as to which ones may have attempted to facilitate the emergence of industries that are consistent with latent comparative advantage.

Summing up the research findings on how to achieve sustained growth through structural transformation and the diffusion of ideas and accumulation of knowledge, Romer notes that 'the challenge is to find better forms of government intervention, ones that have better economic effects and pose fewer political and institutional risks' (1990: 66). He also points out that 'the temptation for economists, however, has always been to duck the complicated political and institutional issues that this kind of analysis raises and instead to work backward from a desired policy conclusion to a simple economic model that supports it'. In fact, the real challenge for economists and policy-makers in any country may be instead to identify the new industries that are consistent with the economy's comparative advantage, which evolves as the endowment structure changes.

A common feature of the industrial upgrading and diversification strategies adopted by successful countries (the most advanced ones and the East Asian NIEs in the post-War period) was the fact that they targeted mature industries in countries not too far advanced compared with their own levels of per capita income. This may have been the single most important cause for their success. Throughout human history, it appears that pioneer countries have always played (and often unwillingly) the role of an 'economic compass' for latecomers. Going back to the sixteenth century, the Netherlands played that role for Britain, which in turn served as a model and target for the US, Germany, and France in the late nineteenth and early twentieth centuries and for Japan in the mid-twentieth century. Likewise, Japan was imitated by Korea, Taiwan-China, Hong Kong-China, and Singapore in the 1960s and 1970s. Mauritius picked Hong Kong-China as its 'compass' in its catch-up strategy in the 1970s. China chose Korea, Taiwan-China, and Hong Kong-China in the 1980s.

Two main lessons can be drawn from these successful cases of state-led structural-change strategies. First, it appears that the government implemented policies to facilitate the development of new industries in a way that was consistent with the country's latent comparative advantage as determined by its endowment structure. Therefore, firms, once established with government support in information, co-ordination, and sometimes limited subsidies, have turned out to be competitive.[21] Second and even more important, to ensure that they would tap into their latent and evolving comparative advantage, the government targeted mature industries in countries that were, on average, about 100% higher than their own level of per capita income, measured in purchasing power parity.[22] When Britain applied industrial policies to catch up with the Netherlands in the sixteenth and seventeenth centuries, its per capita income was about 70% that of the Netherlands. When Germany, France, and the US used industrial policy to catch up with Britain in the nineteenth century, their per capita incomes were about 60 to 75% that of Britain. Similarly, when Japan's industrial policy targeted the US automobile industry in the 1960s, its per capita income was about 40% that of the US. When Korea and Taiwan-China adopted industrial policies to facilitate their industrial upgrading in the 1960s and 1970s, they targeted industries in Japan instead of the US, and for a good reason: their per capita incomes were about 35% that of Japan and only about 10% that of the US at the time.[23]

Looking closely at the elements of successful catch-up strategies, it appears that the specifics of policy interventions depended on the particular binding constraints for these new industries and on country circumstances.

But while the interventions were often different, the patterns of industrial development were similar across countries. They all started from labour-intensive industries, such as garments, textiles, toys and electronics, in the early stage of development and proceeded to move up the industrial ladder step by step to more capital-intensive industries.[24] The East Asian NIEs, for instance, exploited the fact that their endowment structures were similar to Japan's to follow its development in a flying-geese pattern (Akamatsu, 1962; Kim, 1988). This was possible because the per capita income gaps with their target-country were not large (Ito, 1980).[25]

The story of Korea is a particularly good illustration of this strategy. The government took a pro-active approach to industrial upgrading, and adjusted its strategy to enter industries that were consistent with the country's latent (and evolving) comparative advantage. In the automotive sector, for example, early in Korea's growth period, domestic manufacturers concentrated mostly on assembly of imported parts, which was labour-intensive and in line with their comparative advantage at the time. Similarly, in electronics, the focus was initially on household appliances, such as TVs, washing machines and refrigerators, and then moved to memory chips, the least technologically complex segment of the information industry. Korea's technological ascent has been rapid, as has its accumulation of physical and human capital due to the conformity of its main industrial sectors with the existing comparative advantage and, hence, its changes in underlying comparative advantage.[26] As a result, Korea has achieved remarkable GDP growth rates in the past forty years and has performed impressively in industrial upgrading into such industries as automobiles and semiconductors.

Developing countries in other regions of the world pursued the same path with excellent results. Chile, one of the Pacific Rim countries, successfully targeted industries that were consistent with its comparative advantage determined by its natural endowment, as well as industries that were already mature in more advanced countries. While free-market reforms introduced in the early 1970s brought many benefits to the country, they were slowly accompanied by market failures (Diaz-Alejandro, 1985). In recognition of these problems, the government has supported private-sector growth through a number of policy instruments, including the provision of agricultural public goods by a state institution (Servicio Agricola

Granadero); guarantees for loans to small enterprises; a semi-public entrepreneurial institution (Fundacion Chile) responsible for the development of the salmon industry; the 'simplify drawback' mechanism, which provided subsidies to new exports; the various programmes of the national development agency (Corporacion de Fomento de la Produccion, CORFO); and the National Council on Innovation for Competitiveness.

In recent years, the country has experienced 'a burst of export discoveries of new comparative advantages' (Agosin et al., 2008) and dynamic growth. Key to this success has been the diversification of Chile's traditional resource-based industries of mining, forestry, fishing and agriculture, coupled with a strong drive to increase exports. The initial dependence on copper has been gradually reduced in favour of aluminum smelting. Forestry products have been expanded into salmon aquaculture and agriculture into wine production, as well as freezing and canning fruits and vegetables. Manufacturing has been less successful but many foreign firms have chosen to locate in Chile as it offers a secure platform from which to supply other markets across South America.

Mauritius, one of the most successful African economies, took off in the 1970s by targeting labour-intensive industries such as textiles and garments. These industries were mature in Hong Kong, its 'compass economy'. Both economies share the same endowment structure and the per capita income in Mauritius was about half that in Hong Kong-China in the 1970s.[27] The Mauritius Industrial Development Authority (MIDA) and Export Processing Zones Development Authority were created by the government to attract Hong Kong-China's investment in its export processing zone. The vision was to position Mauritius as a world-class export hub on the Hong Kong-China model. Together, they have contributed to the country's emergence as an economic powerhouse.

By contrast, many countries designed and implemented catch-up strategies that were too ambitious for establishing the 'commanding heights', given their level of development. Historical examples of such mistakes go back to countries such as Hungary or Russia, which tried to replicate industries in place in Britain in the late nineteenth century (Gerschenkron, 1962). While GDP statistics are scarce for individual countries, purchasing power parity estimates by Maddison (2006) indicate that their per capita

GDP represented 25% and 30% that of Britain in 1900. Such a large gap made any attempt by the former to develop British industries unrealistic.[28]

Most developing countries fell into the same trap after World War II. They often targeted advanced industries in advanced economies when their per capita incomes represented only a very small fraction of that of high-income countries. After gaining their independence from colonial powers, many countries considered the development of advanced heavy industries as a key symbol of their freedom, a sign of strength, and a political statement of their reputation on the international scene. Across Latin America, Africa and South Asia, some of these newly independent countries were run by political leaders with leftist inclinations who chose to follow the prevailing Stalinist model of state-led industrialisation through the development of advanced heavy industries, regardless of their political denominations. State resources were used in the industrialisation push, with resources directly allocated to various investments, and large public enterprises set up in almost every sector of the economy—all deemed strategic for the survival and modernisation of the nation. Under the 'macroeconomics of nationalism' (Monga, 2006), the criteria for designing industrial policies and selecting specific sectors for government intervention were mostly political.

In parallel to political aspirations for heavy-industry development, there was an obsession with 'market failure' in academic circles—especially in Latin America where many influential economists and policy-makers (Albert Hirschman, Raul Prebisch, Roberto Campos and Celso Furtado, among others) argued that industrialisation and growth could not take place spontaneously in developing countries because of structural rigidities and co-ordination problems.[29] They recommended that government support be provided to the manufacturing industry for these countries to catch up with developed countries, regardless of the large income gap between the two.

Too often, such industrial policy defied the prevailing comparative advantage of many poor countries where factor endowments were characterised by the abundance of labour. By implementing the capital-intensive heavy industry-oriented development strategy, they were not able to build firms capable of surviving in open, competitive markets. Because of their high capital needs and their structurally high production costs, these public enterprises were not viable. Even when they were well managed, they could not earn a socially acceptable profit in an undistorted and competitive market. A good example is Egypt's industrialisation programme in the 1950s, which featured heavy industries such as iron, steel and chemicals. The country's per capita income represented about 5% that of the US, the world's most important steel producer at the time. Unless the government continuously provided costly subsidies and/or protection, Egyptian firms could not attract private investment. The limited fiscal resource capacities of the state made such large-scale protection and subsidies unsustainable. In such situations, governments have had to resort to administrative measures—granting market monopolies to firms in the so-called priority sectors, suppressing interest rates, over-valuing domestic currencies, and controlling the prices of raw materials—in order to reduce the costs of investment and continuous operation of their non-viable public enterprises (Lin, 2009).

These various experiments provide valuable lessons for economic policy. They highlight conditions under which industrial policies can succeed or fail. Failures occur when countries target industries that are too advanced, far beyond their latent comparative advantage. In such circumstances, government-supported firms cannot be viable in open, competitive markets. Their survival depends on heavy protection and large subsidies through various means such as high tariffs, quota restrictions and subsidised credit. The large rents embedded in these measures easily become the targets of political capture and create difficult governance problems (Lin, 2010).[30]

## 4. A Framework for Growth Identification and Facilitation

The historical and contemporary evidence showing that governments always play an important role in facilitating industrial upgrading and diversification in all successful countries may not be enough to validate an idea that has been mired in controversy for so long. Many economists who agree with the general notion that government intervention is an indispensable ingredient of structural transformation have maintained their opposition to industrial policy because of the lack of a general framework that can be used to guide policy-making. As Charles Schultze, chairman of the Council of Economic Advisers under US President Jimmy Carter, once put it:

> The first problem for the government in carrying out an industrial policy is that we actually know precious little about identifying, before the fact, a 'winning' industrial structure. There is not a set of economic criteria that determine what gives different countries preeminence in particular lines of business. Nor is it at all clear what the substantive criteria would be for deciding which older industries to protect or restructure. (Schultze, 1983)

It is therefore useful to draw on the theories of comparative advantage and backwardness advantage as well as the successful and failed experiences of industrial policies discussed in Section 3 to codify some basic principles that can guide the formation of successful industrial policy. The first step is to identify new industries in which a country may have latent comparative advantage, and the second is to remove the constraints that impede the emergence of industries with such advantage and create the conditions to allow them to become the country's actual comparative advantage. Here, we propose a six-step process:

- First, the government[31] in a developing country can identify the list of tradeable goods[32] and services that have been produced for about 20 years in dynamically growing countries with similar endowment structures and a per capita income that is about 100% higher than their own.[33]
- Second, among the industries in that list, the government may give priority to those which some domestic private firms have already entered spontaneously,[34] and try to identify: (i) the obstacles that are preventing these firms from upgrading the quality of their products; or (ii) the barriers that limit entry to those industries by other private firms.[35] This could be done through the combination of various methods such as value-chain analysis or the Growth Diagnostic Framework suggested by Hausmann et al. (2008). The government can then implement policy to remove these binding constraints and use randomised controlled experiments to test the effects of this so as to ensure the effectiveness of scaling up these policies at the national level (Duflo, 2004).
- Third, some of those industries in the list may be completely new to domestic firms. In such cases, the government could adopt specific measures to encourage firms in the higher-income countries identified in the

first step to invest in these industries, so as to take advantage of the lower labour costs. The government may also set up incubation programmes to catalyse the entry of private domestic firms into these industries.[36]

- Fourth, in addition to the industries identified on the list of potential opportunities for tradeable goods and services in step 1, developing-country governments should pay close attention to successful self-discoveries by private enterprises and provide support to scale up these industries.[37]

- Fifth, in developing countries with poor infrastructure and an unfriendly business environment, the government can invest in industrial parks or export processing zones and make the necessary improvements to attract domestic private firms and/or foreign firms that may be willing to invest in the targeted industries. Improvements in infrastructure and the business environment can reduce transaction costs and facilitate industrial development. However, because of budget and capacity constraints, most governments will not be able to make the desirable improvements for the whole economy within a reasonable timeframe. Focusing on improving the infrastructure and business environment in industrial parks or export processing zones is, therefore, a more manageable alternative.[38] Industrial parks and export processing zones also have the benefits of encouraging industrial clustering.

- Sixth, the government may also provide incentives to domestic pioneer firms or foreign investors working within the list of industries identified in step 1 in order to compensate for the non-rival public knowledge created by their investments. These incentives should be limited both in time and in financial cost. They may take the form of a corporate income-tax holiday for a limited number of years,[39] direct credits to co-finance investments, or priority access to foreign reserves[40] to import key equipment. The incentives should not and need not be in the form of monopoly rent, high tariffs, or other distortions. The risk of rent-seeking and political capture can therefore be avoided.[41] For firms in step 4 that discovered new industries successfully by themselves, the government may award them special recognition for their contribution to the country's economic development.[42]

The industries identified through the above process should be consistent with the country's latent comparative advantage. Once the pioneer firms come in successfully, many other firms will enter these industries as well. The government's facilitating role is mainly restricted to provision of information, co-ordination of hard and soft infrastructure improvement, and compensation for externalities. Government facilitation through the above approach is likely to help developing countries tap into the potential of the advantage of backwardness and realise a dynamic and sustained growth.

## 4.1 Possible Ways of Identifying Binding Constraints

The facilitation of industrial growth has been the subject of a rich body of research and several approaches have recently been suggested by various authors.[43] While these are all likely to yield useful results, none of them focuses specifically on the identification of industries in which a developing country may have latent comparative advantage. The intellectual legacy of the failure of industrial policies based on development strategies that were inconsistent with comparative advantage has certainly led many economists to conclude that it may be impossible for any government to 'pick winners' successfully.

In the absence of a framework for industrial identification, the existing literature has been limited to exploring ways of improving the business environment and infrastructure, which indeed affect firms' operations and transaction costs. There is a robust empirical knowledge based on quantitative data on firm performance and perceptions-based data on the severity of a number of potential constraints facing firms in the developing world. It points out that in most of sub-Saharan Africa, for instance, firms tend to consider many areas of the investment climate major obstacles to business development and the adoption of more sophisticated technology. Finance and access to land seem to be areas of particular concern to smaller firms; larger firms tend to perceive labour regulations and the availability of skilled labour as the main constraints to their activity; firms across the board are concerned about corruption and infrastructure—especially network utilities such as electricity, telecommunications, transportation and water (Gelb et al., 2007).

Despite their usefulness, investment-climate surveys, which try to capture the policy and institutional environment within which firms operate, can be misused or misinterpreted. Just as individual perceptions of well-being are subjective and do not necessarily correlate with objective measures such as income or consumption, firms' perceptions of binding constraints to their development often differ from actual determinants of performance. This limitation is due to the very nature of the investment-climate data and the way they are often used. In a typical survey, the managers of a sample of firms are asked to rate each dimension of the investment climate (such as 'infrastructure', 'access to financing', 'corruption', etc.) on a scale of 1 to 4, corresponding to the degree to which it is an obstacle to firm performance.[44] High mean reported values for particular dimensions of the investment climate are then interpreted as evidence of the severity of obstacles to growth.

However, this may not be the case. Despite their intimate knowledge of their business processes and operating environment, firms may not fully recognise the true origin of their main problems and mistakenly identify as a constraint something which is in fact a symptom of another less obvious problem. Because of these shortcomings, investment-climate constraints are increasingly complemented by the World Bank's 'Doing Business' indicators, which are based on expert surveys (not just firm-level perceptions) and provide a more comparable cross-country perspective across a detailed range of regulation.

The problem remains, as survey results often vary depending on whether respondents are asked to rate their most important constraints, or to rank them. While ranking appears to be favoured by researchers who have examined different methodologies, since it forces stronger expression and relationships (Alvin and Krosnick, 1985), it may not be entirely reliable: firms or experts asked to rank constraints may not have a good basis for determining whether their top-ranked constraint is serious or not. Ranking without a solid and meaningful benchmark against which local firms can rate the severity of a particular constraint may not provide useful information. In addition, there are instances where picking any single quantitative criterion could be misleading, as firms often face several constraints simultaneously. Ranking all of them as important may not be very helpful for policy-making. In order to account for the major role of firm heterogeneity in growth analysis, one must go beyond extracting means of investment-climate variables from firm-level surveys. Careful econometric modelling of firm performance is therefore needed to identify which particular variable has the biggest effect on growth. In other words, the policy variables with the greatest economic impact can be quite different from those with the highest perceived values.[45]

Investment-climate surveys have two more limitations. They do not provide information about industries that do not yet exist, but in which a country has latent comparative advantage. And the existing industries that are surveyed may not be consistent with the country's comparative advantage, either because they are too advanced (as a legacy of a development strategy that defied comparative advantage), or because they have become fundamentally uncompetitive (as a result of a general wage increase that accompanied the country's development). These two additional limitations make it highly desirable for investment-climate surveys to cover only a sample of firms that meet the criteria of viability, and can represent the economy's true potential.

Another important problem with the recognition of obstacles to growth is the fact that many other constraints to business development are endogenous to the industries that might be targeted by a developing country. Good examples are specific types of human capital, financing instruments, or infrastructure that may be needed only by firms moving to specific industries. Identifying and removing them may require the use of several complementary analytical tools. One useful tool is the Growth Diagnostics Framework suggested by Hausmann et al. (2008). It is based on the observation that, when presented with a laundry list of needed reforms, policy-makers either struggle to try to solve all of the problems at once or start with reforms that are not critical to their country's growth potential. Because reforms in one area may create unanticipated distortions in another, focusing on the one that represents the biggest hurdle to growth is the most promising avenue to success. Countries should therefore figure out the one or two most binding constraints on their economies and focus on lifting those.

The Growth Diagnostics approach provides a decision-tree methodology to help identify the relevant binding constraints for any given country. It starts with a taxonomy of possible causes of low growth in developing countries, which generally suffer from either a high cost of finance (due either to low economic and social returns or to a large gap between social and private returns), or low private return on investment. The main step in the diagnostic analysis is to figure out which of these conditions more accurately characterises the economy in question. The use of this framework highlights the fact that, in some countries, the growth strategy should identify the reasons for the low returns on investment, while it must explain why domestic savings do not rise to exploit large returns on investment in other countries. While the Growth Diagnostics Framework attempts to take the policy discussion of growth forward, its focus and the specification of its model remain quite macroeconomic. This is understandable; after all, growth is a macroeconomic concept and taking the analysis to a sector level would raise issues of sector interactions and trade-offs.

Moreover, the Growth Diagnostic Framework is also imprecise in its links to the institutions that facilitate the growth process. The methodology proposed for the identification of the binding constraints to growth is not always straightforward. Even if data on shadow prices were widely available, it is not obvious that this would accurately identify areas in which progress is most needed in each country. For example, one could imagine a simple model of growth for a low-income country where technology and human capital are complementary. In such a country, the returns to education and technology adoption would both be low due to low levels of human capital and technology. An exclusive focus on shadow prices and an ignorance of cross-country comparison of levels would then suggest no need to improve education levels and encourage technology adoption.

In fact, even in situations where the Growth Diagnostics approach leads to relative certainty about the binding constraints to growth in any given country, there is still a wide range of policy options available to choose from. It is therefore necessary for policy-makers to rely not just on one approach but to use several different macro and micro tools to identify binding constraints to growth. Microeconomic analyses of growth show that differentiated firm dynamics drive a good part of aggregate productivity growth and capital accumulation. Establishing a diagnostic at the aggregate level requires a good knowledge of what happens at the micro level. In particular, monitoring the entry and exit of firms and the policy variables that affect them is essential to understanding overall gains in productivity in economies subject to strong structural changes (Bourguignon, 2006). One must take account of heterogeneity in country circumstances and among micro agents. This can more effectively be done through country-specific analyses.

Finally, even if one could identify relevant binding constraints to industrial development in industries with comparative advantage and induce improvements in a country's business environment, the crucial issues of externality encountered by first movers and of co-ordination would remain unresolved. Despite the removal of the constraints, a country may then find its industrial upgrading and diversification process stalled. It is therefore necessary that the Growth Diagnostics Framework and other methods of targeting obstacles to industrial upgrading be used in conjunction with the growth identification and facilitation approach.

## 5. Conclusion

The current crisis has inflicted heavy costs on economies around the world. Unemployment is at record levels in many countries, fiscal fragility is a legacy of the crisis in many countries, and capacity-utilisation rates in industry remain substantially below pre-crisis levels. Many developing countries have the potential to grow faster than developed countries and are now confronted with the challenge of finding new sources of growth in the context of a world of multi-polar growth (Zoellick, 2010). In this regard, the role of developing-country governments in inducing and accompanying structural change (industrial upgrading and economic diversification) to promote growth, employment and poverty reduction must regain centre stage. Indeed, historical evidence and economic theory suggest that while markets are indispensable mechanisms for allocating resources to the most productive sectors and industries, government intervention—through the provision of information, co-ordination of hard and soft infrastructure improvement, and compensation for externalities—is equally indispensable for helping economies move from one stage of development to another (Lin, 2010).

Because of the many failures observed throughout the world in the post-World War II period, industrial policy has raised serious doubts among economists and policy-makers. Taking into consideration O'Brien and Keyder's recommendation that 'countries should (if possible) be studied in terms of some unique capacity for development at different stages of their history' (1978: 15), this article has examined the mechanics of structural change in today's advanced economies and the reason for success in a few developing countries in East Asia and elsewhere, as well as suggesting a framework for government intervention in the economy.

The article has argued that the failure of industrial policy is most likely to arise from mistakes made by policy-makers in the growth-identification process. Industrial policies implemented by governments in developed and developing countries usually fall into one of two broad categories: (i) they attempt to facilitate the development of new industries that are either too advanced and thus far from the comparative advantage of the economy, or too old and have lost comparative advantage; or (ii) they try to facilitate the development of new industries that are consistent with the latent comparative advantage of the economy. Only the latter type of policy is likely to succeed. High-performing developed and developing countries are those where governments were able to play an active role in the industrial upgrading and diversification process by helping firms take advantage of market opportunities. They have generally done so by overcoming the information, co-ordination, and externality issues, and by providing adequate hard and soft infrastructure to private agents. It is expected that the growth identification and facilitation approach put forward in the article can help governments in developing countries identify the right industries in their attempts to facilitate structural transformation in the development of their countries.

## Notes

† Célestin Monga, a native of Cameroon, is a Senior Advisor to the World Bank Senior Vice President and Chief Economist. In his 13-year career in the World Bank, he has held positions in both operations and in the research department. He has also served on the Board of Directors of MIT's Sloan School of Management (Sloan Fellows) and taught at Boston University and the University of Bordeaux (France).

1. To protect jobs, governments in both developed and developing countries may also support old, declining industries, which have already lost their comparative advantages. Such policies will fail as well.

2. Examples of hard infrastructure are highways, port facilities, airports, telecommunication systems, electricity grids and other public utilities. Soft infrastructure consists of institutions, regulations, social capital, value systems, and other social and economic arrangements. For further discussion on their impacts on economic development, see Lin (2010).

3. Technology is defined here as knowledge (intangible intellectual capital) of how to transform basic inputs into final utility. It differs from human or physical capital by its non-rival nature. Efficiency is the way technology is used—with the goal of optimality, especially in the allocation of resources.

4. In the growth literature, structural change has not received as much attention as technological change because of the use of a one-sector model, which is incapable of handling issues related to structural change, in the standard growth accounting and regression research.

5. Maddison (2006) estimated that, in Western Europe, the annual per capita income growth rate before the 18th century was about 0.05%, accelerated to about 1% in the 18th and 19th centuries, and reached 2% in the 20th century. The required time for doubling per capita income thus reduced from 1400 years before the 18th century to 70 years in the 18th and 19th centuries, and further to 35 years in the 20th century.

6. The difference between factors of production and infrastructure is that the supply and demand of the former are determined individually by households and firms, whereas the latter in most cases is supplied by the community or governments by collective actions.

7. For example, the application of chemical fertilisers in rice and wheat require modern semi-dwarf varieties to avoid the lodging problem, and the use of modern seeds often requires timely irrigation. Individual farmers will not be able to do this by themselves. There is also a need for access to credits beyond individual farmers' capacity. Similarly, the diversification from farm to non-farm industries or from small-scale traditional to modern industries also requires the provision of many new inputs and improvements in hard and soft infrastructure, which cannot be internalised in any individual firm's decision.

8. The success of Ecuador's cut flowers export in the 1980s is a good example. The fact that Ecuador had latent comparative advantages in producing and exporting cut flowers to the US market was known in the 1970s. But the industry did not expand and exports did not take off until the government helped arrange regular flights and investment in cooling facilities near airports in the 1980s (Harrison and Rodríguez-Clare, 2010). A similar story applies to Ethiopia's cut flowers export to the European market. In issues related to the provision of skilled labour, Germany's dual system of vocational education and training has been a major factor in the country's economic success over the past six decades.

9. In a recent field study in Zambia, we found that a local entrepreneur successfully started the production of corrugated roofing sheets. Within a year, more than 20 firms had joined in.

10. Precisely because of such positive information externalities, governments in developed countries also provide various forms of targeted support to firms

engaged in innovation, such as funding of basic research, preferential taxes, mandates, defence contracts, and procurement policies.

11. The possibility of borrowing existing knowledge does not mean that developing countries need not engage in indigenous innovation. To be successful, they need to undertake a process of innovation that makes the borrowed technology suitable to local conditions, and also to carry out product innovation in sectors where they are already world leaders, or not too far behind the world leader. For further discussion, see Lin and Ren (2007).

12. List's book covers the rise of economic powerhouses in a variety of contexts, from Italian cities such as Venice to Hanseatic cities such as Hamburg or Lübeck, and countries such as the Netherlands, England, Spain, Portugal, France, Germany and the United States.

13. The ban lasted until 1825. See Landes (1969).

14. For a theoretical exposition, see Jones et al. (1990) and World Bank (1995).

15. The Meiji period (1868-1912) marked the beginning of an era of major political, economic, and social change which, according to conventional wisdom, brought about the modernisation and Westernisation of Japan. See Beasley (1972).

16. A common reason for the failure of state-owned enterprises is the government's attempt to use them as a vehicle to develop industries or adopt technologies inconsistent with the country's comparative advantage (Lin and Tan, 1999). Such attempts create a policy burden for state-owned firms which the state is compelled to provide with subsidies and protection. Information asymmetry prevents governments from knowing exactly what level of subsidies and protection would be adequate and state-owned firms use the policy burden as an excuse to ask for more subsidies and protection, which gives rise to the problem of soft-budget constraint (Kornai, 1986).

17. During the 1984 presidential campaign, Democratic candidate Walter Mondale argued that the economic policies of the country were 'destroying industry— not building it', and that federal aid should be directed to 'those communities and regions hit hardest by economic change' (quoted by McKenzie, 2007). Economists Bluestone and Harrison (1982) argued that the ongoing process of deindustrialisation amounted to a 'wide-spread, systematic disinvestment in the nation's productive capacity'. Pointing to the post-War economic success of Japan, which he credited to industrial policies orchestrated by its Ministry of International Trade and Industry (MITI), Thurow (1980) worried that, if left alone, 'our economy and our institutions will not provide jobs for everyone who wants to work', and that 'we have a moral responsibility to guarantee full employment'. He observed that 'major investment decisions have become too important to be left to the private market alone ... Japan Inc. needs to be met with U.S.A. Inc'. Others recommended various measures such as the creation of national and regional economic development banks similar to Herbert

Hoover's Reconstruction Finance Corporation, which would use subsidies and federal loan guarantees to slow the contraction of declining industries and speed the development of emerging industries; the launch of 'Tripartite councils' at the national, regional, and firm levels, which would be composed of representatives from management, labour and government and would seek consensus on how capital investment should be allocated. While often conceding on protectionist proposals, other economists and political leaders have maintained strong opposition to any coherent industrial-policy programmes.

18. The European Coal and Steel Community (ECSC) was created in 1951 and the European Atomic Energy Community (EURATOM) in 1957.

19. In October 2005, the European Commission announced seven new horizontal initiatives in order to: '(1) consolidate the EU's legal framework in the area of intellectual property, (2) take into account the links between the issues of competitiveness and environmental protection, (3) adapt the trade policy with a view to developing the competitiveness of European industry, (4) simplify the law governing certain industrial sectors (i.e. construction, food industry), (5) remedy the shortage of skilled labour in certain sectors (i.e. new technologies, textiles), (6) anticipate and support the structural changes in industry, by taking this objective into consideration in other EU policies (structural funds, in particular), and (7), adopt an integrated European approach to industrial research and innovation.'

20. Several proposals are currently under consideration to stimulate innovation and growth. The recently issued Juppé-Roccard report by two former Prime Ministers (a socialist and a conservative) recommends that France raises 35 billion euros (US$52 bn) through public borrowing to be spent on universities and research (providing them with endowments and incentives to merge or become independent and private), the green economy and high-tech to propel growth. Among the projects are plans to expand the high-speed Internet, develop green cities, and support innovative small businesses and France's cutting-edge aerospace and nuclear industries. Of the 35 bn euros to be raised, 13 bn will come from the reimbursed bailout packages given to French banks, with the remaining 20 bn to be raised on the financial markets.

21. The idea of a dynamic comparative advantage is often used to justify industrial policy and government support to firms (Redding, 1999). In our analysis, however, the argument is valid only if the government's support is limited to overcoming information and co-ordination costs and the externalities associated with the pioneer status of first-movers. The targeted industry should be consistent with the comparative advantage of the economy and the firms in the new industry should be viable, otherwise they will collapse once the government support is removed. If the targeted industry is outside the country's comparative advantage, the required open-ended support to the subsidised firms will crowd out the resources

available to other firms that operate in industries consistent with the comparative advantage. This will obviously slow down economic growth and capital accumulation, and it will take more time for the economy to reach the stage targeted by the dynamic-advantage policy than an economy that follows a comparative-advantage strategy (Lin and Zhang, 2007).

22. For the purposes of this article, the use of per capita income measured in purchasing power parity is better than that of the market-exchange rate because, in cross-country comparisons, the former reflects the level of development and the cost of production better.

23. For a discussion of industrial policies in these countries, see Chang (2003); and for the estimations of per capita income for the above countries, see Maddison (2006).

24. Countries in similar stages of development may specialise in different industries. However, the level of capital intensity in their industries will be similar. For example, in recent years, China is achieving dynamic growth by specialising in the labour-intensive manufacturing industries, such as electronics, toys and textiles, whereas India's growth has relied on specialising in call centres, programming, and business process services, which are labour-intensive activities within the information industry.

25. In a similar spirit, Hausmann and Klinger (2006) recently investigated the evolution of a country's level of sophistication in exports and found that this process was easier when the move was to 'nearby' products in the product space. This is because every industry requires highly specific inputs such as knowledge, physical assets, intermediate inputs, labour skills, infrastructure, property rights, regulatory requirements, or other public goods. Established industries somehow have sorted out the many potential failures involved in assuring the presence of all of these inputs. The barriers preventing the emergence of new industries are less binding for nearby industries, which only require slight adaptations of existing inputs.

26. For the debate on the conformity of Korea's industrial upgrading with its evolving comparative advantage, see the exchange between Lin and Chang (2009).

27. According to Maddison (2006), Hong Kong's per capita income in 1970 measured in 1990 international dollars was 5,695, whereas that of Mauritius was 2,945.

28. As discussed earlier, a similar policy was pursued successfully in Germany, France and the US at the same time. Their per capita incomes ranged from 60% to 75% that of Britain.

29. The new field of development economics was regarded as covering underdevelopment because 'conventional economics' did not apply (Hirschman, 1982). Early trade and development theories and policy prescriptions were based on

some widely accepted stylised facts and premises about developing countries (Krueger, 1997). These included: (i) developing economies' production structures were oriented heavily towards primary-commodity production; (ii) if developing countries adopted policies of free trade, their comparative advantage would forever lie in primary-commodity production; (iii) the global income elasticity and the price elasticity of demand for primary commodities were low; (iv) capital accumulation was crucial for growth and, in the early stage of development, it could occur only with the importation of capital goods. Based on these facts and premises, it was a straight step to believing that the process of development was industrialisation, which consisted primarily of the substitution of domestic production of manufactured goods for imports (Chenery, 1958).

30. The other reason for the failure of industrial policy in developing countries is that the policy targets industries that have already lost comparative advantage, but governments want to protect them for sociopolitical reasons (such as providing employment, often in urban areas).

31. The government refers to both the central and local governments. The process discussed here can also be used by multilateral development agencies and non-governmental organisations to promote industrial upgrading and diversification in developing countries.

32. The tradeable goods refer to manufactured products, agricultural products, and fishery as well other natural-resources products. Because of the ascendance and dominance of international production networks in manufacturing industries, the manufactured goods here refer not only to the final products but also to intermediate inputs of final products in manufacturing industries.

33. As discussed in Section 3, this is the most important principle for a developing country to reap the advantage of backwardness in its industrial upgrading and diversification. This is because, for a dynamically growing economy, its wage rate is increasing rapidly and is likely to start losing comparative advantage in the industries that it has produced for many years. Therefore, the industries will become the latent comparative advantage of countries with a similar endowment structure but with a lower wage. The principle also means that when a country grows beyond the income level of 50% of the most advanced country, it will become increasingly difficult to identify industries that are likely to be its latent comparative advantage. The country's industries will locate increasingly close to the global frontier and its industries' upgrading and diversification will increasingly rely on indigenous innovations. Therefore, the government's policies to support industrial upgrading and diversification will increasingly resemble those of the advanced countries. The chance of those policies failing to achieve the intended goal will also increase. As for low-income countries with per capita income measured at about $1,000 in purchasing power parity (PPP) terms currently, in addition to identifying matured tradeable goods in countries

at about $2,000 currently, it may also identify tradeable goods produced in countries that had similar per capita income levels 20 or so years ago and have been growing dynamically since then. In particular, China, Vietnam and India had a similar or even lower income levels 30 years ago than most of today's poor sub-Saharan countries. Therefore, for today's poor countries, they may identify the list of goods and services produced in China, Vietnam and India 20 years ago as references. They may also review their imports and identify the list of simple manufacturing goods, which are labour-intensive, have limited economies of scale, and require only small investments, as the targets of their industrial upgrading and diversification. The idea put forward is similar to that of monkeys jumping to nearby trees (Hausmann and Klinger, 2006), but the step proposed here is much easier to implement than the product-space analysis proposed by them.

34. This is because every industry requires some highly specific inputs such as knowledge, physical assets, intermediate inputs, labour skills, and so on. The existence of some private firms in the industry indicates that the economy at least partially possesses these crucial inputs.

35. Chile has produced wine for a long time. Its recent success in the wine industry is a good example. The change from a negligible wine exporter to the world's fifth-largest exporter in the 1970s benefitted greatly from the government's programmes to disseminate foreign technology to local farmers and vineyards through Grupos de Transferencia Tecnológica and to promote Chilean wine abroad through Export Promotion Office, ProChile (Benavente, 2006).

36. Lessons from successful Asian countries can be of relevance here. When local Asian firms had no historical knowledge in a particular industry, the state often attracted foreign direct investment and/or promoted joint ventures. After the transition to a market economy in the 1980s, China, for instance, pro-actively invited direct investment from Hong Kong-China, Taiwan-China, Korea and Japan—a promotion policy which helped the local economy to get started in various industries. Bangladesh's vibrant garment industry also started with direct investment from Daewoo, a Korean manufacturer, in the 1970s. After a few years, enough knowledge transfer had taken place and the direct investment became a sort of 'incubation', local garment plants mushroomed, and most of them could be traced back to that first Korean firm (Mottaleb and Sonobe, 2009; Rhee, 1990; Rhee and Belot, 1990). The booming cut-flower export business in Ecuador from the 1980s on also started with three companies founded by Colombia's flower growers (Sawers, 2005). The government can also set up an industrial park to incubate new industries. Taiwan-China's Hsingchu Science-based Industrial Park for the development of electronic and IT industries (Mathews, 2006) and the Fundacion Chile's demonstration of commercial salmon farming (Katz, 2006) are two successful examples of the government's incubation of new industries.

37. India's information industry is a good example. Indian professionals in Silicon Valley helped Indian companies to take advantage of expanding opportunities for outsourced IT work in the 1980s. Once the potential of software exports was demonstrated, the Indian government helped build a high-speed data-communications infrastructure that allowed overseas Indians to return home and set up offshore sites for US clients. The Indian software industy has grown more than 30% p.a. for 20 years, with 2008 exports close to $60 billion (Bhatnagar, 2006). Ethiopia's success in cut flowers exports is another example. Before the government's identification of cut flowers export and the provision of supports in its industrial policy in the 1990s, a local pirate firm had exported cut flowers to the European market for over 10 years. Asparagus in Peru is also a good example. The possibility of growing asparagus, a foreign crop, was discovered by Peruvian farmers in the 1950s. However, the industry and exports did not take off in earnest until 1985 when USAID provided a grant for a farmers' association to obtain advice from a specialist from the University of California, Davis, who had recently invented the UC-157 variety suitable for the US market, and from another expert who showed members of the association's experimental station how to set up seedbeds for large-scale production and package the products for export. The state also supported cooperative institutions such as the Peruvian Asparagus Institute and Frío Aereo Asociación Civil for engaging in research, technology transfer, market studies, export drives, and quality promotion, and invested in the freezing and packing plants that handled 80% of fresh asparagus exports. With these interventions, Peru has overtaken China and become the largest asparagus exporter in the world (O'Brien and Rodriguez, 2004).

38. In addition to infrastructure, many African countries, for instance, also face the constraint of rigid labour regulation. To overcome this, Mauritius has allowed employment to be flexible in the export process zone, while maintaining the existing regulation for the domestic economy (Mistry and Treebhoohun, 2009).

39. The measure commonly used in China to attract FDI is to exempt from corporate income tax for the first two years and reduce the tax by half for a further three years.

40. Direct credits and access to foreign reserves are desirable measures in countries with financial depressions and foreign-exchange control.

41. The likelihood of capture is proportional to the magnitude of protection and subsidies. If the targeted industries are consistent with the country's inherent comparative advantages, and the protection and subsidies are used to compensate the pioneer firms for their positive information externalities, the magnitude of protection and subsidies should be small, and the elites will not have the incentives to use their political capital to capture the small rent. In addition, once the pioneering firms are successful, many new firms will enter and the market will become competitive, which will further reduce

the danger of capture by elites. Alternatively, if the government's goal is to support the development of industries that go against the country's comparative advantages, the firms in the targeted industries will not be viable in competitive markets and the required subsidies and protections will be large, and are likely to become the target of rent-seeking and political capture (Lin, 2009).

42. We owe this *ex-post* reward idea to Professor Shang-jin Wei.

43. See, for example, Di Maio (2008) and Agosin et al. (2009).

44. Ayyagari et al. (2008) present the mean reported values for a number of investment-climate variables in a sample of over 6,000 firms in 80 countries. In the overall sample, taxes and regulation, political instability, inflation and financing are reported as being the greatest obstacles to firm growth.

45. Bourguignon (2006) observes: '"Extracting means" is the way I would characterize the Investment Climate Assessment exercises that the Bank is now carrying out. Like the "Doing Business" indicators, these are undoubtedly useful. However, what they give us is essentially new and better right-hand side variables in cross-country regressions, not necessarily better data for country-specific analysis. The goal should be to use investment climate surveys to measure the sensitivity of firms of different types to investment climate variables, as another way of determining exactly which variable corresponds to a major obstacle to growth.'

# References

Aghion, P. (2009) *Some Thoughts on Industrial Policy and Growth*. Working Paper No. 2009–09. Paris: OFCE-Sciences Po.

Agosin, M., Larraín, C., and Grau, N. (2009) 'Industrial Policy in Chile', Working Papers wp294, University of Chile, Department of Economics.

Akamatsu, K. (1962) 'A Historical Pattern of Economic Growth in Developing Countries,' *The Development Economies*, Preliminary Issue No. 1: 3–25.

Alvin, D. F. and Krosnick, J. A. (1985) 'The Measurement of Values in Surveys: A Comparison of Ratings and Rankings', *Public Opinion Quarterly* 49 (4): 535–52.

Amsden, A. H. (1989) *Asia's Next Giant*. New York and Oxford: Oxford University Press.

Ayyagari, M., Demirgüç-Kunt, A. and Maksimovic, V. (2008) 'How Well Do Institutional Theories Explain Firms' Perceptions of Property Rights?', *Review of Financial Studies* 21 (4): 1833–71.

Bhatnagar, S. (2006) 'India's Software Industry', in Vandana Chandra (ed.), *Technology, Adaptation, and Exports: How Some Developing Countries Got It Right*. Washington, DC: World Bank.

Beasley, W. G. (1972) *The Meiji Restoration*. Stanford, CA: Stanford University Press.

Benavente, Jose Miguel (2006) 'Wine Production in Chile', in Vandana Chandra (ed.), *Technology, Adaptation, and Exports: How Some Developing Countries Got It Right*. Washington, DC: World Bank.

Bluestone, B. and Harrison, B. (1982) *The Deindustrialization of America: Plant Closings, Community Abandonment, and the Dismantling of Basic Industry*. New York: Basic Books.

Bourguignon, F. (2006) *Economic Growth: Heterogeneity and Firm-Level Disaggregation*. PREM Lecture. Washington, DC: World Bank.

British Government (2009) 'Going for Growth: Our Future Prosperity'. London (www.bis.gov.uk/wp-content/uploads/2010/01/GoingForGrowth.pdf).

Chang, H.-J. (2003) *Kicking Away the Ladder: Development Strategy in Historical Perspective*. London, Anthem Press.

Chenery, H. B. (1961) 'Comparative Advantage and Development Policy', *American Economic Review* 51 (1): 18–51.

Chenery, H. B. (1958) 'The Role of Industrialization in Development Programmes' in A. N. Agarwala and S. P. Singh (eds.), *The Economics of Underdevelopment*. Bombay: Oxford University Press.

Diaz-Alejandro, C. (1985) 'Good-Bye Financial Repression, Hello Financial Crash', *Journal of Development Economics* 19: 1–24.

Di Maio, M. (2008) *Industrial Policies in Developing Countries: History and Perspectives*. Working Paper No. 48-2008. Italy: Macerata University, Department of Finance and Economic Sciences.

Duflo, E. (2004) 'Scaling Up and Evaluation' in: F. Bourguignon and B. Pleskovic (eds), *Annual World Bank Conference on Development Economics 2004*. Washington, DC: World Bank.

Evans, P. (1996) 'Using Cross-country Income Differences' in P. Aghion and S. N. Durlauf (eds), *Handbook of Economic Growth*, vol. 1. Amsterdam: North-Holland.

Gelb, A. et al. (2007) *What Matters to African Firms? The Relevance of Perception Data*. Policy Research Working Paper No. 4446. Washington, DC: World Bank.

Gerschenkron, A. (1962) *Economic Backwardness in Historical Perspective: A Book of Essays*. Cambridge, MA: Belknap Press of Harvard University Press.

Harrison, A. and Rodríguez-Clare, A. (2010) 'Trade, Foreign Investment, and Industrial Policy for Developing Countries', *Handbook of Development Economics* 5: 4039–213.

Hausmann, R. and Klinger, B. (2006) *Structural Transformation and Patterns of Comparative Advantage in the Product Space*. Working Paper No. 128. Cambridge, MA: Harvard University Center for International Development.

Hausmann, R. and Rodrik, D. (2003) 'Economic Development as Self-Discovery', *Journal of Development Economics* 72 (December).

Hausmann, R., Rodrik, D. and Velasco, A. (2008) 'Growth Diagnostics' in N. Serra and J. E. Stiglitz (eds.), *The Washington Consensus Reconsidered: Towards a New Global Governance*, New York: Oxford University Press.

Hirschman, A. O. (1982) 'The Rise and Decline of Development Economics' in M. Gersovitz and W. A. Lewis (eds), *The Theory and Experience of Economic Development*. London: Allen and Unwin.

Howitt, P. and Weil, D. (2010) 'Economic Growth' in S. N. Durlauf and L. E. Blume (eds), *Economic Growth*. New York: Macmillan Palgrave.

Ito, T. (1980) 'Disequilibrium Growth Theory', *Journal of Economic Theory* 23: 380–409.

Jäntti, M. and Vartiainen, J. (2009) *The Finnish Developmental State and its Growth Regime*. Research Paper No. 2009/35. Helsinki: United Nations University.

Jones, L. et al. (1990) *Selling Public Enterprises: A Cost-Benefit Methodology*. Cambridge, MA: MIT Press.

Ju, J., Lin, J. Y. and Wang, Y. (2009) *Endowment Structures, Industrial Dynamics and Economic Growth*. Policy Research Working Paper No. 5055. Washington, DC: World Bank.

Katz, J. (2006) 'Salmon Farming in Chile', in Vandana Chandra (ed.), *Technology, Adaptation, and Exports: How Some Developing Countries Got It Right*. Washington, DC: World Bank.

Kim, Y. H. (1988) *Higashi Ajia Kogyoka to Sekai Shihonshugi (Industrialisation of East Asia and World Capitalism)*. Tokyo: Toyo Keizai Shimpo-sha.

Kindleberger, C. (1978) 'Germany's Overtaking of England, 1806–1914' in *Economic Response: Comparative Studies in Trade, Finance, and Growth*. Cambridge, MA: Harvard University Press.

Kornai, J. (1986) 'The Soft Budget Constraint'. *Kyklos* 39 (1): 3–30.

Kosonen, K. (1992) 'Economic Growth' in J. Pekkarinen et al. (eds.), *Social Corporatism*. Oxford: Clarendon Press.

Krueger, A. O. (1997) 'Trade Policy and Economic Development: How We Learn', *American Economic Review* 87 (1): 1–22.

Krueger, A. O. and Tuncer, B. (1982) 'An Empirical Test of the Infant Industry Argument', *American Economic Review* 72: 1142–152.

Krugman, P. (1979) 'A Model of Innovation, Technology Transfer, and the World Distribution of Income', *Journal of Political Economy* 87 (2): 253–66.

Kuznets, S. (1966) *Modern Economic Growth: Rate, Structure and Spread*. New Haven, CT and London: Yale University Press.

Lal, D. (1994) *Against Dirigisme: The Case for Unshackling Economic Markets*. San Francisco: International Center for Economic Growth, ICS Press.

Landes, D. (1969) *The Unbound Prometheus: Technological Change and Industrial Development in Western Europe from 1750 to the Present*. Cambridge: Cambridge University Press.

Lin, J. Y. (2010) *New Structural Economics: A Framework for Rethinking Development*. Policy Research Working Paper No. 5197. Washington, DC: World Bank.

Lin, J. Y. (2009) *Economic Development and Transition: Thought, Strategy, and Viability*. Cambridge: Cambridge University Press.

Lin, J. Y. and Chang, H.-J. (2009) 'DPR Debate: Should Industrial Policy in Developing Countries Conform to Comparative Advantage or Defy It?', *Development Policy Review* 27 (5): 483–502.

Lin, J. Y. and Ren, R. (2007) 'East Asian Miracle Debate Revisited' (in Chinese), *Jingji Yanjiu* (*Economic Research Journal*) 42 (8): 4–12.

Lin, J. Y. and Tan, G. (1999) 'Policy Burdens, Accountability, and the Soft Budget Constraint', *American Economic Review: Papers and Proceedings* 89 (2): 426–31.

Lin, J. Y. and Zhang, Pengfei (2007) *Development Strategy, Optimal Industrial Structure and Economic Growth in Less Developed Countries*. CID Working Paper No. 19. Cambridge, MA: Harvard University Center for International Development.

List, F. (1841 [1930]) *Das Nationale System der Politischen Ökonomie* (*The National System of Political Economy*). *Vol. 6. Schriften, Reden, Briefe*. A. Sommer (ed.). Berlin: Reinmar Hobbing.

Maddison, A. (2006) *The World Economy*. Paris: Organisation for Economic Cooperation and Development.

Maddison, A. (2001) *The World Economy: A Millennial Perspective*. Paris: OECD.

Mathews, J. A. (2006) 'Electronics in Taiwan: A Case of Technological Learning' in Vandana Chandra (ed.), *Technology, Adaptation, and Exports: How Some Developing Countries Got It Right*. Washington, DC: World Bank.

McKenzie, R. B. (2007) 'Industrial Policy' in D. R. Henderson (ed.), *The Concise Encyclopedia of Economics*. Liberty Fund (www.econlib.org/library/Enc1/IndustrialPolicy.html).

Mistry, P. S and Treebhoohun, N. (2009) *The Export of Tradeable Services in Mauritius: A Commonwealth Case Study in Economic Transformation*. London: Commonwealth Secretariat.

Monga, C. (2006) 'Commodities, Mercedes-Benz, and Adjustment: An Episode in West African History' in E. K. Akyeampong (ed.), *Themes in West Africa's History*. Oxford: James Currey.

Mottaleb, K. A. and Sonobe, T. (2009) 'Inquiry into the Rapid Growth of the Garment Industry in Bangladesh'. Tokyo: Foundation for Advanced Studies on International Development (mimeo).

Mowery, D. and Rosenberg, N. (1993) 'The US National Innovation System' in R. Nelson (ed.), *National Innovation Systems: A Comparative Analysis*. Oxford: Oxford University Press.

O'Brien, T. M. and Rodriguez, A. D. (2004) 'Improving Competitiveness and Market Access for Agricultural Exports through the Development and Application of Food Safety and Quality Standards: the Example of Peruvian Asparagus'. San Jose: Agricultural Health and Food Safety Program, Inter-American Institute for Cooperation on Agriculture.

O'Brien, P. and Keyder, C. (1978) *Economic Growth in Britain and France 1789–1914: Two Paths to the Twentieth Century*. London: George Allen and Unwin.

Otsuka, K., Ranis, G. and Saxonhouse, G. (1988) *Comparative Technology Choice in Development: The Indian and Japanese Cotton Textile Industries*. London: Macmillan Press.

Owen, G. (1966) *Industry in the USA*. London: Penguin Books.

Pack, H. and Saggi, K. (2006) 'Is There a Case for Industrial Policy? A Critical Survey', *World Bank Research Observer* 21 (2): 267–97.

Pritchett, L. (1997) 'Divergence, Big Time', *Journal of Economic Perspectives* 11 (3): 3–17.

Redding, S. (1999) 'Dynamic Comparative Advantage and the Welfare Effects of Trade', *Oxford Economic Papers* 51 (1): 15–39.

Rhee, Y. W. (1990) 'The Catalyst Model of Development: Lessons from Bangladesh's Success with Garment Exports', *World Development* 18 (2): 333–46.

Rhee, Y. W. and Belot, T. (1990) *Export Catalysts in Low-income Countries*. World Bank Discussion Papers No. 72. Washington, DC: World Bank.

Rodrik, D. (2009) 'Industrial Policy: Don't Ask Why, Ask How', *Middle East Development Journal* 1 (1): 1–29.

Romer, P. M. (1990) 'Endogenous Technological Change', *Journal of Political Economy* 98 (5): part II, S71–S102.

Sawers, L. (2005) 'Nontraditional or New Traditional Exports: Ecuador's Flower Boom', *Latin American Research Review* 40 (3): 40–66.

Schultze, C. (1983) 'Industrial Policy: A Dissent', *Brookings Review* October: 3–12.

Shapiro, H. and Taylor, L. (1990) 'The State and Industrial Change', *World Development* 18 (6).

Thurow, L. (1980) *The Zero-Sum Society: Distribution and the Possibilities for Change*. New York: Basic Books.

Trebilcok, C. (1981) *The Industrialization of Continental Powers, 1780–1914*. London: Longman.

Wade, R. (1990) *Governing the Market*. Princeton, NJ: Princeton University Press.

World Bank (1995) *Bureaucrats in Business: The Economics and Politics of Government Ownership*. New York: Oxford University Press.

Zoellick, R. B. (2010) *The End of the Third World? Modernizing Multilateralism for a Multipolar Growth*. Washington, DC: World Bank.

# COMMENTS AND REJOINDER*

## Introduction, by Dirk Willem te Velde[†]

Assessing the role of the state in the dynamics of structural change, as Lin and Monga do, is not new. However, the novel and noteworthy contribution of their article is that it provides a practical procedure to identify and facilitate growth through a six-step procedure. This approach complements existing approaches such as the growth diagnostics approach (Hausmann et al., 2005), the competitiveness approach (Porter and Schwab, 2008), the investment-climate survey approach (World Bank, 2005), or the capability approach (Cantore et al., 2011):

- Step 1: Governments should select dynamically growing countries with a similar endowment structure and with about 100% higher per capita income than their own average. They must then identify tradeable industries that have grown well in those countries for the previous 20 years.
- Step 2: If some private domestic firms are already present in those industries, they should identify constraints to technological upgrading or further firm entry, and take action to remove such constraints.
- Step 3: In industries where no domestic firms are present, policy-makers may try to attract foreign direct investment (FDI) from countries listed in step 1, or organize new firm-incubation programmes.

* Adapted from "DPR Debate: Growth Identification and Facilitation: The Role of the State in the Dynamics of Structural Change," *Development Policy Review,* 29 (3), May 2011 (DOI: 10.1111/ j.1467-7679.2011.00534.x). © 2011 Lin, J., Monga, C., te Velde, D. W., Tendulkar, S. D., Amsden, A., Amoako, K. Y., Pack, H., and Lim, W. © 2011 Overseas Development Institute. Reprinted with the permission of John Wiley and Sons / Blackwell Publishing.

- Step 4: In addition to the industries identified in step 1, the government should also pay attention to spontaneous self-discovery by private enterprises and support the scaling up of the successful private innovations in new industries.
- Step 5: In countries with poor infrastructure and a bad business environment, special economic zones or industrial parks may be used to overcome barriers to firm entry and FDI and encourage the formation of industrial clusters.
- Step 6: The government should be willing to compensate pioneer firms in the industries identified above with tax incentives for a limited period, cofinancing for investments, or access to foreign exchange.

Without reviewing the article in detail, one can pose some obvious questions regarding the framework. For example, the first step of the new framework requires a country to identify sectors in which it has a comparative advantage on the basis of goods and services that have been produced for 20 years in similar countries. But what happens if the current circumstances have changed so fundamentally that a comparison with the past is less informative (for example, the rise of emerging power, new communications technology including fiber optic cables, new production processes, new global rules and institutions, climate change)? What if demand patterns have shifted so fundamentally (for example, the rise of the middle classes in China and India, global financial crisis) that different products are now more successful compared with those in the past? What if there are measurement issues, for example information communication technology (ICT) service exports may be quite difficult to measure but this might be just the export in which small landlocked countries with access to a good quality fiber optic cable have a comparative advantage? What if comparator countries are actually very different geographically or institutionally? So one could have doubts that step 1 would actually be sufficiently informative under all these circumstances.

Or with respect to step 2, the argument is made for government support (to remove binding constraints to growth), but it is not clear how a country knows which policy or instrument works best in which case (a comment which can also be made on the growth diagnostics literature, for example). So even if the right industry and constraints are identified, the wrong policy instrument might still lead to an unintended outcome. This links to a wider point which is underemphasized in the article, namely, that the conditions under which policies are implemented (government capacities, political incentives, the nature of state-business relations) can also be crucial for the success of industrial policies as the need for policies to follow the comparative advantage of a country (which is implicit in steps 1–6).

However, these issues aside, the growth identification and facilitation framework is presented as an alternative to the existing frameworks for analysis. We asked five distinguished experts to comment.

## Comments from Experts

Suresh Tendulkar, professor of economics, retired, at the Delhi School of Economics, University of Delhi, comments on the distinction between the roles of the state in facilitating growth and in identifying sources of growth. Tendulkar accepts that there is an important role for growth facilitation, but is less certain about the role of the state in growth identification. He asks how the over-enthusiastic government can be restrained from taking on much more than it can effectively handle, and refers to the South Asian context. He also cautions that time-bound incentives are not straightforward.

Alice Amsden of the Massachusetts Institute of Technology makes three points. First, she argues that industrial policies in countries ranging from the Middle East's energy belt to the Asian manufacturing corridor and the BRIC (Brazil, Russia, India and China) economies have been more successful in practice than is portrayed by Lin and Monga. Secondly, she suggests that the authors' two-track approach (identification and facilitation) is better than Michael Porter's value-chain approach and Ricardo Hausmann's 'jumping-monkey' model, because it involves building up business knowledge which is a more complete approach than is embodied in the other concepts. Thirdly, she argues that Lin and Monga's model can be enhanced by using industrial policy to invest overseas and attract skills.

K. Y. Amoako, founder and president of the African Center for Economic Transformation (ACET) in Accra, argues that Lin and Monga's approach is a practical and useful starting guide, suggesting that such a pragmatic approach is to be welcomed especially because it comes from the World Bank which traditionally has not believed in a proactive industrial policy. However, Amoako also argues that the article pays too much attention to supporting products that follow a comparative advantage and too little attention to the acquisition of new technological capabilities and learning. Successful industrialisation has not always been based on competitive markets, and African countries have not always succeeded, despite following their comparative advantage.

Howard Pack, Department of Business and Public Policy at the Wharton School, University of Pennsylvania, suggests that the algorithm involved in selecting industries on the basis of a selection in richer comparable countries and then following the country's comparative advantage is problematic. This is in part because the economic structure of the richer country could be the result of distorting policies, and in part because a formidable set of policies is required for successful policies which go beyond the mere identification of potential products. Governments should address a whole list of issues which are likely to go beyond the capacity of any government.

Wonhyuk Lim, director of policy research at the Center for International Development, Korea Development Institute, agrees that policy advice based on the ideas of comparative advantage, self-discovery and the facilitating state will help policy-makers in the early stage of development, but argues that more needs to be done to move a country beyond the middle-income trap. South Korea defied its comparative advantage by moving into heavy and chemical industries by means of building specific skills, filling specific gaps in the value chain, relying on a select set of business groups and strategic choice.

*Rejoinder*

Lin and Monga close the debate with a rejoinder. They answer many of these points directly, for example by arguing that growth identification and facilitation go hand in hand implicitly. They also agree with many of the constructive comments made, for example those by Professor Amsden on the importance of gaining experience in managing business organizations, or on the way the model can be enhanced by using industrial policy to invest overseas.

But there are also some points where the reader is invited to make up his or her own mind. For example, Lin and Monga repeat time and again that their model focuses on 'development of industries consistent with latent comparative advantages'. It is unlikely that many will object to this being indeed their intent, but they might object to whether it can be achieved in practice. Or, when Lin and Monga say that it 'simply points to the necessity to set clear, transparent and rigorous criteria that mitigate ... support [for] uncompetitive industries', few would doubt that that is important, but many would rather question the ability of governments to implement these criteria successfully, as Tendulkar emphasized.

A further discussion, which has not been completely closed, is to what extent countries should follow a path consistent with their static comparative advantages or whether they should create dynamic comparative advantages (as implied by Amoako).

Another debate left somewhat open concerns knowledge (as brought up by Pack). Government officials are unlikely to know enough to be able to support industries in the way that is intended and to target the development of industries consistent with latent comparative advantages. When do they know enough?

## Conclusion

The article by Lin and Monga introduces a useful and practical 6-step plan for governments to facilitate growth which seems a credible alternative to the existing frameworks (growth diagnostic framework, competiveness analysis, capability analysis, investment-climate analysis). In doing so, it reinvigorates the debate on the appropriate role of growth policy in development, which has once again become a topical issue in development economics.

Most comments on Lin and Monga's contribution to the literature agree with the importance attached to the role of the state in growth facilitation. Many also value the practical policy advice embodied in the approach. However, there is some disagreement about the capacity of the state to deliver on growth identification.

Furthermore, the two-track approach in Lin and Monga relies on countries following their comparative advantage, and several comments suggest that countries actually need to defy their comparative advantage involving a more complex set of policies than that suggested by the framework.

In conclusion, most agree that the approach could establish useful ingredients in successful industrial development and comes close to a recipe for growth. But there are doubts about the ability of the cooks to use the recipe and turn the ingredients into a fully cooked meal. Nonetheless, it is hoped that the application of the six-step procedure will produce relevant information that can help countries to grow faster. Indeed, apart from questions on what is the binding constraint in a country, developing-country policymakers often ask: how did other countries achieve in the past what we would like to achieve now?

## Note

†    Dirk Willem te Velde is head of Investment and Growth and Trade Programmes at the Overseas Development Institute, London.

## References

Cantore, N., Ellis, K., Massa, I., and te Velde, D. W. (2011) 'Managing Change and Cultivating Opportunity: The Case for a Capability Index Measuring Countries' Ability to Manage Change Effectively'. KPMG-ODI report. London: KPMG and Overseas Development Institute.

Hausmann, R., Rodrik, D., and Velasco, A. (2005) *Growth Diagnostics*. Cambridge, MA: Harvard University Center for International Development (www.hks.harvard.edu/fs/rhausma/new/growthdiag.pdf).

Porter, M. and Schwab, K. (2008) *The Global Competitiveness Report 2008–2009*. Geneva: World Economic Forum.

World Bank (2005) *World Development Report on the Investment Climate*. New York: Oxford University Press for the World Bank.

## Suresh D. Tendulkar[†]

Lin and Monga rightly admit that economists have been intrigued by the mystery of economic growth. Gone are the days of self-assurance and confidence of Walter Rostow in the 1950s who provided a predictable and certain roadmap of growth for every underdeveloped country. A large number of economic theoretical analytical models flourished shortly thereafter. While Rostow did not remain uncontested in his time (Kuznets and Gerschenkron readily come to mind), economists have been much more circumspect since then, despite or possibly because of the wealth of data becoming available. And rightly so. The growth brigade started with 1.5 to 2.0% a year in per capita terms in the eighteenth century with the Netherlands and Britain. It was joined by the United States, Germany and France in the nineteenth century, and the bar was raised significantly by the latecomers: Japan in the 1950s, Hong Kong, Singapore, South Korea and Taiwan in the 1960s, China, Thailand, Malaysia and Indonesia in the 1970s, India in the 1980s, and other emerging economies since then. With the two most populous countries, China and India, joining the brigade, the population-weighted inter-country inequality in per capita GDP has shown a welcome decline. The number of countries in the brigade, however, remains countable. While we are reasonably certain about common ex-post descriptive features associated with rapid growth, very few countries have managed to grow rapidly (say, 3% or higher in per capita annual terms) in a sustained fashion over more than two decades. Nor do we know nor can we predict with certainty what triggers spurts of sustained growth in any given country.

Undeterred, Lin and Monga embark on the ambitious and admirably persuasive enterprise of setting a two-fold agenda for government intervention in growth facilitation (provision of hard and soft infrastructure) and growth identification (continuing technological upgrading and diversification through anticipatory industrial policy) for developing countries striving for rapid economic growth for poverty reduction. The objective is indeed laudable beyond doubt. What is also on their side is the lessons they seek to draw from well-documented ex-post analyses of the successes as well as failures of state interventions during the pre- as well as post-World War II period. While my heart wants their enterprise to succeed, my head remains uncomfortable. Let me therefore express the sources of my discomfort with introspective comments which are indeed coloured by my South Asian, especially Indian, lenses, while recognizing that the authors have an East and South-East Asian, including Chinese, perspective.

Less contentious and more readily acceptable is the important role of the government in growth facilitation, that is, the provision of hard (adequate networks of road, rail and air transport and communications, electricity grids and other public utilities) and soft (basic governance including competitive market institutions, financial system and regulation, basic health, and primary and secondary education services including vocational training) infrastructure. Because of externalities and their public good character, this is indeed the core legitimate domain of the government. The adequacy of physical facilities and the cost-effectiveness of operation and delivery of corresponding public services cut down the transaction costs of exchange for the private sector and impart competitive edge to the economic structure.

More difficult, uncertain and hence contentious is the role of growth identification. Lin and Monga's excellent historical analysis brings out many failures and fewer successes, more over-enthusiastic though often well-intended policy excesses, more heavy-handed than 'right' mixes of non-intrusive interventions, persistence of once successful policies being indiscriminately extended beyond their effective time span, indiscriminate extension of the public sector well beyond the minimum core and discretionary controls often stifling the dynamism of functioning markets and leading to rampant rent-seeking activities. While one may readily concede that some ex-ante judgments regarding the choice of industries consistent with endowment structure and potential comparative advantage may go wrong, the discipline of time-bound withdrawal of concessions in the face of ineffectiveness and even timely exit from some patently unsuccessful policies including subsidies and tariff protection is difficult to obtain. The question ironically becomes: how do you control the over-enthusiastic government from taking on much more than it can effectively handle? In my assessment, growth identification and consequent ex-ante nurturing of picked winners and keeping them under a tight, time-bound leash are a much more difficult and risky enterprise based on the South Asian experience in this context. This does not rule out occasional, lucky successes, but this has to be ascertained by the experience of actual experiential judgment and confidence about the existence of warranted discipline.

## Note

† Suresh Tendulkar is Professor of Economics (Retd.), Delhi School of Economics, University of Delhi, India.

## Alice Amsden[†]

In their critical essay on the role of the state, Justin Lin and Célestin Monga concentrate on the concept of comparative advantage as the clue to slaying the dragon of underdevelopment. Are they moving ahead or simply standing still?

Comparative advantage can be construed deductively or inductively, as an abstract theory or as something that bubbles up from below. Economists mostly conceive of it deductively. Lin and Monga argue that pervasive failures in developing countries are mostly due to the inability of governments to come up with good criteria for identifying industries that are appropriate for their country's endowment structure and level of development, i.e., their 'latent' comparative advantage. But the two vast de-colonised regions with the most successful industrial policies, fast GDP growth and steeply falling poverty, the Far East and Middle East, followed their comparative advantage by nosing around their neighbours; if an industry grew next door, this was taken as de facto proof of its comparative advantage—what more concrete evidence can there be? If an export-processing zone works, if a national oil company raises domestic supply and tax revenues more than an international oil company, other countries try to follow suit, and having a blueprint to follow (imitation has been overwhelmingly South-South) makes it easier for them to succeed.

Two great regional role models have evolved, whose meaning of 'industrial policy', unlike a theory's, meanders, depending on who has joined and exogenous jolts. (The World Trade Organization's restrictions on subsidies, I would argue, have driven the industrial policies of 'emerging' and 'emerged' economies underground, creating a sort of 'level playing field' of subterfuges.) The OPEC development role model (as distinct from the OPEC price cartel), which started in Iran and Saudi Arabia with Mexico's 1938 oil nationalisations as example, employs millions of workers from as far away as Bangladesh and approximates the 'labour-scarce, resource-rich economy' described in the 1950s by Hla Myint. The Far East role model, running along the lines of the labour-surplus economy analyzed by W. Arthur Lewis, formed around post-War Japan, which was neither developed nor underdeveloped at the time and which targeted industries according to simpler criteria than Lin's or Monga's: government support went to industries with dense linkages and high productivity growth rates internationally, first silk and cotton textiles (see Amsden and Suzumura, 2001). Large countries like the BRICs have industrial policies that straddle Asia's manufacturing corridor and the Middle East's energy belt, so in fact industrial policy has probably been more successful than the premise of Lin and Monga's article, that 'most have failed'.

Industrial policy has failed in the peasant export economy, the third prototype of Lewis, Myint and other classical economists, but it is questionable if this is a viable economic formation, given hyper-fast population increases (the 30 countries in 2005-10 with the highest estimated population growth rates include 24 smallholder-type economies, 23 from Africa). Landlessness, unemployment and underemployment are high, but labour costs are not low enough and manufacturing experience is not deep enough to compete against labour-surplus economies like India. What, besides population planning, is the best industrial policy to help peasant economies, many of which have newly discovered energy and mineral resources such as Sudan, Angola, Cameroon and Ghana: the OPEC development role model, with nearby Nigeria teaching what not to do, or Lin and Monga's 'important distinction' between two types of government intervention? The latter differentiate policies that facilitate structural change by overcoming information, and coordination and externality issues' from those that aim at protecting certain selected firms and industries that defy the comparative advantage determined by the existing endowment structure (once called dynamic comparative advantage). Their distinction seems sensible but vague, at least for the vast energy and mining sector, the great hope of the defunct peasant economic configuration.

Developing countries without unlimited labour supplies, rich natural resources or a credible role model close by, such as Colombia, Morocco, Nicaragua and Nepal, are in need of advice about how to 'pick winners'. Lin and Monga's criteria face competition from those of Michael Porter (the value chain) and Ricardo Hausmann (the jumping monkey). I think Lin and Monga's two-track approach is better than theirs because, if I understand its broad implications, comparative advantage boils down to having 'knowledge of a business', an empirical construct that rests on a roadmap of where an industry is going, production engineering skills, and project execution capabilities to get an investment up and running. (Taiwan's electronics firms invested in producing CD-ROMs, despite falling world prices, once government R&D had skirted restrictive patents and there was a sense that Japan would graduate to producing DVDs.) By contrast, where a monkey jumps or where a country situates itself on a value chain largely involves decisions determined by the narrow criterion of factor proportions.

The challenge Lin and Monga face is how to accelerate the growth of professionally managed business organizations and their unique skills. Business knowledge depends on experience, which I would say is the critical missing element in economies deprived of East Asia's pre-War manufacturing culture (which was fortuitously strengthened by Japan's regional war preparations). Experience can be understood using a learning curve, except that learning is not repetitive. Experience depends on gaining tacit and undocumented knowledge of multiple activities that may change simultaneously—a harder task than gaining 'information' (a fact). How can an industrial policy hasten the acquisition of experience?

Two possibilities that I think would move Lin and Monga's argument forward would be to follow what the role models of East Asia and the Middle East are doing, and use industrial policy to: (i) invest overseas (outward foreign direct investment); and (ii) reverse the flow of talented brain drain (and create a level playing field for local talent), which may change a small country's comparative advantage overnight. When Malaysia's government reformed its industrial policy towards its Malay population—instead of subsidising Malay-owned enterprises in Malaysia, it began acquiring foreign companies and giving Malays equity in them—it developed skills to choose a specific overseas asset to buy, the same 'knowledge of a business' it needs to target a successful investment at home. Similarly with SABIC, Saudi Arabia's state-owned petrochemical company, which acquired General Electric's chemical business in China, the feedstock costs of both petrochemicals and chemicals draw on intelligence of the supply of and demand for oil. An outward FDI can thus have positive spillovers on domestic income, employment, income distribution (as in Malaysia's case) and picking winners.

Reversing talented brain drain by creating economic opportunities at home is a costly challenge, but one with potentially high returns, because embedded in returnees' experience is an inductive clue as to the specific industries a government should support. Globalism's imperfections, moreover, have created a willingness on the part of some professionals to return home, opportunities permitting. Morris Chang, a top executive in Texas Instruments, went back to Taiwan to run its new state-owned semiconductor company because he claimed that at TI he had hit a 'yellow glass ceiling'. West African executives in Unilever talk about a 'black glass ceiling'. Industrial policy is inherently nationalistic, and the role of government is to nurture nationalism of a productive type.

## Note

† Alice Amsden is Barton L. Weller Professor of Political Economy, Massachusetts Institute of Technology (MIT), Cambridge, MA.

## Reference

Amsden, A. H. and Suzumura, K. (2001) 'An Interview with Miyohei Shinohara: Nonconformism in Japanese Economic Thought', *Journal of the Japanese and International Economies* 15: 341–60.


# K. Y. Amoako[†]

Lin and Monga's article emphasizes the importance for sustained growth of technological innovation, industrial upgrading and diversification, and improvements in infrastructure and institutions. It notes that, while the market mechanism is essential for efficient resource allocation, it may not be sufficient to enable firms to overcome the problems of information, co-ordination and externality that often stand in the way of achieving the above-listed requirements for sustained growth in developing countries. It then points out that the historical evidence shows that governments in almost all the successful countries (i.e., the industrialized countries and the recent East Asian success stories) played and are continuing to play pro-active roles in helping firms in their economies to overcome these problems. It further states that governments in almost all developing countries have also tried to intervene in their economies for similar reasons, but most have failed. The article's central thesis is that the failures were due to the fact that the governments intervened by trying to defy their economies' existing comparative advantage, meaning that they tried to promote products that did not reflect their relative factor endowments, particularly of capital and labour. To address this, it proposes a process that policy-makers in developing countries may follow to pick industries or products to promote or facilitate.

The authors argue that, for a developing country to diversify its exports, the government should '… identify the list of tradeable goods and services that have been produced for about 20 years in dynamically growing countries with similar endowment structures and per capita income that is about 100% higher than their own', and then remove the binding constraints or take necessary measures to facilitate their export development, including attraction of Foreign Direct Investment (FDI). The government should also look for successful discoveries by domestic enterprises and provide appropriate support. The article provides examples of the type of facilitation or support that may be given.

Overall, I find this proposal a very practical and useful starting guide for a government keen on diversifying and upgrading its country's exports. It is to be welcomed that an article that looks at the role for the state in late-industrialisation in such a pragmatic manner emanates from the World Bank, which spent a great part of the 1980s and 1990s denying any positive or pro-active role for the state in industrialisation and promoting liberalization and privatization programmes to support that view. With the demonstrably superior economic performance of the East Asian countries (for example, Korea, Taiwan, Singapore and Hong Kong) in recent times, in the first three of which the governments pursued active industrial policies, the Bank has had to revise its position, starting with the East Asian Miracle Study (World Bank, 1993). It is to be hoped that this article by Lin and Monga will help move the Bank further along on the line of pragmatism. As they write, paraphrasing Rodrik (2009), "... instead of advising the governments in developing countries to give up playing the facilitating role, it is 'more important to understand better why some countries have been able to succeed while most others have failed, so that it is possible to advise the governments to do the right things and avoid the mistakes'".

While I fully share the authors' view that the state has a positive role to play in facilitating industrialisation and commend their proposal, I would have liked to see a little more flexibility in the way they use comparative advantage (i.e., relative factor proportions) to review the cases of success and failure in diversification and industrial upgrading. The apparent use of the Hecksher-Olin-Samuelson (HOS) framework to interpret industrial policy appears to me to be too confining theoretically, and also does not seem to adequately explain the country experiences.

Conceptually, the idea that a country should try to focus on products for which it has the required factors in relative abundance makes eminent sense. However, this assumes competitive markets, both internationally and domestically, which may not be the case. It is also very static and may not take account of the likely demand, price, and prospects of technological change and learning of products on the world market. The fact that a country's factor endowments enable it to produce product A more cheaply today relative to product B does not necessarily mean that, in the medium to long term, it is better off producing A instead of B, if in fact B has better demand and technological change and learning prospects. Admittedly, producing A today is more likely to raise national income and, presumably, thereby savings, which would enable the country to augment its capital. However, if the country is aiming to 'catch up' in industrialisation, it would at some point have to defy its existing comparative advantage and take non-marginal steps away from its current productive structure (i.e. try to produce B). Certainly, this would be a more risky move, but it would be taking high risks for potential high rewards. For me, therefore, the policy questions are twofold: (i) what should be the mix of the A and B products in industrial policy at any given time, and how should they change over time? And (ii) having chosen a particular mix, especially a mix including B products, what are the complementary policies that minimize the risks and enhance the chances of success? The latter question brings to the fore the issue of the acquisition of technologies and technological capabilities. In the HOS framework, which seems to inform Lin and Monga's article, this issue is side-stepped by the assumption that technologies are equally accessible and can be efficiently operated by all producers. This assumption is clearly problematic. In fact, to my mind, the core development problem that industrial policy should address is precisely the access, efficient deployment, absorption and adaptation of technology (Lall, 2003, 2004). To meet this challenge takes more than focusing on existing comparative advantage as determined by existing relative capital-labour ratios.

In fact, if each country diversified and upgraded its industries only by trying to break into markets that countries ahead of it on the 'industrial ladder' were becoming less competitive due to rising labour costs, then one would expect the industrial rankings of countries to be rather static over time. There would be hardly any instances of 'catch up' or overtaking; the US and Germany would not have overtaken Britain in industrialisation; Japan would not have become dominant in automobile exports; nor would Korea have become among the most efficient steel producers. My reading of the experiences of Japan and the East Asian countries is that the governments promoted a mixture of A and B types of industries, with the mix changing over time, but supported the industries with a host of fiscal, exchange-rate, trade and credit instruments. They also built strong institutions, pursued active technology and FDI policies, aggressively developed skills, and pro-actively engaged in industrial restructuring. One cannot be sure that what arose from all these government interventions could always be character-ized as competitive markets that enabled firms to develop according to com-parative advantage (see Johnson, 1982; Amsden, 1989; Wade, 1990; Evans, 1995; World Bank 1993, and Chang, 2006). It should also be noted that in Africa many of the industries established during the import-substitution era failed, although a large number of them were engaged in manufactures of textiles and other simple consumer goods that reflected the comparative advantage of the countries in terms of relative factor endowments.

What can be taken from all this is that following comparative advan-tage is very important, but is only one of a whole host of policies, institu-tions, capacities and arrangements that have to be deployed together in order to increase the chances of success of industrial policy. And for a country that wants to accelerate its industrial catching-up, it may be nec-essary for it to defy its current comparative advantage to some extent and promote a carefully selected small sub-set of products that are 'high-tech' (i.e., from the point of view of the country's current production structure). This would require a government that is capable, organized, disciplined and prepared to work closely with the private sector, and yet be able to subject it to rigorous performance criteria.

The above are just questions of nuance. As has already been noted, I do think the article makes a valuable contribution by providing a practical and sensible way for countries to initiate industrial policy. At the African Center for Economic Transformation (ACET), we are engaged precisely in exploring ways for African countries to transform their economies through, among other things, sensible industrial policy. We therefore welcome this contribution from Lin and Monga.

## Note

†   K. Y. Amaoko is Founder and President, African Center for Economic Trans-formation (ACET), Accra, Ghana.

## References

Amsden, A. H. (1989) *Asia's Next Giant*. New York and Oxford: Oxford University Press.

Chang, H.-J. (2006) *The East Asian Development Experience: The Miracle, the Crisis and the Future*. London: Zed Books, and Penang, Malaysia: Third World Network.

Evans, P. (1995) *Embedded Autonomy – States and Industrial Transformation*. Princeton, NJ: Princeton University Press.

Johnson, C. (1982) *MITI and the Japanese Miracle: The Growth of Industrial Policy, 1925–1975*. Stanford, CA: Stanford University Press.

Lall, S. (2004) 'Selective Industrial and Trade Policies in Developing Countries: Theoretical and Empirical Issues' in C. Soludo, O. Ogbu and Ha-Joon Chang (eds.), *The Politics of Trade and Industrial Policy in Africa – Forced Consensus?* Trenton, NJ and Asmara, Eritrea: Africa World Press, Inc.

Lall, S. (2003) 'Reinventing Industrial Strategy: The Role of Government Policy in Building Industrial Competitiveness'. Paper prepared for the Intergovernmental Group on Monetary Affairs and Development (G-24).

Rodrik, D. (2009) 'Industrial Policy: Don't Ask Why, Ask How', *Middle East Development Journal* 1 (1): 1–29.

Wade, R. (1990) *Governing the Market*. Princeton, NJ: Princeton University Press.

World Bank (1993) *The East Asian Miracle: Economic Growth and Public Policy*. New York: Oxford University Press.

## Howard Pack[†]

Lin and Monga have covered an enormous range of issues in this intriguing article. They correctly argue for a rethinking of whether a more activist policy is necessary to stimulate manufacturing development in the least industrialised economies, especially in sub-Saharan Africa which has a relatively low level of manufacturing share of GDP and also surprisingly little small-scale manufacturing. It is worth noting that the same is true of the Arab economies (Noland and Pack, 2007). Given the growth in population and labour force and the need to find new sources of employment, the issue is of great importance. The main contribution of the article is a reiteration of the need to conform with comparative advantage in development, an argument made cogently in Lin's Marshall lectures, while seeking to transform the economy to more advanced activities. The new argument is an algorithm for identifying successful sectors; this seems to be deeply influenced by East Asian experience. Phrased perhaps too baldly, the algorithm suggests looking at the industries in nations that are more advanced but not too much so—for Korea and Taiwan targeting Japan's structure as Japan was 'only' three times richer.

This algorithm is problematic. First, the structure of the richer nation may not be economically optimal even for that country, but is itself the result of distorting policies. Some of Japan's industrial development between 1868 and 1941 reflected a felt urgency to develop a serious military potential which did allow the Japanese to deploy battleships in the Russo-Japanese War of 1905. Japan's metallurgical capabilities, reflected partly in post-1950 industrial development, built upon the skills developed in the 1930s that contributed to Japan's initial success in World War II. Similarly, the USSR in the 1920s and '30s emphasized heavy industry in an attempt to build up military capacity but also as a perceived path to industrial success. India in the early 1950s emulated the Soviet path which deeply influenced some Indians such as Mahalanobis, then chair of the Planning Commission. India violated the Lin-Monga dictum of pursuing labour-intensive industry, but that experience, replicated in many other nations pursuing import-substituting industrialisation, does suggest one of the perils of emulating more 'advanced' nations; the body politic may be tempted to throw aside strict economic rationality and pursue technologically advanced and capital-intensive sectors, steel in the 1950s and '60s and high technology today. Once started down the road of emulation, technocrats may not be able to rein in their bosses. Korea's economists have shown the considerable cost to the heavy and chemical industry programme of the 1970s and '80s and it is possible that the interim costs were sufficiently large that the protection failed to satisfy the Mill-Bastable test (Yoo, 1990).

Moreover, the industrial policy of these nations was embedded within a macroeconomic framework that was conducive to growth, including (World Bank, 1993):

- exceptionally high saving and investment rates which continued for four decades, leading to the high growth rates of the capital-labour ratios;
- a rapid increase in education measured in years, but also high achievement in science and mathematics measured in international tests and growing tertiary education enrolments in science and engineering;

- an enormous expansion of infrastructure including transportation, ports and roads that was not sectorally targeted;
- an emphasis on transferring technology from the rest of the world, whether in the form of technology licensing, FDI, the use of foreign consultants, or in some cases reverse engineering;
- the use of export growth as the sine qua non for the continuation of aid to firms, government programmes benefiting firms being contingent on exporting. This forced firms to increase their productivity and was the impetus for the demand for importing more advanced technologies. But export growth was also abetted by macro policies that limited domestic absorption and maintained a relatively constant real exchange rate that allowed potential exporters to gauge potential profitability without worrying about exchange-rate volatility. These macro aspects had a uniform impact, not one that varied among sectors. The fact that the bureaucracy charged with implementing export promotion was largely insulated from political pressure from firms, while there was a simultaneous close monitoring of firms that provided considerable information about their problems.

Such policies are not easily emulated in most of the countries that need to expand their industrial base.

Other problems emerge as well. For example, Yamamura (1986) (in an exhaustive study of Japanese industrial policy in the early 1950s) identified the criteria used by MITI to identify potential competitors with the US. Products encouraged were those with high income elasticities (so that additional supply by Japan would not drive down the initial international price) and a large market so that scale economies could be realized. To implement this policy the Japanese government: (a) provided interest-rate subsidies; (b) protected the domestic market by tariffs; (c) limited or precluded entry of new local competitors so that favoured firms would not lose their ability to realize scale economies; (d) forbade foreign direct investment in the promoted sector; and (e) precluded potential local competitors from borrowing from local financial institutions to avoid the loss of scale economies by favoured firms. Korea and Taiwan, the other model nations that might be cited as having pursued a successful industrial policy, implemented some but not all of these measures. Clearly this is a formidable set of policies to implement and the complete programme is more complex than simply looking at a nation that is richer. This programme would be difficult to implement in any nation, and especially in those with a poor education base, limited government legitimacy and the widespread corruption characteristic of many of the least industrialized nations.

When Japan embarked on its policies, it targeted stable products whose characteristics were changing slowly. There are few such sectors nowadays. Even inexpensive clothing and shoes undergo remarkably rapid changes in style which demand that a successful firm be part of an international supply chain that can keep the supplier up-to-date on fashions and quality standards. Moreover, it is not clear how officials trying to foster an individual sector would even choose a product. Looking at international trade statistics, one does not find 'shoes' but 50 or more categories, each employing a different technology and requiring different production and marketing skills. How many government employees in a ministry of industry could make such choices and carry out the calculation of a social cost/benefit analysis? Moreover, to choose among products would require extraordinary knowledge of both other sectors and the international prospects of the industry with respect to both likely prices and cost structures. Lin and Monga correctly identify lacunae that the government should address to promote structural transformation, in particular, 'information, co-ordination and externality issues, which are intrinsic to industrial upgrading and diversification'. Kamal Saggi and I (2006) have provided a partial list of the requisite knowledge to deal with these problems, based on our synthesis of the industrial-policy literature. These include knowledge of:

- which firms and industries generate knowledge spillovers
- which firms and industries benefit from dynamic scale economies—what is the precise path of such learning and the magnitude of the cost disadvantage at each stage of the learning process
- which sectors have a long-term comparative advantage
- the size of scale economies of different firms and sectors in order to facilitate investment co-ordination
- an ability superior to that of individual firms to learn about their potential competitiveness
- the nature and extent of capital-market failures
- the magnitude and direction of inter-industry spillovers

- the relative amount of learning by individual firms from others and from their own experience
- the extent to which early entrants generate benefits for future entrants
- the extent of heterogeneity of firms' learning abilities
- whether firms trying to reduce production costs also begin a simultaneous effort to improve their product's quality in order to obtain a better reputation
- the potential effects of FDI or international trade in solving some of the coordination problems, including a detailed knowledge of which of tens of thousands of intermediates are tradeable
- forecasting which firms can create new knowledge and discover better production methods
- the spillover effects of FDI as well as the likely intensity of their purchase of domestic intermediates.

This is obviously a formidable list. It is unlikely that, even if a government hired several major international consulting firms, they would possess the ability to undertake this programme, despite having many PhDs and MBAs on their staffs. The implication for much more poorly educated and compensated government staff with considerably fewer resources is obvious. If this characterization is valid, alternatives to government direction have to be sought. None of this implies that Lin and Monga are incorrect in their insistence on a positive role of government in building hard infrastructure such as roads and soft infrastructure such as a legal system and an environment conducive to business. But these critical requirements are likely to exhaust the capabilities (and finances) of almost all national governments of the least industrialized nations.

## Note

† Howard Pack is Professor of Business and Public Policy, The Wharton School, University of Pennsylvania.

## References

Noland, Marcus and Pack, Howard (2007) *The Arab Economies in a Changing World*. Washington, DC: The Peterson Institute for International Economics.

Pack, Howard and Saggi, Kamal (2006) 'Is There a Case for Industrial Policy? A Critical Survey', *World Bank Research Observer*, Fall.

World Bank (1993) *The East Asian Miracle: Economic Growth and Public Policy.* New York: Oxford University Press.

Yamamura, Kozo (1986) 'Caveat Emptor: The Industrial Policy of Japan' in Paul R. Krugman (ed.), *Strategic Trade Policy and the New International Economics.* Cambridge, MA: MIT Press.

Yoo, Jung-Ho (1990) 'The Industrial Policy of the 1970s and the Evolution of the Manufacturing Sector.' Working Paper No. 9017. Seoul: Korea Development Institute.

## Wonhyuk Lim[†]

Development may be conceptualized as the result of synergies between enhanced human capital and new knowledge, involving complementary investments in physical and social capital. The fundamental policy challenge is for the state to work with non-state actors and markets to address innovation and co-ordination externalities while minimizing negative government externalities. Since the time of the Industrial Revolution, countries that have effectively responded to the innovation and coordination challenges have become successful. The key is for a country to retain the ownership of its development and progressively build up its capabilities to add value and respond to shocks, even as it actively learns from, and engages with, the outside world. The reinforcement of successful experiments through the feedback mechanism of performance-based rewards can lead to dramatic changes over time (Lim, 2011).

Developing countries typically export primary commodities or start their industrialisation in the assembly and production segment of the value chain in such labour-intensive industries as garments. Most countries fail to move to higher value-added segments along the value chain (such as product design) or to shift to higher value-added sectors (such as machinery and equipment) for two reasons. They either neglect to address externalities in technical education, R&D, and infrastructure development or rush to promote sophisticated industries without the requisite accumulation of skill and scale economies. International benchmarking based on endowment structures and close consultation between the government and the private sector is key to solving information and incentive problems at this stage, when countries try to upgrade their comparative advantage.

Drawing on development history and economic theory, Justin Yifu Lin and Célestin Monga offer practical advice to developing countries faced with the challenge of identifying promising sectors and facilitating structural transformation. They note that successful developing countries have typically targeted *mature* industries in countries with an endowment structure similar to theirs and with a level of development not much more advanced than theirs' (emphasis added). Specifically, they propose that the government in a developing country focus on 'tradeable goods and services that have been produced for about 20 years in dynamically growing countries with similar endowment structures and a per capita income [measured in purchasing power parity] that is about 100% more than their own, while also paying close attention to successful experiments in other sectors. They also advise the government to encourage the experimentation, self-discovery, and scale-up efforts of private enterprises by removing constraints, supporting pilots, and providing direct incentives to pioneer firms.

Building on the ideas of comparative advantage, self-discovery, and the facilitating state, this set of policy recommendations will help policy-makers in developing countries 'to reap the advantage of backwardness' in the early stages of development. However, more is likely to be needed if they are to move beyond 'the middle-income trap', when catch-up economies may have to take considerable strategic risks to jump into non-mature industries to compete with advanced economies. This is not an easy task. In fact, countries tend to move through the product space by developing goods close to those they currently produce, and can reach the core 'only by traversing empirically infrequent distances', which may explain why poor countries fail to converge with the income levels of rich countries (Hidalgo et al., 2007: 482).

Korea's case is illustrative in this regard. Korea exploited its latent comparative advantage to develop mature, labour-intensive downstream industries in the 1960s, much in line with the advice provided by Lin and Monga. However, it did not just wait for its income and skill levels to rise to move into higher value-added industries. Instead, it systematically studied what had to be done to fill the missing links in the domestic value chain and move up the quality ladder, and made conscious and concerted efforts to aim for international competitiveness from the outset. It sought to indigenize intermediate inputs imported from foreign upstream industries, through the acquisition of technology, the development of human resources, and the construction of optimal-scale plants aimed at the global market. For instance, in the chemical-textile value chain, it systematically built the linkages backwards from the export of textiles to the production of synthetic fibers, and the development of basic petrochemicals.

Korea had a strong and increasing revealed comparative advantage in light industries when it made the decision to promote heavy and chemical industries in 1973. After benchmarking advanced industrial nations with natural endowments similar to its own, such as Japan, Korea recognized that it had a potential comparative advantage in machinery and equipment industries and began to remove the obstacles to achieving this objective, such as lack of technicians and engineers with the requisite skills in sophisticated industries. The government drafted a plan to increase the supply of technicians from 240,000 in 1969 to 1,700,000 in 1981, and established mechanical technical high schools offering full scholarships to poor but talented young students. National universities were called upon to focus on one specialized engineering field related to a nearby industrial complex.

In promoting upstream industries in the 1970s, Korea had to make a strategic choice. It could play safe and develop heavy and chemical industries for the small domestic market and risk the inefficiency resulting from sub-optimal scales and entrenched protectionism. Alternatively, it could promote these industries for the global market and risk capacity under-utilization and financial distress. It chose the latter option because, despite considerable risks, this promised a dynamically efficient growth trajectory if the country managed to develop the requisite skills before the financial burden associated with scale economies and complementary investments became overwhelming. To minimize time and exploit scale economies in establishing capital-intensive industries, the government decided to rely on a select group of state-owned enterprises and family-based business groups (chaebol) with successful track records. It considered that scale economies called for regulated monopoly or oligopoly in these industries until demand became large enough to support effective competition (Lim, 2011).

Although Korea's case is but one example, it shows that industrial upgrading requires much more than international benchmarking based on comparative advantage and self-discovery and scale-up efforts. Innovation and co-ordination externalities in structural transformation demand strategic risk-taking by the public and private sectors.

## Note

† Wonhyuk Lim is Director of Policy Research, Center for International Development, Korea Development Institute.

## References

Hidalgo, C.; Klinger, A. B.; Barabasi, A.-L. and Hausmann, R. (2007) 'The Product Space Conditions the Development of Nations', *Science* 317: 482–7.
Lim, Wonhyuk (2011) 'Joint Discovery and Upgrading of Comparative Advantage: Lessons from Korea's Development Experience' in Shahrokh Fardoust, Yongbeom Kim and Claudia Sepulveda (eds.), *Postcrisis Growth and Development: A Development Agenda for the G-20*. Washington, DC: World Bank.

## Rejoinder by Justin Yifu Lin and Célestin Monga

We are grateful to Professors Amsden, Tendulkar and Pack, and Drs Amoako and Lim for their insightful comments on our article. We first discuss some of the general themes emerging from their analyses. We then respond to some specific comments by each of them.

## 1 General Comments

**1.1 On Scope and Justification.** It is useful to start by stressing that every country in the world, intentionally or not, pursues industrial policy. This is true not only of the usual suspects such as China, Singapore, France and Brazil, but also of the United Kingdom, Germany, Chile and the United States. This is surprising only if one forgets that industrial policy broadly refers to any government decision, regulation or law that encourages ongoing activity or investment in a particular industry. After all, economic development and sustained growth are the result of continual industrial and technological upgrading, a process that requires public-private collaboration. The theoretical case for industrial policy is quite strong and has been acknowledged in the literature at least since Adam Smith in the lesser known Book 5 of *The Wealth of Nations* (in which he discusses factor endowments and infrastructure endowments), and Alfred Marshall, who outlined the analytical framework for understanding externalities and co-ordination.

Nowadays, a new wave of skepticism rests on the idea that industrial (sectoral) policy and competition policy are contradictory or at best substitutes. This argument is implicit in some of the comments by Professors Tendulkar and Pack and Dr Amoako. We believe that industrial policy based on the Growth Identification and Facilitation Framework (GIFF) actually enhances competition. By facilitating co-ordination and addressing externality issues, industrial policy helps many domestic and foreign firms to enter sectors that are consistent with the country's latent comparative advantage and turn them into overt comparative advantages, and thereby intensifies competition within the industries and enhances the economy's competitiveness internationally (Lin and Chang, 2009). Moreover, as shown by Aghion et al. (2010), competition weeds out bad projects, and thus reduces the danger of picking the wrong winner. Also, firms may naturally try to differentiate horizontally in order to increase their competitiveness in the market. In such situations, the more intense product market competition is within sectors, the more innovative and competitiveness-enhancing it will be.

*1.2 On Discipline and Implementation.* The political-economy difficulties of implementing any type of public policy are well known. The comments received highlight some of them: the fact that the body politic may be tempted to ignore economic rationality and pursue more sophisticated sectors in its zeal to emulate advanced countries; and the possibility of extending even successful policies well beyond their effective timespan, thus creating opportunities for rent-seeking activities. These general governance issues are increasingly well studied in the economic and political-science literature (Tollison and Congleton, 1995; Robinson and Torvik, 2005).

These concerns are legitimate but only for the traditional type of industrial policy which encourages firms to enter industries that defy comparative advantage. Firms in these industries are not viable in an open, competitive market. Their entry and continuous operation often depend on large subsidies and protection, which create opportunities for rent-seeking and corruption, and make it difficult for the government to abandon interventions and exit from distortions (Lin and Tan, 1999). The GIFF promotes something quite different: the development of industries that are consistent with the economy's latent comparative advantage. Firms are viable once the constraints to their entry and operation are removed. The incentives provided by the government to the first movers are to be temporary and small, solely for the purpose of compensating for their information externality. In that context, the issues of pervasive rent-seeking and the persistence of government intervention beyond its initial timetable can be mitigated.

## 2 Specific Comments

Professor Tendulkar comments on the distinction between the roles of the state in facilitating growth and in identifying new industries for growth. He accepts the state's important role in growth facilitation, but is more uncertain about its role in growth identification. Referring specifically to the South Asian context, he also asks how the over-enthusiastic government can be prevented from taking on much more than it can effectively handle.

We believe that without identification it is hard to determine the type of facilitation that would be desirable. The appropriate hard and soft infrastructures needed to foster industrial upgrading are often industry-specific. For the state to play its role in determining and providing the necessary infrastructure (facilitation), government officials must form a judgment and make decisions about which particular industries will need it (identification). The two roles are therefore complementary and some-times difficult to disentangle. Moreover, because resources and capacity are limited, governments must prioritise their interventions—and explicitly or implicitly engage in some form of growth identification.

The issue of over-enthusiastic governments is not specific to South Asia. Many countries in Latin America, Africa and Asia (even China before 1979) exhibited the zealous state syndrome, with governments doing too much in their attempts to promote development. That risk, which is real, does not invalidate the need to deal with externalities and co-ordination. It simply points to the necessity to set clear, transparent and rigorous criteria that mitigate the propensity of governments to over-intervene or to support uncompetitive industries. We offer the GIFF precisely to advise political leaders and the general public on the right way of carrying out industrial policy, and identify clearly what would be the wrong way, so that the probability for governments being over-enthusiastic is reduced.

Professor Amsden argues that industrial policies in countries ranging from the Middle East's energy belt to Asia's manufacturing corridor and the so-called BRIC economies (Brazil, Russia, India and China) have been more successful in practice than is portrayed in our article. Admittedly, many OPEC countries avoided the resource curse and managed to reach commendable levels of per capita income. However, most of them failed to use the resource rents to facilitate structural transformation in their countries, as carried out by the other resource-rich countries, such as the Scandinavian countries, the United States, Canada or Australia.

We submit that the performance of resource-rich countries could be further enhanced if they used the GIFF to support structural transformation. This would require them to invest an appropriate share of revenues from their natural resources in human, infrastructural and social capital, and create incentives for domestic or foreign firms to facilitate the development and upgrading of industries in the non-resource sector. Their strategy should not be limited to maintaining good governance, keeping natural-resource revenues in sovereign funds and investing in foreign equity markets to insure against commodity price fluctuations, as is often the case.

Professor Amsden also questions the applicability of the GIFF to a peasant export economy where the pace of population growth is rapid and landlessness, unemployment and underemployment are high, but where labour costs are not low enough and manufacturing experience is not deep enough to compete against labour-surplus economies like India. Regarding population growth, the same could have been said about Asian economies before their economic take-off in the 1960s. Children represent old-age insurance for many families in poor countries, and the increase in per capita income generally reduces fertility rates because that insurance is less needed and the opportunity cost of raising children rises with the increase in wages. East Asian economies did not have Mainland China's restrictive family planning system but they experienced similar reductions in population growth rates. African governments should have devoted the same focus on promoting economic growth as they did on various interventions to reduce child mortality. As for the labour costs, those in the formal sector may not be low, especially in some African countries, as observed by Amsden. But the informal-sector labour costs are unlikely to be high. Moreover, one way out of that dilemma is for those countries to follow the practice of Mauritius in the 1970s (Subramanian and Roy, 2003), namely, allowing wage flexibility in the special economic zones so as to promote the development of new competitive, labour-intensive industries.

Professor Amsden stresses the importance of experience in managing business organizations, which is important indeed. By facilitating the development of latent comparative advantage industries, the GIFF would allow more entrepreneurs to enter competitive manufacturing sectors, gain experience, and prepare their firms to upgrade to higher-level industries. Many successful business giants in Japan (Toyota, Sony, Honda), Korea (Samsung, LG, Daewoo), Taiwan-China (Formosa Plastics), or Hong Kong (Tyco-on Li Kasing) started as small businesses with a few employees and a few thousand dollars of investment. They overcame the odds because their promoters were gifted leaders, but they also acquired experience in business management because they operated in an environment that was conducive to sustained growth.

She also notes that our model can be enhanced using industrial policy to invest overseas and attract skills. We agree. In a country that is recording dynamic growth, the government can employ outward investments to facilitate: (i) the relocation of firms that operate in its sunset sectors to other lower-income countries with a similar endowment structure so as to use those countries as export bases and benefit from their cheaper labour and/ or to get access to their domestic markets; (ii) the acquisition by domestic firms of foreign firms in related sectors in higher-income countries, in order to get access to their technology, management experiences and market channels; and (iii) the acquisition of resources by domestic firms (in resource-scarce countries) from countries where they are abundant.

Dr Amoako argues that successful industrialisation has not always been based on competitive markets, and that African countries have not always succeeded despite following their comparative advantage. The GIFF provides a dual-track strategy for government intervention. Following comparative advantage, which is only the first track of the GIFF, is a necessary condition for a successful industrial policy. However, that is not sufficient. For industrial policy to contribute to a country's growth and structural transformation, the government also needs to play the facilitation role by providing incentives to the first movers and to help them by removing binding constraints to their growth and by coordinating investments in the soft and hard infrastructures that are needed. The likely reason why some African countries have not succeeded despite following their comparative advantage is because their governments failed to play their facilitation role.

By arguing that the article pays too much attention to supporting products that follow a comparative advantage and too little attention to the acquisition of technological capabilities and learning, he also seems to assume that the GIFF approach promotes static comparative advantage. Actually it does the opposite. Our framework promotes upgrading and diversification to new industries and is therefore dynamic in nature. There is a major difference between the GIFF and the theory of dynamic comparative advantage which Dr Amoako has in mind. The latter typically attempts to help firms to enter industries that are a country's future comparative advantage. Because of endowment constraints, firms in those industries would not yet be viable in a competitive market even if the government helped them with the co-ordination and externality compensation. By contrast, the GIFF aims at helping firms enter industries with latent comparative advantage. Under that scenario, firms would be viable and require no subsidies or protection once the government provides coordination and externality compensation. It should be noted that if African countries cannot be successful in industries with latent comparative advantage, their probability of success in industries without comparative advantages will be quite small.

With the GIFF approach, developing countries can tap into the potential advantage of backwardness, record higher rates of growth and upgrade their industrial structure, income level, and endowment structure faster than the high-income countries. Once their income levels and endowment structures are close to those of high-income countries, they will have gained comparative advantage in advanced industries, which will enable them to compete directly with and even overtake the high-income countries. Therefore, contrary to Dr Amoako's prediction that 'if each country diversified and upgraded its industries only by trying to break into markets that countries ahead of it on the "industrial ladder" were becoming less competitive in due to rising labour costs, then one would expect the industrial rankings of countries to be rather static over time', it is actually a faster way for a latecomer to catch up with the more advanced countries.

Professor Pack believes that targeting industries in richer comparable countries and then following the country's comparative advantage accordingly is a problematic algorithm. His reasoning is two-fold: first, the economic structure of the richer country could be the result of distorting policies; and second, a formidable set of policies is required for successful policies which go beyond the mere identification of potential products. In support of his skepticism, he offers the examples of Japan and the USSR (which India tried unsuccessfully to emulate). This is a valid warning. Even in successful cases, industrial policy is never a smooth process. It always involves trial and error from governments that put in place good mechanisms and channels to learn from mistakes, adjust economic strategies, and minimize the potential costs of bad decisions.

However, our framework recommends not only that target countries be richer but also that they have recorded dynamic growth for a long period and where higher incomes and productivity gains in successful industries eventually raise wages and make them less competitive. If they have succeeded in growing dynamically for several decades, it is unlikely that they have followed strategies that defy their comparative advantage.

After the Meiji restoration, Japan took the German kingdom of Prussia as a model. According to estimates by Angus Maddison (2010), Germany's per capita income in 1890 was US$2,428 and Japan's $1,012.[1] Japan's was 42% that of Germany, hence Japan's strategy was consistent with the approach proposed in the GIFF. While Professor Pack's summary of MITI's policies in the 1950s and 1960s is quite instructive, the story behind the numbers is fully consistent with the GIFF analysis as well: Japan's per capita income in 1950, 1960 and 1965 was $1,921, $3,986, and $5,934 respectively, whereas those of the US were $9,561, $10,961, and $13,419. The ratios were as follows: 20%, 36% and 44%. The numbers for 1960 and 1965 are consistent with the principle of the GIFF. The 1950 figure was lower than the normal threshold that the GIFF suggests. This is probably due to the fact that Japan was still recovering from the war and its human capital and soft and hard infrastructure were greater than those indicated by its per capita income; a strong indication is the fact that Japan's per capita income in the 1930s had already reached about 40% that of the US (for example, $2,120 vs. $5,467 in 1935).

In contrast to Japan's story, the USSR in the 1950s was the wrong model for India for two reasons. First, the two countries did not have a similar endowment structure; the USSR was a resource-rich country while India was a resource-poor country. Secondly, the USSR was too far advanced compared with India. According to Maddison, the USSR's per capita income in 1955 was $3,313, while India's was $676 (only 20% that of its reference country). The GIFF recommends that latecomers be realistic (and even modest) in their choice of reference countries and target industries.

Professor Pack also observes that world trade has undergone remarkably rapid changes in style and that there are fewer stable products and industries to be targeted today compared with several decades ago. We believe that, despite changes in style and product customization, the division of labour among countries at different levels of development is still the same. For example, television evolved from black and white to colour and to flat panel today. The main producing countries have changed from the US before the 1950s to Japan in the 1960s-80s, to Korea in the 1980s-2000s, and China today. A latecomer entering the market today could go into labour-intensive assembly of the flat-panel TV production first, just as forerunners did a few decades ago when they decided to compete successfully in the black and white and colour TV markets.

Globalization provides huge potential for industrialisation through specialization. Several decades ago, many low-income countries faced the constraints of their limited market size, high transportation costs and trade barriers, and could not take advantage of the opportunities offered by large-scale manufacturing. With globalization, virtually any country can identify production activities for which it has overt or latent comparative advantage, scale them up and create its own niche in the world market. Precisely because of globalization, the economic development strategy in every country should follow comparative advantage closely. Multinational firms are more likely to exploit any small difference in production costs in the determination of their locations of production or procurement systems. Globalization also makes the government's role in the facilitation process even more important because only with good hard and soft infrastructures, which reduce transaction costs, can the cost advantage based on endowment structure and specialization be realized.

Professor Pack provides an impressive list of knowledge requirements about targeted industries that government officials would need to know in order to design a successful industrial policy. He questions the capacity of governments in developing countries to meet those requirements. First, all countries at low-income levels tend to lack high capacity by definition. Chang (2008) reminds us that, not so long ago, it was not unusual to refer to 'Lazy Japanese and Thieving Germans'. With the process of economic development taking place, capacity will be enhanced in any society. More important, some of the requirements he identifies are likely to be relevant only for more advanced industries in high-income countries. For industries with low technical content, the list should be streamlined considerably. Moreover, instead of analyzing the technical nature of various industries to find out the knowledge underpinning them, the private sector and government officials can rely on the advantage of backwardness and observe what the dynamically growing countries with similar endowment structures are already doing. These successful countries must have already overcome those knowledge challenges either by trial and error or by analysis.

Dr Lim agrees that policy advice based on ideas of comparative advantage, self-discovery and the facilitating state will help policy-makers in the early stage of development, but argues that more needs to be done to move beyond the middle-income trap. Korea, he writes, defied its comparative advantage by moving into heavy and chemical industries by building specific skills, filling specific gaps in the value chain, and relying on a select set of business groups and strategic choice. We agree with his observation that dynamically growing middle-income countries will have some industries that have already reached the global technology frontier and will eventually face the challenge of taking risks in technology and product innovation. For such industries, the government should continue to play its facilitating role, and use policy instruments similar to those in high-income countries, such as subsidising the R&D activities of individual firms by funding basic research in universities or public institutions, granting patents for new inventions, offering preferential taxes and defense and other government procurements, etc. But for other industries that remain well within the global technological frontier even at that level of development, the GIFF could be used to address externalities and co-ordination issues.

The Korean government's encouragement of the development of more capital/technology-intensive industries in the 1970s, as discussed by Lim, is in fact consistent with the need for industrial upgrading due to the change in comparative advantages. The textile, garment, plywood, wigs and other labour-intensive industries were Korea's comparative advantages and very competitive internationally in the 1960s. The success of these labour-intensive industries allowed the country to accumulate human and financial capital. As a result Korea's endowment structure was upgraded. That process led to a gradual loss of comparative advantage in the original industries and allowed the economy to move into new, more capital- and technology-intensive industries. Lim's account of Korea's industrial upgrading process in the 1970s, which targeted mature industries in Japan instead of the most advanced industries in the United States, is in fact a good illustration of how the GIFF approach explains the country's economic success.

## Note

1.  All the estimates of per capita income here are measured in 1990 International Geary-Khamis dollars, taken from Maddison (2010).

## *References*

Aghion, P.; Dewatripont, M.; Du, L.; Harrison, A.; and Legros, P. (2010) 'Industrial Policy and Competition: Disproving a Fallacy?'. Unpublished presentation. Washington, DC: World Bank.

Chang, H.-J. (2008) *Bad Samaritans: The Myth of Free Trade and the Secret History of Capitalism.* New York, Bloomsbury Press.

Lin, J. Y. and Chang, H.-J. (2009) 'DPR Debate: Should Industrial Policy in Developing Countries Conform to Comparative Advantage or Defy It?', *Development Policy Review* 27 (5): 483–502, (Reprinted in chapter II of this volume.)

Lin, J. Y. and Tan, G. (1999) 'Policy Burdens, Accountability, and the Soft Budget Constraint', *American Economic Review: Papers and Proceedings* 89 (2): 426–31.

Maddison, A. (2010) 'Historical Statistics of the World Economy: 1–2008 AD' (www.ggdc.net/maddison/).

Robinson, J. A. and Torvik, R. (2005) 'White Elephants', *Journal of Public Economics* 89: 197–210.

Subramanian, A. and Roy, D. (2003) 'Who Can Explain the Mauritian Miracle? Mede, Romer, Sachs, or Rodrik?' in D. Rodrik (ed.), *In Search of Prosperity: Analytic Narratives on Economic Growth*. Princeton, NJ: Princeton University Press.

Tollison, R. D. and Congleton, R. D. (eds.) (1995) *The Economic Analysis of Rent-Seeking*. Cheltenham: Edward Elgar Publishing.

# APPLYING THE GROWTH
# IDENTIFICATION
# AND FACILITATION
# FRAMEWORK:
# THE CASE OF NIGERIA

# APPLYING THE GROWTH IDENTIFICATION AND FACILITATION FRAMEWORK: THE CASE OF NIGERIA

### WITH VOLKER TREICHEL[†]

## Introduction

Nigeria faces a growing employment crisis. Notwithstanding sustained, high and broad-based growth in the non-oil economy, unemployment has not fallen materially since 1999. More importantly, youth unemployment has markedly risen over the same period. While the number of jobs seems to have grown in line with the labor force, most of these jobs have been created in informal family agriculture. Wage employment, however, has declined. Nigeria needs a strategy aimed at increasing the employment intensity and sustainability of its growth performance.

How to promote economic growth has been a topic for economic discourse and research for a long time. Modern economic growth is a process of continuous technological innovation, industrial upgrading and diversification, and of improvements in the various types of infrastructure and institutional arrangements that constitute the context for business development and wealth creation. While past theories have long emphasized that market mechanisms are essential to getting relative prices right and thereby facilitating an efficient allocation of factors, the growth experience in many countries shows that governments often play a crucial role in facilitating industrial transformation.

New Structural Economics[1] conceptualizes these aspects of growth by integrating some of the insights from the old structural economics, namely the need to take into account, on the one hand, structural features of developing economies in analyzing the process of economic development and, on the other hand, the role of the state in facilitating structural change in developing countries. The key innovation of the approach is that it considers structural differences between developed and developing countries to be endogenous to their endowment structure. With the economy's structure of factor endowment—defined as the relative composition of natural resources, labor, human capital and physical capital—being given at each stage of development and different from one stage to another, the optimal industrial structure will be different at different stages of development. To move from one stage to another, the market requires industrial upgrading and corresponding improvements in hard and soft infrastructure.

The Growth Identification and Facilitation Framework (GIFF) operationalizes key insights of New Structural Economics by developing a methodology for identifying sectors where the country may have a latent comparative advantage and removing binding constraints to facilitate private firms' entry into those industries. The purpose of this paper is to apply the GIFF to Nigeria. The reason for choosing Nigeria is that, in addition to facing a growing employment crisis, Nigeria is also Africa's most populous country and a regional growth pole.[2]

Following an overview of Nigeria's recent economic performance and its impact on employment, the paper describes the basic rationale underlying the GIFF and its methodology. The third section discusses, based on a range of criteria proposed by the GIFF, which sectors or products would be compatible with Nigeria's latent comparative advantage and should therefore be promoted using industrial policy. The fourth section reviews the binding constraints to growth in each of these sectors and discusses specific interventions the government could undertake—in collaboration with the private sector—in order to alleviate these constraints. In view of the fact that shortcomings in governance have in the past often undermined the effectiveness of policy interventions in Nigeria, this section also discusses how the measures could be implemented to ensure accountability and transparency.

## I. Recent Economic Developments in Nigeria

Since 2001, Nigeria has had the longest period of sustained expansion of the non-oil economy since independence. Growth has occurred across all sectors of the economy and has been accelerating. While non-oil growth averaged about 3–4 percent in 1995-2000, it more than doubled to over 7 percent and rose to 8–9 percent in recent years. Even in spite of the current global financial crisis, growth of the non-oil economy remained above 8 percent in 2009 and 2010. While the oil economy contracted in recent years owing to unrest in the Niger Delta, since 2009, the contribution of the Niger Delta has improved as a result of positive effects of the amnesty on oil production (table IV.1).

Moreover, over the last five years, the growth of Nigeria's non-oil economy has been superior to that of most oil-exporting and non-oil exporting countries in Sub-Saharan Africa (table IV.2).

An analysis of the sources of growth shows that, while total factor productivity (TFP) seems to have improved significantly since 2000, relative to the US it has been declining and has only recently improved (figures IV.1 and IV.2).

**Table IV.1: Macroeconomic Aggregates, 2003–2009**
*(percent)*

| Aggregate | 2003 | 2004 | 2005 | 2006 | 2007 | 2008 | 2009 |
|---|---|---|---|---|---|---|---|
| Real GDP | 10.2 | 10.5 | 6.5 | 6.0 | 6.4 | 6.00 | 7.0 |
| Oil GDP | 23.8 | 3.3 | 0.5 | −4.4 | −4.5 | −6.2 | 0.5 |
| Non-Oil GDP | 5.8 | 13.2 | 8.6 | 9.4 | 9.5 | 9.0 | 8.3 |
| Inflation Rate (CPI annual average) | 14.0 | 15.0 | 17.9 | 8.0 | 5.4 | 11.6 | 12.5 |

*Source:* World Development Indicators and various IMF reports.

**Table IV.2: Real Non-Oil GDP Growth, 2003–2009**
*(percent per year)*

| Country | 2003 | 2004 | 2005 | 2006 | 2007 | 2008 | 2009 |
|---|---|---|---|---|---|---|---|
| Nigeria | 5.8 | 13.2 | 8.6 | 9.4 | 9.5 | 9.0 | 8.3 |
| Oil producers | | | | | | | |
| Angola | 10.3 | 9 | 14.1 | 27.5 | 20.1 | 14.7 | 8.1 |
| Cameroon | 4.9 | 4.9 | 3.2 | 2.9 | 4.1 | 3.2 | 3.0 |
| Gabon | 0.8 | 2.3 | 4.3 | 4.9 | 6.2 | 3.0 | 2.3 |
| Chad | 6.0 | −0.5 | 11 | 4.7 | 3.1 | 3.2 | −0.5 |
| Congo, Rep. | 5.4 | 5.0 | 5.4 | 5.9 | 6.6 | 5.4 | 3.9 |
| Equatorial Guinea | 3.7 | 15.4 | 25.8 | 29.8 | 47.2 | 18.1 | 27.6 |
| Non-oil producers | | | | | | | |
| Ghana | 5.2 | 5.6 | 5.9 | 6.4 | 6.3 | 7.3 | 3.5 |
| Kenya | 2.9 | 5.1 | 5.7 | 6.1 | 6.9 | 2.1 | 3.8 |
| Tanzania | 5.7 | 6.7 | 7.4 | 6.7 | 7.1 | 7.4 | 6.0 |
| South Africa | 3.1 | 4.8 | 5.1 | 5.0 | 4.8 | 3.7 | −1.8 |

*Source:* WDI/Various IMF reports.

**Figure IV.1: Evolution of Total Factor Productivity**
*Base Year 1960 = 1*

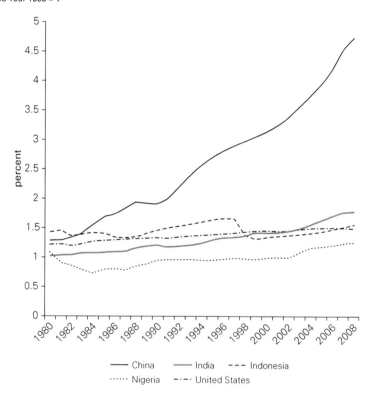

*Source:* Bosworth & Collins, 2003.

**Figure IV.2: Total Factor Productivity Relative to the United States**

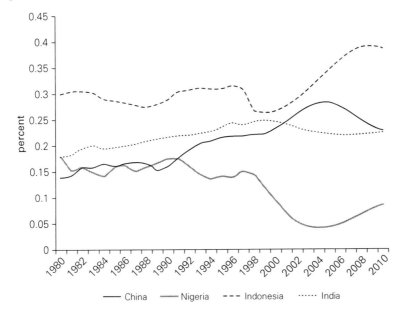

Source: UNIDO, World Productivity Database.

The growth of the non-oil economy was largely driven by the agriculture sector, which contributed on average more than 50 percent (table IV.3).

The contribution of agriculture was followed by that of the wholesale and retail sector (about 20 percent), the manufacturing and financial sectors (4–5 percent), and the telecommunications sector (about 3–4 percent).

Since 2001, changes in the services sector have led to a structural change in Nigeria's economy, manifested in substantial growth of the telecommunications, transportation, hotel and restaurants, construction and real estate, and financial sectors.

The fastest-growing sector has been telecommunications (at an average rate of over 30 percent), followed by the wholesale and retail sectors (about 15 percent) and construction (about 13 percent). Solid minerals grew by over 10 percent on average and manufacturing by about 8–9 percent. Agriculture grew by 6–7 percent on average, the strongest sustained growth performance in more than a decade.

Notwithstanding Nigeria's strong economic performance over the past 10 years, its export and production structure has shown little

**Table IV.3: Contribution to Non-Oil GDP**
*(percent)*

| Sector | 2004 | 2005 | 2006 | 2007 | 2008 | 2009 |
|---|---|---|---|---|---|---|
| Agriculture | 55.3 | 54.5 | 53.5 | 52.3 | 51.1 | 49.9 |
| Solid Mineral | 0.4 | 0.4 | 0.4 | 0.4 | 0.4 | 0.4 |
| Manufacturing | 5.0 | 5.0 | 5.0 | 5.0 | 5.0 | 5.0 |
| Telecommunication | 1.6 | 1.9 | 2.4 | 2.9 | 3.5 | 4.4 |
| Finance & Insurance | 5.5 | 5.2 | 5.0 | 4.8 | 4.6 | 4.4 |
| Wholesale and Retail Trade | 17.4 | 18.2 | 19.2 | 20.2 | 21.1 | 21.7 |
| Building and Construction | 2.0 | 2.01 | 2.1 | 2.1 | 2.2 | 2.3 |
| Others | 13.1 | 13.0 | 12.7 | 12.5 | 12.2 | 12.1 |

*Source:* WDI/IMF.

diversification. Nigeria's exports are concentrated in oil and gas (98 percent), while the structure of the non-oil economy is dominated by the agriculture, wholesale, and retail sectors that serve the domestic market.

## How Have Employment and Incomes Responded to This Strong Growth Performance?

Table IV.4 shows how the labor force has evolved since 1999.

A key feature of Nigeria's working-age population is the high share (approximately one-fourth) of the population that is not in the labor force. As in other African countries, formal unemployment (measured as job seekers who cannot find a job) is extremely low. The vast majority of people outside the labor force are either discouraged job seekers or have not embarked upon a job search, as they do not consider the prospects to be promising. The share of people outside the labor force is a more suitable indicator of unemployment than the official unemployment rate, which consists of individuals who are looking for, but are unable to find, employment. Nonetheless, actual unemployment will be less than 25 percent given that there are individuals not in the labor force who are genuinely not interested in work. However, given the pervasive poverty in Nigeria, that figure is not likely to be high.

Table IV.4 shows that despite the high growth performance, the share of the population that is not in the labor force has remained broadly unchanged. That means that the number of jobs has risen broadly in line with the labor force and that unemployment has remained basically unchanged.

**Table IV.4: Labor Force Status**
*(percent, weighted)*

| Labor force status | 1999 | 2004 | 2006 |
|---|---|---|---|
| Not in the labor force | 25.3 | 23.0 | 25.2 |
| In the labor force | 74.7 | 77.0 | 74.8 |
| Unemployment status | | | |
| Employed | 97.8 | 97.0 | 97.4 |
| Unemployed | 2.2 | 3.0 | 2.6 |

*Source:* Francis Teal / Luke Haywood NLSS 2003-2004 and General Household Survey
(GHS) 1999–2006. Sample includes population aged 15–65 not in schooling.

Table IV.5 shows the evolution of employment broken down by family agriculture, non-agriculture self-employed (that is, mostly urban) and wage employment.

From 1999 to 2006, the most important structural changes that have occurred in Nigeria's labor force have been a shift *into* agriculture employment and *out of* wage employment: the proportion of the sample population aged 15 to 65 (excluding those in full-time education) with wage jobs *declined* over this period (from 15 percent in 1999 to 10 percent in 2006). The same is also true for those classified as non-agriculture self-employed (their share of the population fell from 24.1 to 22.9 percent). The category that saw a major increase in this share of the population was family agriculture, which rose from 30.8 to 37.8 percent.[3]

Table IV.6 provides further insights into the development of wage employment since 1999: Wage employment in parastatals, ministries and public companies has declined, while employment in the private sector and others (including NGOs, international organizations and associations) has risen.

The decline of wage employment reflects three developments: (i) the retrenchment of civil servants and the privatization of many parastatals led to a sharp decline in public service employment, which has long dominated employment in the formal sector and continues to represent the largest share of wage employment; (ii) many private industries with large wage employment, notably the textile industry, have been in decline for a number of years and have shed a considerable part of their work force; and (iii) sectors of the economy that have grown quickly, such as wholesale/retail, construction and agriculture, have been, to a significant extent, in the informal sector, while those in the formal sector, for example, the

**Table IV.5: Types of Employment as a Percentage of the Sample Population**
*(percent, weighted)*

| Type of employment | 1999 | 2004 | 2006 |
|---|---|---|---|
| Family agriculture | 30.8 | 36.6 | 37.8 |
| Non-agriculture self-employed | 24.1 | 25.8 | 22.9 |
| Non-agriculture unpaid family work | 0 | 0.1 | 0.1 |
| Wage employment | 15.0 | 10.4 | 10.0 |
| Apprenticeship | 2.1 | 1.1 | 1.9 |
| Unemployed | 1.7 | 2.4 | 1.9 |
| Not in the labor force | 26.4 | 23.7 | 25.5 |

*Source:* Francis Teal / Luke Haywood NLSS 2003-2004 and GHS 1999–2006.

**Table IV.6: Types of Wage Employment**
*(percent, weighted)*

| Type of employment | 1999 | 2004 | 2006 |
|---|---|---|---|
| Other | 22.8 | 25.2 | 29.6 |
| Parastatals and ministries | 48.6 | 42.2 | 45.6 |
| Private companies | 17.0 | 20.5 | 18.0 |
| Public companies | 11.6 | 12.0 | 6.9 |

*Source:* Francis Teal / Luke Haywood NLSS 2003–2004 and GHS 1999–2006.

financial services and hospitality industries, either are not very employment intensive or added labor from a very low base, failing to make a
significant difference in the growth of wage employment.

Two features stand out:

- Among the young, the share of family agriculture almost doubled from
  1999 to 2006.
- By 2006, the share of young people outside the labor force in the urban
  areas had appreciably increased. A more detailed review of the share of
  the people outside the labor force suggests that most of them consist of
  women engaged in household work and men who have never had any
  employment experience.

This picture generally supports the conclusion that youth unemployment has been on the rise since 1999, an alarming trend in view of the
strong growth performance in recent years.

The pattern of growth in Nigeria and its relation to the evolution of
Nigeria's labor market can be described as follows:

- Nigeria's strong growth in recent years has been dominated by the agriculture sector. In the labor market this has been reflected in a shift of

employment into family agriculture. The considerable growth of employment in the agriculture sector is consistent with the absence of improvements in agricultural productivity.

• Creation of contractual wage jobs in the rapidly growing sectors of the economy was unable to compensate for the loss of wage jobs in the public sector, parastatals and ministries, leading to a decline in wage employment.

With the share of population outside the labor force unchanged for the population as a whole and rising for the lowest age bracket, Nigeria's growth performance has clearly not responded to the aspirations of its population.

Nigeria's strong growth performance reflected primarily two factors: (i) sound macroeconomic policies that created a more favorable environment for private investment, and (ii) sectoral policies, such as the banking consolidation exercise that directly boosted growth in specific sectors of the economy. Both macroeconomic and structural policies contributed to confidence in a new era in the Nigerian economy and thus promoted investment, substantially fueled by foreign direct investment and remittances.

However, this investment was more focused on capital-intensive than employment-intensive industries. Investment occurred primarily in the oil and gas and the telecommunications industries, where returns were particularly high. Hence, few productivity improvements occurred in sectors that are employment-intensive and consistent with the comparative advantage of the economy, such as the labor-intensive manufacturing sector. As a result, the infrastructure constraints became more binding in these sectors of the economy, limiting improvements in their productivity and competitiveness and hence their ability to generate employment. A forward-looking growth strategy needs to focus on improving productivity in the employment-intensive sectors of the economy.

The next section identifies the sectors that Nigeria should target based on the methodology proposed by the Growth Identification and Facilitation Framework.

## II. The Growth Identification and Facilitation Framework

New Structural Economics notes that modern economic growth is a process of continuous technological innovation, industrial upgrading and diversification, and improvements in the various types of infrastructure and institutional arrangements that constitute the context of business development and wealth creation. At any given point in time, the structure of a country's endowment, that is, the relative abundance of factors that the country possesses, determines relative factor prices and thus the optimal industrial structure. A low-income country with abundant labor or natural resources and scarce capital will have comparative advantage and be competitive in labor-intensive or resource-intensive industries. Hence, the optimal industrial structure in a country which will make the country most competitive is endogenously determined by its endowment structure. For a developing country to reach the income level of advanced countries, it needs to upgrade its industrial structure to the same relative capital-intensity of the advanced countries.

A country's endowment structure is not static, but will depend on the rate of capital accumulation and technological progress. The change in relative prices associated with these changes will affect the type of industries in which the country has a latent comparative advantage and hence the optimal industrial structure, given that, in order to be competitive, the new industry needs to be consistent with a country's latent comparative advantage.[4] Of particular importance to the latent comparative advantage is the wage level. By imitating or licensing to obtain technology—a process that is less expensive than inventing the technology on their own—low-income countries will be able to produce the same commodities at a significantly lower cost than developed countries provided the enabling conditions have been created. That way the country can exploit the latecomer advantages by developing matured industries in dynamically growing, more advanced countries with endowment structures similar to theirs. By following carefully selected lead countries, latecomers can emulate the leader-follower, flying-geese pattern that has served well all successful economies since the 18th century.

The process of upgrading the industrial structure to a higher level consistent with the factor endowment cannot rely solely on the market mechanism. For example, starting a new industry may be difficult because of the lack of complementary inputs or adequate infrastructure for the new industry even if the targeted industry is consistent with the economy's comparative advantage. Private firms will not be able to internalize those investments in their decision to upgrade or diversify. Therefore, the government has an important role in providing or coordinating investments in necessary infrastructure and complementary inputs.

In addition, innovation which underlies the industrial upgrading and diversification process is a risky process, as it presents a first-mover problem. Both failure and success of a first mover create externalities. For example, firms that are first movers pay the cost of failure and produce valuable information for other firms. At the same time, when first movers succeed, their experience also provides valuable information to other market participants about the type of industries that can be profitable in the specific country. However, if new firms enter on a large scale this may largely eliminate the possible rents that the first mover may enjoy. In a developed country, a successful first mover can in general be rewarded with a patent and enjoy the rent created by a matured industry. However, in a developing country, a new patent may not be available, as the industry may already be located within the global industrial frontier. Therefore, the first mover will not be able to obtain a patent for its entry into a new industry in its economy, and, as a result, some form of direct support by the government to pioneer firms may be justifiable.

The GIFF proposes a new approach to help identify industries where the economies may have a latent comparative advantage and remove binding constraints to facilitate private firms' entry into those industries, or facilitate industries that are already active in the country to grow fast. In this context, the GIFF argues that picking winners is inevitable because the binding constraints may be sector specific and removing them may not be possible for the private sector alone. Therefore the main issue is to minimize the error margin of picking the wrong industry. The key risk in this regard is that countries target industries that are too advanced and far beyond the latent comparative advantage or target industries in which the country has already lost its comparative advantage.

The GIFF proposes a six-step approach to growth identification and facilitation. Three of these steps aim at the selection of sectors. After the sectors are selected, value-chain analyses can be used to identify the binding constraints for private firms' entry and growth in those sectors (box IV.1).

## Box IV.1:  Applying the GIFF: Comparative Value Chain Analysis

A forthcoming report by the World Bank on Light Manufacturing in Africa (World Bank 2011) demonstrates how to implement an innovative form of value chain analysis to both determine the competitiveness of a sector as well as assist governments and the private sector in identifying the constraints which most impact the cost competitiveness of domestically produced products on the global market.

In the usual value-chain analysis, the advantages, bottlenecks and policy issues would be analyzed within the country of study with some comparison between sectors within the economy. In the comparative approach, however, China and Vietnam are being chosen as benchmark countries in order to compare the cost competitiveness of African production of particular products, chosen to be as like-for-like as possible.

After applying the GIFF to arrive at several sub-sectors which could potentially be successfully produced in SSA (Ethiopia, Tanzania and Zambia were the sample countries), in-depth value chain analyses were conducted for particular products in each of those sub-sectors in order to gain a representative view of the competitiveness and constraints of the sub-sector. The analysis included a quantitative breakdown of the proportion and cost of inputs, efficiency input use, logistic costs, labor productivity, production wastage and efficiency etc. This data was gathered from a reasonable sample of firms in all five countries producing similar products in each of the five identified sub-sectors. Each component which impacts the cost and competitiveness of the firms was compared between China, Vietnam and SSA. The results were conclusive in identifying the cost elements which vary significantly between East Asia and SSA, thereby identifying the priority areas for intervention. The results also screened out those sectors where the country does not have comparative advantage by calculating the domestic resource costs.

For Nigeria, value chain analyses have been conducted in recent years for several key sectors which have been valuable in highlighting the constraints and opportunities in the sectors studied. However, the new approach proposed in this paper is to use the GIFF to identify sectors where Nigeria may have some comparative

*(Box continued next page)*

**Box IV.1: Continued**

advantage, latent or revealed. A comparative value chain analysis could then be undertaken in those identified sectors which will provide rigorous evidence and support for a prioritized program by government and private sector to overcome key constraints in targeted sectors. For example, the comparative value chain provides some more conclusive evidence on the wage difference in specific sectors as well as the difference in labor productivity in those sectors. That way, conclusions can be drawn on both the poverty-reducing employment effect of expansion in a sector, as well as the labor cost advantage (or disadvantage) which can be a crucial aspect in determining competitiveness of a sector.

- The first step consists of identifying tradable goods and services that have been growing dynamically for about 20 years in fast-growing countries with similar endowment structures that have a per capita GDP about 100 to 300 percent higher than their own. In many cases, given that wages tend to rise in the growth process, a fast-growing country that has produced goods and services for about 20 years may begin to lose its comparative advantage in this sector.[5] In addition, Nigeria could domestically produce simple manufacturing goods which are labor-intensive, have limited economies of scale, require only small investments, and are imported. This step also allows the identification of industries that are new to the country, but may be good business opportunities for Nigeria.
- Second, among the industries on the list, the government may give priority to those in which some domestic private firms have already entered spontaneously, and try to identify: (i) the obstacles that are preventing these firms from upgrading the quality of their products; or (ii) the barriers that limit entry to those industries by other private firms. For such industries, the government could also adopt specific measures to encourage foreign direct investment in the higher-income country to invest in these industries.
- Third, in addition to the industries identified on the list of opportunities for tradable goods and services in step 1, developing country governments

should pay close attention to successful self-discoveries by private enterprises and provide support to scale up those industries.

The application of this methodology to Nigeria is discussed below.

## III. Selecting Sectors

### Selecting a Country with a Per Capita Income 100–300 percent above Nigeria's

Table IV.7 shows a list of countries that have a per-capita GDP of 100 to 300 percent of that of Nigeria. Removing slowly growing countries, i.e., countries growing at less than 6 percent per year, leaves the following countries: Indonesia, China, Vietnam and India.

Using the criterion of factor endowment, among these countries Indonesia would stand out as the country with the greatest similarity with Nigeria because it is a natural resource-rich country and a former member of OPEC, but also specializes in labor-intensive production.[6] Indonesia has effectively used both its natural resources as well its abundant labor supply to develop industries that correspond to its latent comparative advantage. As discussed in a blog by Justin Lin (March 2011), a resource-rich, labor-abundant country can use both resource-rich and labor-abundant countries as comparators.[7]

While not a resource-rich country, Vietnam's high growth rate makes it an appropriate comparator, especially in view of its labor-intensive

**Table IV.7: GDP Per Capita PPP in 2009**
*(constant 2005 international $)*

| Country | GDP per capita | Percent of Nigeria |
|---|---|---|
| Nigeria | 2,001 | 100 |
| Vietnam | 2,682 | 134 |
| India | 2,970 | 148 |
| Philippines | 3,216 | 161 |
| Indonesia | 3,813 | 191 |
| Morocco | 4,081 | 204 |
| Paraguay | 4,107 | 205 |
| Egypt, Arab Rep. | 5,151 | 257 |
| China | 6,200 | 310 |
| Tunisia | 7,512 | 375 |

*Source:* World Development Indicators.

economy. Its strong growth performance and consequent rise in labor costs could also quickly erode Vietnam's cost advantage in certain labor-intensive industries.

Another country that lends itself as a comparator is China. China has a per capita income that is about 300 percent higher than that of Nigeria and is not a natural-resource-rich country. However, given its fast growth, large population size and domestic market, as well as fast ascent on the technological value-added ladder, its production structure may be suited for imitation given that it may be in the process of losing its cost advantage in some of the industries that have in the past driven its growth performance. This is especially true if Nigeria can use the rent from natural resources to improve its infrastructure and education.

A further comparator country is India. While India has not consistently followed its comparative advantage of abundant unskilled labor, the availability of skilled labor has been successfully used for several new sectors, such as call centers. Hence in some areas, India's production structure has been in line with its latent comparative advantage.

## Which Commodities Do These Countries Export?

Table IV.8 identifies industries in these comparator countries where production is labor intensive or requires natural resources, and provides brief comments on Nigeria's potential in these industries.

### Imports of Labor-Intensive Manufactured Goods Have Limited Economies of Scale, and Require Only Small Investments

A review of imports of labor-intensive manufactured goods with limited economies of scale shows the following commodities (at the 4-digit SITC level) (table IV.9).

### Industries Where the Private Sector Is Already Active and Where Successful Self-Discovery Has Taken Place

A third criterion for selection is to choose sectors in which Nigeria's private sector has become increasingly active and where successful self-discovery has already taken place, such as ICT, light manufacturing, food processing, wholesale and retail, construction and car parts, meat and poultry, oil palm, and cocoa. None of these industries currently produces for export.

**Table IV.8: Identifying Sectors for Growth: Key Exports of China, India, Vietnam, and Indonesia**

| China | Vietnam | India | Indonesia | Nigeria potential |
|---|---|---|---|---|
| Rubber manufactures | Crude rubber | | Palm oil | Large domestic production. High potential established in detailed value chain analysis. However, low export value of USD 300,000 in 2009. Tire industry closed several years ago as it could not compete with imports. Natural rubber is Nigeria's 10th largest export. Large rubber plant exists in Calabar, Cross River. |
| Apparel & clothing accessories; textile yarn, fabrics etc.; dyeing & tanning | Apparel & clothing accessories; textile yarn, fabrics etc. | Apparel & clothing accessories; textile yarn, fabrics etc. | Apparel & clothing accessories; textile yarn, fabrics etc. | Textiles is a failing industry primarily because competitiveness with imports is undermined by high costs of power in Nigeria, as well as a small wage differential to comparator countries which produce at large volumes. |
| Footwear; travel goods, handbags; leather manufactures | Footwear | | | Leather – already private sector momentum, goat/kidskin leather is the 4th largest export. Industry already in place in Kano that needs better enabling conditions. |
| Telecommunications & sound recording equipment; photographic | | Telecommunications & sound recording equipment | Telecommunications & sound recording equipment | Since December 2010, two operators have begun TV assembly in Lagos on CKD basis. Large potential for scaling up exists, provided land is being made available. |
| Office machines & automatic data projectors | Electronic integrated circuits, telecoms. | | Printed circuits, electronically integrated circuits, insulated wire and optical fiber | IT –Knock-down of computers is successfully taking place. |
| Manufactured fertilizers | | | | Indigenous fertilizer plants exist and are growing fast; Nigeria has refineries and fertilizer plants, but requires enabling conditions, such as the removal of the petroleum subsidy. Also, production of petrochemicals needs to match with specific type of refining capacity. |

| | | | | |
|---|---|---|---|---|
| Fish, crustaceans prepared | Fish, crustaceans prepared | Fish, crustaceans prepared | Fish, crustaceans prepared | Food & beverages: booming sector oriented to the domestic market; Cocoa beans are 3rd largest export; frozen crustaceans 5th largest export. |
| Vegetables & fruit | Cereals & cereal preparations; coffee, tea, cocoa, spices manufactured | Cereals & cereal preparations; vegetables and fruit | Fixed vegetable oils and fats; coffee, tea, cocoa, spices manufactured | Both already active in Nigeria; to scale up, enabling conditions, especially power and a cold chain, are required. |
| Road vehicles | | Road vehicles; other transport equipment | | Onitsha cluster in Anambra state focuses on car parts; motorcycles and tractors are assembled in a knock-down assembly already. |
| Furniture and parts thereof; cork and wood manufactures | Furniture and parts thereof | | | Furniture industry active in Nigeria and rapidly growing. |
| Paper, paperboard etc. | | | Paper, paperboard etc. | Already active and growing. Logistical support could help accelerate growth. |
| Medicinal and pharmaceutical products | | medicinal and pharmaceutical products | | Industry established; but fragmented. Mergers could help reduce cost. |
| Machinery - electrical, metalworking or power-generating | Machinery - electrical, industrial | Machinery - electrical, general industrial, power-generating | electrical machinery | Metal industry in place; but too small and scattered to be cost effective. Scaling up could be facilitated through creation of clusters. |
| Organic chemicals; chemical materials & products; artificial resins, plastic materials; inorganic chemicals | | Organic chemicals | | Organic chemicals industry could benefit from abundant supply of raw materials; however, petroleum subsidy is major distortion blocking larger foreign direct investment. |

*Source:* Authors' calculations using declining export shares based on Comtrade data.

**Table IV.9: Nigeria's Top Imports, 2010**

| Product (4-digit) | 1,000 of US$ | percent |
|---|---|---|
| Cereals and cereal preparations | 863,917 | 10.7 |
| Telecommunications & sound recording | 330,136 | 4.1 |
| Fish, crustaceans, mollusk, preparation | 276,152 | 3.4 |
| Other transport equipment* | 255,846 | 3.2 |
| Medicinal and pharmaceutical products | 241,312 | 3.0 |
| Manufactures of metal | 214,157 | 2.7 |
| Artificial resins, plastic materials, cellulose | 151,868 | 1.9 |
| Essential oils & perfume material | 104,932 | 1.3 |
| Professional, scientific & controlling equipment | 101,065 | 1.3 |
| Dairy products and birds' eggs | 99,125 | 1.2 |
| Miscellaneous manufactured articles | 98,169 | 1.2 |
| Rubber manufactures, n.e.s. | 96,489 | 1.2 |
| Paper, paperboard, articles of paper | 91,269 | 1.1 |
| Textile yarn, fabrics, made-up articles | 82,120 | 1.0 |
| Beverages | 58,480 | 0.7 |

*Source:* COMTRADE database, 4-digit SITC Revision 2.

* Since transport equipment may be protected by patents, Nigeria could start by producing generic products.

However, all of them have significant employment and growth potential and could be upgraded for exports.

Figure IV.3 highlights how the growth and employment potential of a sector may differ on a regional or geographical basis. For example, rice production has a lower employment and growth potential in Kano than in Kaduna. And the wholesale and retail sector has greater growth potential in Lagos, given the very large domestic market, than in Kano, where the market is smaller. Such detailed regional analysis is very important, given the great disparity in Nigeria.

In addition to these sectors, there are a number in which successful self-discovery has already taken place. For example, production of suitcases has recently successfully started and is expanding rapidly. At this stage, 60 percent of the required parts are being produced domestically, which has allowed for the unit cost to fall significantly; also about 50 percent of the domestic demand is being met through domestically produced suitcases. A further area of successful self-discovery is TV assembly, which began as recently as December 2010. Both areas of production could be further expanded rapidly, including for exports, if the government provided assistance toward scaling up, e.g., through better access to finance.

**Figure IV.3:  Prioritization of Value Chains for Further Investigation**

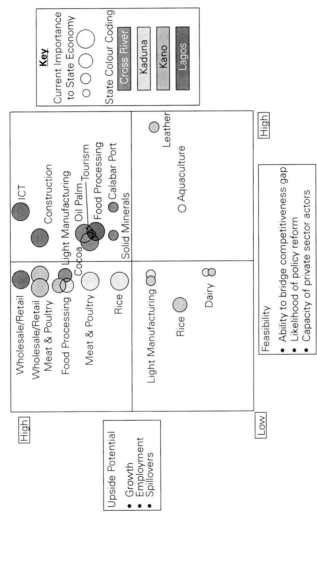

## What Are the Sectors in Which Nigeria Has a Potential Comparative Advantage Based on This Analysis?

The sections above use three different criteria to identify sectors with high growth and employment potential that could be the subject of targeted interventions. First is the identification of dynamically growing tradable industries in fast-growing countries with similar factor endowment and a per capita income 100 to 300 percent above that of Nigeria. Second is the review of Nigeria's imports to identify sectors that require only small investments and have limited economies of scale and could therefore be manufactured domestically. Third is the identification of domestic sectors where successful self-discovery has already taken place or that are already growing fast, but have a high employment impact and could grow faster.

Upon application of the first criterion, seven sectors emerge quite clearly for further analysis, as they represent industries in countries with a similar endowment structure: footwear, including sports shoes; textiles; TV recorders; aquaculture; motor vehicle parts; vegetable oil; and fertilizers. Additional sectors are motorcycles; meat, meat products, and oil seeds; fertilizers, petroleum products; leather; travel goods; office machines; pharmaceutical products; and organic chemicals.

Based on the second criterion, the following four sectors would be prioritized: vehicles parts; color TV receivers; tires; and metal manufacture.

The third criterion, which focuses on sectors that are already growing fast, yields a list of target sectors that is slightly different from that identified through the first two criteria: light manufacturing, food processing, meat and poultry, palm oil and rice, telecommunications, leather, wholesale and retail, and construction.

Nigeria is a country rich in natural resources, in particular oil and gas, but also solid minerals. Industries associated with these natural resources, in particular refined petroleum products, petrochemicals, cosmetics and plastics, are currently not particularly active in Nigeria. However, given that they are imported in large quantities, and raw materials are available in abundance, they should be subject to a detailed value chain analysis aimed at assessing whether they can be produced at a comparative advantage in Nigeria.

How should the targeted sectors be selected from this list? The key criteria will be the upside potential of the sector in terms of growth and employment creation, as well as the feasibility of growth in terms of private sector capability and the public sector regulatory framework. These questions can ultimately be answered only through detailed value chain analysis, along the lines of the methodology described in Box 1. However, as a first approximation, the list of potential target industries can be narrowed down further by applying a set of pre-screening criteria developed in the context of the forthcoming report on light manufacturing in Africa.

First, sectors with very high capital requirements and only small domestic markets should be eliminated, given that Nigeria is not a capital abundant country and initially success will be in catering to the large domestic market. Second, goods should ideally be produced by small and medium-size enterprises in the comparator countries, given that large enterprises are currently not prevalent in Nigeria. However, to the extent that Nigeria's business environment could be made conducive to attracting large-scale foreign direct investment, the goods could also be produced by large companies in comparator countries. Third, a supply chain should exist for each product in the domestic market. Fourth, raw materials should be available in the domestic market or be easily imported. And fifth, labor skills should be easily transferable.

Table IV.10 shows whether the pre-selected sectors meet the criteria: Wholesale/retail and construction sectors have not been included, as they are not sectors that would be imitated from other countries, but may still benefit from targeted interventions to make them more responsive to higher demand and more employment-intensive.

Most of these sectors meet the pre-screening criteria, that is, they have some upside potential for growth and meet feasibility criteria. A notable exception is sportswear—unavailability of PVC in the domestic market creates a comparative disadvantage and has already resulted in the closure of domestic production. Its competitiveness may depend on the establishment of a domestic petrochemical industry. Also, in the comparator countries, fertilizer and petrochemical production as well as TV production may not take place in small or medium-size enterprises; however, targeted foreign direct investment may be able to attract investments to establish larger firms, including through joint ventures, provided enabling conditions have been put in place.

**Table IV.10: Criteria for Screening Potential Subsectors**

| Product groups | Criteria 1: Production has low capital requirements and there is a significant domestic market | Criteria 2: Production in comparator countries is by small and medium-size enterprises | Criteria 3: There is some factor endowment in Nigeria — supply chain exists in the domestic market (domestic or imported raw materials); labor skills should be easily transferable. |
|---|---|---|---|
| Footwear, including sports shoes, Travel bags | Yes | Yes | Leather supply chain exists; however, PVC required for sports shoes does not exist. Leather shoes and travel bags are already being manufactured and see strong growth. |
| TV electronics | Yes | In some cases | Raw materials can be easily imported. Not a high-skills type of production. |
| Tires and motor vehicle parts | Yes | Yes | Rubber and associated supply chain exists. International companies were active in Nigeria. |
| Vegetable oil, aquaculture, palm oil and rice; food processing, meat and poultry | Yes | Yes | Yes |
| Motorcycles and tractors | Yes | Yes | Yes |
| Fertilizers, petrochemicals, organic chemicals | Yes | No | Nigeria is abundant in oil and gas. Labor skills are transferable. |
| Light manufacturing | Yes | Yes | Yes. Vibrant domestic industry with relevant skills already in place. |
| Leather | Yes | Yes | Yes |
| Pharmaceuticals | Yes | Yes | Yes |
| Paper board | Yes | Yes | Yes |

*Source:* World Bank 2011.

In a second step, Nigeria's basic wage competitiveness in these sectors needs to be reviewed to determine whether that would allow Nigeria to reap the advantage of backwardness.

Table IV.11 summarizes wage data for China, Vietnam, and Nigeria on a sectoral basis.

**Table IV.11: Average Wage, Including Benefits, by Industry (US$)**

| Sector | Skilled labor | | | | | Unskilled labor | | | | |
|---|---|---|---|---|---|---|---|---|---|---|
| | Nigeria | Ethiopia (ICA) | Ethiopia | Vietnam | China | Nigeria | Ethiopia (ICA) | Ethiopia | Vietnam | China |
| Food | 135 | 82 | 89–141 | 181–363 | 398–442 | 87 | 45 | 26–52 | 78–207 | 192–236 |
| Garments | 85 | 82 | 37–185 | 119–181 | 331–370 | 54 | 48 | 26–48 | 78–130 | 237–296 |
| Textiles | 120 | 71 | | | | 71 | 20 | | | |
| Machinery & equipment | 163 | | | | | 125 | | | | |
| Chemicals | 212 | | | | | 127 | | | | |
| Electronics | 119 | | | | | 79 | | | | |
| Non-metallic minerals | 106 | | | | | 66 | | | | |
| Wood, wood products & furn | 102 | 151 | 81–119 | 181–259 | 393–442 | 67 | 35 | 37–52 | 85–135 | 206–251 |
| Metal & metal products | 107 | | 181 | 168–233 | 265–369 | 82 | | 89 | 117–142 | 192–265 |
| Other manufacturing | 130 | 154 | | | | 87 | 67 | | | |

Source: Nigeria – Productivity and Investment Climate Survey, 2009; Ethiopia Investment Climate Survey, Manufacturing 2006 (reported values are mean over sample); Others – Light Manufacturing in Africa (2001), vol. II (values reported are the range reported by sample firms).

Note: Ethiopia has been included to provide another African country as a reference for Nigeria.

These data confirm Nigeria's relative cost advantage in cheap labor in the industries identified above.

## IV. How Can Growth in the Selected Value Chains Be Promoted?

In addition to proposing the above methodology to identify target sectors, the GIFF also identifies a number of steps to encourage growth in these targeted sectors. As discussed above, the government can try to identify the obstacles that are preventing these firms from upgrading the quality of their products or the barriers that limit entry to those industries through value chain analysis or the Growth Diagnostic studies suggested by Hausmann, Rodrik, and Velasco (2005). In addition, the government can adopt specific measures to encourage firms in the higher-income countries identified in the first step to invest in these industries. Moreover, in developing countries with poor infrastructure and an unfriendly business environment, the government can invest in industrial parks or export processing zones. Such industrial parks or EPZs typically provide conditions that are specifically targeted at certain sectors or industries, e.g., IT or light manufacturing, and are often built around already existing industry clusters. Lastly, the government can also provide limited incentives to domestic pioneer firms or foreign investors that work within the list of industries identified in step 1 in order to compensate for the non-rival public knowledge created by their investments. These steps may include corporate income tax holidays, directed tax credits, or priority access to foreign reserves to import key equipment. In the literature, the former type of intervention is referred to as soft and the latter as hard industrial policy.

The following discusses key constraints in the selected value chains and what specifically could be done about it in the Nigerian context. Available value chain studies provide an analysis of the binding constraints to growth in a number of these value chains.[8] The binding constraints can be broadly categorized in 5 categories: (i) physical infrastructure, in particular lack of power and roads; (ii) business environment (cumbersome procedures); (iii) lack of access to finance; (iv) lack of a technical and vocational education system that corresponds to the needs of the market; and (v) restrictive trade policy. The annex table summarizes binding constraints and the measures that could be undertaken to address them in a number of selected value chains.

Specific measures to be undertaken for each category of constraints to growth could be as follows:

*Physical Infrastructure.* Construction of industrial parks with dedicated power supply and transportation. Construction of independent power plants (IPPs) in geographical areas with high growth potential that already have a high concentration of promising value chains, possibly through the Bank of Industry in close collaboration with state governments.

*Business Environment.* Selective capacity-building in key government agencies, such as the Standards Organization of Nigeria that enforce quality, and reform of business licensing as well as land transactions.

*TVET (Technical and Vocational Education and Training).* Linking growth sectors to skills development through promotion of Innovation Enterprise Institutions (IEI)—an initiative promoted by the Nigeria Board of Technical Education. Developing a National Vocational Qualification framework and calibrating the National Youth Service to assign youth corp participants to jobs matching their qualifications. Encouraging the development and adoption of training standards in traditional apprenticeships through trade associations.

*Access to Finance.* Mobilizing mortgage-based finance by enhancing the availability of mortgages through reform of the land allocation system. Introducing directed credit schemes at concessional interest rates.

*Trade Policy Reform.* Import bans and high tariffs adversely affect competitiveness of a number of value chains. Replacing import bans that adversely affect certain sectors with the highest growth potential with tariffs could be very beneficial to the development of industries. Some protection may still be necessary for sectors with high growth potential that still need to develop.

## Key Constraints for Each Sector

One of the most important challenges for government and the private sector is to identify the most important constraint, which, if alleviated, is likely to allow for the sector to grow faster. The annex table highlights various constraints for each value chain and how they could be addressed in each individual case. The section below discusses some of the findings from meetings with entrepreneurs in Lagos. Lack of electric power is a pervasive constraint in almost every industry and is therefore not specifically mentioned. It is imperative for the Nigerian government to promote construction of IPPs in industrial zones as the main tool for addressing the high cost of power.

On a general note, entrepreneurs call for greater protection from imports through tariffs. In the past, Nigeria has consistently protected domestic industry through high tariffs or import bans. However, the desired improvement in domestic output has not materialized, as key constraints to greater productivity have remained unaddressed, in particular the lack of power. Against this background, it would be preferable if continued protection was associated with a pre-commitment on the part of government to gradually phase out protection and address some of the key binding constraints in a comprehensive package of measures, e.g., the construction of independent power plants, the establishment of a fast-track window for imports of manufacturers and specific financial interventions to facilitate access to finance of key value chains. Import bans should be replaced by tariffs, given the fact that most import bans cannot be enforced and only encourage smuggling.

**Food processing** (including fruit juices, meat and poultry, noodles and spaghetti and tomato paste) has experienced strong growth in recent years and producers are confident about prospects for further growth. Tomato paste producers indicate that their growth potential would sharply improve if domestic production of tomatoes could be scaled up. In addition, specific government incentives such as for research and development, the full operationalization of the Export Expansion Grant (EEG) and assistance in distributing seeds could allow production to further expand.

**Construction** has a very significant potential for job creation. The primary constraint for faster growth is the unavailability of mortgage financing. Specific interventions to improve the availability of such financing through reform of the land transaction process and the development of mortgage-related financial instruments would be critical to facilitate faster growth. In addition, the industry suffers from shortages of skilled technical labor. Targeted interventions to substantially upgrade the quality of vocational training would help youth unemployment and reduce the cost of construction firms.

**Motorcycle, tractor and TV assembly** are set for rapid expansion. Key constraints are the lack of adequate trade facilitation leading to delays in clearance of imports and the need for land to allow expansion of production and reap benefits from economies of scale.

**Computer assembly** is also growing rapidly. Partnership between the public and private sectors to help reduce the skills gap would be crucial to reduce cost. In addition, the government may facilitate the adoption of broadband internet access in universities and schools.

Following years of decline owing to lack of competitiveness with imports, the **tire industry** ceased production in 2008. Key constraints to greater productivity include (i) the need for natural gas to power an IPP; (ii) the need to rehabilitate the Warri refinery to facilitate availability of black carbon, a key input for tire production; and (iii) the need for a bail-out fund to address the large amount of unserved debt. Gas had not been available owing to the turmoil in the Niger Delta, while the rehabilitation of the refinery had not proceeded on a timely basis. An injection of fresh capital from the government could be crucial to bailing out the industry, especially if packaged with other measures, in particular the rehabilitation of the Warri refinery and concessional loans (based on a performance agreement with the private contractor).

**The metal industry** has been suffering from power shortages and lower price competition from abroad. Nonetheless, some segments of the production, like cast iron and manganese steel, have been prospering, while others, such as aluminum, have been in decline. One of the key obstacles, in addition to the power supply, has been the customs administration which has been delaying the clearance of imported raw materials. However, the most important challenge in facilitating the growth of this industry is the lack of power.

## V. How Should Governance Issues Be Addressed in Implementing These Measures?

One of the most important criticisms against industrial policy is the potential for elite capture of the interventions in a way that could seriously undermine

244 I New Structural Economics

the effectiveness of any policy intervention. Nigeria has a poor track record in governance, traditionally ranking near the bottom of the global Corruption Perception Index. In this context, it is important to establish some principles that would allow proper management of governance-related issues in the implementation of these targeted policy measures. Based on experience in other countries, the following seem to be components that could help improve the governance aspect of these measures:

- Transparency and accountability is best ensured through a public process of agreement and follow-up on the implementation of the agreed measures. For example, as a first step a jobs summit could be held in which private and public sector representatives for key sectors meet, discuss and agree on critical interventions aimed at boosting growth in the individual sector, including selection criteria and appropriate implementation mechanisms. These Memoranda of Understanding could then be published and their implementation reviewed in public fora on a regular basis.
- The agreements should also explicitly specify the results that are to be expected. In addition, they should say that if the results are not achieved, the intervention should be retracted.
- A further measure helping to foster transparency and accountability is to limit the scale of the intervention. Smaller interventions stand a greater chance of transparency than large schemes. This is because the potential for elite capture is directly proportional to the magnitude of rents from government subsidies and other forms of protection and therefore smaller interventions stand a better chance.
- The selection of industries could be delegated to a consulting firm, rather than be handled by the government (as has been the case in Chile).

## VI. Conclusions

This paper has aimed to identify sectors with high growth and employment potential and targeted interventions to remove binding constraints to growth in each of these sectors. The paper concludes that a number of sectors, some of which are already active in Nigeria and some new to Nigeria, may hold significant potential for growth and employment creation and should be subject to detailed value chain analyses that would identify the type of interventions that would allow Nigeria to effectively compete with its competitors. Targeted interventions to promote growth should primarily focus on (i) providing physical infrastructure, especially power, water and sewerage; (ii) improving the business environment; (iii) developing targeted vocational and educational skills programs; (iv) improving the business and regulatory environment; (v) reforming trade policy; and (vi) providing some tax incentives, access to finance, and access to foreign exchange for the targeted sectors.

Of crucial importance in implementing these targeted interventions is the adoption, in parallel, of a range of measures to support good governance as highlighted above. Provided such policies are undertaken in parallel, Nigeria should be in a good position to maintain its strong growth performance, as well as to increase the employment intensity of growth.

# Annex

**Table IV.A1: Growth-Inhibiting Cross-Cutting Constraints, Interventions and Expected Outcomes**

| Potential sectors | Growth constraints | Intervention approach | Low quality & unproductive labor inputs | Finance | Distortionary trade policy | Lack of regulatory enforcement on product standards | Poor environmental practices & enforcement | Unreliable & high cost infrastructure | Poor logistics & handling | Onerous administrative procedures | Technology and information asymmetries |
|---|---|---|---|---|---|---|---|---|---|---|---|
| Real estate & construction: rising demand and emerging middle class provides significant upside potential | Unreliable and high-cost infrastructure services (power, water, transport); poor logistics & handling. under-developed freight transport services system | Public-private partnerships and sectoral reforms in the power sector and other key infrastructure areas (tariff and regulatory reform) | | | | | | X | X | | |
| | | Construction of independent power plants in geographical areas with high growth potential that already have a high concentration of promising value chains | | | | | | | | | |
| | Distortionary trade policy accompanied by poor border controls, import bans on factor inputs; tariff and duties to protect domestic goods. | Replace import bans on key inputs, such as rebar steel, with tariffs (15% tariff would maximize incentives for formalizing trade) | | | X | | | | | | |
| | | Reform customs procedures, including through risk-based customs clearances | | | | | | | | | |
| | Onerous administrative procedures, planning approvals & building permits; burdensome business regulatory compliance, including EEG | Initiate administrative reform program to simplify individual procedures in relevant agencies to speed up the compliance/approval process | | | | | | | | X | |

(continued next page)

| Issue | Recommendation | | | | | | | |
|---|---|---|---|---|---|---|---|---|
| | Redesign or reengineer procedures through careful process mapping and streamline legal basis as necessary | | | | | | | |
| | Provide strong technical assistance in the preparation/design stage followed by hands-on implementation with stakeholders | | | | | | | |
| Low-quality and unproductive labor inputs: shortage of skilled labor, lack of vocational training, unskilled labor exhibits low productivity | Explore possibility of using the Innovative Enterprise Institutions to deliver training programs | X | | | | | | |
| | Develop new and strengthen existing vocational institutions to increase access to unskilled, informal labor sector including programs designed for practical teaching programs (e.g. Vocational Training Centre of Excellence in Lagos for the construction sector) | | | | | | | |
| Lack of regulator Enforcement on Product Standards, SON, Local Town Planning Authority | Deliver capacity building program to strengthen inspection activities of relevant government authorities pertaining to quality and safety standards of products in the construction industry | | | | | X | | |
| Inadequate development of the mortgage market | Facilitate development of mortgage-related financial services through reform of land transactions and development of the financial sector | | X | | | | | |

**Table IV.A1:** *(Continued)*

| Potential Sectors | Growth constraints | Intervention approach | Low quality & unproductive labor inputs | Finance | Distortionary trade policy | Lack of regulatory enforcement on product standards | Poor environmental practices & enforcement | Unreliable & high cost infrastructure | Poor logistics & handling | Onerous administrative procedures | Technology and information asymmetries |
|---|---|---|---|---|---|---|---|---|---|---|---|
| | Poor environmental practices and enforcement; inadequate procedures for disposal of construction materials | Provide technical assistance to the State Ministry of Environment to develop the appropriate level of resources and expertise, as well as the institutional authority to enforce environmental regulations under its statutory responsibility | | | | | | X | | | |
| Food processing: rising incomes have spurred demand for alcoholic and non-alcoholic beverages and for processed foods | Raw material costs sources locally are high because of import bans, leading to high and uncompetitive prices of products, produced with imported raw material | Replace import bans on key inputs with tariffs and reform customs procedures, including through risk-based customs clearances | | X | | | | | | | |
| | Coordination failures, weak linkages between processors and producers | Industry associations to address information and knowledge transfers to SME processors | | | | | | | | | X |

| Constraint | Recommendation | | | | | | |
|---|---|---|---|---|---|---|---|
| Onerous administrative procedures, land registration | Initiate administrative reform program to simplify individual procedures in relevant agencies to speed up compliance/approval process | | | | | | |
| | Redesign or reengineer procedures through careful process mapping and streamline legal basis as necessary | | x | | | | |
| | Provide strong technical assistance in the preparation/design stage followed by hands-on implementaton with stakeholders | | | | | | |
| Poor logistics & handling; poor rural roads to dispersed small scale farms; poor handling practices (no temperature control, improper bagging, storage etc.); under-developed freight transport services system; business environment (power, water, roads) is lacking; IPP and other dedicated infrastructure for industrial areas with high volumes of food processing | Deliver an integrated logistics program for the food sector from farm gate to the processing stage covering farm storage, drayage, wholesale markets, rural roads and line haul transport to the processor, complete with temperature control equipment as warranted | | | x | x | | |

(continued next page)

**Table IV.A1:** *(Continued)*

| Potential Sectors | Growth constraints | Intervention approach | Low quality & unproductive labor inputs | Finance | Distortionary trade policy | Lack of regulatory enforcement on product standards | Poor environmental practices & enforcement | Unreliable & high cost infrastructure | Poor logistics & handling | Onerous administrative procedures | Technology and information asymmetries |
|---|---|---|---|---|---|---|---|---|---|---|---|
| | Lack of skilled labor: support to the technical and vocational training system for food technology training; Low quality and unproductive labor inputs: shortage of skilled labor, lack of vocational training, unskilled labor exhibits low productivity. | Explore possibility of using the Innovative Enterprise Institutions to deliver training programs | | | | | | | | | |
| | | Develop new and strengthen existing vocational institutes to increase access to unskilled, informal labor sector including programs designed for practical teaching programs (e.g. Vocational Training Centre of Excellence in Lagos for the construction sector); MAN and NASSI to provide outreach for private sector interventions | X | | | | | | | | |
| | | Sponsor technical advisory trips to locations that incorporate religious and traditional practices of the domestic target groups, e.g. Islamic run abattoirs and butchers in Dubai, Malaysia, South Africa | | | | | | | | | |

| | Issue | Recommendation | | | | | | |
|---|---|---|---|---|---|---|---|---|
| | Lack of regulator Enforcement on Product Standards - SON; State Dept of Agriculture; Veterinary Services; Livestock & Poultry services; Agric Services, Pest control, produce inspection and fisheries; NAFDAC | Deliver capacity building program to strengthen inspection activities of relevant government authorities pertaining to quality and safety standards of products in the agriculture, animal livestock and food industries. In particular, harmonize roles of food inspection agencies for seamless cooperation (State Ministry of Agriculture, State Ministry of Health, and NAFDAC) | | | X | | | |
| | Poor environmental practices and enforcement, improper environmental control of animal waste at public abattoirs | Provide technical assistance to the State Ministry of Environment to develop the appropriate level of resources and expertise, as well as the institutional authority to enforce environmental regulations under its statutory responsibility | | | | X | | |
| **Meat & Poultry:** urbanization, emerging middle class, and high income elasticity have created high demand for meat; fast food industry very important as source of demand | Abattoirs are dysfunctional | Privatization of abattoirs | | | X | | | |
| | Import bans are undermining competitiveness | Removal of import ban on meat | | X | | | | |
| | Public sector institutions are weak, especially for veterinary services and other support services | Targeted capacity-building for key government institutions | | | X | | | |
| Aquaculture: growing steadily from a low base reflecting increased demand | Information on technology options and prices | Support with technical training and establishment designs | | X | | | | |

(continued next page)

**Table IV.A1:** *(Continued)*

| Potential Sectors | Growth constraints | Intervention approach | Low quality & unproductive labor inputs | Finance | Distortionary trade policy | Lack of regulatory enforcement on product standards | Poor environmental practices & enforcement | Unreliable & high cost infrastructure | Poor logistics & handling | Onerous administrative procedures | Technology and information asymmetries |
|---|---|---|---|---|---|---|---|---|---|---|---|
| | Access to finance | Increase access to term lending for micro and small businesses | | X | | | | | | | |
| | Input supply and business development services | Commercial stakeholders' capacity to be developed through infrastructure, technology, information systems | | | X | | | | | | X |
| | Unreliable and high cost infrastructure services (power, water, transport); poor logistics & handling; poor rural roads to dispersed small scale farms | Construction of Independent Power Plants in geographical areas with high growth potential that already have a high concentration of promising value chains | | | | | | X | X | | |
| Leather: high-quality products with potential for international marketability that needs upgrading | Distortionary trade policy accompanied by poor border controls: import bans on factor inputs; tariff and dustiest to protect domestic goods; porous borders undermine trade policy | Replace import bans with tariffs (15% tariff would maximize incentives for formalizing trade) | | | X | | | | | | |
| | | Reform customs procedures, including through risk-based customs clearances | | | | | | | | | |

| Constraint | Recommended action | | | | | |
|---|---|---|---|---|---|---|
| Onerous administrative procedures: burdensome business regulatory compliance, including EEG | Initiate administrative reform program to simplify individual procedures in relevant agencies to speed up compliance/approval process | | | | | |
| | Redesign or re-engineer procedures through careful process mapping and streamline legal basis as necessary | | | X | | |
| | Provide strong technical assistance in the preparation/design stage followed by hands-on implementation with stakeholders | | | | | |
| Low-quality and unproductive labor inputs: shortage of skilled labor, lack of vocational training, unskilled labor exhibits low productivity | Explore possibility of using the Innovative Enterprise Institutions to deliver training programs | | | | | |
| | Develop new and strengthen existing vocational institutions to increase access to unskilled, informal labor sector including programs designed for practical teaching programs (e.g. Vocational Training Centre of Excellence in Lagos for the construction sector) | X | | | | |
| | Sponsor technical advisory trips to locations that incorporate religious and traditional practices of the domestic target groups, e.g. Islamic run abattoirs and butchers in Dubai, Malaysia, South Africa | | | | | |

(continued next page)

**Table IV.A1:** *(Continued)*

| Potential Sectors | Growth constraints | Intervention approach | Low quality & unproductive labor inputs | Finance | Distortionary trade policy | Lack of regulatory enforcement on product standards | Poor environmental practices & enforcement | Unreliable & high cost infrastructure | Poor logistics & handling | Onerous administrative procedures | Technology and information asymmetries |
|---|---|---|---|---|---|---|---|---|---|---|---|
| | Poor environmental practices and enforcement: improper chemical disposal practices by leather tanneries (3 out of 6 have no chemical treatment facilities) | Provide technical assistance to the State Ministry of Environment to develop the appropriate level of resources and expertise, as well as the institutional authority to enforce environmental regulations under its statutory responsibility | | | | | X | | | | |
| | Lack of regulator Enforcement on Product Standards: Veterinary Services; Livestock & Poultry services | Deliver capacity building program to strengthen inspection activities of relevant government authorities pertaining to quality and safety standards of products in the agriculture and animal livestock industries | | | | X | | | | | |

| Sector | Constraints/issues | Policy recommendations | | | | | | |
|---|---|---|---|---|---|---|---|---|
| ICT: crucial role in increasing productivity for other sectors by reducing communications and transactions costs; strong links with financial sector; large market attracts FDI; recent increase in competition has led to productivity increases & product innovation; opportunities for regional investment; language skills allow for opening of call centers. | Policy & regulatory reforms: NCC issues new licenses for new operators to enter exceeding the capacity of the market. Spectrum management plan to be issued. Enforcement capacity and ability to assess proper levels of service charges lacking; confusion over role of telecoms agencies | Targeted capacity-building for communications regulator; new streamlined regulations | | X | | | | |
| | Market failures to access debt and equity financing | Specific financing windows for the telecommunications sector | | | X | | | |
| | Skills shortages | Targeted training | | | | X | | |
| Light manufacturing (metal, wood processing, furniture): rising demand in construction increases demand for structural timber and steel products | High cost of raw materials (uncompetitive steel producers) | Replace import bans with tariffs | | | | | X | |
| | Skills shortages | Targeted investment in vocational training, especially through IEI's | | | | X | | |
| | Policy neglect at local government level results in low level of public sector investment | Power needs of clusters should be met more effectively through IPP's, dedicated water and roads supply | | | X | | | |
| | Unequal access to information especially for micro and small businesses | Industry associations should increase the flow of market intelligence to the industry; improve technology transfer mechanisms by sharing information on successful innovation | X | | | | | |
| | Lack of access to finance | Increased access to term lending | | | | | | X |

(continued next page)

**Table IV.A1:** *(Continued)*

| Potential Sectors | Growth constraints | Intervention approach | Low quality & unproductive labor inputs | Finance | Distortionary trade policy | Lack of regulatory enforcement on product standards | Poor environmental practices & enforcement | Unreliable & high cost infrastructure | Poor logistics & handling | Onerous administrative procedures | Technology and information asymmetries |
|---|---|---|---|---|---|---|---|---|---|---|---|
| Tires | Access to finance | Consider establishment of a bail-out fund and of a credit line at concessional rates; construction of an IPP | | | | | | | | | |
| | Power and water infrastructure | Rehabilitate refinery in Warri | | | | | | | | | |
| | Lack of access to black carbon because refinery in Warri is dysfunctional | | | | | | | | | | |
| Car parts, motor cycle assembly | Skills upgrade | Reduce training costs | | | | | | | | | |
| | Power and water infrastructure | Build IPP in industrial zone | | | | | | | | | |
| | Customs procedures | Reform fast-track manufacturing line | | | | | | | | | |
| Pharmaceutical goods | Too small and fragmented to operate competitively | Encourage mergers and acquisitions | | | | | | | | | |
| Color TV receivers | Customs procedures | Activate fast-track lane for manufacturers | | | | | | | | | |
| | Access to land | Facilitate acquiring of land | | | | | | | | | |

*Source:* World Bank/DFID (2008).

# Notes

†    The authors wish to thank Doerte Doemeland, Hinh Dinh, John Litwack, Ngozi Okonjo-Iweala, Brian Pinto, David Rosenblatt and Sunil Sinha for comments and suggestions. Excellent research assistance was provided by Frances Cossar and Dimitris Mavridis.

    Volker Treichel has been a Lead Economist in the World Bank's Office of the Senior Vice President and Chief Economist from December 2010. Prior to that, he served as Lead Economist in Nigeria. Before 2007, he worked at the IMF, including as mission chief for Togo and resident representative in Albania.

1.   See chapter I of this volume.

2.   See also Global Development Horizons (2011).

3.   It is important to note that this finding does not necessarily imply that people in wage employment moved into family agriculture. It could also mean that those who previously reported no activity (that is, outside the labor force) but were at least temporarily involved in agriculture, became engaged in agriculture to an extent that they now reported employment in family agriculture. That means they moved from under-employment to employment. Rodrik (2010) finds evidence that labor moved from the wholesale/retail sectors (which have a reasonably high productivity) to agriculture.

4.   See chapter II of this volume.

5.   Countries with a similar endowment structure should have a similar comparative advantage. The country with a lower wage level than the comparator country is hence able to produce a commodity at a lower cost than its competitor. Within the same industry, the complexity of the associated technology may differ widely; as a result, in some specific products a country may have comparative advantage and others not. For example, when Korea entered the memory chip industry in the 1980s, Japan's memory chip industries were still expanding. What made Korea's entry successful was that it started with simple, technologically matured chips which Japan had produced 10 years ago. Also, an industry can be divided into different segments with different capital-intensity. For example, the IT industry can be divided, according to capital intensity, R&D, chips, spare parts, and assembly. The lower-income countries can enter the industry starting from labor-intensive assembly.

6.   The similarities between Nigeria and Indonesia had earlier been recognized in a World Bank publication which reviewed the economic performance of the two countries over the period 1960-85 (see Bevan, Collier, and Gunning 1999).

7.   See Lin (2011).

8. A jobs summit that took place in Abuja in August 2010 identified binding constraints to growth for each of the key value chains. How to alleviate these constraints has been agreed upon in a Memorandum of Understanding between the public and the private sector. These measures have subsequently been ratified by the government and are currently being implemented.

## References

Bevan, David, Paul Collier, and Jan Willem Gunning. 1999. *The Political Economy of Poverty, Equity, and Growth: Nigeria and Indonesia.* New York: Oxford University Press.

Bosworth, Barry, and Susan Collins. 2008. "Accounting for Growth, Comparing China and India," *Journal of Economic Perspectives* 22, no. 1 (Winter): 45–66.

Hausmann, Ricardo, Dani Rodrik and Andres Velasco, 2008. "Growth Diagnostic," *The Washington Consensus Reconsidered: Towards a New Global Governance,* eds. Narcis Serra and Joseph E. Stiglitz. Cambridge, Massachusetts.

Lin, Justin Yifu. 2011. "Economic Development in Natural Resource-Rich, Labor-Abundant Countries," Let's Talk Development Blog, February 28 (http://blogs.worldbank.org/developmenttalk/economic-development-in-resource-rich-labor-abundant-economies).

Rodrik, Dani. 2010. "Globalization, Structural Change and Productivity Growth." Working Paper 17143. National Bureau of Economic Research, Cambridge, MA.

Treichel, Volker, ed. 2010. *Putting Nigeria to Work: A Strategy for Employment and Growth.* Washington, DC: World Bank.

World Bank. 2011. *Global Development Horizons: Multipolarity: The New Global Economy.* Washington, DC: World Bank.

World Bank. Forthcoming. "Light Manufacturing-Focused Policies to Enhance Private Investment and Create Productive Jobs." Washington, DC: World Bank.

World Bank/DFID. 2008. "Nigeria Valua Chain Analysis: Sector Choice and Market Analysis Report." EME consultants, London.

# FINANCIAL STRUCTURE AND ECONOMIC DEVELOPMENT

# FINANCIAL STRUCTURE
# AND ECONOMIC
# DEVELOPMENT*

## WITH LIXIN COLIN XU†

## Introduction

Financial structure differs greatly across countries. In bank-based financial systems such as in Germany, Japan, and India, banks offer the main financial services in mobilizing savings, allocating capital, monitoring corporate managers, and providing risk management services. In market-based systems such as in the United Kingdom, the United States, and Malaysia, both stock markets and banks play important roles in all financial services. There are vast variations in financial structure. Using comprehensive cross-country data on financial structure, Demirgüç-Kunt and Levine (2001) classify a large number of countries into four categories—bank- or market-based systems in financially developed or underdeveloped countries. Bank-based financially-underdeveloped countries include

* Adapted from a paper presented at the Sixteenth World Congress of the International Economic Association in Beijing, China, in July 2011.

Bangladesh, Nepal, Egypt, Costa Rica, Kenya, Sri Lanka, Indonesia, Colombia, Pakistan, Zimbabwe, Greece, Argentina, Venezuela, India, and Ireland. Market-based financially-underdeveloped countries include Denmark, Peru, Chile, Brazil, Mexico, Philippines, and Turkey. Bank-based financially-developed economies include Tunisia, Portugal, Austria, Belgium, Italy, Finland, Norway, Japan, France, Jordan, Germany, Israel, and Spain. Finally, market-based financially-developed countries include the Netherlands, Thailand, Canada, Australia, South Africa, Korea, Sweden, Great Britain, Singapore, the United States, Switzerland, Hong Kong, and Malaysia.

What explains financial structure? Does the combination of institutions and markets that constitute the financial system have any impact on economic development? These questions have fascinated economists for decades. One of the earliest attempts to address these questions was Goldsmith (1969), who 40 years ago tried to document the change in financial structure over time and to assess the impacts of financial development on economic development. He states that "one of the most important problems in the field of finance, if not the single most important one, almost everyone would agree, is the effect that financial structure and development have on economic growth." With data from 35 countries for the pre-1964 period, he finds positive correlation between financial development and economic growth. But data constraints prevented him from going far on financial structure: he could rely only on careful comparisons of Germany and United Kingdom. Obviously, it is hard to extend the conclusions from case studies to the rest of the world.

Since Goldsmith wrote, there has been great progress in the research on financial structure. Having collected comprehensive cross-country data on financial structure themselves (along with their coauthors), Demirgüç-Kunt and Levine (2001) find from this new data set that financial systems become more complex as countries become richer with both banks and markets getting larger, more active, and more efficient. But in general, the structure becomes more market-based in higher-income countries. They also find strong and consistent evidence that what matters for economic development is the level of financial development, and that the relative mix of banks and stock market does not matter much (Beck et al. 2001).

This conclusion that financial structure is irrelevant for development faces significant challenge. Several authors argue theoretically that financial structure should matter a great deal. After all, economic development increases the demand for the services provided by securities markets relative to services provided by banks (Allen and Gale 2000; Boyd and Smith 1998). Moreover, banks and stock markets exhibit distinct effectiveness in delivering corporate governance and investor protection (Stulz 2001). In particular, banks are better at reducing the market frictions related to financing standardized, shorter-run, lower-risk, and well-collateralized projects, while security markets are better at financing more innovative, longer-run, and higher-risk projects that rely more on intangible inputs such as human capital (Allen and Gale 2000). Furthermore, the fact that stock markets become significantly more active and important as economies develop also conjures up the notion that stock markets may become more useful as income levels rise.

In this paper, we summarize some recent progress, both theoretical and empirical, that suggest that financial structure does indeed matter for economic development, that banks and stock markets play different roles at countries at different development stages, and that there might be optimal financial structure associated with each development stage. We also offer evidence that the actual financial structure in a country may deviate from its optimum due to politics.

In the rest of this paper, we first summarize conventional wisdom and findings about financial structure. We then proceed to discuss some new ideas on this topic, along with empirical support for these new ideas.

## Traditional View of Financial Structure and Economic Development

While the literature on the relative merits of banks versus markets is large, it can be summarized by four views (Beck et al. 2001; Levine 2002; Stulz 2001). The first is *the financial-structure-irrelevancy view.* In a perfect capital market with risk-neutral agents, the interest rate determines which investment opportunities are worth taking up, and all investment opportunities yielding positive net return (after capital costs) will be taken (Stulz

2001). If there is imperfect capital mobility, that is, if capital flows across borders are hindered by worries about country-specific risks, then what matters for job creation, firm growth, and efficient allocation of resources is whether the financial system can provide efficient financial services and sufficient access to finance; the mix of banks and markets does not matter. According to this view, only financial depth, not financial structure, matters for economic performance.

A particular version of the financial-structure-irrelevance view is *the law and finance view*, which argues that the primary determinant of the soundness of the financial system is the legal system (La Porta et al. 2000). In particular, this view holds that what is relevant for growth is not financial structure, but rather whether it is bank-based or market-based. The overall financial development is determined by the legal system and the origins of law. The legal system may affect external finance because good legal protection increases investors' confidence that they would reap at least some return on their investments (managed by firms) and as a result, they are more likely to provide investment funds to firm managers (La Porta et al. 2000; Stulz 2001).

Underlying the financial-structure-irrelevancy view are strong assumptions that may not hold in reality. When the financial system fails to direct savings to its more efficient uses, financial structure becomes important (Stulz 2001). Two key market imperfections destroy perfect financial markets (Stulz 2001): managers have an information advantage over investors about the firm's activities ("hidden information"), and managers' actions cannot be observed by investors ("hidden action"). Hidden information and action allow managers to pursue its own objectives. And managers cannot credibly commit to return investment returns to investors, who in turn may fail to finance projects that may have positive returns to them in a perfect-information world. With these two issues in mind, financial structure leads to real consequences when it changes information and transaction costs, affects the cost of capital, and alters the incentives and monitoring of management.

*The bank-based view* emphasizes the positive role of banks in mobilizing resources, identifying good projects, monitoring managers, and managing risks, and highlights the shortcomings of the stock market (Beck et al. 2001). One of the pioneers in research on financial structure,

Gerschenkron (1962), suggests that banks are more important than markets in the early stage of economic development when the institutional environment cannot support market activities effectively. The reason is that even in countries with weak legal and accounting systems and frail institutions, powerful banks can force firms to reveal information and pay their debts, thereby helping industrial growth. Moreover, banks may be better than markets at providing external finance to new firms requiring staged financing: banks can more credibly commit to making additional funding available as the project proceeds, while markets find it more difficult to make credible, long-term commitments. In contrast, a good stock market quickly and fully reveals information in public markets, which decreases the incentives for investors to acquire information. Good market development may thus impede incentives for identifying innovative projects and thereby hinder efficient resource allocation. Moreover, liquid markets also lead to a myopic investment sentiment—all investors need to do is to watch stock prices without having to actively monitor firm managers, which hinders corporate control.

In contrast, *the market-based view* regards stock markets as crucial in promoting economic success (Beck et al. 2001). Markets allow investors to diversify and manage risks more effectively, thereby encouraging more supply of external finance. Market-based systems also facilitate competition, which induces stronger incentives for R&D and growth. Thus, market-based systems may be especially effective in promoting innovative and R&D-based industries (Allen and Gale 2000). Liquid stock markets also allow investors to build and seek large stakes, therefore enabling hostile takeovers to discipline shirking or incompetent managers (Stulz 2001). This market-based view also emphasizes the negative roles played by banks. By spending expensive resources on information about firms, banks can extract large rents from firms, which reduces the incentives for firms to undertake high-risk, high-return projects since firms lose a large share of the rents to the banks. Moreover, because of the nature of the debt contracts—banks do not benefit from high returns but are harmed by low returns—banks prefer to finance safe and low-return projects, retarding innovation and growth. Moreover, powerful banks may collude with firm managers to prevent entry by other investors, a practice that reduces competition and effective corporate control and therefore growth.

## Conventional Empirical Results

Demirgüç-Kunt and Levine (2001) use the new cross-country database on financial structure to document how financial structure evolves with economic development. They characterize financial structure by ratios of banking sector development (measured by size, activity and efficiency) relative to stock market development (similarly measured), with a higher ratio meaning a more bank-based structure. They then classify countries into bank-based or market-based countries. Austria, France, Germany, Great Britain, Hong Kong, Japan, the Netherlands, and Switzerland have comparatively large, active banking systems. In contrast, Argentina, Colombia, Costa Rica, Ghana, Nepal, Nigeria, Peru, Turkey, and Zimbabwe have particularly small, inactive banking systems. In terms of stock market development, some countries emerge as particularly well-developed by all measures (Australia, Great Britain, Hong Kong, Malaysia, the Netherlands, Singapore, Sweden, Switzerland, Thailand, and the United States), while other countries, such as Chile and South Africa, are large and illiquid. A few countries, such as Germany and Korea, have active but small stock markets.

Demirgüç-Kunt and Levine find that banks, nonbanks, stock markets, and bond markets are larger, more active, and more efficient in richer countries, confirming the findings of Goldsmith (1969) with a smaller sample of countries in earlier periods. Thus financial systems on average are more developed in richer countries. In addition, stock markets in higher-income countries tend to be more active and efficient relative to banks. Furthermore, financial structure is more market-oriented in countries with common law tradition (as distinct from a civil law tradition), strong protection of minority shareholder rights, good accounting systems, low levels of corruption, and no explicit deposit insurance. This is consistent with theories that argue that higher information costs and worse legal protection of property rights tend to favor banks over markets (Allen and Gale 2000; Stulz 2001).

Beck et al. (2001) provide comprehensive evidence that financial structure does not matter but that financial depth does. They combine the new cross-country database of financial structure with both firm-level and cross-country industry level data. Relying on evidence about financial structure and economic performance at three levels (pure cross-country comparisons, cross-industry, cross-country methods, and firm-level data across many countries), they obtain consistent results. They find no evidence that financial structure helps explain country economic performance: "Countries do not grow faster, financially dependent industries do not expand at higher rates, new firms are not created more easily, firms' access to external finance is not easier, and firms do not grow faster in either market-based or bank-based systems." In contrast, they write, "distinguishing countries by overall financial development does help explain cross-country differences in economic performance. Measures of bank development and market development are strongly linked to economic growth. More specifically, the data indicate that economies grow faster, industries depending heavily on external finance expand at faster rates, new firms form more easily, firms' access to external financing is easier, and firms grow more rapidly in economies with a higher level of overall financial-sector development." They also find that the part of financial development explained by the legal system consistently explains firm, industry, and national economic success, consistent with the law and finance view of financial structure.

## New Waves of Theoretical Arguments

Does financial structure really not matter for development? Recent developments cast doubt that this is the case. First, economists have come to realize that there is often no one-size-fits-all recipe for development (Kremer 1993). The reform areas with the largest payoffs differ from country to country, and there are often development "bottlenecks," which can be likened to the famous failure of the space shuttle *Challenger*: with thousands of components, it "exploded because it was launched at a temperature that caused one of those components, the O-rings, to malfunction" (Kremer 1993). Consistent with this notion of country-specific and development-stage-specific bottlenecks, some research has found policy complementarity in various contexts. In particular, Xu (2011) summarizes evidence suggesting that the effects of the business environment on development tend to be heterogeneous depending on the stage of development, and that in particular, bad infrastructure and labor inflexibility—as in the case of India—tend to be key bottlenecks because of their negative indirect effects.

Second, the theory on financial structure has evolved. Relying on the comparative experience of Germany, Japan, the United Kingdom, and the United States, Allen and Gale (2000) examine whether financial structure matters. They conclude that since banks and markets offer distinct financial services, economies at different stages of development require distinct mixtures of these financial services to work efficiently. They conjecture that a country will require different mixtures of financial services (that is, banks and stock markets) as it grows richer (Boyd and Smith 1998), and that when a country's actual financial structure differs from the optimal mixture of banks and markets, its economy will not obtain the appropriate mix of financial services, hurting economic growth.

Lin, Sun, and Jiang (2011) also argue that financial structure has to matter for development but from a different angle. The key reason, they contend, is that an efficient financial structure must reflect the demand of the real economy. Fundamentally, factor endowments (labor, capital, and natural resources) determine industrial structure, which in turn needs the support of a certain development-stage-specific financial structure. In particular, at each stage of development a country has a specific combination of factor endowments. That combination determines factor prices, which in turns determines the optimal industry structure, the nature of its associated risk, and distribution of firm size (Lin 2009). Since enterprises that operate in different industries differ in size, risk, and financing needs, the demands of the real economy for financial services at some development stages can be systematically different from those of the same economy at other stages. When the characteristics of financial structure match those of an economy's industrial structure, the financial system can perform its fundamental functions most efficiently and thus contribute to sustainable and inclusive development. Therefore, there is an optimal financial structure for an economy at each stage of development.

With respect to developing economies, the key characteristic of their endowment structures is the relative abundance of unskilled labor (and scarcity of capital). Labor-intensive industries and labor-intensive sections of capital-intensive industries have the comparative advantage and should thus dominate in these economies. Since the experiences from developed economies can be mimicked, the industries, products, and technologies that are appropriate in developing economies are relatively mature. With respect to firm size, firms in labor-intensive industries are usually smaller, especially in terms of capital, relative to firms in capital-intensive industries. The efficiency of the financial system in developing countries therefore depends on its ability to serve the financing needs of labor-intensive, small, and mature businesses. Since those firms also tend to be more opaque due to their lack of standard financial information, screening firms and monitoring firm managers become the major concerns for providers of external funds to these firms. In such an economic environment, banks, especially small local banks, have more strengths than stock markets, due to their superior abilities to harness local information, assess "soft" information regarding creditworthiness, and engage in long-term relationships with borrowers. In addition, banks are particularly attractive to firms in low-income countries because banks represent lower costs of capital to firms in such countries: (i) when borrowing from no more than a few banks, these firms do not need to have public information such as financial statements and external auditing ready for the lenders, thus saving precious capital; (ii) interest rate payments for loans tend to be lower than returns to shares in the stock market due to lower risks associated with bank loans, a fact that again saves precious capital from the perspective of firms in developing countries. Thus, if there are no distortions, the financial systems in these economies are likely to be characterized by the dominance of banks.

It is likely that small regional banks play an especially significant role in efficiently serving small firms in developing countries. Recent evidence suggests that there is a match between bank size and the size of firms that these banks serve. Large banks tend to shy away from small businesses but rather focus on large businesses, while small banks tend to target small businesses. Large banks can save transaction costs if making loans mainly to large businesses—since making a loan, no matter how large or small, involves the same procedures and forms. Making a few large loans to large businesses, rather than many smaller loans to small firms, therefore lowers the unit costs of loans for large banks. Serving small firms is thus left to small banks in developing countries.

In contrast, the key characteristics of the endowment structure in developed countries are the relative abundance of skilled labor and capital. The comparative advantage of these countries is then capital-intensive industries. Firms in such industries tend to be large, demanding more external financing. Since these countries are already at or near the technological frontier, firms there would spend much more on R&D and innovation, and bear higher technological and product innovation risks.[1] With larger firm sizes, firms can afford the (more or less) fixed costs of providing standard financial information to the market, and specialized financial agencies can make sufficient money and become viable in providing specialized financial and auditing information. Thus with standard financial information available, stock markets, bond markets, and big banks become the main finance providers to these capital-intensive firms.

Moreover, there are arguments that stock markets are better suited to richer countries. For firms with new technologies or innovative projects, investors do not have much information and often have diverse opinions about the prospects of these new technologies. Decentralized stock markets allow people to agree to disagree about the future prospects of these firms, and these firms, as a result, are more likely to be funded (Allen and Gale 2000). Furthermore, stock markets can take advantage of the standard financial information—information available only in richer countries—to reduce the information asymmetry between the managers of a firm and the external investors, which allows investors to make more informed decisions about what firms to invest in and in which firms they are more likely to have safer returns. Venture capital is often involved in the early stage of high-risk innovative and capital-intensive firms, but stock markets remain crucial by providing exit options for venture capital and by financing further development of these high-tech businesses. Banks can also offer staged investment once venture capital has identified good projects as demonstrated by good initial returns. Thus, for rich countries, the optimal financial structure is likely characterized by a large and active stock market, augmented with many large banks.[2]

As a result, for a country at a certain stage of its economic development, some specific financial structure will be more efficient in mobilizing and allocating capital. In other words, there is a certain optimal financial structure at a specific stage of development, in which the composition and relative importance of available financial arrangements can most efficiently allocate financial resources to viable firms in the competitive sectors of the optimal industrial structure, which is in turn determined by its endowment structure. The optimal financial structure for developing countries tends to feature a stronger role for banks (especially small banks) than for stock markets, while the opposite is true for developed countries. Moreover, the optimal financial structure is dynamic. As the endowment structure changes with physical and human capital accumulation, the optimal industrial and financial structure changes accordingly. There is, therefore, no unique financial structure that fits all countries. For future reference, we call this view of optimal financial structure specific to each development stage the new structural view.

## Some New Empirical Results

Several fairly recent papers offer evidence supporting the premise that financial structure matters in various ways for economic development. The first and the key piece of evidence is based on a cross-country study by Demirgüç-Kunt, Feyan and Levine (2011). Noting that the past literature has not been successful in identifying the importance of financial structure, they explore whether deviations from an optimal financial structure are associated with the speed of development. They use data from 72 countries from 1980 to 2008 to reassess the role of financial structure in economic development. More specifically, they assess whether the sensitivity of economic development to increases in bank securities market development change during the process of economic development, and whether each level of economic development is associated with an optimal financial structure. Financial structure here is measured as the ratio of private credit (as a share of GDP) to security market capitalization (as a share of GDP) and some of its variants.

The authors use quantile regressions to assess how the sensitivities of economic activity to bank and securities market development evolve as countries grow. The quantile regressions provide information on how the associations between economic development and both bank and securities market development change as countries grow richer. In contrast, the conventional cross-country studies tend to focus on the association between economic development and financial structure for the "average" country. The reliance on quantile regression, which implicitly insists that the effects of financial structure have distinct effects for countries at different income levels, proves to be the key for finding that financial structure matters.

A measure of optimal financial structure at each level of development is constructed by regressing a measure of financial structure as a share of GDP per capita for the sample of OECD countries, while also controlling for key institutional, geographic, and structural traits of those countries. The maintained hypothesis is that conditional on these traits, the OECD countries provide information on how the optimal financial structure varies with economic development. Next, the authors use the coefficients from the regression to compute the estimated optimal financial structure for each country in each year. They then compute a "financial structure gap," which is equal to the natural logarithm of the absolute value of the difference between the actual and the estimated optimal financial structure.

They find that as economies develop, both banks and markets become larger relative to the size of the overall economy. More importantly, as countries become richer, the sensitivity of economic development to changes in bank development decreases, while the sensitivity of economic development to changes in securities market development increases. Thus the relative demand for the services provided by the stock market increases as an economy develops, and these services differ from those the banks provide, as suggested by Allen and Gale (2000).

Demirgüç-Kunt, Feyan, and Levine (2011) find some support for the notion that there is appropriate financial structure for countries at distinct stages of development. In particular, deviations in an economy's actual financial structure from its estimated optimal one (that is, the size of the financial development gap) are associated with reduced economic output. Even when controlling for the level of bank development, securities market development, a standard set of controls, and country fixed effects, there is a robust and negative relationship between the financial structure gap and economic activity. They also look at whether it matters if the non-optimal financial structure is due to too much bank orientation or too much market orientation, and find that neither matters. Magnitudes of the effects of deviations from the optimal financial structure are non-trivial: an increase of one standard deviation in the financial structure gap is associated with a drop in log real GDP per capita of 0.06, or a 6 percent reduction in economic activity. Further controlling for country and period fixed effects and some standard controls, the magnitude drops by 50 percent but remains significant. The magnitude, at face value, is interesting: it is certainly non-trivial, but the magnitude is not overwhelmingly important.

It is useful to point out that this paper does not deal with the potential endogeneity of the financial structure. If financial structure does respond to income level, as the theory would suggest, then there may be bias for the estimated effects of financial structure. Moreover, it is not clear that using OECD countries to infer optimal financial structure is completely convincing. After all, OECD countries are all rich, and it is unclear that this group of countries can form the base to infer the optimal financial structure in much poorer countries. Still, the paper offers plausible empirical support for the new structural view of financial structure and is a nice first step toward disentangling the mystery of the impact of financial structure.

The second clue of the effects of financial structure comes from a large firm-level dataset. Cull and Xu (2011) use firm-level data across 89 countries, looking at how labor growth rates of firms vary with their country's financial structure. An important advantage of combining firm-level data and cross-country indicators of financial structure is the ability to examine how various types of firms may be affected differently by financial structure. This allows us to distinguish between the efficiency-based (that is, the new structural view) and the political-economy based approach of explaining the evolution of financial structure.

Cull and Xu (2011) regress firm-level labor growth rates to country-level measures of bank and stock market development (after controlling for basic firm and country characteristics). They are concerned about the potential endogeneity of financial structure in the labor growth equation for two reasons. First, there might be omitted variables that are correlated with both financial structure and labor growth rates. Such variables might, for instance, include non-finance business environment variables (Xu 2011). Second, causality might go both ways, from finance to firm growth, or vice versa. They thus resort to instrumental variables to deal with such issues. In particular, they consider potential instrumental variables including natural resource dependence, the level of trust in a society, cereal plantation patterns, settler mortality, and so on, and choose a subset of these potential instrumental variables that are related to financial structure yet pass the over-identifying restrictions test. Beside the instrumental variable approach, they also use the Rajan-Zingales difference-in-difference approach to examine whether firms in industries that rely more heavily on external finance benefit more in terms of firm growth from financial development at the country level, holding constant both country and industry fixed effects, therefore controlling for all country- and industry-specific factors. This approach significantly reduces the extent of omitted variable bias.

Relating firm growth to firm and country characteristics and financial structure, and taking into account the potential endogeneity of financial structure, Cull and Xu (2011) find that labor growth is swifter in low-income countries that have a higher ratio of private credit to GDP, and the growth-spurring effects of banking development are especially pronounced in industries that heavily rely on external finance. In high-income countries, labor growth rates are increasing in the level of stock market capitalization. Both patterns are consistent with predictions from the new structural view and some earlier theoretical conjectures (Allen and Gale 2000; Boyd and Smith 1998; Lin, Sun, and Jiang 2011).

The third clue about the effects of financial structure emerges from examining the impact of financial structure on poverty. Financial structure might affect poverty because entrepreneurs have trouble obtaining finance due to information asymmetry between them and investors—the entrepreneurs know more about the prospects of the projects than banks and atomistic investors in the stock market. A number of researchers argue that banks are better able to reduce this information asymmetry problem than stock markets. One reason is that banks form long-term relationship with borrowers and can benefit from the value of the information obtained from this long-term relationship. In contrast, well-established stock markets quickly and publicly reveal information, thereby reducing the incentives for individual investors to acquire information. Banks therefore may have better capacity to reduce the information asymmetry issue and make external financing possible. Moreover, since stock markets rely more strongly on the legal and accounting framework to safeguard necessary returns to investors, the effects of stock markets may depend on institutions to a greater extent, whereas banks can more effectively force firms and households to honor their contracts than stock markets (Gerschenkron 1962, Boyd and Smith 1998), and are therefore especially important in poorer countries with weak contract enforcement.

Based on the above logic, Kpodar and Singh (2011), using data from 47 developing countries from 1984 to 2008, show that financial deepening through banks is associated with reduced poverty levels, while market-based measures of financial development are associated with higher incidence of poverty in this sample. In addition, the interaction between institutional quality and the sized-based measures of the importance of stock markets relative to banks is negative and significant in their regressions, indicating that as institutions improve, the positive link between market-based financial development and poverty incidence phases out, and even reverses after some threshold of institutional quality is reached. Conversely, the results suggest that in weak institutional environments bank-based financial systems tend to reduce poverty more than market-based ones. The authors have dealt with the endogeneity of financial structure for poverty by using the system GMM estimator, which controls for country fixed effects, and allows financial structure and other variables to be endogenous and predetermined.

## The Deviation from the Optimal Financial Structure

Besides derived demand based on industrial structure that originates in the endowment structure, there are other determinants of financial structure that cause the actual financial structure to deviate from the optimal one. Earlier research has shown that financial structure is significantly and robustly related to law and legal origins (La Porta et al. 2000; Demirgüç-Kunt and Levine 2001); here we focus on several other factors such as the role of belief and ideas and the role of politics, which have emerged as potentially important in recent studies.

The first factor stems from the belief of government leaders.[3] In most developing countries, the government plays a very important role in defining the structure of the economy. And the belief of the top government leaders will naturally shape the country's financial structure. A case in point is the financial repression that is widely observed in many developing countries. Countries featuring financial repression tend to adopt policies restricting entry into the banking sector, controlling interest rates, and intervening in the allocation of bank loans. As a result, a few big banks tend to dominate the banking landscape, and capital tends to flow to large firms. Small businesses, which have comparative advantages in these economies, have little access to credit and have to make do with internal capital or resort to informal channels for external finance.

Why do countries adopt such obviously inefficient policies? Inappropriate development strategies adopted by the government are likely the main driving force leading to these repressive policies and distorted financial system.[4] If the government's priority is to promote industries that are inconsistent with the comparative advantages endogenously determined by the economy's endowment structure, it has to use distortional policies to channel scarce resources into the priority sectors. As a result, government interventions and consequent repression of the financial system are inevitable. Due to inertia of institutional change, such distorted policies can have prolonged influence on the evolution of the financial system.

A good example of this practice is China. In the 1950s, the factor endowments in the Chinese economy were characterized by extreme scarcity of capital and enormous abundance of labor. The government, however, decided to adopt an ambitious comparative-advantage-defying development strategy in which establishment and development of heavy industries took the first priority. To push the development of heavy industries, which are very capital-intensive, the government had to deliberately distort prices of various products and production factors including labor, capital, and foreign exchange; replace market mechanisms with a government planning system to control the allocation of production factors; nationalize private businesses; and collectivize agricultural production with the People's Communes. In this centrally planned economic regime, banks were closed or merged into the People's Bank of China, which became the only financial institution in the whole economy until the end of 1970s. After the reform and opening in the late 1970s, the government adopted a dual-track approach to the transition: on one hand, some transitory protections and subsidies were provided to firms in the old priority sectors, and, on the other hand, entry to sectors that were consistent with the economy's comparative advantages and were repressed in the old strategy were liberalized. As part of the economic reform, four big state-owned banks were established in the early 1980s. A dozen joint-stock commercial banks were also set up in the late 1980s and early 1990s. But interest rates are still under the control of the state, and domestic entry into the banking sector is rigidly restricted by the government. The market share of the four big state-owned banks has slowly declined, but they still hold a dominant position in the banking system today. Because of this serious mismatch of financial structure with optimal industrial structure, labor-intensive small businesses have very limited access to formal financial credit, a situation that reduces job creation and contributes to widening inequality of income distribution in China.

A second factor behind the deviation of actual financial structure from its optimal one stems from the belief of many policy advisors in the benefits of financial liberalization and the possibility of leapfrogging in financial development. As a policy prescription to correct financial repression, financial liberalization has been generously prescribed by theorists and exercised by many developing countries. While those repressive policies should be removed, some new, less noticeable policy distortions may be introduced in the process of financial liberalization. It is not rare that developing countries are advised to establish and develop a financial system similar to those in the advanced economies. The U.K. and U.S. financial systems, where financial markets are highly active, are often taken as the model that developing countries should follow. This model is often justified by the supposed superiority of financial markets. As a result, some small, low-income economies are eager to develop stock markets, consolidate small banks into large banks. and repress the development of local banks.

However, as the new structural view has argued—and with supporting evidence emerging—the optimal financial structure for poor countries is likely to be systemically different from that for advanced economies. Thus imitating the financial model of advanced economies will not lead to improved efficiency of the financial system nor generate better economic performance in poor countries. Such imitation may even result in destructive consequences such as financial crises. Such policy advice is also inconsistent with the growth experience of those successful economies in their industrialization periods. For instance, in the British Industrial Revolution, industrial enterprises were typically very small and mainly internally financed at both the start-up and expansion stages. In the case of external finance, personal contacts played a crucial role. The role of the banking system in financing long-term investment in industrial sectors was insignificant. The British banks were typically small and locally based with a limited number of offices until at least the mid-19th century. Bank merger movement in England did not develop until the 1860s, with the peak of merger activity occurring in the late 1880s and early 1890s.

When it comes to the role of capital market, history shows that capital markets started to play an important role in financing industrial sectors only at the end of 19th century. In the United States before 1890, industrial firms were numerous, small, and closely owned. Industrial securities, except in the coal and textile industries, were almost unknown. A capital market for industrial preferred stocks did not develop until the 1887–1904 merger wave. And public markets for common stocks developed even later. Therefore, while financial markets are a prominent element of the current U.K. and U.S. financial systems, this was not the case at the early stage of economic development in these countries. According to Cull et al. (2006), during the 19th and early 20th centuries, it was a variety of local financial institutions that emerged to meet the needs of small- and medium-sized firms in the economies of the North Atlantic Core. These financial intermediaries were able to tap into local information networks and so extend credit to firms that were too young or small to get funds from large, financial center banks.

The third factor causing deviation of reality from optimal financial structure is politics, as argued by Calomiris and Haber (2011) in the case of bank crisis—in which case the financial structure is clearly not optimal. Many under-banked economies repeatedly supplied credit imprudently: once a crisis was over, banks appeared to continue misallocating scarce credit to firms and households that were prone to default. Why? Calomiris and Haber rely on reasoning rooted in political economy that can explain the prevalence of fragile banking systems that allocate credit narrowly. The key reason is that government actors face inherent conflicts of interest when it comes to the operation of the banking system, and those conflicts can lead to banking instability and undersupply of credit. Specifically, governments regulate and supervise banks to limit risk taking but they also rely on banks as a source of risky public finance (by borrowing from and taxing them). In addition, while governments enforce contracts that discipline bank borrowers, they also depend on bank debtors for votes or political support. Finally, governments distribute losses among creditors when a bank fails, but they also must depend on the largest creditor group—bank depositors—for their political fate. These conflicts of interest imply that regulatory policies toward banks often reflect the interest of the political coalitions that support the government.

This political economic framework turns out to be very useful for understanding banking structure in a series of historical case studies (Scotland, England, United States, Canada, Mexico, and Brazil). Indeed, formation of viable political coalitions under different types of government dictated the evolution of the banking structure in each of these countries. Adapting the conceptual framework to the historical case studies leads to a number of conclusions. Foremost, the nature of the coalitions that generate barriers to entry in banking varies across types of political regimes. In an autocracy, it is easier to create a stable coalition in favor of tight entry restrictions, in part because potential borrowers from banks do not have a voice in the political process. Autocracies therefore tend to create banking systems that allocate credit narrowly to the government and to enterprises owned by an elite class of government-selected bankers. The narrow allocation of credit under authoritarian regimes has not resulted in greater banking sector stability, however: in times of economic strife, bank insiders and the government expropriate firms and households that are either loosely or not at all affiliated with the coalition (that is, minority shareholders and depositors). In times of extreme difficulty, the autocrat can (and has) expropriated bank insiders.

Mass suffrage, by giving voices to mass economic actors, makes it harder to sustain a banking system that allocates credit narrowly to an elite group. It does not, however, necessarily guarantee banking stability. Bank borrowers can vote for representatives that expand the supply of credit, improve the terms on which credit is offered, and then forgive those debts when they prove difficult to repay. This was largely the story of the U.S. subprime crisis. Under any type of political system, banking systems are fragile. Therefore, only a small share of countries has been able to enjoy stable banking along with broad credit supply, because this outcome requires political institutions that allow for mass suffrage, but also limit the authority and discretion of the parties in control of the government.

To shed light on whether real financial structure tends to deviate from the optimal financial structure, Cull and Xu (2011) examine the types of firms that benefit more from private credit market development. In particular, they allow the private credit variable (that is, private credit as a share of GDP) to interact with firm characteristics such as firm size and capital intensity in the labor growth equation, estimated at the firm level. The authors find no evidence that small-scale firms in low-income countries benefit most from private credit market development. Rather, the labor growth rates of large and capital-intensive firms increase more with the level of private credit market development. Thus large and more-capital-intensive firms seem to benefit more from banking development in low-income countries. This suggests that the actual financial structure likely deviates from the optimal financial structure. In particular, the likely scenario is that banks in developing countries tend to lend mostly to large and capital-intensive firms, allowing a small segment of elite firms to grow faster. Such a scenario could be due to an over-concentrated banking structure dominated by large banks, which in turn lend largely only to large firms (Lin, Sun and Jiang 2011), or political coalition between political and banking insiders restrict entry into the banking sector, resulting in a bank sector dominated by large banks, which lends largely to affiliated inside firms that tend to be large and capital-intensive (Calomiris and Haber 2011).

## Conclusions

What explains the vast variations across countries in financial structure? Does financial structure have any impact on economic development? There has been some evolution on these questions. The traditional theoretical views tend to argue that financial structure does not matter. The traditional empirical consensus tends to imply that it is financial depth, not financial structure, that determines aggregate economic performance.

Several researchers have recently argued that financial services are endogenous to industrial structure which in turn depends on a country's relative endowment structure, and optimal financial structure should be specific to the particular development stage. And some recent findings seem to support this view. In particular, while both banks and stock markets become larger and more active as a country grows richer, stock markets become relatively more important. Moreover, as economies become richer, the sensitivity of economic development to changes in bank development decreases, while the sensitivity of economic development to changes in stock market development increase, thus the relative demand for the service provided by stock market increases. In addition, deviation of a country from its optimal financial structure is found to be negatively and significantly related to a lower income level. Firm-level evidence also shows that bank development has particularly strong effects in relatively poor countries, especially in those industries heavily relying on external finance, while stock market development has particularly strong effects in relatively rich countries. Banks (relative to stock markets) are also found to be relatively better in reducing poverty in developing countries, especially in institutionally weak countries. On the other hand, there is no evidence that small firms in developing countries benefit more from bank development, due to the deviation of actual financial structure from the optimal one.

The findings have important implications. First, the optimal financial structure changes, becoming more market-oriented, as economies develop. Second, new evidence suggests that indeed different financial structures may be better at promoting economic activity at different stages of a country's economic development. These findings advertise financial structure as an independent financial policy consideration. And if the optimal mixture changes as an economy develops, then this suggests the desirability of appropriately adjusting financial policies and institutions as countries develop. Third, politics, legal origins, and beliefs of government leaders may cause the actual financial structure in a country to deviate from its optimal, resulting in some efficiency and welfare losses to the economy. Improving the understanding of what the optimal is and the efficiency and welfare losses due to the deviation from the optimal, therefore, may mitigate the impact of political and other belief-related factors in the determination of a country's actual financial structure.

## Notes

† This paper benefited from discussions with Robert Cull and Asli Demirgüç-Kunt, and the discussions at the World Bank Conference on Financial Structure held in Washington, D.C., on June 17, 2011.

   Lixin Colin Xu is a Lead Economist in the Development Research Group of the World Bank.

1. Technological innovation risks are those related to successfully developing new products, while product innovation risks concern those related to successfully getting the new product accepted by the market.

2. There would also be numerous small banks offering services to small labor-intensive firms in the non-tradable sectors.

3. The next four paragraphs draw heavily from Lin, Sun, and Jiang (2011). See also references therein.
4. See Lin (2009) for detailed discussion of development strategy and its impact on the development of financial institutions.

# References

Allen, Franklin, and Douglas Gale. 2000. *Comparing Financial Systems.* Cambridge, MA: MIT Press.

Beck, Thorsten, Asli Demirgüç-Kunt, Ross Levine, and Vojislav Maksimovic. 2001. "Financial Structure and Economic Development: Firms, Industry, and Country Evidence." In *Financial Structure and Economic Growth: A Cross-Country Comparison of Banks, Markets, and Development,* eds. Demirgüç-Kunt and Levine. Cambridge, MA: MIT Press.

Boyd, John H., and Bruce D. Smith. 1998. "The Evolution of Debt and Equity Markets in Economic Development." *Economic Theory* 12: 519–60.

Calomiris, Charles, and Stephen Haber. 2011. "Fragile Banks, Durable Bargains: Why Banking Is All about Politics and Always Has Been." Stanford University, Stanford, CA.

Cull, Robert, and Lixin Colin Xu. 2011. "Firm Growth and Finance: Are Some Financial Institutions Better Suited to Early Stages of Development than Others?" World Bank, Washington, DC.

Cull, R., L. E. Davis, N. R. Lamoreaux, and J. Rosenthal. 2006. "Historical Financing of Small- and Medium-sized Enterprises." *Journal of Banking and Finance* 30: 3017–42.

Demirgüç-Kunt, Asli, Erik Feyen, and Ross Levine. 2011. "Optimal Financial Structures and Development: The Evolving Importance of Banks and Markets." World Bank, Washington, DC.

Demirgüç-Kunt, Asli, and Ross Levine. 2001. "Bank-Based and Market-Based Financial Systems: Cross-Country Comparisons." In *Financial Structure and Economic Growth: A Cross-Country Comparison of Banks, Markets, and Development,* eds. Demirgüç-Kunt and Levine. Cambridge, MA: MIT Press.

Gerschenkron, Alexander. 1962. *Economic Backwardness in Historical Perspective, a Book of Essays.* Cambridge, MA: Harvard University Press.

Goldsmith, Raymond W. 1969. *Financial Structure and Development.* New Haven, CT: Yale University Press.

Kpodar, Kangni, and Raju Singh. 2011. "Does Financial Structure Matter for Poverty? Evidence from Developing Countries." International Monetary Fund, Washington, DC.

Kremer, Michael. 1993. "The O-Ring Theory of Economic Development." *Quarterly Journal of Economics* 108: 551–75.

La Porta, Rafael, Florencio Lopez-de-Silanes, Andrei Shleifer, and Robert W. Vishny. 2000. "Investor Protection and Corporate Governance." *Journal of Financial Economics* 58: 3–27.

Levine, Ross. 2002. "Bank-Based or Market-Based Financial Systems: Which Is Better?" *Journal of Financial Intermediation* 11: 1–30.

Lin, Justin Yifu. 2009. *Economic Development and Transition: Thought, Strategy, and Viability.* New York: Cambridge University Press.

Lin, Justin Yifu, Xifang Sun, and Ye Jiang. 2011. "Toward a Theory of Optimal Financial Structure." World Bank, Washington, DC.

Stulz, René. 2001. "Does Financial Structure Matter for Economic Growth? A Corporate Finance Perspective." In *Financial Structure and Economic Growth: A Cross-Country Comparison of Banks, Markets, and Development,* eds. Demirgüç-Kunt and Levine. Cambridge, MA: MIT Press.

Xu, Lixin Colin. 2011. "The Effects of Business Environments on Development: A Survey of New Firm-Level Evidence." *World Bank Research Observer* 26: 310–40.

# DEVELOPMENT STRATEGY, INSTITUTIONS, AND ECONOMIC PERFORMANCE

# DEVELOPMENT STRATEGY, INSTITUTIONS, AND ECONOMIC PERFORMANCE

## PART 1[*][†]

### Introduction

Since the Industrial Revolution in the eighteenth century, the world's countries have evolved into two groups. The first group includes rich, industrialized, developed countries (DCs). The second group includes poor, agrarian, less-developed countries (LDCs). The wealth of developed countries results from their industrial and technological advantages. Since the nineteenth century, political leaders and intellectuals alike have debated how to modernize LDCs (Gerschenkron 1962; Lal 1985). After World War II, many LDC governments adopted various policy measures to industrialize their economies. However, only a small number of economies in East Asia have actually succeeded in raising their level of per capita income to the level in DCs.[1]

* Adapted from "Development Strategy, Viability, and Economic Convergence," by Justin Yifu Lin, originally published in *Economic Development and Cultural Change* (2003) 51 (2): 277–308. Reprinted with the permission of The University of Chicago. Copyright © 2003 The University of Chicago. All rights reserved.

I argue here that the failure of most LDCs to converge with DCs in terms of economic performance can be explained largely by their governments' inappropriate development strategies. After World War II, most LDC governments pursued development plans that placed priority on the development of certain capital-intensive industries. However, an economy's optimal industrial structure is endogenously determined by that economy's endowment structure. Often the firms in a government's priority industries are not viable in an open, competitive market because these industries do not match the comparative advantage of their particular economy. As such, the government introduces a series of distortions in its international trade, financial sector, labor market, and so on, to support nonviable firms. It is possible with such distortions to establish capital-intensive industries in developing countries, but the economy becomes very inefficient because of misallocation of resources, rampant rent seeking, macroeconomic instability, and so forth. Consequently, convergence—that is, convergence of LDC economic indicators to levels akin to those in DCs—fails to occur. I argue that the government of an LDC should focus development efforts on upgrading the country's endowment structure instead of on upgrading its industry/technology structure. Once the endowment structure is upgraded, profit motives and competitive pressures will lead firms to upgrade their technologies and industries. The upgrading of the endowment structure means faster accumulation of capital—both physical and human—than the growth of labor and natural resources in the economy. Capital accumulation depends on the economic surplus (or, alternatively, the profits) and the savings propensity in an economy. If an LDC develops its industries in accordance with its comparative advantages, its economy will have the largest possible economic surplus and the highest savings propensities and will therefore achieve the highest possible upgrade in its endowment structure. Following this strategy, an LDC could achieve faster upgrades in endowment, technology, and industrial structures than the DCs and realize convergence. A firm's choice of industry/technology depends on the relative prices of capital, labor, and natural resources in the economy. Therefore, only if the price structure of the economy can reflect the relative abundances of capital, labor, and natural resources will firms choose their industries and technologies according to comparative advantage. The price structure will reflect the relative abundance of each factor only if the prices are determined in competitive markets. Therefore, the government's primary function for economic development is to maintain well-functioning markets.

I first present a brief overview of recent theoretical developments and debates on economic growth and convergence. I then discuss the determinants of a firm's viability and an economy's comparative advantages and their relations to the economy's factor endowments. After analyzing a government's alternative development strategies, I present the statistical measurement of a development strategy and the econometric estimation of the impact of the development strategy on economic growth. The policy implications of the analyses are set forth in a concluding section.

## Growth Theories: An Overview

When the field of development economics started to take shape in the postwar period, development economists encouraged LDC governments to adopt interventional policies to accelerate capital accumulation and to pursue "inward-looking" strategies oriented toward heavy industry or import substitution aimed directly at closing the industry-technology gap with DCs (Chenery 1961; Warr 1994). These economists were strongly influenced by the Soviet Union's initial success in nation-building, by the pessimism surrounding the export of primary products born during the Great Depression, by the lack of confidence in markets, and by neoclassical growth theory (Rosenstein-Rodan 1943; Prebisch 1959). Since the 1950s, most LDCs in both socialist and capitalist camps have adopted some variation of these strategies (Krueger 1992).

According to seminal work by Robert Solow (1956) and others, neoclassical growth theory, with its assumption of the same given technology to DCs and LDCs, has suggested that LDCs would grow faster than DCs and that the gap in per capita income between DCs and LDCs would narrow because of the diminishing returns to capital in DCs. However, empirical evidence shows that, while convergence occurred within the different states in the United States and among the DCs (Barro and Sala-i-Martin 1992; Baumol 1986), most LDCs failed to narrow the gaps between their per capita incomes and those of the DCs (Pearson 1969; Romer 1994).

Unsatisfied with neoclassical growth theory's inability to explain the continuous growth of DCs and the failure of most LDCs to converge with DCs, Paul Romer (1986) and Robert Lucas (1988) pioneered a new growth theory. Their theory treats technological innovation as endogenously determined by the accumulation of human capital, research and development (R&D), learning by doing, and so on. This new growth theory is insightful for explaining the continuous growth of DCs, which use the most advanced technologies. However, the new growth theory cannot satisfactorily explain the extraordinary growth and convergence during the last three decades of the twentieth century of the newly industrialized economies (NIEs) in Asia, including South Korea, Taiwan, Hong Kong, Singapore, and, recently, China (Pack 1994; Grossman and Helpman 1994). During the catch-up process, these NIEs' investments in R&D, human capital, and learning by doing were much lower than those of DCs.

The LDCs generally use technologies that are inside the technology frontier of the DCs (Caselli and Coleman 2000). Technological innovation in a DC that adopts technology on the new frontier can be obtained only through R&D or other knowledge-generating mechanisms. For an LDC, however, technological innovation can be the result of technology transfer or the imitation of existing technology held by DCs. The costs of technological innovation through R&D are obviously much higher than the costs of imitation or other ways of technological borrowing. Therefore, technology diffusion from DCs to the LDCs will facilitate the growth of LDCs. It is futile, when attempting to understand convergence, to focus primarily on mechanisms that generate new technology.

However, the technological gap between DCs and LDCs is filled with a whole spectrum of different technologies. An LDC is faced with the question of which technology is appropriate to imitate or borrow.

The idea of appropriate technology was first introduced in neoclassical trade theory by Anthony Atkinson and Joseph Stiglitz (1969), who formalized "localized learning by doing." E. F. Schumacher (1973) made a similar argument in development economics. The study of appropriate technology has been revived recently by I. Diwan and D. Rodrik (1991), Susanto Basu and David Weil (1998), and Daron Acemoglu and Fabrizio Zilibotti

(1999).[2] However, the models based on the idea of appropriate technology are inconclusive on the issue of convergence. Basu and Weil (1998) consider the relatively low capital stock in an LDC as a barrier to adopting the advanced technology of DCs. They conclude that an LDC will experience a period of rapid growth by raising its savings rate to take advantage of the advanced technology. However, their arguments cannot explain why governmental interventions to improve the savings rate in Latin America, Africa, and Asia—excluding the "Four Little Dragons"—failed to accelerate the growth rate. In a cross-country study, Francisco Rodríguez and Dani Rodrik show that causality runs from growth to savings, not vice versa. It would be quite difficult for a rise in the savings rate to trigger rapid growth. By contrast, Acemoglu and Zilibotti (1999) stress the disadvantages of importing technology. In their framework, technology in DCs is used by skilled workers. When the technology is transferred to an LDC, the technology is used by unskilled workers. This mismatch between labor skill and technology can lead to sizable differences in output per capita and total factor productivity (TFP). To Acemoglu and Zilibotti, improving the skill base and human capital of workers, the same argument made by Lucas (1993), is critical to income convergence. The assumption adopted by Acemoglu and Zilibotti is, however, too strong: they assume that LDCs always adopt DCs' frontier technologies rather than some technologies inside the frontier.

The appropriate technology argument does not answer the question of the appropriate role of LDC government in the process of economic growth. Although the linkage of knowledge diffusion with an appropriate technology suggests an alternative development path that differs from the development practices followed by many LDCs, it is not clear if the government's intervention matters to economic growth. Moreover, it is not clear if governments should adopt policies to improve the savings rate and human capital stock of the private sector or if they should subsidize the adoption of high technology industries directly.

## Viability, Comparative Advantage, and Endowment Structure

A country's per capita income is a function of the prevailing technologies and industries found in the country. If two countries have an identical technology-industry structure, the two countries should have a similar level of per capita GDP. To understand how the income of an LDC converges to that of DCs, we need to understand how an LDC can narrow the technology/industry gap between it and DCs. I will first define the meaning of a firm's viability and the relationship between a firm's viability and its industry/technology choice.

I define the term *viability* with respect to the expected rate of profit of a normally managed firm in an open, free, and competitive market. If, without any external subsidies or protections, a normally managed firm is expected to earn a socially acceptable profit in a free, open, and competitive market, the firm is viable. Otherwise, the firm is nonviable. It is obvious that no one will invest in a firm if it is not expected to earn a socially acceptable normal profit. Such a firm will exist only if the government gives it support.

In a competitive market, the management of a firm will affect its profitability. This statement is a known proposition. However, the expected profitability of a firm also depends on its industry/technology choice.

My discussion begins by presenting a simple economy that possesses two given factor endowments, capital and labor, and produces only one good. Each point on the isoquant shown in figure VI.1 represents a technology of production or a combination of capital and labor required to produce a given amount of a certain product. The technology represented by A is more labor-intensive than that of B; C, C1, D, and D1 are isocost lines. The slope of an isocost line represents the relative prices of capital and labor. In an economy where capital is relatively expensive and labor is relatively inexpensive, as represented by isocost lines C and C1, the adoption of technology A to produce the given amount of output will cost the least. When the relative price of labor increases, as represented by the isocost lines by D and D1, production will cost least if technology B is adopted.

In a free, open, and competitive market economy that produces only one product as illustrated in figure 1, a firm will be viable only if it adopts the least-cost technology in its production. In figure VI.1, if the relative prices of capital and labor can be presented by C, the adoption of technology A costs the least. The adoption of any other technology, such as B, will cost more. Market competition will make firms that adopt technologies other than A nonviable. Therefore, in a competitive market with given

**Figure VI.1: Relative Price of Production Factors and Technique Choice**

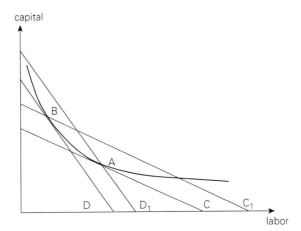

relative prices of labor and capital, the viability of a firm depends on its technology choice.

In a competitive market, the relative prices of capital and labor are determined by the relative abundance or scarcity of capital and labor in the economy's factor endowments. When labor is relatively abundant and capital is relatively scarce, the isocost line will be similar to that of line $C$ in figure VI.1. When capital becomes relatively abundant and labor relatively scarce, the isocost line will change to something like line $D$. Therefore, the viability of a firm in a competitive market depends on whether its choice of technology is on the least-cost lines determined by the relative factor endowments of the economy.

This discussion can be extended to an economy with one industry that has many different products and an economy that has many different industries. As shown in figure VI.2, lines $I1$, $I2$, and $I3$ represent the isoquants of three different products that have the same output value in industry $I$. The average relative capital intensity of the three products is increasing from $I1$ to $I3$. As shown in figure VI.2, the viability of a firm is determined by whether or not its product and technology choices are on the least-cost line, which is determined by the relative factor endowments of the economy.

**Figure VI.2: Product Choice in an Industry**

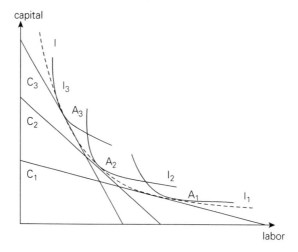

An industry can be represented by an isovalue line, which is the enve-
lope of the isoquants of all different kinds of products in the industry. On
the isovalue line of an industry, each point represents a specific product in
the industry that is produced by a specific technology and has the same
value as any other product in the same line. Figure VI.3 shows an economy that has three different industries, which are represented by the three
industrial isovalue lines $I$, $J$, and $K$, respectively. These three lines have the
same value. If labor is relatively abundant and the isocost line is indicated
by $C$, the economy has a comparative advantage in industries $I$ and $J$, and
a firm will be viable if it enters industry $I$ (or $J$) and adopts a corresponding technology to produce product $I1$ (or $J1$). Suppose that the relative
abundance of capital increases such that the isocost line changes to line $D$.
The comparative advantage of the economy will change accordingly, and
a firm will be viable if it upgrades its product-technology from $J1$ to $J2$
in industry $J$ or it migrates to industry $K$ and produces $K1$. The firm that
produces $I1$ in industry $I$ will become nonviable.

From the above discussion, one sees that the concept of a firm's viability and the concept of an economy's comparative advantage are closely
related. Viability refers to a firm's expected profitability, while comparative
advantage refers to the competitiveness of an industry in an open economy.

**Figure VI.3: Industry and Product Choices in an Economy**

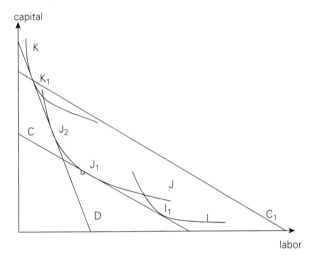

Both are endogenously determined by the economy's relative factor endowments. In a closed economy, however, the concept of viability is still relevant while the concept of comparative advantage is not. This discussion leads to the conclusion that, if an LDC wants to close the industry-technology gap, it needs to start by focusing on narrowing the factor endowment gap.

## Alternative Development Strategies

The government is the most important institution in any economy. Its economic policies shape the macro incentive structure that firms in the economy face. With the aim of explaining the success or failure of convergence in an LDC, I analyze government economic policies toward industrial development. I group these policies into different development strategies and then broadly divide the development strategies into two mutually exclusive groups: the comparative-advantage-defying (CAD) strategy, which attempts to encourage firms to ignore the existing comparative advantages of the economy in their entry/choice of industry/technology, and the comparative-advantage-following (CAF) strategy, which attempts to facilitate the firms' entry/choice of industry/technology according to the economy's existing comparative advantages.[3] No one country has ever followed either strategy consistently or without amendment. However, some countries have followed a strategy close enough to be a model of that strategy. A country that follows a particular strategy may also abandon it. A switch in strategy provides a good opportunity for careful comparison of the impact of different strategies.

## The Characteristics of Development Strategies

**The CAD Strategy.** Most LDCs are characterized by relatively abundant labor and scarce capital. Therefore, in a free, open, and competitive market, firms in LDCs enter relatively labor-intensive industries and adopt relatively labor-intensive technologies in their production.[4] However, political leaders and intellectuals in LDCs often equate industrialization, especially heavy industrialization, with modernization and push their countries to develop capital-intensive heavy industries and adopt the most advanced technologies in their production as quickly as possible. They want the economy to develop some industry like $K$ and produce product $K1$ when the isocost line determined by their endowment structure is $C$ (see figure VI.3).[5] With the given endowment structure, a firm producing product $K1$ will not be viable in a free, open, and competitive market. If a free, open, and competitive market is maintained, a firm following its government's strategy will incur a loss equivalent to the distance between isocost lines $C$ and $C1$. I call this loss a policy burden on the firm. Because the government is responsible for the firm's entry-adoption of the industry/technology, the government is accountable for the firm's loss. Therefore, for implementing the CAD strategy, the government must give the firm a policy subsidy to compensate for losses incurred (Lin and Tan 1999; Lin, Cai, and Li 1998, 2001).

How large the subsidy needs to be to compensate for the policy burden in the real world depends on how distant the promoted industry-technology is from the economy's comparative advantages. If the distance is small, the government can rely on tax incentives or direct fiscal transfer to subsidize the firm. However, this distance is often very large when the government in an LDC pursues a CAD strategy and special institutional arrangements are required for achieving the strategy's goal.

When an LDC government pursues a CAD strategy, the most frequently used method of subsidy is to suppress interest rates by regulation in order to reduce the project's capital costs. In addition, the equipment for the CAD project, in general, cannot be produced domestically in an LDC and needs to be imported from DCs. Therefore, access to foreign exchange is also required for the CAD project. However, foreign exchange in an LDC is generally scarce and expensive because the LDC's exports are limited and consist mainly of low-value agricultural products and resources. To lower the costs of equipment imports for the CAD project, governments also tend to overvalue domestic currency and undervalue foreign exchanges.[6]

On the one hand, the distortions in the interest rate and the foreign exchange rates will stimulate firms in both the priority and nonpriority sectors to demand more capital and foreign exchange. On the other hand, distortions will suppress the incentives to save and export and, thus, reduce the availability of capital and foreign exchange in the economy. Therefore, there will be shortages in capital and foreign exchange, and the government will need to use administrative measures to ration capital and foreign reserves in order to guarantee that the CAD firms will have the resources to perform strategic tasks. The resource allocation function of markets is thus constrained, or even replaced by, direct government rationing.[7]

Theoretically, the government that adopts a CAD strategy is responsible only for giving a subsidy to compensate for the loss arising from the policy burden. Given information asymmetry, however, the government cannot distinguish losses induced by the policy burden from operational losses. The firms will use the policy burden as an excuse and use resources to lobby the government for ex ante policy favors, such as access to low-interest loans, tax reductions, tariff protection, legal monopolies, and so on, to compensate for policy burdens. In addition to policy favors, if the firms still incur losses, they will also request that the government offer some ex post, ad hoc administrative assistance, such as more preferential loans. The economy will be full of rent-seeking or directly unproductive profit-seeking activities.[8] Because the firms can use the policy burdens as an excuse to bargain for more government support and because it is hard for the government to shun such responsibility, the firm's budget constraints become soft.[9] When a soft budget constraint exists, the manager of the firm will have no pressure to improve productivity and will have more on-the-job consumption and other moral hazards. The subsidies could actually end up much higher than those required to compensate for the original policy burdens.

*The CAF Strategy.* The government in an LDC could adopt the alternative CAF strategy to encourage firms to enter the industries for which the country has comparative advantages and to adopt the technology in production that will make these firms viable. As discussed above, the industries for which the economy has comparative advantages and the technologies that are appropriate for production are all determined by the country's relative factor endowments. However, the managers of firms, as micro agents, have no knowledge or concern of the actual endowments. Their only concerns are the prices of their outputs and the costs of their production. They will enter the industry and choose the technology of production appropriately only if the relative factor prices correctly reflect the relative factor abundances, which can be achieved only if the markets are competitive. Therefore, when the government in an LDC adopts a CAF strategy, its primary policy is to remove all possible obstacles to the functioning of free, open, and competitive product and factor markets.

The above discussions assume that the information about the product markets, industries, and production technologies is freely available to the firms in the economy. Therefore, when the factor endowment structure of the economy is upgraded, the firms can upgrade their product-technologies or smoothly upgrade from a less capital-intensive industry to a relatively more capital-intensive industry. Such information may not be available, however, so it is necessary to invest resources to search for, collect, and analyze industry, product, and technology information. If a firm carries out the activities on its own, it will keep the information private, and other firms will be required to make the same investment to obtain the information. There will be repetition in the information investments. The information has a public goods aspect, however. After the information has been gathered and processed, the cost of information dissemination is close to zero. Therefore, the government can collect the information about the new industries, markets, and technology and make it available in the form of an industrial policy to all firms.

The upgrading of technology and industry in an economy often requires the coordination of different firms and sectors in the economy. For example, the human capital or skill requirements of new industries and technologies may be different from those used with older industries and technologies. A firm may not be able to internalize the supply of the new requirements and will need to rely on outside sources. Therefore, the success of a firm's industry-technology upgrade also depends on the existence of an outside supply of new human capital. In addition to human capital, the firms that are upgrading may also require new financial institutions, trading arrangements, marketing, distribution facilities, and so on. Therefore, the government may also use industrial policy to coordinate among firms in different industries and sectors for the upgrade of industry and technology in the economy.

The upgrading of industry and technology is an innovation, and it is risky by nature. Even with the information and coordination provided by the government's industry policy, a firm's attempt to upgrade may fail because the upgrade is too ambitious, the new market is too small, the coordination is simply inadequate, and so forth. The failure will indicate to other firms that the targets of the industrial policy are not appropriate and, therefore, they can avoid that failure by not following the policy. That is, the first firm pays the cost of failure and produces valuable information for other firms. If the first firm succeeds, the success will also provide externalities to other firms, prompting them to engage in similar upgrades. These subsequent upgrades will also dissipate the possible rents that the first firm may enjoy, so there is an asymmetry between the costs of failure and the gains of success that the first firm may have. To compensate for the externality and the asymmetry between the possible costs and gains, the government may provide some forms of subsidy, such as tax incentives or loan guarantees, to the firms that initially follow the government's industrial policy.

It is worth noting that there is a fundamental difference between the industrial policy of the CAF strategy and that of the CAD strategy. The promoted industry/technology in the CAF strategy is consistent with the comparative advantage determined by changes in the economy's factor endowments, whereas the priority industry/technology that the CAD strategy attempts to promote is not consistent with comparative advantage. Therefore, the firms in the CAF strategy should be viable, and a small, limited-time subsidy should be enough to compensate for the information externality. By contrast, firms following a CAD strategy are not viable, and their survival depends on large, continuous policy favors and support from the government.[10]

A comparison of the successes and failures of industrial policies on automobile production in Japan, South Korea, India, and China is a good illustration of the differences between the CAF and CAD industrial policies. The automobile industry is a typical capital-intensive heavy industry, and its development is the dream of every LDC. Japan adopted an industrial policy to promote its automobile industry in the mid-1960s and achieved great success. Japan's experience is often cited as a supporting argument by advocates of an industrial policy for heavy industries in developing countries. South Korea instituted an industrial policy for automobile production in the mid-1970s and has also achieved a limited degree of success in automobile production. The automobile industries in China and India were started in the 1950s, and the industry in both countries has required continuous protection from the government since that time. How does one explain why a similar industrial policy can yield success in one instance and failure in another? This becomes clear once one compares the per capita income of these countries with the per capita income of the United States at the time when they initiated their policies (table VI.1).

Per capita income is a good proxy for the relative abundances of capital and labor in an economy. Capital is abundant and wage rates are high in a high-income country. In a low-income country, the opposite holds true. Table VI.1 indicates that, when Japan initiated its automobile production policy in the mid-1960s, its per capita income was more than 40 percent that of the United States. The automobile industry was not the most advanced, capital-intensive industry at that time, nor was Japan a

**Table VI.1: Level of Per Capita Income
(in 1990 Geary-Khamis $)**

| Year | United States | Japan | South Korea | India | China |
|------|---------------|-------|-------------|-------|-------|
| 1955 | 10,970 | 2,695 | 1,197 | 665 | 818 |
| 1965 | 14,017 | 5,771 | 1,578 | 785 | 945 |
| 1975 | 16,060 | 10,973 | 3,475 | 900 | 1,250 |

Source: Maddison 1995.

Note: The Geary-Khamis dollar is a multilateral purchasing power parity measurement of income. The use of the Geary-Khamis technique to convert income in different countries ensures cross-country comparisons, base country invariance, and additivity of the measurements.

capital-scarce economy. The Ministry of International Trade and Industry (MITI) gave support only to Nissan and Toyota. However, more than 10 firms—ignoring MITI's prompting not to enter the industry—also started automobile production and were successful, even though they did not receive any support from MITI. The above evidence indicates that the Japanese automobile firms were viable and that the MITI's promotion of the automobile industry in the 1960s was a CAF strategy. When Korea initiated its automobile industry development policy in the 1970s, its per capita income was only about 20 percent that of the United States and about 30 percent that of Japan. This may explain why the Korean government needed to give its automobile firms much greater and longer support than the Japanese government did its firms. Despite the support, two of the three automobile firms in Korea recently fell into bankruptcy. When China and India initiated their automobile industry development policies in the 1950s, their per capita incomes were less than 10 percent that of the United States. The automobile firms in China and in India were not viable at all. It is still the case today that their survival depends on heavy government protection.[11]

## Human Capital and Economic Development

The previous discussion focused on the accumulation of physical capital and its determining effect on an economy's industry-technology upgrading. The role of human capital in the process of development has received much attention in the development literature in recent years. Recent empirical work that attempts to explain cross-country income differences has included human capital as an explanatory variable in the production function and has found that human capital has a positive effect on economic growth (Mankiw, Romer, and Weil 1992; Caselli, Esquivel, and Lefort 1996; Klenow and Rodriguez 1997; Barro 1997).

What is the role of human capital accumulation in the development strategy of an LDC? If an LDC adopts a CAF strategy, the upgrading of its factor endowments will occur rapidly, and, consequently, the upgrading of its industry/technology will also be very rapid. Upgrading is an innovation by nature, even though the process is an imitation of an existing industry or technology from more advanced countries. The managers/workers will face and will need to handle uncertainty in skills, production, marketing, and so on in the upgrading process. They will also need to make many adaptations in the borrowed technologies to fit them to local conditions. Increasing the manager's or worker's human capital will increase his or her ability to handle these kinds of uncertainties and to carry out necessary adaptations (Schultz 1975). When a developing country narrows its industry/technology gap with DCs, it will move from mature industries and technologies closer to newer, less mature, and more uncertain industries and technologies. The requirement for human capital increases with economic development because human capital becomes increasingly complementary to physical capital in the new, frontier industries and technologies.[12] Given the complementary relationship between physical capital and human capital, it is necessary to accumulate human capital along with the accumulation of physical capital in the convergence process. Human capital is not a substitute for physical capital, however. An overaccumulation of human capital will lead to waste. After World War II, many scientists and engineers migrated to the United States from India and Latin America and other developing countries, but they made little direct contribution to the economic growth of their mother countries. These scientists and engineers are not to be blamed, however, because the low factor endowment structures in their mother countries made it impossible for many of them to find suitable positions that would utilize their human capital at home.

## Comparison of CAF Strategy and CAD Strategy

The attempt to catch up with DCs is justifiable for any LDC. The CAD strategy is appealing to political leaders and the general public in LDCs, including elite intellectuals, because most people directly observe the differences between industry-technology structures in DCs and those of their own countries and notice the correlation between industry-technology and per capita income. However, a CAF strategy enables an LDC to catch up with DCs, while a CAD strategy in effect stifles an LDC's opportunity to catch up. Many other theories have also attempted to explain an LDC's success or failure in achieving sustained economic development. The CAF/CAD strategy framework provides a unified explanation.

*Capital Accumulation.* An economy's optimal industry-technology structure is endogenously determined by its endowment structure. Therefore, if an LDC wants to attain the industry/technology structure of a DC, it first needs to narrow the gap between their respective factor endowment structures. The upgrading of the factor endowment structure means an increase in capital relative to labor. Capital accumulation depends on the size of surplus/profits accrued by firms and the rate of savings of economic agents in the economy. When, following the CAF strategy, a firm in an economy enters an industry in which that economy has a comparative advantage and adopts the least-cost technology in its production, the firm will be competitive, occupy the largest market share, and have the largest surplus/profits. Meanwhile, the capital in the economy employed in the industries following comparative advantage will have the highest possible rate of return. Therefore, economic agents' incentives to save will be highest. Moreover, the government will not distort the prices of factors and products, nor will the government use administrative powers to create legal monopolies. Therefore, there will be no scope for wasteful rent-seeking activities. The firm will have a hard budget constraint and will need to earn profits by improving management and competitiveness. The CAD strategy will result in just the opposite of what the CAF strategy promises regarding competitiveness, rates of return, rent-seeking activities, and the softness of budget constraints in firms in the priority industries. Therefore, upgrading the endowment structure will be faster under the CAF strategy than under the CAD strategy.

*Technology Transfer.* Upgrading the endowment structure in an economy will provide the basis for upgrading the industry-technology structure (Basu and Weil 1998). The targeted industry-technology will be new to the firms in an LDC and will need to be transferred from DCs. The learning costs will be smaller under the CAF strategy than under the CAD strategy because the distance between the new industry/technology and the old industry/technology is smaller under the former strategy than under the latter strategy (Barro and Sala-i-Martin 1992). Moreover, the patent protections for many of the targeted technologies under the CAF strategy may have already expired. Even if a technology is still under patent protection, the license fee will be lower with the CAF strategy than with the CAD strategy because the targeted technology for the CAF strategy is older than the CAD strategy ceteris paribus. In some cases, the firm under the CAD strategy will not be able to obtain the technology from DCs and will need to "reinvent the wheel" and invest in costly and risky R&D of technology by themselves. Therefore, the acquisition costs of the technology will be lower under the CAF strategy than under the CAD strategy.

*Openness in International Trade.* A number of empirical studies show that more open countries exhibit stronger convergence tendencies than do closed countries (Harberger 1985; Dollar 1992; Warr 1994; Ben-David 1993; Sachs and Warner 1995; Harrison 1996; Michaely 1977; Frankel and Romer 1999). International trade is expected to facilitate technology diffusion among countries. Jong-Wha Lee (1995) finds that countries importing more capital goods tend to grow faster, which means that new technologies may be embodied in the capital goods. However, Rodríguez and Rodrik (1999) argue that "methodological problems with the empirical strategies employed in this literature leave the results open to diverse interpretations." The role of trade policies is unclear. If the importation of equipment facilitates technology transfer, should the government adopt measures to promote it, or is it best to pursue trade liberalization in the sense of lower tariffs and nontariff barriers to trade?

In this framework, a country adopting a CAF strategy will rely on importing products for which it does not have a comparative advantage and exporting products for which it has comparative advantage. For this country, openness is endogenously determined by the country's factor endowment structure instead of by an exogenously determined policy for imports and exports. If the government in an LDC adopts the CAD strategy and attempts to substitute the importation of capital-intensive manufactured goods by domestic production, not only will the country's import trade be reduced but also its export trade will be suppressed. The latter consequence results from the transfer of resources away from the industries for which the economy has a comparative advantage. Also, exchange rates may be overvalued to facilitate the development of priority industries, effectively hampering export opportunities. Socialist economies, India, and many Latin American countries exemplify this case. The growth performance of these countries is miserable compared with economies that have followed the CAF strategy more closely. The government in an LDC may adopt the CAD strategy and, at the same time, encourage its firms in the priority capital-intensive industries to export. In this case, exports will be unprofitable even though the firms may have a high ratio of exports to foreign markets and may achieve fast technology improvements.[13] The firms' survival relies on the protection of domestic markets, preferential loans from banks, and other policy support. The country will have poor external accounts, accumulate foreign debt, and be easily affected by external shocks. It may be better for an LDC to adopt a CAD strategy that encourages exports rather than a CAD strategy that encourages import substitution. However, the overall economic performance of an economy that adopts the export-promotion strategy will be poorer than that of an economy that adopts the CAF strategy.[14] Therefore, it is not true that more exports in a country necessarily lead to higher GDP growth.[15]

*Financial Deepening.* Since the pioneering works by E. S. Shaw (1969) and R. Mckinnon (1973), many researchers have argued that there exists causality between financial deepening and economic growth in an economy. The indicator often used to measure financial deepening is either the ratio of the money supply (M2) to GDP, or the total amount of credits from financial intermediaries to private sector divided by GDP. The empirical findings have supported the above hypothesis (Levine 1997; Rajan and Zingales 1998).

However, the degree of financial deepening in an LDC is, to a large extent, endogenous to a government's development strategy. Under the CAD strategy, the carriers of a government's development strategy are the large-sized firms. To support the financial needs of nonviable large-sized firms, the government often nationalizes the firms and uses direct fiscal appropriation—skipping financial intermediation—to support these firms. Such was the case in the former socialist planned economies and continues to be the case in India and many other LDCs. Even if the government relies on private firms to carry out the CAD strategy, the CAD needs of large-sized firms will be significant and can only be met by a heavily regulated oligopolistic banking system; consequently, interest rates will be suppressed. In either case, the financial system in the country will be underdeveloped. However, the most competitive and dynamic firms in LDCs are the labor-intensive small- and medium-size firms, which are discriminated against and often denied access to financial services by large banks. The financial system is, thus, very inefficient. Moreover, the priority-sector firms that receive preferential access to bank loans are not viable and may not be able to repay loans. The banks often accumulate large amounts of bad debts from the large firms in the priority sectors, thus contributing to or even triggering an economic crisis. A precondition for financial deepening in an LDC is, therefore, a change in the government's development orientation from a CAD strategy to a CAF strategy.

*Macroeconomic Stability.* The bulk of empirical studies show that volatility in the macroeconomy could hamper long-run growth (Barro and Sala-i-Martin 1997). If the government in an LDC adopts the CAD strategy, firms in priority industries will not be viable and will rely on preferential loans, trade barriers, and other policy support for their survival. Because existing comparative advantages are not utilized, the economy as a whole will not be competitive, no dynamic changes in the economy's comparative advantage can be sustained, and the economic performance of the economy will be poor. The economy will have a weak financial sector and poor external accounts. Fiscal deficits, debt burdens, and financial fragility will accumulate, and macroeconomic stability will become unsustainable. A country that follows the CAF strategy will have better external accounts, will have healthier financial and fiscal systems, will be better equipped to resist external shocks, and will have a much better record of macroeconomic stability.[16]

*Income Distribution.* The relationship between income distribution and economic development is one of the oldest subjects in development economics. Simon Kuznets (1955) proposed an inverted-U hypothesis, suggesting that inequality tends to widen during the initial stages of economic development with a reversal of this tendency in the later stages. There is mixed evidence for this hypothesis. A number of cross-sectional studies support this hypothesis (Paukert 1973; Cline 1975, Chenery and Syrquin 1975; Ahluwalia 1976). However, the study of 43 episodes in 19 countries by Gary Fields (1991) finds that there is no tendency for poorer countries to yield increased rather than decreased inequality or for richer countries to yield decreased rather than increased income inequality, while a case study by John Fei, Gustav Ranis, and Shirley W. Y. Kuo (1979) shows that the Taiwanese economy achieved growth with equity. I propose that the adoption of the CAF strategy in an LDC will alleviate income inequality, whereas the adoption of the CAD strategy will aggravate income inequality. The most important asset that the poor have in an LDC is their own labor. The CAF strategy will result in sustained economic growth through the development of more-labor-intensive industries, creating more job opportunities for the poor, increasing wage rates, and allowing the poor to have a share in the benefits of growth. In contrast, the CAD strategy, by facilitating the development of more-capital-intensive industries, will reduce job opportunities for the poor and suppress wage rates of the working poor. Growth will not be sustainable, and when the economy breaks down, the poor will suffer the worst hardship, as evidenced by the recent East Asian financial crisis (Stiglitz 1998).

## The Choices of Development Strategy

When development economics started to take shape in the mid-twentieth century, the dominant view among development economists was to advise LDC governments to ignore their own comparative advantages and to adopt an inward-looking variation of the CAD strategy, such as the heavy-industry-oriented strategy or the import-substitution strategy. Proponents of the CAD strategy have often confused the causality of the dynamic change of comparative advantage. They have urged LDCs to disregard the constraint of relative capital scarcity in its factor endowments and to establish directly the same capital-intensive industries as those of DCs. They worked with the understanding that economic development can be accelerated if LDCs bypass development of labor- or resource-intensive industries.

I argue that the alignment of industry/technology with an economy's comparative advantage is key to facilitating the international diffusion of appropriate technology, to accelerating the rate of economic growth, and to realizing convergence. The dynamic change in an economy's comparative advantage depends on the dynamic change in the economy's endowment structure, which itself depends on the rapidity of capital accumulation in the economy. Capital accumulation, in turn, depends on how well economic agents in the economy exploit existing comparative advantages in their choices of industry/technology. An LDC that responds to comparative advantages present in its own factor endowments as the guiding principle in its choice of industry/technology will minimize imitation costs, experience faster shifts in its endowment structure, and sustain a continuous upgrade in its industrial structures. The development experience of the East Asian Four Little Dragons is a good illustration of the merits of the CAF strategy.

Like many other developing economies, Taiwan, South Korea, Hong Kong, and Singapore were very poor after World War II. In the early 1950s, their levels of industrialization were low, their capital and foreign exchange reserves were extremely limited, and their per capita incomes were very low. Like any other developing economy, they also faced the problem of choosing an appropriate development path. Taiwan, South Korea, and Singapore initially adopted an import-substitution CAD strategy but gave up the attempt to develop heavy industries while still in their initial stages. Instead, based on their factor endowments, they energetically developed labor-intensive industries, promoted exports, and expanded their outward-oriented economies to use their comparative advantages to the full extent.

At the time, many European countries, the United States, and Japan were gradually replacing labor-intensive industries with technology- and capital-intensive ones because of an increasing abundance of capital and increases in wage rates. The Four Little Dragons had abundant, inexpensive labor. Therefore, when developed countries' comparative advantages changed to more capital- and technology-intensive industries, the four East Asian countries were able to capitalize on the dynamic opportunities. Through trade linkages and the openness of their economies, labor-intensive industries in developed countries were relocated to these Asian economies. Because of the intensive use of their comparative advantages, the Four Little Dragons were very competitive and were thus able to achieve rapid capital accumulation. Along with the accumulation of capital and the change in comparative advantages, they gradually upgraded to more capital- and technology-intensive industries. As a result these four countries were able to sustain more than 30 years of rapid growth, first becoming newly industrialized economies and then reaching or nearly reaching the level of developed economies. Their extraordinary achievements in economic development have attracted worldwide attention.

Most developing economies adopted the CAD strategy in the 1950s and maintained that strategy for quite a long time. Why has Hong Kong never tried the CAD strategy, and why did Taiwan, South Korea, and Singapore switch to the CAF strategy shortly after trying the CAD strategy? Are these little dragons just lucky, or is their choice of the CAF strategy attributable to the wisdom of their political leaders? Gustav Ranis and Mahmood Syed (1992) attribute the success to their poor natural resources. In addition, I propose it is also attributable to their small populations. The CAD strategy is very inefficient and costly. The length of time this strategy can be maintained in an LDC depends on how many resources the government can mobilize to support it. The larger the per capita natural resources or the larger the population in an economy, ceteris paribus, the more resources government can mobilize to maintain the inefficient CAD strategy. For an economy with poor natural resources and a small population, the adoption of the CAD strategy will precipitate immediate economic crisis. By that time, the government will have no choice but to carry out reforms and change its strategy (Edwards 1995). In effect, influenced by the prevailing economic thoughts in the 1950s and motivated by the dream of nation building, many political leaders and intellectuals in Taiwan and Korea never gave up their desires to accelerate development of capital-intensive heavy industries. However, their per capita natural resources were extremely poor, and their populations were very small. The implementation of the CAD strategy in the early 1950s in Taiwan led to an immediate and enormous fiscal deficit coupled with high inflation, and the government was forced to give up the strategy (Tsiang 1984). When South Korea decided to push the heavy machinery and heavy chemical industries in the 1970s, similar results occurred and the push was postponed (Stern et al. 1995). Singapore and Hong Kong were both too small in population and too poor in natural resources to implement the CAD strategy.

## The Transition Strategy

If the government adopts a CAD strategy, the development of labor-intensive sectors—in which developing countries have comparative advantage—is repressed. The growth performance during the transition from a socialist economy to a market economy depends, therefore, on the country's ability to create an enabling environment for the development of labor-intensive sectors and at the same time find a way to solve the viability issue for firms inherited from the previous development strategy, paving the way for eliminating previous distortions and interventions. However, in many countries that adopted a CAD strategy, many nonviable enterprises exist that were unable to survive in an open and competitive market. If government distortions and interventions are eliminated abruptly, these nonviable enterprises will become bankrupt. At the same time, the originally suppressed labor-intensive industries will thrive, and newly created employment opportunities in these industries can surpass the losses from the bankruptcy of nonviable firms. As a result, the economy can grow dynamically soon after implementing the shock therapy, with at most a small loss of output and employment initially.

On the other hand, if the number of nonviable firms is too large, the output value and employment of those firms will make up too large a share in the national economy and shock therapy may be inapplicable. Its application will result in economic chaos due to large-scale bankruptcies and dramatic increases in unemployment. To avoid such dramatic increases in unemployment or to sustain these "advanced" nonviable enterprises, some governments, for example in Eastern Europe, continued their protection and subsidies for these firms—either explicitly or implicitly—and in the end, the economy can find itself in an awkward situation of shock without therapy (Kolodko 2000).[17]

The Chinese government opted for a dual-track approach, which is arguably better than shock therapy (McKinnon 1993). Instead of following the "macro-institution-first" approach proposed by the Washington Consensus, the Chinese government employed a 'micro-first' approach to improve incentives for farmers and state-owned enterprise workers. It adopted the individual household-based farming system to replace the collective farming system,[18] introduced profit-retention and managerial autonomy to state-owned enterprises,[19] making farmers and workers partial residual claimants. This reform greatly improved the incentives and productivity in agriculture and industry (Groves et al. 1994; Jefferson, Rawski, and Zheng 1992; Jefferson and Rawski 1995; Lin 1992; Li 1997; Weitzman and Xu 1995). Then the government allowed collective township-and-village enterprises (TVEs),[20] private enterprises, joint ventures, and state-owned enterprises to use the resources under their control to invest in labor-intensive industries that had been suppressed in the past. Meanwhile, the government required farmers and state-owned enterprises to fulfill their obligations to deliver certain quotas of products to the state at preset prices. The former reform improved the efficiency of resource allocation, and the latter ensured the government's ability to continue subsidizing the nonviable firms. Therefore, economic stability and dynamic growth were achieved simultaneously.

# Notes

† This is the inaugural D. Gale Johnson Lecture, presented at the University of Chicago on May 14, 2001. I am grateful for the helpful comments by Gary Becker, Kang Chen, James Heckman, Ralph Huenemann, Keijiro Otsuka, George Rosen, Jan Svejnar, Yingyi Qian, Kislev Yoav, Hao Zhou, and participants at the lecture. I am indebted to Mingxing Liu, Qi Zhang, and Peilin Liu, who provided invaluable help in reviewing the literature, assembling the data sets, and running the regressions.

1. Starting from very low levels, Japan's per capita income, measured in current U.S. dollars, exceeded that of the Unites States in 1988, and Singapore's per capita income exceeded that of the United States in 1996. Taiwan, South Korea, and Hong Kong have all significantly narrowed the income gap between themselves and the DCs.

2. Other economists also hold similar ideas about appropriate technology. Drawn from the lessons of the East Asian Miracle, some economists, such as K. Akamatsu (1962) and Ito Takatoshi (1998), suggested the "flying geese pattern" metaphor to describe the characteristics of industrial structure and technological diffusion during different development stages. But distinct policy proposals cannot be obtained from this metaphor.

3. Other ways of classification exist. For example, Griffin (1999) classifies development strategies into six alternatives: monetarism, open economy, industrialization, green revolution, redistribution, and socialist strategy.

4. For simplicity, I neglect the endowment of natural resources in the discussion. The propositions derived from the discussion remain valid if natural resources are also considered.

5. Heavy industry was the most advanced sector in the past. Nowadays, the priority of the CAD strategy in an LDC is focused on information technology and other high-tech industries, which are the most capital-intensive industries now.

6. The distortions in the interest rate and the foreign exchange rate are universal for LDCs that pursue a CAD strategy. Socialist countries and other LDCs that adopted a development strategy oriented toward heavy industry often distorted the prices of raw materials and living necessities along with wages.

7. The government that adopts a CAD strategy can also ration capital to the firms that are not in the priority industries. This is, in fact, the practice in the socialist planned economy. Certainly, the firms in the nonpriority industries will receive less capital than if the government does not adopt this strategy. Alternatively, the government can allow the market to allocate capital after the firms in the priority industries have been guaranteed rations. The interest rate will consequently be higher than it is when all capital is allocated by the market. On the contrary, the wage rate in the market will be lower because of the low labor

absorption of the firms in the priority industries. Therefore, the firms in the nonpriority industries will adopt a more labor-intensive technology in their production than if there is no government intervention. The above analyses are also applicable to the allocation of foreign exchange to firms in nonpriority industries. The distortions of interest rates and foreign exchange rates and the use of administrative allocations will lead to rent-seeking or directly unproductive profit-seeking activities.

8. The loss from rent-seeking or directly unproductive profit-seeking activities is estimated to be much larger than the loss from misallocation.

9. Kornai (1986) was the first economist to analyze the phenomenon of the soft budget constraint. He attributed the existence of the soft budget constraint in a state-owned enterprise in a socialist country to the patriarchic nature of the socialist government. However, I argue that soft budget constraints arise from the government's accountability for the nonviability of an enterprise caused by the government's development strategy. My hypothesis can explain why the phenomenon of the soft budget constraint also exists in firms of nonsocialist countries, such as South Korea's *chaebols*, and why the soft budget constraint phenomenon continues to exist in the Eastern European and former Soviet Union countries after their state-owned firms were privatized and the socialist system was abandoned. See also Lin and Tan (1999).

10. The dynamic comparative advantage is an often-used argument for the government's industrial policy and support to the firms (Redding 1999). In our framework, however, it is clearly evident that the argument is valid only if the government's support is limited to overcoming information and coordination costs and the pioneering firm's externalities to other firms. The industry should be consistent with the comparative advantage of the economy, and firms in the new industry should be viable, otherwise they will collapse once the government's supports are removed.

11. Most big-push attempts by the LDCs in the 1950s and 1960s failed. However, there has been a renewed interest in the idea after the influential articles by Murphy, Shleifer, and Vishny (1989a, 1989b). Their papers show that a government's coordination and support are required for setting up a key industry and that the demand spillovers from the key industry to other industries will enhance economic growth. For the "big push" strategy to be successful, however, the industry being promoted must be consistent with the comparative advantage, which is determined by the relative factor endowment of the economy, and the firms in the promoted industry must be viable after the push. Deviation from comparative advantage in the promoted industries and the consequent lack of viability of the chosen firms are the reasons why so many big-push attempts by the LDCs in the 1950s and 1960s failed.

12. In recent years, a variety of papers have argued that different technologies may display different degrees of skilled-labor or unskilled-labor bias. This idea

of skill complementarity has been employed to explain the increase in wage inequality in the 1980s and 1990s in the United States.

13. I met a senior manager of Hyundai Automobile Company in the United States in the early 1990s. He told me that Hyundai was still losing money after 10 years of successful exportation of cars to the U.S. market.

14. Taiwan and South Korea are good examples for comparison. Taiwan has followed the CAF strategy consistently, whereas Korea has often attempted to switch from the CAF strategy to the CAD strategy. The GDP growth rate, income distribution, macro stability, and other development indicators in Taiwan are better than those of South Korea.

15. In the development literature, export promotion and import substitution are often used as a classification of development strategy. There are some similarities between this classification and the CAF/CAD classification. Any country's level of export will be higher under a CAF strategy than that under a CAD strategy. However, the level of trade in any economy is endogenously determined by the economy's endowment structure. It is inappropriate to use an endogenous variable as a policy target or instrument.

16. In the recent East Asian financial crisis, Taiwan, Hong Kong, Singapore, and Malaysia were affected slightly whereas Korea, Indonesia, and Thailand were hard hit. One reason for the different performances among these two groups of economies is the difference in their development strategies. The first group followed the CAF strategy closely, whereas the latter group leaned toward the CAD strategy; see Lin (2000).

17. The difference in the shares of nonviable firms in the economy might explain why the shock therapy recommended by Sachs succeeded in Bolivia but not in the economies of Eastern Europe and the former Soviet Union. Bolivia is a poor, small economy; therefore, the resources that the government could mobilize to subsidize the nonviable firms were small, and the share of nonviable firms in the economy was also relatively small. Stiglitz (1998) questioned the universal applicability of the Washington Consensus. He pointed out that it advocated use of a small set of instruments—including macroeconomic stability, liberalized trade and privatization—to achieve a relatively narrow goal of economic growth. He encouraged governments to use a broader set of instruments—such as financial regulations and competition policy—to achieve a broader set of goals, including sustainable development, equity of income distribution and so on. Stiglitz's arguments are based on information asymmetry and the need for government to overcome market failures. However, he did not discuss how to deal with the issue of nonviable firms in developing and transitional economies and the implications of nonviability for choices of transition path and policies.

18. When reform started at the end of 1978, the government originally proposed to raise the agricultural procurement prices, to liberalize rural market fairs,

and to reduce the size of production teams of 20–30 households to voluntarily-formed production groups of 3–5 households, but explicitly prohibited the replacement of the production team system with an individual household-based farming system. However, a production team in a poor village in Fengyang County, Anhui Province, secretly leased the collective-owned land to individual households in the team in the fall of 1978 and harvested a bumper increase in outputs in 1979. Seeing the effects of an individual-household-based farming system, the government changed its policy and endorsed this approach as a new direction of reform (Lin 1992). Initially, the collectively-owned land was leased to farm households for one to three years, extended to 15 years in 1985, and further extended to 30 years in 1994. The farm household was obliged to deliver certain amounts of agricultural produce at the government-set prices to fulfill its quota obligation until the late 1990s.

19. The state-owned enterprise reform proceeded from the profit-retention system in 1979, the contract-responsibility system in 1986, and the modern corporation system from the 1990s to now. Each system was experimented in a small group of enterprises first before that system was extended nationwide (Lin, Cai, and Li 1994).

20. The TVE was another institutional innovation by the peasants in China during the transition process. After the Household Responsibility System (HRS) reform, farmers obtained a substantial amount of residuals and saw profitable investment opportunities in consumer-products sector. However, due to the ideological reason at that time, the form of private enterprise was prohibited and the farmers used the collective TVE as an alternative to tap into the profitable opportunity. The government initially put many restrictions on the operation of TVEs for fear of TVEs' competition with state-owned enterprises for credits, resources, and markets. Only after the government was convinced by the evidences that the TVE was good for increasing farmers' income and for solving the shortages in the urban markets, did the government give green light to the development of TVEs in rural China (Lin, Cai, and Li 1994).

## References

Acemoglu, Daron, and Fabrizio Zilibotti. 1999. "Productivity Differences." Working Paper 6879 National Bureau of Economic Research, Cambridge, Mass.

Ahluwalia, Montek S. 1976. "Inequality, Poverty, and Development." *Journal of Development Economics* 3 (December): 307–12.

Akamatsu, K. 1962. "A Historical Pattern of Economic Growth in Developing Countries." *Developing Economies*, preliminary issue, no. 1 (March–August): 3–25.

Atkinson, Anthony B., and Joseph E. Stiglitz. 1969. "A New View of Technological Change." *Economic Journal* 79 (September): 573–78.

Barro, Robert J. 1997. *Determinants of Economic Growth: A Cross-Country Empirical Study.* Cambridge, Mass.: MIT Press.

Barro, Robert J., and Xavier Sala-i-Martin. 1992. "Convergence." *Journal of Political Economy* 100 (April): 223–51.

———. 1997. "Technological Diffusion, Convergence, and Growth." *Journal of Economic Growth* 2 (March): 1–26.

Basu, Susanto, and David N. Weil. 1998. "Appropriate Technology and Growth." *Quarterly Journal of Economics* 113 (November): 1025–54.

Baumol, William J. 1986. "Productivity Growth, Convergence, and Welfare: What the Long-Run Data Show." *American Economic Review* 76 (December): 1072–85.

Ben-David, Dan. 1993. "Equalizing Exchange: Trade Liberalization and Income Convergence." *Quarterly Journal of Economics* 108 (August): 653–79.

Caselli, Francesco. 1999. "Technological Revolutions," *American Economic Review* 89 (March): 78–102.

Caselli, Francesco, and Wilbur John Coleman II. 2000. "The World Technology Frontier." Working Paper 7904. National Bureau of Economic Research, Cambridge, Mass.

Caselli, Francesco, Gerardo Esquivel, and Fernando Lefort. 1996. "Reopening the Convergence Debate: A New Look at Cross-Country Growth Empirics." *Journal of Economic Growth* 1 (September): 363–89.

Chenery, Hollis B. 1961. "Comparative Advantage and Development Policy." *American Economic Review* 51 (March): 18–51.

Chenery, Hollis B., and M. Syrquin. 1975. *Pattern of Development, 1950–70.* New York: Oxford University Press.

Cline, William. 1975. "Distribution and Development: A Survey of the Literature." *Journal of Development Economics* 1 (February): 359–400.

Diwan, I., and D. Rodrik. 1991. "Patents, Appropriate Technology, and North-South Trade." *Journal of International Economics* 30: 27–47.

Dollar, David. 1992. "Outward-Oriented Developing Economies Really Do Grow More Rapidly: Evidence from 95 LDCs, 1976–1985." *Economic Development and Cultural Change* 40, no. 3 (April): 523–44.

Edwards, Sebastian. 1995. *Crisis and Reform in Latin America: From Despair to Hope.* New York: Oxford University Press.

Fei, John, Gustav Ranis, and Shirley W. Y. Kuo. 1979. *Growth with Equity: The Taiwan Case,* New York: Oxford University Press.

Fields, Gary. 1991. "Growth and Income Distribution." In *Essays on Poverty, Equity, and Growth*, ed. George Psacharopoulus. Oxford: Pergamon, pp. 1–52.

Frankel, Jeffrey, and David Romer. 1999. "Does Trade Cause Growth?" *American Economic Review* 89 (June): 379–99.

Gerschenkron, A. 1962. *Economic Backwardness in Historical Perspective.* Cambridge, MA: Harvard University Press.

Griffin, Keith. 1999. *Alternative Strategies for Economic Development,* 2d ed. London: St. Martin's Press.

Grossman, Gene M., and Elhanan Helpman. 1994. "Endogenous Innovation in the Theory of Growth." *Journal of Economic Perspectives* 8 (Winter): 23–44.

Groves, Theodore, Yongmiao Hong, John McMillan, and Barry Naughton. 1994. "Autonomy and Incentives in Chinese State Enterprises." *Quarterly Journal of Economics* 109 (1): 183–209.

Harberger, Arnold C., ed. 1985. *World Economic Growth.* San Francisco: ICS.

Harrison, Ann. 1996. "Openness and Growth: A Time-Series, Cross-Country Analysis for Developing Countries." *Journal of Development Economics* 48 (March): 419–47.

Jefferson, Gary H., and Thomas G. Rawski. 1995. "How Industrial Reform Worked in China: The Role of Innovation, Competition, and Property Rights." *Proceedings of the World Bank Annual Conference of Development Economics.* Washington DC: World Bank, pp. 129–56.

Jefferson, Gary H., Thomas G. Rawski, and Yuxin Zheng, 1992. "Growth, Efficiency, and Convergence in China's State and Collective Industry." *Economic Development and Cultural Change* 40 (2): 239–66.

Klenow, Peter, and A. Rodríguez-Clare. 1997. "The Neoclassical Revival in Growth Economics: Has It Gone Too Far?" In *NBER Macro Annual 1997,* ed. Ben S. Bernanke and Julio Rotemberg. Cambridge, Mass.: MIT Press, pp. 73–114.

Kolodko, Grzegorz W. 2000. *From Shock to Therapy. Political Economy of Postsocialist Transformation.* New York: Oxford University Press.

Kornai, Janos. 1986. "The Soft Budget Constraint." *Kyklos* 39, no. 1: 3–30.

Krueger, A. O. 1974. "The Political Economy of the Rent-Seeking Society." *American Economic Review* 64 (June): 291–303.

———. 1992. *Economic Policy Reform in Developing Countries.* Oxford, U.K.: Blackwell.

Kuznets, Simon. 1955. "Economic Growth and Income Inequality." *American Economic Review* 45 (March): 1–8.

Lal, Deepak. 1985. "Nationalism, Socialism and Planning: Influential Ideas in the South." *World Development* 13 (June): 749–59.

Lee, Jong-Wha. 1995. "Capital Goods Imports and Long Run Growth." *Journal of Development Economics* 48 (October 1): 91–110.

Levine, Ross. 1997. "Financial Development and Economic Growth: Views and Agenda." *Journal of Economic Literature* 35 (June): 688–726.

Li, Wei. 1997. "The Impact of Economic Reform on the Performance of Chinese State Enterprises, 1980–1989." *Journal of Political Economy* 105 (5): 1080–106.

Lin, Justin Yifu. 1992. "The Needham Puzzle: Why the Industrial Revolution Did Not Originate in China." UCLA Economics Working Paper 650. UCLA Department of Economics, Los Angeles.

———. 2000. "The Financial and Economic Crisis in Asia: Causes and Long-Term Implications." In *The New Social Policy Agenda in Asia: Proceedings of the Manila Social Forum* (Manila: Asian Development Bank), pp. 9–17.

Lin, Justin Yifu, and Guofu Tan. 1999. "Policy Burdens, Accountability, and the Soft Budget Constraint." *American Economic Review: Papers and Proceedings* 89 (May): 426–31.

Lin, Justin Yifu, Fang Cai, and Zhou Li. 1994. "China's Economic Reforms: Pointers for Oher Economies in Transition." Policy Research Working Paper 1310, World Bank, Washington, DC.

———. 1998. "Competition, Policy Burdens, and State-Owned Enterprise Reform." *American Economic Review: Papers and Proceedings* 88 (May): 422–27.

———. 2001. *China's State-Owned Firm Reform*, trans. by the authors (Hong Kong SAR, China: Chinese University of Hong Kong Press, 2001; originally published as *Zhongguo Guoyou Qiye Gaige*. Taipei: Linking Press, 2000).

Lucas, Robert E. 1988. "On the Mechanism of Economic Development." *Journal of Monetary Economics* 22 (March): 3–42.

———. 1993. "Making a Miracle." *Econometrica* 61 (March): 251–72.

Maddison, Angus. 1995. *Monitoring the World Economy, 1820–1992*. Paris: OECD, pp. 196–205.

Mankiw, N. Gregory, David Romer, and David N. Weil. 1992. "A Contribution to the Empirics of Economic Growth." *Quarterly Journal of Economics* 107 (May): 407–37.

McKinnon, R. 1973. *Money and Capital in Economic Development*. Washington, D.C.: Brookings Institution.

———. 1993. *The Order of Economic Liberalization: Financial Control in the Transition to a Market Economy*, 2d ed. Baltimore: Johns Hopkins University Press.

Michaely, Michael. 1977. "Exports and Growth: An Empirical Investigation." *Journal of Development Economics* 4 (March): 49–53.

Murphy, Kevin M., Andrei Shleifer, and Robert W. Vishny. 1989a. "Income Distribution, Market Size, and Industrialization." *Quarterly Journal of Economics* 104 (August): 537–64.

———. 1989b. "Industrialization and Big Push." *Journal of Political Economy* 97 (October): 1003–26.

Pack, Howard. 1994. "Endogenous Growth Theory: Intellectual Appeal and Empirical Shortcomings." *Journal of Economic Perspectives* 8 (Winter): 55–72.

Paukert, Felix. 1973. "Income Distribution at Different Levels of Development: A Survey of Evidence." *International Labour Review* 108 (August–September): 97–125.

Pearson, Lester B. 1969. *Partners in Development: Report of the Commission on International Development.* New York: Praeger.

Prebisch, Raul. 1959. "Commercial Policy in the Underdeveloped Countries." *American Economic Review: Papers and Proceedings* 49 (May): 251–73.

Rajan. R. G., and L. Zingales. 1998. "Financial Dependence and Growth." *American Economic Review* 88 (June): 559–86.

Ranis, Gustav, and Mahmood Syed. 1992. *The Political Economy of Development Policy Change.* Cambridge, Mass.: Blackwell.

Redding, Stephen. 1999. "Dynamic Comparative Advantage and the Welfare Effects of Trade." *Oxford Economic Papers* 51 (January): 15–39.

Rodríguez, Francisco, and Dani Rodrik. 1999. "Trade Policy and Economic Growth: A Skeptic's Guide to the Cross-National Evidence." Working Paper w7081. National Bureau of Economic Research, Cambridge, Mass; subsequently published in National Bureau of Economic Research. 2000. *NBER Macroeconomics Annual, 2000,* ed. B. Bernanke and K. Rogoff. Cambridge, Mass.: MIT Press, pp. 261–325.

Romer, Paul. 1986. "Increasing Returns and Long-Run Growth." *Journal of Political Economy* 94 (October): 1002–37.

———. 1994. "The Origins of Endogenous Growth." *Journal of Economic Perspectives* 5 (Winter): 3–22.

Rosenstein-Rodan, P. 1943. "Problems of Industrialization of Eastern and Southeastern Europe." *Economic Journal* 53 (June–September): 202–11.

Sachs, Jeffrey D., and Andrew Warner. 1995. "Economic Reform and the Process of Global Integration." *Brookings Papers on Economic Activity,* no. 1: 1–95.

Schultz, T. W. 1975. "The Value of the Ability to Deal with Disequilibria." *Journal of Economic Literature* 13 (September): 827–46.

Schumacher, E. F. 1973. *Small Is Beautiful: Economics as If People Mattered.* New York: Harper & Row.

Shaw, E. S. 1969. *Financial Deepening in Economic Development.* New York: Oxford University Press.

Solow, Robert M. 1956. "A Contribution to the Theory of Economic Growth." *Quarterly Journal of Economics* 70 (February): 65–94.

Stern, Joseph J., Ji-hong Kim, Dwight H. Perkins, and Jung-ho Yoo, eds. 1995. *Industrialization and the State: The Korean Heavy and Chemical Industry Drive.* Cambridge, Mass.: Harvard University Press.

Stiglitz, Joseph E. 1998. "Toward a New Paradigm for Development: Strategies, Polices, and Processes." 1998 Prebisch Lecture at the United Nations Conference on Trade and Development, Geneva, October 19.

Takatoshi, Ito. 1998. "What Can Developing Countries Learn from East Asia's Economic Growth?" In *Annual World Bank Conference on Development Economics, 1997*, ed. Boris Pleskovic and Joseph E. Stiglitz. Washington, D.C.: World Bank, pp. 183–200.

Tsiang, Sho-chieh. 1984. "Taiwan's Economic Miracle: Lessons in Economic Development." In *World Economic Growth: Case Studies of Developed and Developing Nations*, ed. Arnold C. Harberger. San Francisco: ICS.

Warr, Peter G. 1994. "Comparative and Competitive Advantage," *Asian Pacific Economic Literature* 8 (November): 1–14.

Weitzman, Martin L., and Xu Chenggang. 1994. "Chinese Township-Village Enterprises as Vaguely Defined Cooperatives." *Journal of Comparative Economics* 18 (2): 121–45.

# PART 2*

## Strategy Choice and Economic Performance: Empirical Testing

The previous sections discussed the effects of development strategy on institutional arrangements, economic growth, income distribution, and transition performance in a country. From those discussions, I derive several testable hypotheses.

Hypothesis 1. A country that adopts a CAD strategy will require various government interventions and distortions in its economy.

Hypothesis 2. Over an extended period, a country that adopts a CAD strategy will have poor growth performance.

Hypothesis 3. Over an extended period, a country that adopts a CAD strategy will have a volatile economy.

Hypothesis 4. Over an extended period, a country that adopts a CAD strategy will have less equitable income distribution.

Hypothesis 5. In the transition to a market economy, a country's overall economic growth will be improved if it creates conditions to facilitate the development of formerly repressed labor-intensive industries.

## Estimating the Choice of Development Strategy Using the Capital Intensity in the Manufacturing Sector

To expand the set of countries and testable hypotheses, Lin and Liu (2004) propose another technology choice index (TCI), which is defined as follows:

$$TCI_{i,t} = \frac{AVM_{i,t}/LM_{i,t}}{GDP_{i,t}/L_{i,t}} \tag{VI.1}$$

where $AVM_{i,t}$ is the added value of manufacturing industries of country $i$ at time $t$; $GDP_{i,t}$ is the total added value of country $i$ at time $t$; $LM_{i,t}$ is

* Adapted from "Development Strategy, Development and Transition Performances: Empirical Analysis," in *Economic Development and Transition: Thought, Strategy, and Viability*, by Justin Yifu Lin. Reprinted with the permission of Cambridge University Press. Copyright © 2009 Cambridge University Press. The conclusion was adapted from "Development Strategy, Viability, and Economic Convergence." See disclaimer on the first page of part 1 of this chapter.

the labor in the manufacturing industry and $L_{i,t}$ is the total labor force. If a government adopts a CAD strategy to promote its capital-intensive industries, TCI in this country is expected to be larger than otherwise. This is because if a country adopts a CAD strategy, in order to overcome the viability issue of the firms in the prioritized sectors of the manufacturing industries, the government might give the firms monopoly positions in the product markets—allowing them to charge higher output prices—and provide them with subsidized credits and inputs to lower their investment and operation costs. The above policy measures will result in a larger $AVM_{i,t}$ than otherwise. Meanwhile, investment in the prioritized manufacturing industry will be more capital intensive and absorb less labor—*ceteris paribus*. The numerator in equation VI.1 will therefore be larger for a country that adopts a CAD strategy. As such, given the income level and other conditions, the magnitude of the TCI can be used as a proxy for the extent that a CAD strategy is pursued in a country.[1] The data for calculating the TCI are taken from the World Bank's *World Development Indicators* (2002) and the United Nations Industrial Development Organisation's *International Yearbook of Industrial Statistics* (2002). The means and variations of the TCI for each of the 122 countries in the period 1962–99 are reported in annex table VI.1.

## Development Strategy and Institutions

To assess the effects of development strategy on the government's distortions and interventions in the economy—as postulated in Hypothesis 1—I use several proxies for the institutions: 1) the "black-market premium" is used as an index of price distortion; 2) the index of economic freedom (IEF) and the expropriation risk are used as indexes of government's intervention in property rights institution; 3) the number of procedures required for a start-up firm to obtain legal status and the "executive *de facto* independence" are used as indexes of enterprise autonomy; and 4) the trade dependence ratio is used as an index for openness. The means and variations of each proxy for each country are reported in the annex table.

***Development Strategy and Price Distortions.*** The black-market premium of 105 countries is taken from the *Global Development Network Growth Database* provided by the Development Research Institute of New York

University. The relationship between the TCI and the black-market premium across four decades (1960–69, 1970–79, 1980–89, 1990–99) is shown in figure VI.4.

Figure VI.4 shows that the TCI and the black-market premium had positive relationships throughout the four decades, which implies—as predicted by Hypothesis 1—that a higher degree of CAD strategy is associated with a larger black-market premium.

*Development Strategy and Government Intervention in Resource Allocation.* To measure government's intervention in property rights institution, I use the index of economic freedom and the expropriation risk. The observations of IEF from 91 countries are taken from *Economic Freedom of the World* (Gwartney and Lawson 2007), which are available from 1970 onwards. This index ranges from zero to 10. A higher value means a higher degree of economic freedom. The correlations between the TCI and the IEF averaged across a decade for each country are shown in figure VI.5.

There is a strong negative relationship between the TCI and the IEF in each of the panels, which is consistent with the prediction that the more aggressively a government pursues a CAD strategy, the more government intervention is required, and the less economic freedom there is.

The expropriation risk of 102 countries is adopted from the *International Country Risk Guide.* The expropriation risk is the risk of outright confiscation and forced nationalization of property. This variable ranges from zero to 10. A higher value means that a private enterprise has a lower probability of being expropriated. Figure VI.6 plots the relationship between the TCI and the expropriation risk. Both variables are calculated as the average values from 1982 until 1997.

As shown, there is a negative relationship between the TCI and expropriation risk, which is consistent with the expectation that the more aggressive the government's CAD strategy, the more likely it is that the government will confiscate or nationalize an enterprise.

*Development Strategy and Enterprise Autonomy.* To analyze the relationship between the government's development strategy and enterprise autonomy, the study uses two indexes—including the number of procedures and the executive *de facto* independence used in Djankov and

**Figure VI.4: The TCI and Black-Market Premium**

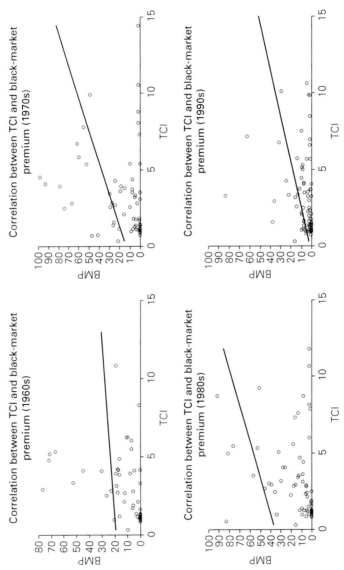

**Figure VI.5: The TCI and the IEF**

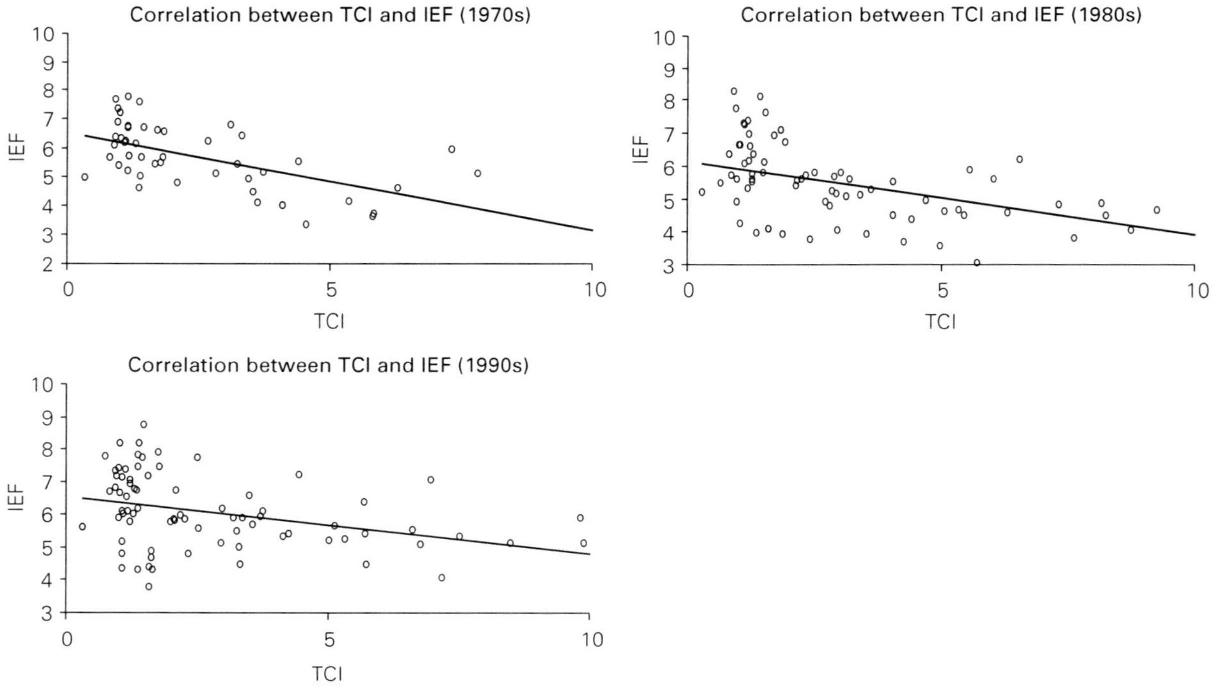
Correlation between TCI and IEF (1970s)
IEF
TCI
10
9
8
7
6
5
4
3
2
0
5
10
Correlation between TCI and IEF (1980s)
IEF
TCI
10
9
8
7
6
5
4
3
0
5
10
Correlation between TCI and IEF (1990s)
IEF
TCI
10
9
8
7
6
5
4
3
0
5
10

**Figure VI.6: The TCI and Expropriation Risk**

Correlation between TCI and expropriation risk

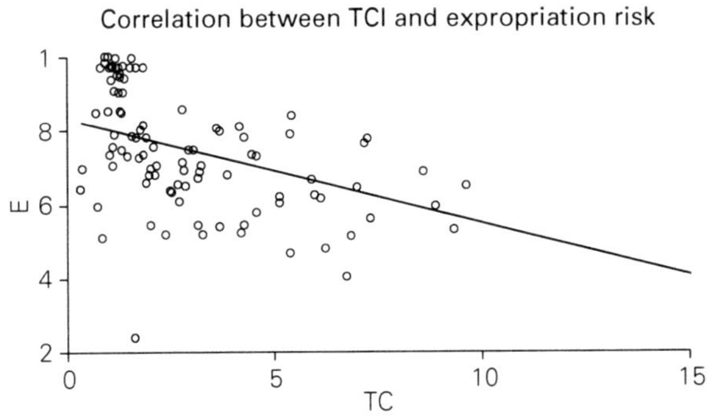

Murrell (2002)—to represent the extent of enterprise autonomy. There are 69 countries in the samples.

The "number of procedures" is the number of administrative procedures that a start-up firm has to comply with in order to obtain legal status—that is, to start operating as a legal entity. "'Executive *de facto* independence*" is an index of "operation (*de facto*) independence of the chief executive," descending from 1 to 7 (1 = pure individual; 2 = intermediate category; 3 = slight to moderate limitations; 4 = intermediate category; 5 = substantial limitations; 6 = intermediate category; 7 = executive parity or subordination). Both indexes are the average values for the years from 1965 until 1998.

The positive relationship between the TCI and the number of procedures and the negative relationship between the TCI and the executive *de facto* independence shown in figure VI.7 indicate that a high degree of CAD strategy is associated with low enterprise autonomy, which confirms the prediction of Hypothesis 1.

*Development Strategy and Openness.* The trade-dependence ratio of 115 countries—taken from Dollar and Kraay (2003)—is used to reflect the openness of a country. The correlations between the TCI and openness averaged across the past four decades in each country are shown in figure VI.8.[2]

We find that the TCI and openness have a negative relationship, which is consistent with the hypothesis that if a developing-country government adopts a CAD strategy, its economy will become more inward-oriented

**Figure VI.7: The TCI and Enterprise Autonomy**

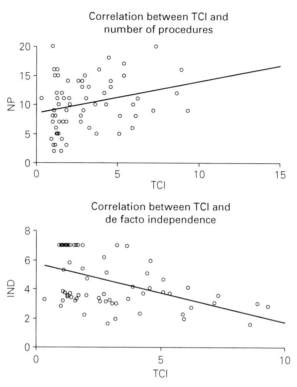

than otherwise. This is because the CAD strategy attempts to substitute the import of capital-intensive manufactured goods with domestic production, causing a reduction in imports. Exports will also be suppressed due to the inevitable transfer of resources away from the industries that have comparative advantage to the prioritized sectors determined by the CAD strategy. The more a country follows a CAD strategy, therefore, the less openness there will be in the country.

## Development Strategy and Economic Growth

Hypothesis 2 predicts that over an extended period, a country adopting a CAD strategy will have a poor growth performance. The following econometric model is used to test the hypothesis:

$$GROWTH_{i,t} = C + \alpha TCI_{i,t} + \beta X + \vartheta \qquad (VI.2)$$

**Figure VI.8: The TCI and Openness**

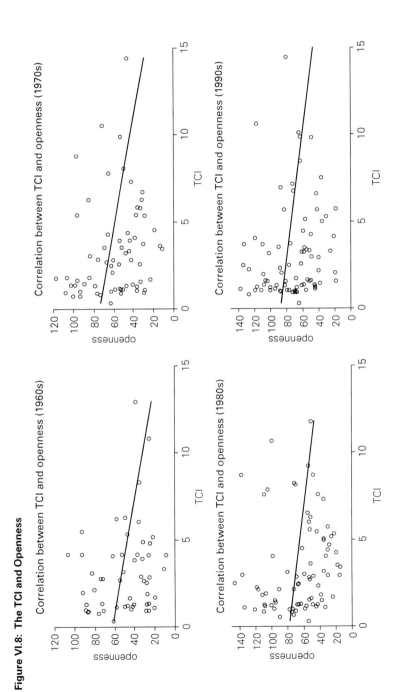

where $GROWTH_{i,t}$ is the economic growth rate in a certain period in country $i$, $X$ is a vector that includes the initial per capita GDP to control the effect of the stage of development, the initial population size to control the effect of market size, the indicator of rule of law to reflect the institutional quality—which was constructed by Kaufmann and Kraay (2002)—the trade-dependent ratio to reflect openness, the distance from the Equator and whether the country is land-locked. The last two explanatory variables are included to capture the effects of geography. The instrumental variable for controlling the endogeneity of institutional quality is the share of population that speaks English and the share that speaks a major European language (Hall and Jones 1999), which are used to capture the long-run impacts of colonial origin on current institutional quality. Similarly, the fitted values of trade predicted by a gravity model are used as the instrument for openness. This approach was proposed by Frankel and Romer (1999) and revised by Dollar and Kraay (2003). In the regressions that use panel data, the instrument for openness is the single-period lagged value of itself. Table VI.2 summarizes the definition of each variable and the data source.

We will use two approaches to test this hypothesis. In the first approach, the dependent variable is the average annual growth rate of per capita GDP for the period 1962–99, and in the second, the dependent variable is the average annual growth rate of per capita GDP for each decade of the 1960s, 1970s, 1980s and 1990s.

Table VI.3 reports the estimates from the first approach. Regression Model 1.1 and Model 1.2 use the OLS approach to obtain the estimates. The explanatory variables in Model 1.1 include only the proxy for the development strategy, LnTCI1, and the initial GDP per capita, LnGDP60, whereas Model 1.2 includes other explanatory variables that capture institutional quality, openness, geographic location and market size. Model 1.3 has the same explanatory variables but the model uses the 2SLS approach in order to control the endogeneity of institutional quality and openness.

The results show that the TCI has the expected negative effect and is highly significant in all three regressions. This finding supports Hypothesis 2 that the more aggressive is the CAD strategy pursued by a country, the worse the growth performance is in that country in the period 1962–99. The estimated coefficients of LnTCI1 have values ranging from –0.66 to –1.25. From the estimates, we can infer that a 10 percent increase from

**Table VI.2: Variable Definitions and Data Source**

| Variable | Definition | Mean | Std dev. | Sources |
|---|---|---|---|---|
| LnGDP60 | Log of real GDP per capita in 1960 | 7.33 | 0.80 | World Bank *World Development Indicators* |
| LnGDP80 | Log of real GDP per capita in 1980 | 7.91 | 1.05 | World Bank *World Development Indicators* |
| LnGDP | Log of real GDP per capita in 1960, 1970, 1980, 1990 | 7.73 | 1.02 | World Bank *World Development Indicators* |
| LnTCI1 | Log of the average technology choice index from 1963 to 1999 | 0.96 | 0.90 | World Bank *World Development Indicators* and UNIDO (2002) |
| LnTCI2 | Log of the average TCI per decade in 1960s, 1970s, 1980s, 1990s | 0.85 | 0.84 | World Bank *World Development Indicators* and UNIDO (2002) |
| LnTCI70 | Log of the average TCI from 1970 to 1979. If not available, we use the log of the average TCI from 1980 to 1985 | 0.91 | 0.92 | World Bank *World Development Indicators* and UNIDO (2002) |
| ΔTCI | Log of the average TCI from 1999 to 1990 minus LnTCI70 | 0.07 | 0.38 | World Bank *World Development Indicators* and UNIDO (2002) |
| RL01 | Rule of law in 2000–01 | 0.003 | 0.95 | Kaufmann and Kraay (2002) |
| LnOPEN1 | Log of the average (exports + imports)/GDP from 1960 to 1999 | −1.11 | 0.81 | Dollar and Kraay (2003) |
| LnOPEN2 | Log of the decadal average (exports + imports)/GDP in 1960s, 1970s, 1980s, 1990s | −1.30 | 0.84 | Dollar and Kraay (2003) |
| LnPOP1 | Log of the total mid-year population from 1960 to 1999 | 15.2 | 2.11 | World Bank *World Development Indicators* |
| LnPOP2 | Log of the total initial-year population in 1960s, 1970s, 1980s, 1990s | 14.93 | 2.12 | World Bank *World Development Indicators* |
| LANDLOCK | Dummy variable taking value of 1 if country is land-locked; 0 otherwise | 0.18 | 0.39 | Dollar and Kraay (2003) |
| LnDIST | Log (DISTEQ+1), where DISTEQ is the distance from Equator, measured as absolute value of latitude of capital city | 2.96 | 0.88 | Dollar and Kraay (2003) |
| ENGFRAC | Fraction of population speaking English | 0.07 | 0.24 | Hall and Jones (1999), taken from Dollar and Kraay (2003) |
| EURFRAC | Fraction of population speaking a major European language | 0.22 | 0.38 | Hall and Jones (1999), taken from Dollar and Kraay (2003) |
| LnFRINST | Instrument variable for LnOPEN | −2.83 | 0.64 | Dollar and Kraay (2003) |
| INST | Predicted value of RL01 in the cross-section estimation (ENGFRAC and EURFRAC as the instruments) | 0.003 | 0.34 | Author's estimation |

**Table VI.3: Development Strategy and Economic Growth—Model 1**

| | Model 1.1 (OLS) | Model 1.2 (OLS) | Model 1.3 (2SLS) |
|---|---|---|---|
| Constant | 7.32*** | 4.66** | 3.26 |
| | (1.60) | (1.87) | (2.15) |
| LnTCI2 | −1.25*** | −0.66*** | −0.92*** |
| | (0.20) | (0.18) | (0.19) |
| LnGDP60 | −0.54*** | −0.99*** | −0.59*** |
| | (0.20) | (0.18) | (0.21) |
| RLO2 | | 0.58*** | |
| | | (0.21) | |
| INST | | | 0.22 |
| | | | (0.41) |
| LnOPEN2 | | 0.70*** | |
| | | (0.22) | |
| TRADE2 | | | 0.93** |
| | | | (0.43) |
| LnDIST | | 0.20 | 0.47*** |
| | | (0.16) | (0.16) |
| LnPOP2 | | 0.33*** | 0.22** |
| | | (0.09) | (0.09) |
| LANDLOCK | | 0.07 | 0.46 |
| | | (0.32) | (0.38) |
| Adjusted-$R^2$ | 0.36 | 0.56 | 0.44 |
| Observations | 85 | 83 | 83 |

\* indicates significance at the 10 per cent level

\*\* indicates significance at the 5 per cent level

\*\*\* indicates significance at the 1 per cent level

*Note:* The dependent variable is the yearly average of per-capita GDP growth rate in 1962–99. Standard errors are reported in parentheses.

the mean in the TCI can result in approximately 0.1 of a percentage point reduction in the country's average annual growth rate of per capita GDP for the whole period 1962–99.

The regression results also show that the initial per capita income and the population size have the expected signs and significant effects on the growth rate. Rule of law, openness and distance from the Equator also have the expected signs. Rule of law, however, is not significant in the 2SLS regression and distance from the Equator is not significant in the OLS regression. Whether the country is land-locked is insignificant in all three regressions.

Table VI.4 reports the results from the second approach, in which the dependent variable is the average annual growth rate of per capita GDP in

**Table VI.4: Development Strategy and Economic Growth—Model 2**

|  | Model 2.1 (OLS) | Model 2.2 (OLS) | Model 2.3 (fixed effect) | Model 2.4 (2SLS) | Model 2.5 (2SLS, fixed effect) |
|---|---|---|---|---|---|
| Constant | 7.15*** (1.61) | 8.36*** (2.16) | 3.83* (2.11) | −0.74 (2.56) | −2.70 (2.37) |
| LnTCI2 | −1.10*** (0.21) | −0.69*** (0.20) | −0.40** (0.19) | −0.69*** (0.24) | −0.47** (0.22) |
| LnGDP | −0.54*** (0.18) | −1.39*** (0.23) | −0.86*** (0.23) | −0.17 (0.27) | 0.17 (0.25) |
| RLO1 | | 1.45*** (0.23) | 1.12*** (0.22) | | |
| INST | | | | −0.38 (0.42) | −0.67* (0.38) |
| LnOPEN2 | | 0.24 (0.23) | 0.35 (0.22) | | |
| TRADE2 | | | | 0.01 (0.29) | −0.06 (0.27) |
| LnDIST | | −0.04 (0.18) | −0.10 (0.17) | 0.27 (0.20) | 0.17 (0.18) |
| LnPOP2 | | 0.32*** (0.10) | 0.41*** (0.09) | 0.22* (0.12) | 0.27** (0.12) |
| LANDLOCK | | −0.31 (0.39) | 0.08 (0.36) | −0.23 (0.46) | 0.02 (0.43) |
| Adjusted-$R^2$ | 0.08 | 0.23 | 0.36 | 0.08 | 0.24 |
| Observations | 315 | 278 | 278 | 213 | 213 |

* indicates significance at the 10 per cent level

** indicates significance at the 5 per cent level

*** indicates significance at the 1 per cent level

*Notes:* Dependent variable is the average growth rate of GDP per capita in the decades 1960s, 1970s, 1980s, 1990s. Models 2.3 and 2.5 include the time dummy. Standard errors are reported in parentheses.

each decade from 1960–99. The regressions to fit the estimates are OLS for Models 2.1 and 2.2, one-way fixed effect for Model 2.3, 2SLS for Model 2.4 and 2SLS and one-way fixed effect for Model 2.5. In the fixed-effect models, time dummies are added to control the time effects, whereas the 2SLS models are used for controlling the endogeneity of institutional quality and openness.

As in the results in the first approach, the estimates for the TCI have the expected negative sign and are highly significant in all regressions. The finding is once again consistent with the prediction of Hypothesis 2 that development strategy is a prime determinant of the long-run economic growth performance of a country.[3]

The results for other explanatory variables are similar to those in table VI.3.

## Development Strategy and Economic Volatility

Hypothesis 3 is about the effect of a CAD strategy on the volatility of the economic growth rate. If a country follows a CAD strategy, there could be a period of investment-led growth, but it will not be sustainable and is likely to cause economic crisis. Therefore, a country that follows a CAD strategy is likely to be more volatile than otherwise. In the empirical testing of this hypothesis, the volatility of a country's per capita GDP growth rate in the period 1962–99 is measured as follows:

$$
V_i = \left[ (1/38) \sum_{t=1962}^{T=1999} \left( \frac{g_{it}}{\left( \sum_{t=1962}^{T=1999} g_{it} \right) \Big/ 38} - 1 \right)^2 \right] \tag{VI.3}
$$

where $g_{it}$ is the growth rate of GDP per capita of $i^{th}$ country in year $t$.

In testing Hypothesis 3, the dependent variable is the log of the above measurement of volatility, $V_i$, and the explanatory variables are the same as those used in testing Hypothesis 2. The approaches to fitting the regression equation are also similar to those used previously. Table VI.5 reports the results from fitting the regression models. As expected, the estimates of the TCI are positive and highly significant in all three regressions. The results support Hypothesis 3 and indicate that the deeper a country follows a CAD strategy, the more volatile is the country's economic growth rate. From the estimates, it can be inferred that a 10 percent increase in the TCI could cause volatility to increase about 4–6 per cent.

The estimates for other explanatory variables show that the quality of institutions, the degree of openness, whether the country is land-locked and the population size all have negative effects on economic volatility. The coefficients on population size, which is a proxy for the size of the economy, are significant in the OLS and 2SLS models. The estimated coefficients of initial per capita income in 1960 and the distance from the Equator are insignificant in all three regressions. The estimated coefficients of all other variables are either significant in the OLS model or the 2SLS model.

**Table VI.5: Development Strategy and Economic Volatility**

|  | Model 3.1 (OLS) | Model 3.2 (OLS) | Model 3.3 (2SLS) |
|---|---|---|---|
| Constant | 0.49 | 3.03** | 3.63** |
|  | (1.06) | (1.44) | (1.56) |
| LnTCI1 | 0.64*** | 0.41*** | 0.56*** |
|  | (0.13) | (0.14) | (0.14) |
| LnGPP60 | −0.04 | 0.17 | −0.07 |
|  | (0.13) | (0.14) | (0.15) |
| RL01 |  | −0.33** |  |
|  |  | (0.16) |  |
| INST |  |  | −0.20 |
|  |  |  | (0.29) |
| LnOPEN1 |  | −0.46*** |  |
|  |  | (0.17) |  |
| TRADE1 |  |  | −0.53 |
|  |  |  | (0.33) |
| LnDIST |  | −0.003 | −0.15 |
|  |  | (0.11) | (0.11) |
| LANDLOCK |  | −0.31 | −0.53* |
|  |  | (0.24) | (0.28) |
| LnPOP1 |  | −0.26*** | −0.18** |
|  |  | (0.06) | (0.07) |
| Adjusted-R² | 0.29 | 0.47 | 0.37 |
| Observations | 103 | 93 | 93 |

* indicates significance at the 10 per cent level

** indicates significance at the 5 per cent level

*** indicates significance at the 1 per cent level

*Notes:* Dependent variable is the log of the growth rate's volatility for GDP per capita from 1962–99. Standard errors are reported in parentheses.

## Development Strategy and Income Distribution

In testing the effect of development strategy on income distribution, the following regression equation is used:

$$GINI_{i,t} = C + \alpha TCI_{2i,t} + \beta X + \varepsilon \qquad (VI.4)$$

where $GINI_{i,t}$ is the index of inequality in country $i$ at time $t$, $TCI$ is a proxy for the development strategy and $X$ is a vector of other explanatory variables.

GINI coefficients are taken from a revised version of the data set in Deininger and Squire (1996). The data set includes the estimation of GINI

coefficients for many countries in the various literature. Some are estimated according to the data on income; others are based on expenditure.
The coverage differs between the different countries' GINI data. Deininger
and Squire (1996) assessed the quality of GINI coefficient estimations; only
those ranked as "acceptable" were used in the regression. The original estimates of GINI coefficients based on income data are left unchanged, but
those based on consumption expenditure are adjusted by adding 6.6, which
is the average difference between the two estimation methods. Matching
this GINI data with the TCI, I end up with a panel of 261 samples from
33 countries. Figure VI.9 shows the relationship between the TCI and the
GINI coefficient.

In order to test alternative hypotheses for the determination of inequality,
I have included the explanatory variables—per capita income, $GDPPC_{i,t}$,
and its reciprocal, $GDPPC\_1_{i,t}$—which test the Kuznets inversed-U hypothesis. If Kuznets' hypothesis holds, the coefficients for these two variables
should be significantly negative.

Based on the data set of Deininger and Squire (1996), Li et al. (1998)
conducted a robust empirical test, and the result showed that the GINI
coefficient for an individual country was relatively constant across different periods. Based on this conclusion, the GINI coefficient in the initial
year in the data set is introduced into the regression, denoted by IGINI.
In this way, the historical factors that could affect income distribution
and those non-observable factors across countries can be excluded. In the

**Figure VI.9: Development Strategy and Income Distribution**

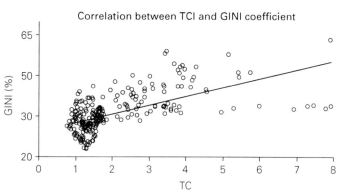

data set, the year of IGINI differs from country to country. In spite of this difference, the higher the IGINI, the higher are the subsequent GINI coefficients—regardless of the initial year. As a result, the coefficient of IGINI is expected to be positive.

Corruption could also affect income distribution. Two explanatory variables are included in the regression: the index for corruption, $CORR_{i,t}$, and the quality of officials, $BQ_{i,t}$. The data for these two variables are taken from Sachs and Warner (2000) and they differ from country to country but remain constant throughout the period studied. The larger the value is, the less is the corruption and the higher is the quality of officials. The coefficients of these two variables are expected to be negative.

Foreign trade could also affect income distribution. It affects the relative prices of factors of production (Samuelson, 1978) and market opportunities for different sectors in the economy. Consequently, trade—through its effect on employment opportunities (Krugman and Obstfeld, 1997)—can affect income distribution. The regression therefore includes an index of economic openness, denoted by $OPEN_{i,t}$, which is the share of total import and export value in nominal GDP, as an explanatory variable. The data are taken from Easterly and Yu (2000). Openness could, however, have different impacts on skilled and unskilled labor, on tradable and non-tradable sectors and in the short run and in the long run. Its sign is therefore uncertain.

Table VI.6 reports the results from five regression models. Model 4.1 includes all explanatory variables: *TCI, IGINI, GDPPC, GDPPC_1, CORR, BQ* and *OPEN*. As *CORR, BQ* and *OPEN* are endogenous, other models exclude these variables to control the endogeneity problem. Because *IGINI, CORR* and *BQ* are time invariant, the one-way effects model is applied in fitting the regression of Models 4.1, 4.2 and 4.4. According to Hausmann tests, the one-way random-effect model is used in the regressions of Models 4.1, 4.2 and 4.4, and the two-way fixed-effect model is used in the regression of Models 4.3 and 4.5.

The estimated coefficients of *TCI* are positive and significant at the 1 percent level in all five regression models. These results strongly support the hypothesis that the more a country pursues a CAD strategy, the more severe will be the income disparity in that country. This result holds whether the initial income distribution is equal or unequal.

**Table VI.6: The Effect of Development Strategy on Inequality**

|  | Model 4.1r | Model 4.2r | Model 4.3f | Model 4.4r | Model 4.5f |
|---|---|---|---|---|---|
| CONSTANT | 6.46 | 8.18*** | 31.5*** | 8.09*** | 32.6*** |
|  | (4.72) | (2.40) | (1.75) | (3.16) | (0.97) |
| TCI | 1.32*** | 1.35*** | 1.84*** | 1.35*** | 1.72*** |
|  | (0.33) | (0.31) | (0.48) | (0.32) | (0.46) |
| IGINI | 0.73*** | 0.71*** |  | 0.71*** |  |
|  | (0.08) | (0.07) |  | (0.07) |  |
| GDPPC | −0.89 |  | 0.43 | 0.74 |  |
|  | (11.3) |  | (12.6) | (10.8) |  |
| GDPPC_1 | 0.40 |  | 1.91 | 3.21 |  |
|  | (1.84) |  | (2.11) | (16.6) |  |
| CORR | 1.03* |  |  |  |  |
|  | (0.58) |  |  |  |  |
| BQ | −0.84 |  |  |  |  |
|  | (0.58) |  |  |  |  |
| OPEN | 0.12 |  |  |  |  |
|  | (1.68) |  |  |  |  |
| R2 | 0.9040 | 0.8941 | 0.5495 | 0.8936 | 0.5780 |
| Hausmann statistics | 3.32 | 1.19 | 23.91 | 1.99 | 7.98 |
| Hausmann P-value | 0.19 | 0.28 | 0.00 | 0.37 | 0.00 |
| Sample | 261 observations from 33 countries | | | | |

f: fixed-effect model

r: random-effect model

* indicates significance at the 10 per cent level

** indicates significance at the 5 per cent level

*** indicates significance at the 1 per cent level

Notes: Null hypothesis of Hausmann test: there is a random effect in countries and time. Standard errors are reported in parentheses.

The estimated coefficients of IGINI are also positive and significant at the 1 percent level in Models 4.1, 4.2 and 4.4. This result is consistent with the finding in Li et al. (1998): that is, the initial income distribution will have a carry-over effect in the subsequent period's income distribution.

The estimated coefficients of *GDPPC* and *GDPPC_1* in Models 4.1, 4.3 and 4.4 are all insignificant and have an unexpected positive sign—except for *GDPPC* in Model 4.1. Kuznets' inversed-U hypothesis of income distribution is therefore rejected.

The results in Model 4.1 show that the coefficient for $CORR_{i,t}$ has an unexpected positive sign. One possible reason for this is that the effect of corruption on distribution is not reflected accurately in the surveys. The coefficient for bureaucracy quality, $BQ_{i,t}$, has an expected, but insignificant, negative sign. The coefficient for openness, $OPEN$, is positive, but not significant.

From the results above, it is clear that development strategy and initial income distribution are the two most important determinants of income distribution in a country. As argued above, for a country in which the government follows a CAF strategy, income distribution will become more equal even if its initial income distribution is unequal. In effect, this is the "growth with equity" phenomenon observed in Taiwan and other newly industrialized economies in East Asia (Fei, Ranis, and Kuo 1979).

## Transition and Economic Performance

As mentioned above, the development of labor-intensive sectors—in which developing countries have comparative advantage—is repressed and many institutions are distorted if the government adopts a CAD strategy, resulting in poor resource allocation and inefficiency. The growth performance during transition to a market economy depends, therefore, on the country's ability to create an enabling environment for the development of labor-intensive sectors and at the same time find a way to solve the viability issue for firms inherited from the previous development strategy so as to pave the way for eliminating previous distortions and interventions. A CAD strategy is associated with a high TCI. If, after the reform/transition, a country is able to successfully develop labor-intensive sectors, resource allocation and growth performance will improve, and the TCI will decline. A successful transition from a CAD strategy is therefore expected to result in a negative change in the TCI. The larger the negative change is, the higher is the expected growth rate. For the purpose of testing Hypothesis 5, therefore, a variable, ΔTCI, is created to measure the difference between the log of average TCI in the period 1990–99 and the log of average TCI in the period 1970–79—as the transition in socialist countries and the reforms in other developing countries started in the 1980s.

The dependent variable in the regressions is the log of the average annual growth rate of GDP per capita in the period 1980–99. In addition to ΔTCI, the explanatory variables include the log of average TCI in the

1970s, initial per capita GDP in 1980 and other explanatory variables—representing institutional quality, openness and population size—which are similar to those used in testing Hypothesis 1.

Two approaches are used to test the hypothesis. The first includes observations from all countries in the data set, while the second includes only the developing countries defined by Easterly and Sewadeh (2002). Both approaches try three regressions—two by OLS and one by 2SLS—to control the endogeneity problem of institutional quality and openness. Table VI.7 reports the results from the regressions.

**Table VI.7: Development Strategy and the Performance of Economic Reform/Transition**

|  | Model 5.1 (OLS) | Model 5.2 (OLS) | Model 5.3 (2SLS) | Model 5.4 (OLS) | Model 5.5 (OLS) | Model 5.6 (2SLS) |
|---|---|---|---|---|---|---|
| Constant | 2.53 | 3.79 | -2.94 | 4.28 | -4.50 | -9.03 |
|  | (3.17) | (3.63) | (3.97) | (4.24) | (5.01) | (6.43) |
| $\Delta$TCI | -1.25** | -0.91** | -1.12** | -1.16* | -1.02* | -1.30** |
|  | (0.55) | (0.45) | (0.51) | (0.66) | (0.52) | (0.60) |
| LnTCI70 | -0.84** | -0.38 | -0.52 | -0.61 | -0.26 | -0.31 |
|  | (0.41) | (0.34) | (0.38) | (0.48) | (0.38) | (0.45) |
| LnGDP80 | -0.04 | -1.32*** | -0.31 | -0.34 | -0.78* | -0.12 |
|  | (0.35) | (0.37) | (0.38) | (0.50) | (0.45) | (0.57) |
| RLO1 |  | 1.31*** |  |  | 1.78*** |  |
|  |  | (0.37) |  |  | (0.47) |  |
| INST |  |  | 0.44 |  |  | 0.96 |
|  |  |  | (0.60) |  |  | (1.18) |
| LnOPEN1 |  | 0.71* |  |  | 0.54 |  |
|  |  | (0.36) |  |  | (0.49) |  |
| TRADE1 |  |  | 1.50** |  |  | 2.23* |
|  |  |  | (0.70) |  |  | (1.26) |
| LnDIST |  | 0.16 | 0.57* |  | -0.06 | 0.34 |
|  |  | (0.28) | (0.29) |  | (0.33) | (0.36) |
| LnPOP1 |  | 0.52*** | 0.44*** |  | 0.79*** | 0.78** |
|  |  | (0.17) | (0.16) |  | (0.19) | (0.29) |
| LANDLOCK |  | -0.87 | -0.06 |  | -0.55 | 0.54 |
|  |  | (0.57) | (0.68) |  | (0.73) | (1.15) |
| Adjusted-$R^2$ | 0.13 | 0.43 | 0.27 | 0.03 | 0.45 | 0.24 |
| Observations | 76 | 72 | 72 | 50 | 49 | 49 |

* indicates significance at the 10 per cent level

** indicates significance at the 5 per cent level

*** indicates significance at the 1 per cent level

Notes: Dependent variable is the average growth rate of GDP per capita from 1980–99. The data samples in the regression of Models 6.4–6.6 include only the developing countries defined by Easterly and Sewadeh (2002). Standard errors are reported in parentheses.

As expected, the sign of ΔTCI is negative and the estimates are significantly different from zero in all six regressions. The results support the hypothesis that a larger reduction in the TCI from the level in the 1970s to the level in the 1990s has a larger positive effect on the average per capita GDP growth rate in the period 1980–99. For a country that adopts a CAD strategy, therefore, growth performance will be improved if the government manages well the transition from a CAD to a CAF strategy. From the estimates, we can infer that a 10 percent reduction in the TCI level in the 1990s to the level of the 1970s could cause a 0.1–0.13 percentage point increase in the average annual growth rate of per capita GDP in the period 1980–99.

The other explanatory variables all have the expected signs; however, except for the population size—which is positive and highly significant in all six regressions—the other variables are either insignificant or significant in some regressions but not in others.

In a nutshell, as predicted by Hypothesis 5, the entry of small and medium-size firms into the repressed sectors under a CAD strategy is essential for the economy to achieve dynamic growth during the transition process.

## Concluding Remarks

This chapter argues that most LDCs follow an inappropriate development strategy and that, as a result, convergence is impeded, economic volatility enhanced, and income distribution more unequal. During economic reform and transition, a country's economic performance depends on its government's ability to create an environment that facilitates the growth of labor-intensive industries, which have been suppressed in the past due to the government's pursuit of a CAD strategy. The temptation to close the industry/technology gap as soon as possible is strong for LDCs. At a low level of factor endowment structure, however, LDCs' economies do not have the comparative advantages necessary for capital-intensive industries/technologies, and their firms will not be viable in an open, free, and competitive market if they enter/adopt these industries/technologies. To give priority to the development of non–comparative advantage industries/technologies, the governments in LDCs often adopt a

CAD strategy and give nonviable firms policy support through a series of distortions in interest rates, foreign exchange rates, and other prices. They also use administrative measures to directly allocate resources with distorted prices to the firms in the priority industries. With the above policy measures, an LDC may be able to establish firms that adopt high technologies in advanced industries for which the economy does not have the comparative advantages. However, the development of financial markets will be repressed, foreign trade will be retarded, rent-seeking activities will be widespread, the macroeconomy will be unstable, income distribution will be unequal, the economy will be very uncompetitive, and the country will fail to converge with DCs in terms of income.

I argue here that the optimal industry/technology structure of an economy is endogenously determined by the economy's factor endowment structure and that the CAF strategy is the better one for an LDC's development. The CAF strategy will induce the firms in an LDC to enter industries for which the country has comparative advantages and facilitate the firms adoption of appropriate technology by borrowing at low costs from the more advanced countries. The economy will be competitive. The country will enjoy rapid upgrades in its factor endowment structure and, consequently, its industry/technology structure. As such, the CAF strategy will help an LDC achieve and foster a high rate of growth. Convergence will come true. The empirical findings from the cross-country analyses are consistent with the above hypothesis.

To implement the CAF strategy, a government needs to maintain an open, free, and competitive market. The government can also adopt an industrial policy to facilitate the firms' upgrading of industry/technology. However, the functions of an industrial policy should be limited to information sharing, investment coordination, and compensation for externalities produced by first movers.

The government of an LDC plays an especially important role, for better or for worse, in the country's economic development. As W. Arthur Lewis (1965) has noted, "No country has made economic progress without positive stimulus from intelligent governments... On the other hand, there are so many examples of the mischief done to economic life by governments." Here I would like to propose that, for the government in an LDC to be an intelligent one, its most important task is to get its development strategy right.

# Data Annex

## Table VI.A1: TCI Based on Value Added in the Manufacturing Sector

122 countries

| Economy | TCI (1963–99) Mean | TCI (1963–99) S.D. | Growth rate of GDP per capita (%) (1962–99) Mean | Growth rate of GDP per capita (%) (1962–99) S.D. | Black-market premium (1960–99) Mean | Black-market premium (1960–99) S.D. | Number of procedures (1999) Mean | IEF (1970–2005) Mean | IEF (1970–2005) S.D. | Expropriation risk (1982–97) Mean | Executive de facto independence (1945–98) Mean | Openness (1960–2003) Mean | Openness (1960–2003) S.D. |
|---|---|---|---|---|---|---|---|---|---|---|---|---|---|
| Albania | 1.771 | 0.095 | 1.713 | 9.190 | 7.503 | 6.492 | | 5.483 | 0.742 | 7.264 | | 48.321 | 15.940 |
| Algeria | 2.157 | 0.979 | 1.377 | 8.127 | 147.937 | 137.826 | | 4.363 | 0.481 | 6.763 | | 56.805 | 15.229 |
| Argentina | 2.564 | 0.588 | 0.915 | 5.742 | 40.934 | 77.874 | 14.000 | 5.365 | 1.172 | 6.313 | 3.140 | 16.423 | 6.248 |
| Australia | 1.073 | 0.162 | 2.150 | 2.036 | 0.000 | 0.000 | 2.000 | 7.585 | 0.461 | 9.379 | 7.000 | 32.905 | 5.337 |
| Austria | 1.083 | 0.071 | 2.790 | 1.831 | 0.000 | 0.000 | 9.000 | 7.149 | 0.545 | 9.743 | 7.000 | 69.527 | 15.824 |
| Bahamas | 1.929 | 0.845 | 1.504 | 6.985 | 12.539 | 12.764 | | | | 7.793 | | 129.182 | 10.750 |
| Bangladesh | 4.302 | 0.902 | 1.192 | 4.091 | 96.876 | 66.359 | | 4.990 | 0.969 | 5.413 | | 22.414 | 5.646 |
| Barbados | 1.283 | 0.521 | 2.449 | 4.566 | 7.442 | 4.861 | | 5.615 | 0.142 | | | 118.786 | 14.759 |
| Belgium | 1.017 | 0.122 | 2.626 | 1.959 | 0.000 | 0.000 | 8.000 | 7.316 | 0.179 | 9.686 | 7.000 | 120.602 | 25.441 |
| Belize | 1.067 | 0.072 | 3.256 | 4.168 | 26.857 | 21.769 | | 6.235 | 0.497 | | | 116.954 | 9.390 |
| Benin | 13.694 | 2.026 | 0.861 | 3.185 | 3.424 | 4.533 | | 5.212 | 0.406 | | | 40.868 | 12.273 |
| Bhutan | 4.514 | | 4.247 | 3.278 | 3.045 | 3.521 | | | | | | 68.883 | 10.109 |
| Bolivia | 7.341 | 2.905 | 0.377 | 3.590 | 32.334 | 84.457 | 20.000 | 5.915 | 1.095 | 5.600 | 3.520 | 49.479 | 4.896 |
| Botswana | 1.791 | 0.801 | 6.421 | 5.132 | 13.180 | 11.245 | | 6.578 | 0.681 | 8.007 | | 103.668 | 24.533 |
| Brazil | 5.373 | 1.195 | 2.371 | 4.076 | 29.063 | 36.841 | 15.000 | 5.207 | 0.868 | 7.881 | 3.692 | 17.317 | 4.359 |
| Bulgaria | 1.372 | 0.089 | 1.541 | 5.288 | 7.423 | 10.158 | 10.000 | 5.536 | 0.889 | 9.036 | 3.679 | 90.813 | 16.009 |
| Cameroon | 7.018 | 1.626 | 0.977 | 5.993 | 3.431 | 4.531 | | 5.597 | 0.144 | 6.463 | | 48.559 | 9.062 |
| Canada | 1.531 | 0.199 | 2.110 | 2.097 | 0.000 | 0.000 | 2.000 | 7.858 | 0.282 | 9.721 | 7.000 | 55.645 | 14.057 |

**Table VI.A1:** *(Continued)*

122 countries

| Economy | TCI (1963–99) | | Growth rate of GDP per capita (%) (1962–99) | | Black-market premium (1960–99) | | Number of procedures (1999) | IEF (1970–2005) | | Expropriation risk (1982–97) | Executive de facto independence (1945–99) | Openness (1960–2003) | |
|---|---|---|---|---|---|---|---|---|---|---|---|---|---|
| | Mean | S.D. | Mean | S.D. | Mean | S.D. | Mean | Mean | S.D. | Mean | Mean | Mean | S.D. |
| Central African Republic | 9.830 | 2.221 | −0.837 | 3.924 | 3.271 | 4.456 | 10.000 | | | 7.800 | 3.667 | 53.552 | 13.560 |
| Chile | 4.307 | 1.223 | 2.595 | 4.798 | 38.157 | 104.680 | 12.000 | 6.554 | 1.345 | 8.114 | 2.321 | 46.041 | 14.844 |
| China | 4.165 | 1.327 | 6.003 | 7.381 | 71.004 | 111.533 | 18.000 | 5.397 | 0.525 | 7.350 | 5.074 | 26.614 | 16.924 |
| Colombia | 4.466 | 0.701 | 1.780 | 2.117 | 7.993 | 7.510 | | 5.282 | 0.256 | | | 30.873 | 5.286 |
| Congo, Rep. | 6.847 | 2.614 | 1.190 | 5.896 | 2.866 | 4.064 | | | | 5.146 | | 104.950 | 19.420 |
| Costa Rica | 2.190 | 0.683 | 1.833 | 3.350 | 40.799 | 67.249 | | 6.730 | 0.755 | 7.038 | | 70.816 | 13.687 |
| Côte d'Ivoire | | | | | | | | | | | | | |
| Croatia | 1.581 | 0.637 | 0.884 | 8.096 | 37.525 | 25.826 | 12.000 | 5.855 | 0.680 | | 3.192 | 102.438 | 19.668 |
| Cyprus | 1.308 | 0.310 | 5.357 | 4.515 | 4.671 | 4.550 | | 6.327 | 0.680 | 8.486 | | 104.364 | 8.351 |
| Denmark | 1.178 | 0.079 | 2.100 | 2.230 | 0.000 | 0.000 | 3.000 | 7.268 | 0.502 | 9.721 | 7.000 | 64.511 | 7.827 |
| Dominican Republic | 2.532 | 0.368 | 2.800 | 5.232 | 31.641 | 36.064 | 21.000 | | | 6.356 | 3.340 | 59.607 | 20.106 |
| Ecuador | 3.878 | 1.238 | 1.263 | 3.381 | 20.225 | 24.613 | 16.000 | 5.300 | 0.592 | 6.763 | 4.148 | 50.157 | 9.744 |
| Egypt, Arab Rep. | 2.012 | 0.238 | 3.013 | 2.913 | 39.256 | 45.442 | 11.000 | | | 6.800 | 3.519 | 48.161 | 13.088 |
| El Salvador | 4.229 | 1.569 | 0.825 | 3.925 | 42.640 | 48.101 | | 6.468 | 1.264 | 5.206 | | 56.661 | 9.927 |
| Ethiopia | 17.921 | 2.621 | 0.326 | 7.127 | 72.262 | 73.517 | | | | 6.047 | | 32.004 | 10.522 |
| Fiji | 1.564 | 0.214 | 1.711 | 4.700 | 1.605 | 1.939 | | | | | | 101.288 | 15.192 |
| Finland | 1.237 | 0.116 | 2.885 | 3.009 | 0.000 | 0.000 | 5.000 | 5.963 | 0.231 | 9.721 | 7.000 | 54.250 | 10.204 |
| France | 1.106 | 0.096 | 2.519 | 1.664 | 0.000 | 0.000 | 15.000 | 7.371 | 0.462 | 9.707 | 5.283 | 38.959 | 9.083 |
| Gabon | 2.119 | 0.759 | 2.538 | 10.245 | 1.740 | 4.035 | | 6.645 | 0.432 | 7.556 | | 93.218 | 15.593 |
| Gambia | 5.442 | 3.157 | 0.595 | 3.398 | 6.511 | 11.907 | | 4.944 | 0.470 | 8.385 | | 101.192 | 17.250 |
| Ghana | 5.962 | 2.075 | 0.071 | 4.253 | 248.144 | 729.713 | 10.000 | 5.159 | 1.390 | 6.219 | 1.943 | 47.462 | 25.698 |
| Greece | 1.337 | 0.087 | 3.200 | 3.878 | 5.412 | 5.028 | 15.000 | 6.394 | 0.532 | 7.481 | 5.792 | 40.066 | 10.166 |

| | | | | | | | | | | | | | |
|---|---|---|---|---|---|---|---|---|---|---|---|---|---|
| Guatemala | 3.303 | 0.279 | 1.230 | 2.500 | 12.346 | 15.467 | | 6.321 | 0.542 | 5.156 | | 39.266 | 7.322 |
| Guyana | 0.733 | | 0.935 | 5.216 | 209.506 | 270.332 | | 6.242 | 0.556 | 5.956 | | 151.372 | 49.475 |
| Honduras | 3.183 | 0.790 | 0.820 | 2.946 | 12.008 | 26.842 | | 6.180 | 0.359 | 5.413 | | 68.718 | 16.915 |
| Hong Kong SAR, China | 0.713 | 0.071 | 5.192 | 4.445 | −0.416 | 1.383 | | | | 8.488 | | 209.386 | 52.589 |
| Hungary | 1.151 | 0.183 | 3.338 | 4.210 | 165.435 | 155.711 | 8.000 | 6.489 | 1.059 | 9.079 | 3.735 | 86.700 | 25.216 |
| Iceland | 0.802 | 0.134 | 2.823 | 3.809 | 1.233 | 1.423 | | 6.906 | 1.102 | 9.700 | | 72.982 | 6.502 |
| India | 3.635 | 0.421 | 2.573 | 3.077 | 26.530 | 24.692 | 10.000 | 5.744 | 0.729 | 8.069 | 6.959 | 15.517 | 6.343 |
| Indonesia | 3.073 | 0.408 | 3.581 | 3.974 | 273.451 | 806.400 | 11.000 | 5.863 | 0.535 | 7.475 | 2.981 | 44.716 | 16.991 |
| Iran, Islamic Rep. | | | 0.231 | 7.115 | 464.833 | 857.111 | | | | 4.694 | | 38.814 | 16.870 |
| Iraq | 1.646 | 0.577 | −2.515 | 18.460 | 851.008 | 2093.052 | 3.000 | | | 2.400 | | | 31.741 |
| Ireland | 1.853 | 0.507 | 4.179 | 2.806 | 0.600 | 3.795 | 5.000 | 7.491 | 0.642 | 9.721 | 7.000 | 105.765 | 23.283 |
| Israel | 1.287 | 0.232 | 2.744 | 3.677 | 14.077 | 17.706 | 16.000 | 5.686 | 1.283 | 8.513 | 7.000 | 79.064 | 8.718 |
| Italy | 1.292 | 0.134 | 2.794 | 2.143 | 0.000 | 0.000 | 6.000 | 6.422 | 0.656 | 9.457 | 7.000 | 40.020 | 15.792 |
| Jamaica | 3.248 | 0.621 | 0.756 | 4.339 | 19.076 | 17.070 | 11.000 | 6.200 | 1.023 | 7.044 | 7.000 | 87.759 | 3.495 |
| Japan | 1.680 | 0.083 | 4.056 | 3.678 | 1.750 | 3.350 | 14.000 | 7.071 | 0.316 | 9.721 | 7.000 | 20.925 | 14.334 |
| Jordan | 1.936 | 0.492 | 1.980 | 7.193 | 3.399 | 2.899 | 11.000 | 6.335 | 0.698 | 6.556 | 2.208 | 119.307 | 7.232 |
| Kenya | 0.335 | 0.030 | 1.241 | 4.785 | 15.722 | 14.031 | 13.000 | 5.973 | 0.786 | 6.406 | 3.250 | 60.309 | 18.238 |
| Korea, Rep. | 2.816 | 0.493 | 5.797 | 3.615 | 15.251 | 24.015 | | | | 8.569 | 3.140 | 53.775 | 11.295 |
| Kuwait | 1.090 | 0.477 | −3.916 | 8.708 | 0.001 | 0.399 | 7.000 | 6.609 | 0.817 | 7.056 | | 96.580 | 20.540 |
| Latvia | 1.638 | 0.010 | 2.893 | 7.074 | 7.233 | 6.266 | | 6.622 | 0.818 | | 3.333 | 104.600 | 33.884 |
| Lesotho | 8.719 | 2.037 | 3.935 | 6.891 | 9.133 | 8.125 | | | | | | 112.698 | 18.966 |
| Libya | 0.836 | 0.176 | 3.425 | 16.053 | 82.000 | 127.559 | | | | 5.088 | | 77.574 | 32.906 |
| Luxembourg | 0.914 | 0.101 | 3.163 | 3.267 | 0.375 | 0.466 | | 7.703 | 0.105 | 10.000 | | 198.318 | 28.830 |
| Macao | 0.384 | 0.060 | 2.666 | 4.375 | | | | | | | | 156.762 | |
| Madagascar | 5.373 | 0.498 | −1.041 | 4.032 | 15.000 | 21.331 | 17.000 | 5.316 | 0.599 | 4.686 | 3.684 | 40.325 | 9.212 |
| Malawi | 8.631 | 2.923 | 1.309 | 5.380 | 36.658 | 31.917 | 12.000 | 5.038 | 0.397 | 6.863 | 1.571 | 60.909 | 8.653 |
| Malaysia | 1.854 | 0.191 | 3.926 | 3.483 | 1.172 | 1.634 | 7.000 | 6.819 | 0.382 | 8.150 | 5.381 | 122.600 | 49.604 |
| Malta | 1.143 | 0.091 | 5.196 | 4.244 | 2.724 | 5.448 | | 6.236 | 0.663 | 7.875 | | 162.837 | 27.787 |
| Mauritius | 1.121 | 0.447 | 4.355 | 1.678 | 4.892 | 7.090 | | 6.669 | 0.893 | | | 116.900 | 13.110 |

(continued next page)

**Table VI.A1:** *(Continued)*

122 countries

| Economy | TCI (1963–99) | | Growth rate of GDP per capita (%) (1962–99) | | Black-market premium (1960–99) | | Number of procedures (1999) | IEF (1970–2005) | | Expropriation risk (1982–97) | Executive de facto independence (1945–98) | Openness (1960–2003) | |
|---|---|---|---|---|---|---|---|---|---|---|---|---|---|
| | Mean | S.D. | Mean | S.D. | Mean | S.D. | Mean | Mean | S.D. | Mean | Mean | Mean | S.D. |
| Mexico | 2.969 | 0.242 | 1.982 | 3.395 | 4.772 | 8.816 | 15.000 | 6.159 | 0.591 | 7.469 | 3.241 | 31.384 | 16.422 |
| Moldova | 4.073 | 0.611 | -1.986 | 10.241 | 0.000 | | | | | | | 122.079 | 25.610 |
| Mongolia | 3.697 | 0.860 | -0.258 | 6.501 | 0.635 | 3.085 | 5.000 | 5.600 | 0.526 | 7.950 | 3.333 | 120.161 | 32.221 |
| Morocco | 3.201 | 0.383 | 1.926 | 4.544 | 7.673 | 6.987 | 13.000 | 6.239 | 0.351 | 6.713 | 1.930 | 51.277 | 10.001 |
| Namibia | 3.711 | | -0.226 | 2.509 | 1.230 | 2.130 | | | | 5.400 | | 114.971 | 16.921 |
| Nepal | 4.174 | 0.342 | 1.359 | 2.893 | 33.574 | 34.464 | 8.000 | 5.448 | 0.271 | | | 33.297 | 15.010 |
| Netherlands | 1.158 | 0.204 | 2.253 | 1.946 | 0.000 | 0.000 | | 7.620 | 0.305 | 9.979 | 7.000 | 100.484 | 12.498 |
| Netherlands Antilles | 0.767 | 0.110 | -1.846 | 1.312 | -0.333 | 2.417 | | | | | | | |
| New Zealand | 1.061 | 0.188 | 1.420 | 2.906 | 0.600 | 3.795 | 3.000 | 7.656 | 0.900 | 9.736 | 7.000 | 57.134 | 6.072 |
| Nigeria | 9.338 | 6.549 | 0.801 | 7.314 | 86.273 | 109.203 | 9.000 | 4.659 | 0.915 | 5.300 | 2.784 | 49.170 | 24.309 |
| Norway | 0.914 | 0.072 | 3.090 | 1.723 | 0.000 | 0.000 | 4.000 | 6.890 | 0.534 | 9.850 | 7.000 | 73.425 | 3.821 |
| Oman | 1.036 | 0.151 | 6.296 | 16.124 | 0.460 | 1.061 | | 7.125 | 0.440 | 7.321 | | 93.117 | 12.928 |
| Pakistan | 6.114 | 1.221 | 2.564 | 2.397 | 38.871 | 42.583 | 8.000 | 5.190 | 0.632 | 6.150 | 4.083 | 32.965 | 4.991 |
| Panama | 2.738 | 0.550 | 2.186 | 4.133 | 0.000 | 0.000 | 7.000 | 6.811 | 0.590 | 6.063 | 3.611 | 154.750 | 27.245 |
| Papua New Guinea | 7.250 | 1.541 | 1.177 | 4.902 | 15.938 | 15.557 | | | | 7.743 | | 82.113 | 17.158 |
| Paraguay | 2.852 | 0.450 | 1.598 | 3.634 | 25.390 | 37.524 | | 6.041 | 0.405 | 6.900 | | 48.239 | 20.040 |
| Peru | 5.128 | 1.162 | 0.783 | 4.825 | 36.554 | 64.825 | 8.000 | 5.648 | 1.496 | 6.206 | 3.769 | 34.543 | 5.348 |
| Philippines | 4.571 | 1.143 | 1.304 | 3.004 | 9.418 | 13.474 | 14.000 | 6.176 | 0.725 | 5.788 | 4.038 | 56.720 | 24.885 |
| Poland | 1.704 | 0.327 | 3.320 | 3.604 | 351.565 | 270.847 | 11.000 | 5.755 | 1.103 | 7.814 | 3.538 | 51.814 | 5.736 |
| Portugal | 1.265 | 0.257 | 3.684 | 3.804 | 4.263 | 7.944 | 12.000 | 6.635 | 1.028 | 9.006 | 3.538 | 57.577 | 11.450 |
| Puerto Rico | 3.814 | 0.718 | 3.760 | 2.936 | | | | | | | | 133.300 | 24.180 |
| Qatar | 1.595 | 0.387 | | | 0.203 | 0.259 | | | | 7.857 | | 80.400 | 6.756 |
| Romania | 1.086 | 0.046 | 0.400 | 5.217 | 169.469 | 158.714 | 16.000 | 5.149 | 0.711 | 7.557 | 3.180 | 60.521 | 11.528 |

|  | | | | | | | | | | | | | |
|---|---|---|---|---|---|---|---|---|---|---|---|---|---|
| Russian Federation | 0.999 | 0.108 | -1.259 | 7.645 | 520.000 | 576.479 | 20.000 |  |  | 8.500 | 2.796 | 56.640 | 19.001 |
| Saudi Arabia | 1.675 | 1.101 |  |  |  |  |  |  |  |  |  |  |  |
| Senegal | 8.914 | 2.469 | 0.003 | 4.200 | 3.431 | 4.531 | 16.000 | 5.506 | 0.494 | 5.925 | 3.000 | 62.380 | 14.527 |
| Sierra Leone |  |  | -0.780 | 5.760 | 129.831 | 308.869 |  | 4.994 | 0.708 | 5.708 |  | 48.373 | 11.093 |
| Singapore | 1.406 | 0.203 | 5.576 | 4.289 | 0.800 | 0.988 | 7.000 | 8.364 | 0.365 | 9.394 | 3.421 |  |  |
| Slovak Republic | 1.176 | 0.004 |  |  |  |  |  |  |  |  |  |  |  |
| Slovenia | 1.071 | 0.112 | 2.123 | 4.236 | 10.000 | 6.880 | 9.000 | 5.811 | 0.453 | 7.350 | 3.808 | 118.000 | 12.035 |
| South Africa | 1.853 | 0.162 | 0.924 | 3.562 | 4.239 | 11.191 | 9.000 | 6.364 | 0.537 | 9.550 | 7.000 | 50.766 | 5.868 |
| Spain | 1.267 | 0.199 | 3.332 | 2.698 | 2.344 | 2.235 | 11.000 | 6.750 | 0.508 | 6.538 | 3.471 | 35.180 | 12.544 |
| Sri Lanka | 2.728 | 0.341 | 2.831 | 1.983 | 50.615 | 50.224 | 8.000 | 5.720 | 0.407 |  | 6.176 | 70.775 | 10.682 |
| Sudan | 6.761 |  | 1.119 | 5.531 | 87.922 | 155.904 |  |  |  | 4.019 |  | 28.406 | 5.289 |
| Suriname | 2.409 | 0.532 | 0.217 | 6.114 | 14.683 | 8.356 |  |  |  | 5.169 |  | 94.879 | 29.815 |
| Swaziland | 3.817 | 0.733 | 2.008 | 4.193 | 11.283 | 7.128 |  |  |  |  |  | 146.657 | 30.193 |
| Sweden | 1.206 | 0.124 | 2.198 | 1.993 | 0.000 | 0.000 | 6.000 | 6.856 | 0.681 | 9.500 | 7.000 | 58.955 | 13.210 |
| Switzerland | 0.992 | 0.086 | 1.393 | 2.265 | 0.000 | 0.000 | 7.000 | 8.179 | 0.168 | 9.986 | 7.000 | 64.777 | 8.952 |
| Syrian Arab Rep. | 2.058 | 0.755 | 2.559 | 8.022 | 128.798 | 211.522 | 13.000 | 5.213 | 1.183 | 5.413 |  | 51.880 | 13.155 |
| Tanzania | 3.233 | 0.370 | 1.297 | 2.384 | 86.952 | 92.424 | 9.000 | 6.514 | 0.386 | 6.888 | 3.000 | 48.043 | 9.123 |
| Thailand | 7.201 | 2.613 | 4.641 | 3.640 | 0.418 | 2.889 | 9.000 | 4.979 | 0.326 | 7.644 | 3.039 | 60.693 | 28.782 |
| Togo | 9.660 | 2.364 | 1.270 | 6.390 | 3.431 | 4.531 |  |  |  | 6.500 |  | 83.123 | 18.104 |
| Trinidad and Tobago | 1.475 | 0.446 | 2.043 | 4.713 | 30.029 | 20.051 | 13.000 | 5.613 | 0.557 | 7.294 |  | 89.984 | 18.725 |
| Tunisia | 2.891 | 1.243 | 3.117 | 3.613 | 27.354 | 41.695 | 11.000 | 5.181 | 0.812 | 6.506 | 1.625 | 69.147 | 22.894 |
| Turkey | 4.586 | 0.968 | 1.937 | 4.124 | 18.921 | 20.025 |  | 5.332 | 1.640 | 7.288 | 5.943 | 30.608 | 16.899 |
| Uganda | 6.236 | 0.376 | 2.259 | 3.224 | 198.418 | 301.088 | 5.000 |  |  | 4.800 | 2.735 | 35.186 | 9.543 |
| United Arab Emirates | 0.365 | 0.013 | -3.028 | 8.110 | -1.255 | 3.172 | 4.000 | 7.626 | 0.766 | 6.944 |  | 110.931 | 17.137 |
| United Kingdom | 1.358 | 0.154 | 2.149 | 1.795 | 0.000 | 0.000 | 10.000 | 8.135 | 0.273 | 9.764 | 7.000 | 49.873 | 6.861 |
| United States | 1.588 | 0.108 | 2.193 | 1.979 | 0.000 | 0.000 | 14.000 | 6.304 | 0.426 | 9.979 | 7.000 | 17.046 | 5.272 |
| Uruguay | 2.036 | 0.430 | 0.887 | 4.408 | 11.699 | 26.516 |  | 5.254 | 0.900 | 6.938 | 4.712 | 35.923 | 7.589 |
| Venezuela, R. B. | 2.826 | 0.843 |  |  | 26.885 | 62.964 |  |  |  | 7.106 | 5.093 |  |  |
| Zambia | 5.909 | 1.694 | -0.776 | 4.695 | 85.435 | 119.817 | 6.000 | 5.653 | 1.336 | 6.669 | 2.257 | 77.325 | 13.388 |
| Zimbabwe | 5.118 | 1.358 | 0.450 | 5.847 | 52.239 | 56.792 | 5.000 | 3.912 | 0.855 | 6.025 | 4.643 | 53.964 | 16.555 |

*Note:* Standard deviations for number of procedures, expropriation risk, and executive *de facto* independence are not available.

## Notes

1. Lin (2003) constructs another index—based on the ratio of capital intensity in the manufacturing industry and the capital intensity in the whole economy—as a proxy for measuring the degree with which a CAD strategy is pursued. That proxy is correlated highly with the current proxy and the results of empirical analyses based on that proxy are similar to the results reported in this section. The data for capital used in a country's manufacturing industry are, however, available for only a small number of countries. To enlarge the number of countries in the studies, I therefore use the proxy based on the added value of manufacturing industries.

2. The samples are 86 for the 1960s, 97 for the 1970s, 107 for the 1980s and 114 for the 1990s.

3. These findings are similar to the result presented in Lin (2003) using the TCI based on the ratio of capital intensity in the manufacturing industry and the capital intensity in the whole economy. Lin (2003) uses a two stage estimation to estimate the effect of the choice of the development strategy on growth. In the first stage, TCI is regressed on several variables that capture an economy's factor endowment. The residuals from this regression are used as a proxy for an economy's deviations from a CAF strategy. They are expected to be zero if the government adopted a CAF strategy and nonzero if the strategy is CAD. The second stage consists of a cross-country growth equation where the dependent variable is the annual growth rate of per capita real GDP. The results show that the proxy for the development strategy has the expected negative sign and is statistically significant in all regressions. The magnitudes of the impact of the development strategy on the per capita GDP growth rate in the period 1970–80 are twice those of the period 1980–92. The results suggest that if a developing country, for example, India, as shown in the appendix, adopted a CAD strategy causing TCI to be 8.47 and the residual to be 3.60, the annual per capita real GDP growth rate would be reduced 0.47 percent per year over the period 1970–92.

## References

Deininger, K., and L. Squire. 1996. "A New Data Set Measuring Income Inequality." *World Bank Economic Review* 10 (3): 565–91.

Djankov, Simeon, and Peter Murrell. 2002. "Enterprise Restructuring in Transition: A Quantitative Survey." *Journal of Economic Literature* 40 (3): 739–92.

Dollar, David, and Aart Kraay. 2003. "Institutions, Trade, and Growth." *Journal of Monetary Economics* 50 (1): 133–62.

Easterly, W., and M. Sewadeh. 2002. Global Development Network Database, http://www.worldbank.org/research/growth/GDNdata.htm.

Easterly, William, and H. Yu. 2000. "Global Development Growth Network Database." Technical Report, World Bank, Washington, DC.

Fei, John, Gustav Ranis, and Shirley W. Y. Kuo. 1979. *Growth with Equity: The Taiwan Case*, New York: Oxford University Press.

Frankel, Jeffrey, and David Romer. 1999. "Does Trade Cause Growth?" *American Economic Review* 89 (June): 379–99.

Gwartney, James, and Robert Lawson, eds. 2007. *Economic Freedom of the World 2007 Annual Report*. Vancouver: Fraser Institute.

Hall, R. E., and C. Jones. 1999. "Why Do Some Countries Produce So Much More Output per Worker than Others?" *Quarterly Journal of Economics* 114 (1): 83–116.

Kaufmann, Daniel, and Aart Kraay. 2002. "Growth without Governance." Policy Research Working Paper No. 2928, World Bank, Washington, DC.

Krugman, Paul, and Maurice Obstfeld. 1997. *International Economics: Theory and Policy*, Fourth Edition. Reading, MA: Addison-Wesley.

Lewis, W. Arthur. 1965. *Theory of Economic Growth* (New York: Harper & Row), p. 376.

Li, H. Y., L. Squire, and H. Zou. 1998. "Explaining International and Intertemporal Variations in Income Inequality." *Economic Journal* 108: 26–43.

Lin, Justin Yifu, 2003. "Development Strategy, Viability, and Economic Convergence." *Economic Development and Cultural Change* 51(2): 276–308. (Reprinted in part in this chapter.)

Lin, Justin Yifu, and Mingxing Liu. 2004. "Development Strategy, Transition and Challenges of Development in Lagging Regions." China Center for Economic Research Working Paper Series 2004–2. Peking University, Beijing.

Sachs, Jeffrey D., and Andrew M. Warner. 2001. "The Curse of Natural Resources." *European Economic Review* 45 (4–6) (May): 827–38.

Samuelson, Paul A. 1978. *The Collected Scientific Papers of Paul A. Samuelson*, edited by H. Nagasani and K. Crowley. Cambridge, MA: MIT Press.

United Nations Industrial Development Organisation. 2002. *International Yearbook of Industrial Statistics*. Edward Elgar Publishing.

World Bank. Various years. *World Development Indicators*. Washington, DC: World Bank.

# Epilogue: The Path to a Golden Age of Industrialization in the Developing World

"The golden age of finance has now ended," as Barry Eichengreen commented recently in reference to the Great Recession.[1] In my view, however, the golden age of industrialization in the developing world has just begun.

The global financial crisis is still looming large over Europe. Newspapers are carrying daily reports on the anemic recovery, stubbornly high unemployment rates, downgraded sovereign credit ratings, and recurrent debt crises occurring in the wake of the recession in advanced countries on both sides of the Atlantic. Political leaders the world over are just waking up to the fact that over reliance on making financial deals to maintain a high standard of living, without building and rebuilding a strong industrial base, is just a mirage.

For a sustainable global recovery and robust growth in the coming years, the world needs to look beyond the Euro Area and sovereign debt worries to the promise inherent in structural transformation, which, as defined in this volume, is the process by which countries climb the industrial ladder and change the sector employment and production compositions of their economies. Except for a few oil-exporting countries, no countries have ever gotten rich without achieving industrialization first. During my travels in the past three and a half years as the Chief Economist of the World Bank Group, I have been struck by the potential for less developed countries to take a page from the playbook of more successful industrializing East Asian countries, such as China, Indonesia, Japan, Korea, Malaysia, Singapore, and Vietnam, and to dramatically improve their development performance.

My belief in the coming of a golden age of industrialization in the developing world is based on the potential to rapidly expand industrial sectors in developing countries, including those in Sub-Saharan African countries, and on the dynamic relocation of industries in a multipolar growth world. The first force can be envisioned through an improved understanding of the mechanics of economic transformation in modern times ushered in by the Industrial Revolution in the 18th century. In advanced countries technological innovation and industrial upgrading require costly and risky investments in research and development, because their vanguard technologies and industries are located on the global frontier. By contrast, a latecomer country can borrow technology from the advanced countries at low risk and cost. Hence, if a developing country knows how to tap the advantage of backwardness, its industrial upgrading and economic growth can proceed at an annual rate several times that of high-income countries for decades as the country closes its industrial and income gap with advanced countries. The second force is the rapid wage increase in the dynamically growing emerging market economies and the unavoidable relocation of their labor-intensive manufacturing industries to other lower-income countries. Take China, for example: its monthly wage for unskilled worker is about $350. China is likely to maintain high growth in the coming decades (Lin 2011a). Its monthly wage for unskilled worker will reach at least $1,000 in 10 years. Such wage dynamics means China will need to upgrade to higher value added, more capital-intensive sectors, opening up a huge opportunity for other countries with income levels lower than China's to enter the labor-intensive manufacturing industries.

In the UNU-WIDER annual lecture I delivered in Maputo, Mozambique, in May 2011, I explained how developing countries can capture these opportunities to achieve rapid industrialization and economic growth. The winning formula is for them to develop tradable industries that are expanding rapidly in countries that have been growing dynamically for decades and that have higher income and similar endowment structures to theirs. The pattern of flying geese is a useful metaphor to explain my vision. Since the 18th century, the successfully catching-up countries in Western Europe, North America, and East Asia all followed carefully selected lead countries that had per capita income about twice as high as theirs, and emulated the leader-follower flying-geese pattern in their industrial upgrading and diversification before becoming advanced countries themselves (Lin 2011c).

The emergence of large market economies such as Brazil, Russia, India and China (BRIC) as new growth poles in the multipolar world and their likely continuous dynamic growth in the postcrisis world offers an unprecedented opportunity to all developing economies with income levels currently below theirs—including those in Sub-Saharan Africa—to develop manufacturing and jump-start industrialization. China, for example, having been a "follower goose" in East Asia, is on the verge of graduating from low-skilled manufacturing jobs. Because of its size, however, China may become a "leading dragon" for other developing countries instead of a "lead goose" in the traditional flying geese pattern of the international diffusion of industrial development. China will free up 85 million labor-intensive manufacturing jobs, compared with Japan's 9.7 million in the 1960's and Korea's 2.3 million in the 1980s (Lin 2011c).

The benefits of reallocating labor-intensive manufacturing jobs from China and other dynamically growing emerging market economies, such as India and Brazil, to low-income countries, most of which are located in Sub-Saharan Africa, could be enormous. In 2009 alone, China exported $107 billion worth of apparel to the world, compared with Sub-Saharan Africa's total apparel exports of $2 billion (2 percent of Chinese apparel exports). If only 1 percent of China's production of apparel is shifted to lower-wage African countries, African production and exports of apparel would increase by 47 percent. Similarly, employment gains could be significant. Africa's population (north and south of the Sahara) is 1 billion, slightly less than India's 1.15 billion. In 2009 manufacturing value added was 16 percent of GDP in India, 13 percent in Sub-Saharan African countries, and 16 percent in North African countries such as Egypt, Morocco, and Tunisia. India's employment in manufacturing was 8.7 million in 2009. Hence, based on a back-of-the-envelope calculation, it is reasonable to assume that total manufacturing employment in Africa is at about 10 million (Lin 2011c). This suggests that relocation of even a small share of China's 85 million labor-intensive manufacturing jobs to Africa would provide unprecedented opportunities for Africa.

But why are Chinese firms and lower-income country governments that would benefit substantially from a reallocation of firms from China and other emerging market economies not yet organizing themselves to seize these opportunities? From my frequent interactions in the past three years with policy makers in low-income countries in Africa and Asia, as well as with business people and government officials in emerging market economies, I know that policy makers and business communities would be interested in pursuing this opportunity. Some individual firms from emerging markets have linked up with entrepreneurs in low-income countries to develop various labor-intensive manufacturing industries. Still, many industrialists in emerging markets are hesitant to relocate abroad, especially to Africa. They cite the following concerns: (i) social and political instability; (ii) differences in labor laws and qualification; (iii) poor logistics; and (iv) the lack of adequate infrastructure and business conditions. These soft and hard infrastructure concerns add to the risks of their investments, increase the transaction costs of their operations, and outweigh the potential benefits of low labor costs in Africa and other low-income countries.

How to deal with these infrastructure problems? The first two issues can be mitigated through the commitment and broad-based support of recipient governments; the latter two could be addressed effectively through the development of sector-specific cluster-based industrial zones. Why is the latter sector-specific approach—sometimes called "picking winners"—desirable?

First, the required infrastructure improvements are often industry specific. The cut flower and textile industries, for example, require different infrastructure for their exports. Because the government's fiscal resources and implementation capacity in a developing country are limited, the government has to prioritize the infrastructure improvement according to the targeted industries.

Second, to compete in the globalized world, a new industry not only must align with the country's comparative advantage so that its factor costs of production can be at the lowest possible level, but the industry also needs to have the lowest possible transaction-related costs. Suppose a country's infrastructure and business environment are good and industrial upgrading and diversification happen spontaneously. Without the government's coordination, firms may enter into too many different industries that are all consistent with the country's comparative advantage. As a result, most industries may not form large enough clusters in the country and may not be competitive in the domestic and international market. Only in the wake of many failures might a few clusters eventually emerge. Such "trial and error" is likely to be a long and costly process, reducing the individual domestic and foreign firms' expected returns and incentives to enter new industries or relocate to other countries. This in turn can slow down or even stall a country's economic development.

But there exists a long list of failed attempts to pick winners. These failures, as discussed in the previous chapters, were often the result of the inability of government to come up with good criteria for identifying industries that are appropriate for a given country's endowment structure and level of development. In fact, governments' propensity to target industries that are too ambitious and not aligned with a country's comparative advantage largely explains why their attempts to "pick winners" resulted in "picking losers" (Lin, 2011d).

The recipe to economic success therefore is the one that helps policy makers in developing countries identify the industries in which their economies may have a latent comparative advantage and remove binding constraints to facilitate private domestic and foreign firms' entry to and operation in those industries. Chapter III of this book provides the governments in developing countries with a pragmatic and easy-to-follow growth identification and facilitation framework to do so.

Many low-income countries have an abundance of natural resources. They may also benefit from the industrialization opportunity provided by the industrial upgrading in dynamically growing emerging market economies by following the "flying geese" pattern. Resource-intensive industries, such as extraction, provide very limited job opportunities.

In a visit to Papua New Guinea in 2009, I found that its famous OK Tedi copper mine generated 40 percent of the country's public revenues and 80 percent of its exports but provided only 2,000 jobs in 2009. Most of Papua New Guinea's 6.6 million people still live on subsistence agriculture. Their wage rate is low, and wages constitute the major cost of production for labor-intensive industries. Low wage, natural-resource-rich countries could therefore develop labor-intensive industries, creating much needed jobs. Indonesia is a good example showing that this is possible. Labor-intensive manufacturing industries not only offer the potential to absorb surplus labor from the rural subsistence sector, but the development of such industries can also pave the way through continuous upgrading to higher value added industries. Finland's Nokia, for an example, started as a logging company and diversified its operation to the labor-intensive business of producing rubber boots; it then became the original equipment manufacturer of household electronics for Phillips before venturing into mobile phones.

Still, resource-rich countries often suffer from the Dutch Disease, as export receipts from natural resources push up the value of the currency, thus adversely affecting the competitiveness of their other exports. Sometimes also the wealth from natural resources is captured by powerful groups, turning resource richness into a curse. At the same time natural-resource rents can provide a great opportunity for development if managed in a transparent way and prudently invested in human and physical capital, such as infrastructure, and used to diversify to nonresource sectors as suggested in the growth identification and facilitation framework. These investments, if well chosen, can increase labor productivity, reduce production and transaction costs and ultimately cure the Dutch Disease, and turn the abundance in natural resources from a curse to a blessing. This is because such countries have opportunities to accumulate capital, upgrade endowments, improve infrastructure, transform industrial structure, and subsequently raise incomes faster than labor-abundant, resource-poor countries (Lin, 2011b).

The discussion so far has been on the opportunity of and ways to achieve rapid industrialization in low-income countries. The new structural economics also offers new insights to middle-income countries about how to upgrade their industries and achieve dynamic growth. A unique feature of middle-income countries is that some of their industries will still locate within the global frontier and some of their industries will locate on the frontier because of the graduation of higher-income countries from those industries. For the former industries, the government can follow the growth identification and facilitation framework to assist the private firms to tap into the potential of the latecomer's advantage, and for the latter industries, the government should adopt the same measures as those in the advanced countries for supporting innovation in technology and industries. Commonly used measures include support for basic research, providing patent protection, mandated use of new technology/products, and direct government procurement of new products. If a middle-income country can implement these measures to facilitate private firms' industrial upgrading and diversification, the country can not only avoid the middle-income trap but also achieve dynamic growth and catch up to advanced countries in a generation.

The discussion so far has not discussed the technological innovation and productivity improvement in agriculture. In low-income countries, where most people work in agriculture, improving agriculture will be important not only for reducing poverty but also for generating economic surplus to support industrialization. Governments need to facilitate the innovation and extension of agricultural technology and improvement of infrastructure for agricultural production and commercialization.

Finally, as stated in the introduction, I am convinced that, every developing country, including those in sub-Saharan Africa, has the potential to grow at 8 percent or more continuously for several decades, to significantly reduce poverty, and to become a middle-income or even a high-income country in the span of one or two generations, if its government has the right policy framework to facilitate the private sector's development along the line of its comparative advantages and tap into the latecomer's advantages. I hope this book will help developing countries to realize their growth potential. A world without poverty will then become a reality instead of just a dream.

## Note

1.  http://www.project-syndicate.org/series/the_next_financial_order/long_description.

# References

Lin, Justin Yifu. 2011a. "Demystifying the Chinese Economy," Cambridge, UK: Cambridge University Press.

———. 2011b. "Economic Development in Resource-Rich, Labor-Abundant Economies," Feb. 28, 2011, Let's Talk Development Blog, http://blogs. worldbank.org/developmenttalk/economic-development-in-resource-rich-labor-abundant-economies.

———. 2011c. "From Flying Geese to Leading Dragons—New Opportunities and Strategies for Structural Transformation in Developing Countries," WIDER Annual Lecture 15, Helsinki: UNU-WIDER. (A shorter version of this paper is forthcoming in *Global Policy*.)

———. 2011d. "Picking Winners," Let's Talk Development Blog, Oct. 18, 2011, http://blogs.worldbank.org/developmenttalk/node/670.

# INDEX

Boxes, figures, notes, and tables are indicated with b, f, n, and t following the page number.

economic reform favoring privatization, 72

exports of, 55, 68, 77–78, 232–33t, 351

financial structure, 276–77

foreign direct investment in, 174n36

industrialization and comparative advantage, 77–78, 119

industry-specific investment as economic growth strategy, 69

information industry, 127

labor-intensive manufacturing industries, 172n24, 351

labor surplus, 67–68

"micro-first" approach to economic development, 310

new growth theory and, 290

Pareto improvement contributing to economic development, 127

poverty rate, 2

steel industry, 136

transition from "follower goose" to "lead goose" status, 351

transition strategy, 310, 313–14nn18–19

TVEs (township-and-village enterprises), 310, 314n20

wage dynamics, 250

classical economists, 86

classification of countries in "old" structural economics, 28

collective action, 25, 50, 69, 148

college wage premium, 89

Colombia's investment in Ecuador, 174n36

comparative advantage, 8, 113–39

adjustment costs and technological differences undermining, 126–27, 130–31

choice of strategy. See alternative development strategies

comparative-advantage-defying (CAD) approach, 54, 117–18, 127, 138–39, 170n16, 175–76n41, 185

characteristics of, 296–98

compared to CAF strategy, 302–7

defined, 295

drawbacks of, 205

as part of catch-up strategy, 195

transition strategy to CAF approach, 309–10

comparative-advantage-following (CAF) approach, 117, 131–32, 133, 135–37

characteristics of, 298–301

compared to CAD strategy, 302–7

defined, 295

competitive advantage vs., 24, 27, 30, 108–9n19, 118–19

East Asian Four Little Dragons, 308–9. See also Hong Kong SAR, China; Korea, Republic of; Singapore; Taiwan, China

facilitating with vision and realism, 136–37

factor endowments and, 24, 28, 50, 75, 136, 353

as foundation for industrial policy, 25, 50–51, 101–2, 105–6, 129, 288

growth and industrial upgrading, 6, 14, 23–24, 99–100, 113–14

higher-income country exploiting lower-income country's comparative advantage, 40

historical development of theory, 121

latent, 52, 75–76, 78, 145, 155, 163

market failures and, 55, 71, 114–16

"old" structural economics' failure to properly account for, 48, 66

risks of deviating from, 131–32, 138

state assistance to private sector to exploit, 116–17

success of entrepreneurs linked to, 75

viability's relationship to, 291–95, 292–93f, 295f

comparative value chain analysis, 228–29b

compensation mechanisms lacking for trade-adjustment process, 122

competitive advantage, 24, 27, 30, 41n5, 76, 108–9n19, 118–19

competitive markets

price system in, 24, 288–89

technology adoption and, 292–93, 293f

Squire, L., 333–34
stagflation, 4, 18
state's role, 3, 143–68
  in advanced economies, 150–55
  Amoako comments on, 192–96
  Amsden comments on, 188–92
  economic importance of, 295
  facilitating state as best enabler for indus-
    trial upgrading and technological
    advance, 103, 114, 116–17, 121,
    145–50, 353–55
  Growth Identification and Facilitation
    Framework, 69–70, 78, 160–67
  identification of binding constraints, 20,
    163–67
  index of economic freedom (IEF) and
    expropriation risk as indexes for,
    321, 322, 324–25f, 341–45t
  industrial upgrading supported by
    state subsidies, 134–35, 137,
    149–50, 162
    in industrialized nations, 152–53
  Lim comments on, 201–204
  market failures and, 55, 114–16, 155,
    159–60, 192, 288, 353
  in new structural economics, 15, 29, 48,
    54, 100–101
  in "old" structural economics, 28
  Pack comments on, 196–201
  public sector quality, 60
  recipe for success, 29, 57, 155–60
  rejoinder to comments, 204–14
  research support from state, 41n6
  in structuralist approach to economic
    development, 17, 67
  Tendulkar comments on, 186–88
  te Velde comments on, 181–86
  types of government interventions,
    145, 168
steel industry, 135–36, 139
Stiglitz, Joseph E., 56, 58, 59, 66, 67,
  72–75, 78, 290, 313n17
stock markets, 263, 270. See also financial
  structure
structural change
  categories of level of growth for, 26

developing countries' differences from
    developed ones, 53
  in growth literature, 169n4
  importance of, 3, 5, 14, 23
  state's role in dynamics of, 143–68
Sub-Saharan Africa
  agricultural sector, 3
  comparative value chain analysis,
    228–29b
  economic growth, 2, 3, 196
  financial policies, 33
  investment climate as obstacle to business
    development, 163
  manufacturing industries, 352
subsidies. See state's role
Sun, Xifang, 268
sustainable growth, 1, 3
  citizens' long-term benefits and, 61
  commitment needed for, 96
  poverty reduction and, 14
Sweden's compensation mechanisms for
    trade-adjustment process, 122
Switzerland and watch-making industry, 59,
  73–74
Syed, Mahmood, 308

T
Taiwan, China
  comparative advantage and, 190
  comparative-advantage-following (CAF)
    approach, 308–9, 313n14
  East Asian financial crisis (late 1990s),
    313n16
  economic growth, 2
  government support for industrialization,
    198–99
  income distribution, 306
  large firms' advantage, 71
  new growth theory and, 290
  targeting industries in Japan, 156, 197
Takatoshi, Ito, 311n2
technological capabilities. See also
    technology transfer
  catch up with more advanced countries,
    123
  industry-specific nature of, 125

CPSIA information can be obtained at www.ICGtesting.com
Printed in the USA
LVOW081009110212

268219LV00003B/25/P